# THE
# Longman
# Writer's Bible

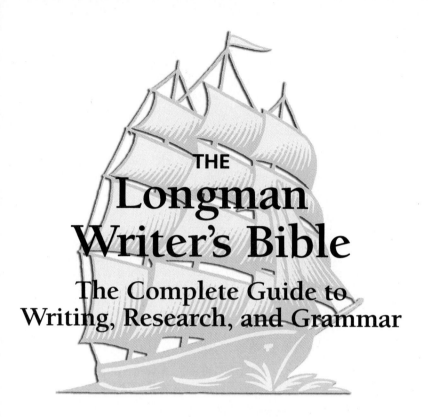

# THE
# Longman
# Writer's Bible

## The Complete Guide to
## Writing, Research, and Grammar

**CHRIS M. ANSON**
North Carolina State University

**ROBERT A. SCHWEGLER**
University of Rhode Island

**MARCIA F. MUTH**
University of Colorado at Denver

PEARSON
Longman

New York   Boston   San Francisco
London   Toronto   Sydney   Tokyo   Singapore   Madrid
Mexico City   Munich   Paris   Cape Town   Hong Kong   Montreal

Cover Designer: Laura Shaw

ISBN 0-321-33348-9

1 2 3 4 5 6 7 8 9 10—CRW—08 07 06 05

# CONTENTS

## PART THREE
# Documenting Sources: MLA Style
*Guides to MLA Formats*

## PART FOUR
# Documenting Sources: APA Style
*Guides to APA Formats*

## PART FIVE
# Editing Grammar: Meeting Community Expectations

## PART SIX

# Editing Sentence Problems:
# Understanding Community Options

**PART SEVEN**

# Editing Word Choice: Matching Words to Communities

**PART EIGHT**

# Editing Punctuation: Following Community Guidelines

## PART NINE

# Proofreading for Mechanics and Spelling: Respecting Community Conventions

# PREFACE

We've prepared this book for people who will be called on to write for different audiences and purposes—in short, for all writers. We know from experience and research that the demands of writing situations vary in important ways. We know, too, that writers need a range of concrete strategies in order to work successfully with the expectations and possibilities posed by each writing situation.

In response, we have produced a handbook filled with advice about writing and revising, creating correct and effective sentences, researching and reasoning, documenting and evaluating sources, representing yourself as a writer and speaker, and navigating the electronic world—all within three important communities: academic, work, and public. And we've made this advice easy to locate and use. We hope that you'll find this handbook to be just what its title promises—a true writer's bible.

This handbook continues to approach written communication as a social act, taking place among communities of writers and readers. Within different communities—academic, work, or public—the kinds of writing employed are likely to vary considerably. So, too, are expectations for style, reasoning, diction, correctness, and documentation.

*The Longman Writer's Bible* is unique among compact handbooks in its attention to writing within different communities. Throughout the text, it emphasizes and integrates the three key communities in which students live and write—academic, workplace, and public. Its concrete strategies help writers understand and respond to the needs of these communities. While the text highlights the importance of the academic setting, it recognizes writing as an essential tool for both occupational success and participation as an involved citizen.

It is hard to correct an error if you don't first recognize it as a problem. We have designed *The Longman Writer's Bible* to help writers develop the ability to recognize problems in their work by viewing it as readers do. We pay attention both to the importance of following conventions and to the way conventions may vary from community to community. Finally, our practical advice about recognizing and editing errors is easy to find and easy for writers to apply to their own texts.

## Acknowledgments

Our special thanks go to the following reviewers of this edition: Laura J. Bird, Northern Illinois University; Stuart Brown, New Mexico State University; Erika Deiters, Moraine Valley Community College; James H. Donelan, UC Santa Barbara; Patricia Gordon, Central Carolina Technical College; Sandra Jamieson,

Drew University; Winnie Kenney, Southwestern Illinois College; Lesley Lydell, University of Minnesota; Marti L. Mundell, Washington State University; Myra Seaman, College of Charleston; Matt Smith, University of Saint Francis; and Deborah Coxwell Teague, Florida State University.

Thank you also to those who worked with us as consultants in the development and revision of selected chapters in previous editions of *The Longman Writer's Companion*—Stevens Amidon; Daniel Anderson, University of North Carolina, Chapel Hill; Ellen Bitterman, SUNY, New Paltz; Mick Doherty and Sandye Thompson; Jim Dubinsky, Virginia Tech; Elizabeth Ervin, University of North Carolina, Wilmington; Mary Finley, University Library at California State University, Northridge; Christina Haas, Kent State University; Eric Pappas, Virginia Tech; Gladys Vega Scott, Arizona State University; Charlotte Smith, Adirondack Community College; and Victor Villaneuva, Washington State University. We remain grateful for the advice, expertise and creativity of all these writers and teachers.

We wish to thank Lynn Huddon, senior acquisitions editor, for overseeing this complicated project and attending to its many details with an imaginative eye and an innovative spirit. Our thanks go to Esther Hollander, editorial assistant, for coordinating the reviewing program and taking care of the endless communications and the personalities interwoven with them. We are especially grateful to Barbara Conover, our truly esteemed development editor, for guiding with clarity and wisdom such a complicated project and for fitting together the many pieces, large and small, textual and visual, typographical and personal. On each page of the text, we can see the contributions of Kathy Smith, and we thank her for her patience and care. We acknowledge, too, the guidance and care of Donna DeBenedictis, who took us from manuscript to printed book.

Chris Anson thanks Geanie, Ian, and Graham for enduring yet another book project and for always being understanding (well, almost always) when long phone calls, hours at the computer, or thickets of manuscripts got in the way of backyard soccer, a leaking faucet, or something more than thirty minutes for dinner. Your patience has been my inspiration.

Bob Schwegler would like to acknowledge above all Nancy Newman Schwegler for sharing her understanding of readers, reading, and writers. "And I'll be sworn up 'y that he loves her; / For here's a paper written in his hand, / A halting sonnet . . ." He would also like to thank Brian and Tara Schwegler for their advice, Christopher for his smiles, Ashley Marie for her inspiration, and Lily for hope.

Marcia Muth thanks her family: her son, Anderson, whose friends, crises, inspirations, and inventive papers continue to enlighten her about the rich and varied lives of student writers, and her husband, Rod, who remains the most patient, steadfast, and inspirational of friends, advisors, and companions.

CHRIS M. ANSON
ROBERT A. SCHWEGLER
MARCIA F. MUTH

# GUIDE TO ESL ADVICE

If your first language is not English, look for special advice integrated throughout the handbook. Each ESL Advice section is labeled and highlighted.

## ADJECTIVES AND ADVERBS

Adjective Forms (18d, 23a)
Adjective Clauses (19c)
Adjectives in a Series (23a)
Adverb Clauses (19c)

## AGREEMENT

Pronoun-Antecedent Agreement (22d)
  Demonstrative Adjectives or
    Pronouns (18b, 22d)
Subject-Verb Agreement (22b, 22c)
  *Other, Others,* and *Another* (22c)
  Paired Conjunctions (22c)
  Present Tense Verb Agreement
    (22b)
  Quantifiers (*each, one, many,*
    *much, most*) (22c)
  Separated Subjects and Verbs (22c)

## ARTICLES AND NOUNS

Articles: *A, An,* and *The* (18a)
Noun Clauses (19c)

## PREPOSITIONS

Prepositions (18f)
*For* and *Since* in Time Expressions (18f)
Prepositions of Place and Time: *At,*
  *On,* and *In* (18f)
Prepositions with Nouns, Verbs, and
  Adjectives (18f)
*To* or No Preposition to Express Going
  to a Place (18f)

## PUNCTUATION AND MECHANICS

Abbreviated Titles (47a)
Quotation Marks (40a)

## SENTENCES

*Because* and *Because of* (25c)
Coordination and Subordination
  (31c)
Position of Modifiers (27a)
Sentence Variety (25c)
*There* and *It* as Subjects (32b)

## VERBALS

Gerunds (19b)
Gerunds vs. Infinitives (19b)
Infinitives (19b)

## VERBS

Verb Forms (20a)
Conditional Statements (20h)
Helping Verbs (20d)
Passive Voice (20i)
Simple Present and Simple Past (20a)
Simple Present and Present
  Progressive Tenses (20e)
Subject-Verb Agreement (22b, 22c)
Third Person *–s* or *–es* Ending (20b)
Verb Tense and Expressions of Time
  (20e, 28b)

## WORDS

Idioms in American English (34b)

## WRITING

Appropriate Formality (4c)
Civic Participation (1a)
Drafting (5a)
Effective Writing (1c)
Paragraph Conventions (7b)
Peer Readers (6c)
Planning (3a)

Boldface numbers refer to sections and chapters in the handbook.

| | |
|---|---|
| abbrev | incorrect abbreviation, **47** |
| add | information or detail needed, **6a, 7e–f** |
| agr | error in subject-verb or pronoun-antecedent agreement, **22** |
| apos | lack of (or incorrect) possessive apostrophe, **39** |
| art | article used incorrectly, **18a** |
| awk | awkward construction, **32** |
| cap | capital letter needed, **43** |
| case | incorrect pronoun form, **21** |
| clear | clearer sentence needed, **32** |
| coh | paragraph or essay coherence needed, **7c–d** |
| coord | faulty coordination, **31** |
| cs | comma splice, **25** |
| cut | unnecessary material, **6a** |
| dev | paragraph or essay development needed, **7a–f** |
| discrm | sexist or discriminatory language, **35** |
| dm | dangling modifier, **27** |
| dneg | double negative, **23b-4** |
| emph | emphasis needed, **32b** |
| focus | paragraph or essay focus needed, **7a–b** |
| frag | sentence fragment, **24** |
| fs | fused sentence, **25** |
| hyph | hyphen (-) needed, **45** |
| inc | incomplete sentence, **29** |
| ital | italics (underlining), **44** |
| lc | lowercase letter needed, **43** |
| link | paragraph linkage needed, **7d, 7g** |
| mixed | grammatically mixed sentence, **29** |
| mm | misplaced modifier, **27** |
| modif | incorrect adjective or adverb, **23** |
| num | incorrect numbering style, **46** |
| // | parallel elements needed, **30** |
| ¶ | new paragraph, **7** |

| | |
|---|---|
| no ¶ | no new paragraph, **7** |
| p | error in punctuation, **37–42** |
| prep | preposition error, **18f** |
| pr ref | pronoun reference error, **26** |
| punc | error in punctuation, **37–42** |
| ⌃, | comma, **37** |
| no ⌃, | no comma, **37l** |
| ; | semicolon, **38a** |
| : | colon, **38b** |
| ' | apostrophe, **39** |
| " " | quotation marks, **40** |
| . | period, **41a** |
| ʔ | question mark, **41b** |
| ! | exclamation point, **41c** |
| ( ) [ ] — | parentheses, brackets, dashes, |
| . . . / | ellipses, slashes, **42** |
| ref | pronoun reference error, **26** |
| reorg | reorganize passage or section, **3b, 6a** |
| rep | repetitious, **33** |
| sent | sentence revision needed, **6a-b, 32** |
| shift | shift, **28** |
| sp | word spelled incorrectly, **48** |
| spell | word spelled incorrectly, **48** |
| sub | faulty subordination, **31b–c** |
| t | wrong verb tense, **20a–g** |
| tense | wrong verb tense, **20a–g** |
| trans | transition needed, **7d, 7f** |
| und | underlining (italics), **44** |
| us | error in usage, **Glossary** |
| var | sentence variety needed, **32** |
| verb | incorrect verb form, **20** |
| wc | faulty word choice, **34** |
| wordy | unneeded words, **33** |
| ww | wrong word, **34** |
| ^ | insert |
| ⤳ | delete |
| ◠ | close up space |
| ∿ | transpose letters or words |
| # | add a space |
| X | obvious error |

**SERIOUS ERROR**

# Ten Serious Errors to Recognize and Revise

## WHY ARE THESE ERRORS SERIOUS?

We asked college instructors which errors are most likely to confuse or distract readers and to undermine their confidence in a writer. Our research identified these errors as most serious in their potential for misleading and irritating readers. Look out for them, and edit them carefully.

## WHAT ARE THEY?

1. **Fragment (see 24a–b)**
   EXAMPLE: The heavy rain turned the parking area to mud. *And stranded thousands of cars.*
   → READER'S REACTION: **The second part seems disconnected. Now I've got to stop reading to figure out how it fits.**

2. **Fused Sentence (see 25b–c)**
   EXAMPLE: The promoters called *the insurance company they discovered* their coverage for accidents was limited.
   → READER'S REACTION: **I'm confused. This seems to be talking about some new insurance company they discovered. That can't be right.**

3. **Unclear Pronoun Reference (see 26a–b)**
   EXAMPLE: After talking with the groundskeeper, the security chief said *he* would not be responsible for the safety of the crowd.
   → READER'S REACTION: **Who's *he*—the groundskeeper or the security chief?**

4. **Double Negative (see 23b–4)**
   EXAMPLE: The local authorities *hadn't scarcely* enough resources to cope with the flooding.
   → READER'S REACTION: ***Hadn't scarcely*—I know double negatives are out of place in formal writing, and they take my attention away from what the writer is trying to say.**

5. **Dangling Modifier (see 27a–b)**
   EXAMPLE: *After announcing the cancellation from the stage, the crowd* began complaining to the promoters.
   → READER'S REACTION: **I know the crowd didn't announce the cancellation, but that's what this says!**

6. **Missing Possessive Apostrophe (see 39a)**
   EXAMPLE: Even the *promoters promise* to reschedule and honor tickets did little to stop the *crowds complaints.*
   → READER'S REACTION: **The apostrophes are missing; this is really distracting and confusing.**

7. **Missing Punctuation Marks (see 37a–d, 37g, 38a, 40a)**
   EXAMPLE: "The grounds are *slippery the* mayor announced, "so please leave in an orderly manner."
   → READER'S REACTION: **I couldn't figure out exactly what the mayor was saying because a comma and quotation marks were missing.**

8. **Lack of Subject-Verb Agreement (see 22a–c)**
   EXAMPLE: Away from the microphone, the mayor said, "I hope the security chief or the promoters *has* a plan to help everyone leave safely."
   → READER'S REACTION: **Promoters *has*? I found this confusing because the sentence parts didn't seem to fit together.**

9. **Shift in Person (see 28a)**
   EXAMPLE: If *people* left the amphitheater quickly, *you* could get to *your* car without standing long in the rain.
   → READER'S REACTION: **Why is this sentence mixing *people* with *you*? Is *you* supposed to mean *me*?**

10. **Unnecessary Commas (see 39i)**
    EXAMPLE: *Although,* the muddy parking area caused problems, all the cars and *people,* left the grounds without incident.
    → READER'S REACTION: **It looks as if the writer just tossed in some commas here—and they make the sentence hard to read.**

xvii

# PART 1

# Joining Communities: Participating as Critical Readers and Writers

 **TAKING IT ONLINE**

**WEB EXHIBITS**
http://www.webexhibits.org
Browse this site for links to interesting reading and visuals on widely varied topics, academic and otherwise.

**GENERAL WRITING CONCERNS (PLANNING/WRITING/REVISING/GENRES)**
http://owl.english.purdue.edu/handouts/general/index.html
Click on the options on this page for valuable advice about writing processes from the popular Online Writing Lab at Purdue University.

**THE ONLINE WRITERY**
http://www.missouri.edu/~writery/
Visit *The Online Writery* at the University of Missouri at Columbia for help with your general questions about writing.

**OVERCOMING WRITER'S BLOCK**
http://leo.stcloudstate.edu/acadwrite/block.html
Can't get started? Try the ideas on this page, or turn to the other suggestions available at *The Write Place.*

**WORKING WITH TOPICS**
http://writing.colostate.edu/references/processes/topic/
Here's advice across the academic disciplines for finding, narrowing, and working with topics.

**DEVELOPING A THESIS STATEMENT**
http://www.english.uiuc.edu/cws/wworkshop
Click on "Tips & Techniques" and then on "Developing a Thesis." This guide uses pairs of original and revised sentences to illustrate how to refine a thesis statement.

# PART 1

# Joining Communities: Participating as Critical Readers and Writers

# 1 Readers, Writers, and Communities

Someone created the Web page you browsed yesterday—writing its text, planning its design, and anticipating readers' reactions. Someone else wrote the newsletter in your mailbox, the forms for your car loan, and the waiver you signed before the technician X-rayed your ankle. Because writing and reading surround us, shaping our lives, choices, responsibilities, and values, this book looks at the roles of writers and readers in contemporary culture. It offers concrete strategies for writing, for critical reading and thinking, and for understanding your readers' expectations.

Whether you're drafting a psychology paper, an email message at work, or a neighborhood flyer, try to envision a **community of readers and writers**, people with shared—though not necessarily identical—goals, settings, preferences, and uses for verbal and visual texts. This book will help you develop your skill at recognizing different needs and expectations of writers, readers, and speakers in the academic, work, and public communities in which you may be active throughout your life.

## 1a Recognizing academic, work, and public communities of readers and writers

In a Denver suburb, pets have been disappearing. The culprits have been coyotes or other predators, crowded by new homes and industrial parks. Alarmed local residents wonder if a young child will be the next victim.

In such situations, problem solving often begins with written and oral presentations. City officials and citizens may turn to the **academic community** for studies of the habitat and feeding habits of coyotes and other predators. Their research documents may sound like this:

> This report summarizes and compares data from two studies of the habits of predators in areas with significant population growth and urbanization over the past ten years.

The scientific reports focus on one question: how do coyotes behave in a shrinking habitat? But parents, pet owners, and others in the **public community** are likely to ask a different question: how can we protect our children and pets without harming local wildlife? Tips created by the Colorado Division of Wildlife apply scientific knowledge to residents' concerns.

*If you see a coyote:*
- Leave it alone; do not approach it.

*If a coyote approaches:*
- Use an animal repellent such as pepper spray to ward off the coyote.
- Throw rocks or sticks at the coyote to scare it away.

- Use a loud, authoritative voice to frighten the animal away.

*How to coexist with coyotes:*
- Keep your pet on a leash.
- Do not let pets out between dusk and dawn, when most predators are active. . . .

*(The Denver Post, 30 July 1998, 15A)*

Neighborhood groups might distribute leaflets and organize meetings.

**COYOTE ALERT!**
**Are your children safe in their own backyards? Coyotes attacked seven dogs and cats last summer. Find out what we can do. Join the Committee to Safeguard Our Children on Tuesday, October 2, at 7:00 p.m. in the high school gym.**

Other reports might circulate in the **work community**, analyzing the frequency of complaints, summarizing business perspectives, or presenting policy options to help people, pets, and coyotes live in balance.

## 1 Consider academic, work, and public communities

Participating within and across academic, work, and public communities means talking, listening, reading, and, especially, writing. Your immediate academic challenge—responding to assignments—helps prepare you to write more thoughtfully in other communities. In the same way, writing at work or in public situations can stimulate or enrich your writing for academic readers.

To communicate effectively within a community of readers and writers, consider its roles, goals, forms, and writing characteristics. (See the chart on the facing page.) Although community considerations sometimes overlap, they can help you recognize both readers' expectations and your limitations and choices as a writer.

## ESL ADVICE:   CIVIC PARTICIPATION

Many schools encourage students to join clubs, participate in campus governance, and volunteer on or off campus. Local civic participation is a rewarding tradition that provides many opportunities to improve your reading, writing, and speaking in English.

| THREE MAJOR COMMUNITIES OF READERS AND WRITERS | | |
| --- | --- | --- |
| **ACADEMIC** | **WORK** | **PUBLIC** |
| **ROLES** Students<br>Teachers<br>Researchers<br>Committees gathering<br>  expert opinions<br>Readers interested in<br>  specialized knowledge | Co-workers<br>Supervisors<br>Organizational work<br>  groups (management,<br>  accounting, public<br>  relations)<br>Clients and customers<br>Government agencies<br>Public target groups | Residents or group<br>  members<br>Possible supporters<br>Public officials or agencies<br>Community activists<br>Local groups<br>Readers interested in an<br>  issue |
| **GOALS** Creation or exchange<br>  of knowledge | Provision of information<br>Analysis of problems<br>Proposal of solutions<br>Promotion of<br>  organization | Persuasion in support of<br>  a cause or issue<br>Participation in democracy<br>Provision of issue-oriented<br>  information |
| **TYPICAL FORMS** Analysis of text or<br>  phenomenon<br>Interpretation of text,<br>  artwork, or event<br>Research proposal<br>Lab report<br>Scholarly article<br>Annotated bibliography<br>Grant proposal<br>Classroom presentation | Description of object,<br>  event, situation, or<br>  problem<br>Proposal<br>Report of findings<br>Memos, letters,<br>  agendas, or minutes<br>  of meetings<br>Guidelines or<br>  instructions<br>Promotional materials<br>Meeting presentation | Position paper<br>Informative report<br>Letter to group, supporters,<br>  officials, agency,<br>  organization, or<br>  publication<br>Flyer, newsletter, pamphlet,<br>  or fact sheet<br>Action or grant proposal<br>Guidelines, charter, or<br>  principles<br>Comments in public<br>  forum |
| **WRITING CHARACTERISTICS** Detailed reasoning<br>Critical analysis<br>Fresh insights or<br>  conclusions<br>Extensive evidence<br>Accurate detail that<br>  supports conclusions<br>Balanced treatment<br>Acknowledgment of<br>  other viewpoints<br>Thoughtful, stimulating<br>  exploration of topic | Concentration on<br>  task, problem, or goal<br>Accurate and efficient<br>  presentation of<br>  problem or issue<br>Concise, direct prose<br>Promotion of product<br>  or service<br>Attention to corporate<br>  image and design<br>  standards | Focus on shared values<br>  and goals<br>Advocacy of cause<br>Fair recognition of others'<br>  interests<br>Relevant evidence that<br>  supports positions<br>Concentration on own<br>  point of view or on need<br>  for information<br>Orientation to actions or<br>  solutions |

## 2 Consider electronic communities

The broad academic, work, and public communities all cohabit the intriguing world of the Internet. A click of a mouse connects you with large and small electronic communities, each organized around a shared interest in a topic, point of view, or issue.

**STRATEGY**  Use TASALS to help you recognize electronic communities.

**T**OPIC. On what subject does the site focus? Do contributors belong to any organization or share any other affiliation?

**A**TTITUDE. Does the site have a clear point of view or set of values? Do contributors have similar perspectives or values?

**S**TRATEGIES. Does the site use a particular written style or visual design?

**A**UTHORITY. Does the site support claims or information? Do contributors reason carefully, offering evidence rather than opinion?

**L**INKS. Do postings or links refer to related online resources?

**S**UMMARIZE. How can you sum up the qualities of the community, its expectations of participants, and its conventions?

## 1b Joining communities of readers and writers

Participating in communities of readers and writers brings personal, academic, and professional rewards whether your involvement just happens or you actively seek it.

**STRATEGY**  Become involved in communities of readers and writers.

- **Become an active, critical reader.** Read widely—newspapers, special-interest magazines, campus newsletters, neighborhood flyers, electronic exchanges, or Web texts. Note especially effective passages. Reread them as a writer, trying to figure out why they work so well.
- **Look for opportunities to write as a citizen, employee, and student.** Create an email study group for a class. Contribute to a company or group newsletter or the school paper. Keep a journal, record ideas in a notebook, or send email messages. Write letters to the newspaper or public figures about issues that simplify or complicate your life as a citizen. Attend public meetings, and voice your ideas.
- **Turn to your readers.** Do they expect your text to be short or long, simple or elaborate? Do they want sources or opinions, analysis or argument, formal style or chatty prose? Ask readers to respond to your draft: Is it clear or confusing? Which parts read well? Which are awkward?
- **Develop a portfolio.** As you look ahead to demonstrating your skills for potential employers, begin building a portfolio. Include samples of your best academic papers, work documents, materials from civic or volunteer activities, and taped oral presentations.

## 1c Recognizing myths and realities about the writing process

Successful writing is almost never a matter of just recording your thoughts in finished form. Instead, it begins with a response: to an idea or a reading, an experience, or a problem. It calls for planning, defining a purpose and thesis, considering community and readers, drafting, revising, editing, and proofreading. And it rarely moves in a straight line. Revising may mean further drafting, or editing may mean collaborating with readers.

Replace your self-defeating habits with reliable strategies that increase your impact and flexibility as you write in different communities.

**Myth:** People easily succeed in the real world without having to write.

**Reality:** It's a popular myth that executives don't need to write because their assistants do this work. In Fortune 500 companies, however, over half the employees spend between eight and forty hours writing each week. As more employees carry laptops and send email, their writing time is likely to increase, making writing ability even more crucial for success.

**Myth:** Writing is easy for people born with the knack.

**Reality:** If we looked over other writers' shoulders, we'd know what researchers know: good writers draft and redraft, succeeding through hard work.

**Myth:** You can be a good writer without doing much reading.

**Reality:** It's not likely. The more you read, the better you understand the writing that works in specific communities and your options as a writer.

**Myth:** It's cheating to ask others to read your paper before you turn it in.

**Reality:** It certainly is cheating if you have someone else write a paper or parts of it and then claim the work as your own. But successful writers always depend on readers for feedback. Especially at work and in civic groups, key documents are likely to be written collaboratively.

**Myth:** Good writing is effective for all readers.

**Reality:** All good writing is clear, coherent, and correct, but what works in one community may not work as well in another. Your sociology research paper will differ in tone, style, and content from the proposal you write at work or the email you send to your running group.

### ESL ADVICE: EFFECTIVE WRITING

Another myth is that you can't be an effective writer if English is not your first language. Of course, the more you read and write, the more your English will improve. But effective writing takes hard work whether you're a native or nonnative speaker. And powerful writing from the heart moves readers no matter what the writer's language background.

# 2  Reading Critically

When you read, you almost always respond. You may highlight in your textbook, revise a collaborative report at work, or jot a civic event on your calendar. Whatever you read—essays, articles, memos, reports, Web pages—responsive reading is bedrock, supporting speaking and writing.

## 2a Reading for understanding

A systematic approach to reading can help you identify expectations of readers and practices of writers. Like most people, you probably begin to read by going to the first page and plunging into the text. By starting "cold," however, you may have too much to do at once: understand the detailed information in the text, grasp the writer's conclusions, and develop your own critical responses. Instead, you may want to "warm up" by previewing a text and developing a reading plan.

### 1 Preread before reading

Begin by figuring out the "big" features that shape a text's meaning, ideas, or relationship to readers before you jump right into the text.

**Preview the form.** Locate features that suggest the text's approach: long paragraphs or short, opening abstract, headings, sidebars, frames, glossary, references, links, visuals, one column or more.

**Preview the organization.** Skim a book's table of contents. Look for headings in articles, reports, or memos. Click on the site map.

**Examine the context.** Consider the author's background, the original readers and situation, the place and date of first publication, or a Web site's sponsor.

**Sample and predict.** Scan the text to activate your own knowledge and prepare for interpreting unfamiliar words and examples in context. Look up baffling words before you read. Recall similar texts; try to predict where the reading will go.

**Learn some background.** Talk to peers, co-workers, or others who know a difficult subject. Find an encyclopedia entry on key concepts.

**Plan ahead.** When you read Web pages or library articles, consider printing or duplicating the text so you can write on your own copy.

## 2 Follow a reading plan

As you read, look for the generalizations and conclusions that will help you make sense of unfamiliar material. Focus on beginnings—the thesis that guides the introduction, general statements that open sections, and topic sentences that begin paragraphs (see 4b, 7b, and 7g). Look also for paragraphs that supply an overview of the main ideas and the organizational plan. In addition, set aside extra time for reading sections devoted to new information and insights.

**Find what's important.** Read first—*without highlighting*—to capture the essentials. Go back again to note or highlight what's *really* important.

**Read the visuals.** Examine graphs, charts, diagrams, or other illustrations; analyze what they say and how they relate to the written text.

**Pause and assess.** Where are you? What have you learned so far? What confuses you? Jot down your answers; then skim what you've just read.

**Summarize in chunks.** Glance back over a section, and state the main point so far. Guess where the reading will go next.

**Share insights.** Meet with classmates or co-workers to discuss a text. Compare reactions, considering how the others reached their interpretations.

## 3 Respond after reading

When you read carefully, you respond to the content and evaluate it according to your purposes and the standards of your community.

**Record main ideas.** Use a file card, journal, or computer file so you can review without leafing through copies, printouts, or books.

**Add your own responses.** Note what you already know as well as your own views about the topic. Don't simply accept what the author says.

**Reread and review.** Reread difficult material, first skimming more quickly and then studying the passages you've highlighted.

**Write in your text.** If a book or other text isn't yours, don't write in it. If it—or a photocopy or printout—is yours, annotate it.

- Interpretations: What does the author or speaker mean?
- Confusions: At what points are you puzzled?
- Questions: What more do you need to know?
- Objections or counterarguments: Where do you disagree?
- Restatements: How can you say it in your own words?
- Evaluations: What do you like or dislike about the reading?
- Applications: What can you use for class, work, or activities?
- Expectations: How does this reading resemble or differ from others typical in your academic, work, or public community?

## 2b Reading analytically and critically

Your purposes and context shape your responses as a reader. If you are gathering details for an oral presentation or essay, your **analytical reading** will focus on *understanding* the content—the ideas, purposes, information, organization, perspective, and approaches. (See 9g.)

These activities can help guide your analytical reading.

- **Summarize:** How can you sum up or restate its key ideas?
- **Paraphrase:** How can you state its main points in your own words?
- **Synthesize:** How can you connect its information with that in other texts?
- **Quote:** Which of the text's exact words make powerful statements?

Next, your **critical reading** will focus on *interacting* with the text, adding to it your knowledge and insight, analyzing what it does—and doesn't —address, relating it to other texts within the community, and assessing its strengths and limitations. (See 9g.) Your critical reading will be active, engaged, and responsive as you ask questions, look for answers, and develop your own perspective.

- **Question:** What answers do you still want or need?
- **Synthesize perspectives:** How can you relate it to other views?
- **Interpret:** What do you conclude about its outlook and bias?
- **Assess:** How do you evaluate its value and accuracy?

The example below illustrates both analytical and critical comments.

| ANALYTICAL COMMENTS | | CRITICAL COMMENTS |
|---|---|---|
| *Compares health care choices to grocery shopping* | How is health care like going to the grocer? The more you put in the cart, the higher the bill. But unlike your grocery expedition, where all you pay for are the items in your own cart, with health care the other customer's cart is on your tab, too. | *Sounds good, but is it fair overall? Need to read more* |
| *Admits benefits but claims costs will increase*  *Supplies supporting evidence* | Nor will the tab get any better with the patient protection legislation being considered in Washington. Sure, Americans will get guaranteed access to emergency rooms, medical clinical trials and specialists. Senate legislation even provides | *Lots of coverage problems—like my emergency room bill* |

the right to sue your insurer
and be awarded up to $5 million
in punitive damages. . . .

*Projects costs
and effects*

The litigation costs, and the
efforts by some employers to
avoid liability, could lead to
an additional 9 million
uninsured Americans by 2010.

*Does everyone
agree on
estimates?*

—"Restrict Right to Sue or
We'll Pay in the End,"
*Atlanta Journal-Constitution*,
July 19, 2001.

*What's this
paper's usual
viewpoint?*

## 2c Using journals to turn reading into writing

A **journal** is a place to explore ideas, develop insights, experiment with your writing, and reflect on your reading. You may want to organize entries around a writing task, a reading assignment, a research question, or a regular schedule for recording observations. Unlike a diary, where you record daily activities, a journal encourages interpretation and speculation as you develop your voice as a writer. (See also 9e, 9f, and 36b.)

You can keep an informal journal in whatever form you prefer—an electronic file, a three-ring notebook, or a small binder—although you may appreciate being able to remove or reorganize pages. Stick to a regular schedule for writing because an abandoned journal soon withers away.

### STRATEGY  Make your thoughts visible in a journal.

Nurture your own voice as a writer, and cultivate your creative insights as you turn reading, listening, and thinking into writing.

- Translate new ideas into your own words, clarifying and speculating about them for an imaginary reader or for yourself.
- Brainstorm, letting one thought lead to the next without immediate criticism or evaluation.
- Extend ideas, developing implications, applications, or solutions.
- Take issue with what you read or hear, flexing your critical thinking muscles as you challenge and critique other views. Then look for balance—areas where you respect or agree with others, too.

# 3  Planning

Imagine trying to build a house without drawing up any plans beforehand or going into the playoffs without a team strategy, just to "see what happens." Success would depend on luck, not design. The same is true for speaking and writing. For almost any formal project—in college, for a civic group, or on the job—you need to "rough out" ideas before you really get started. **Planning** before you write a full draft—often called **prewriting**—gives you a map of where you want to go in your writing.

## ESL ADVICE:  PLANNING

Try planning in your first language; move to English as ideas develop.

## 3a  Generating ideas

Whatever your writing task, you will want to ask, "What do I know about what I'm writing? What else do I need to know?" Gather ideas from your existing resources—your journal or notebook entries, readings annotated with your responses, class or meeting notes, your assignment sheet or job description, and any similar projects. (See also 4a.)

**Freewriting.** Write by hand or at the computer for five or ten minutes *without stopping*, even if you only repeat "I'm stuck." As such empty prose bores you, you'll almost magically slip into more engaging ideas. Or begin **focused freewriting** with an idea you already have—"I guess I support antigambling laws"—to start productively exploring the topic.

**Listing.** Lists can help you draw out your own knowledge, create ideas through association, and generalize from details. For her history paper on Soviet espionage during the Cold War, Annie Hanson listed her main points and, under her final point, key supporting details.

1. Cold War background from Yalta to Berlin Wall
2. Western vs. Soviet technology
3. Role of KGB training operatives and recruiting
4. Espionage examples (Fuchs, De Groot, Philby)

Write your topic at the top of a page, and then list ten thoughts, facts, impressions, ideas, or specifics about it. For example, begin with a general idea or a major part of your project, and list supporting details and new associations. Repeat the process with your other ideas or parts.

**Strategic questions.** Especially for proposals and recommendations, strategic questioning can pull information from your memory and direct you to other ideas to pursue. Brian Corby asked questions as he began his letter to the zoning board opposing a high-rise apartment next to a public park.

What? • Proposed high-rise apt.—18 stories, 102 units
• East side of Piedmont Park by Sunrise Ave.
• Planning by Feb., groundbreaking by June, done in a year

Why? • Developers profit
• Provides medium-cost housing in growing area
• Develops ugly vacant lot by park

Why Not? • "Citifies" one of the few green patches in town
• Traffic, crime rate, park use
• New zoning opens the door to other high-rises

---

**STRATEGY**   Ask strategic questions.

Begin with *what, why,* and *why not.* Ask *who, where, when,* and *how,* if they apply. Continue to ask questions as you develop ideas and probe more deeply.

---

**ESL ADVICE:  CLEAR AND FORCEFUL DETAILS**

Most writing in English tends to be direct rather than abstract. Especially in the academic and work communities, a writer often makes a clear assertion about a topic, a problem, or an event and then supports that idea with facts, details, or research. In a sense, the writer must "prove" the point, and readers won't accept it on faith or by virtue of the writer's authority. If readers find your writing too broad, indirect, or poorly supported, compare their expectations with those of readers in your first language. American teachers and workplace supervisors generally want writers to ask questions about writing projects and are used to explaining what they expect.

---

## 3b  Structuring ideas and information

Ideas and information alone will get you started, but most writing and speaking projects require **structure**—a pattern, outline, or plan to shape and

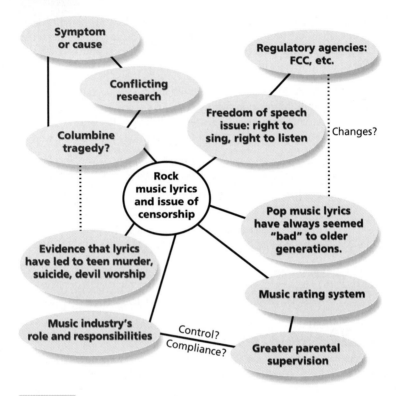

FIGURE 3.1   A simple conceptual cluster

organize. Use the structure expected by readers in projects such as reports, or create a structure from the ideas you've generated.

**Clusters.**   Draw a cluster by circling a concept, idea, or topic in the center of a page. Then jot down associations with this kernel topic, circling and connecting them with lines to the center, like the spokes of a wheel, or to each other to show interconnections. To create clusters in cycles, use each subsidiary idea as a new kernel topic. As she began her researched argument paper, Marianne Kidd used clustering to relate her ideas about censoring rock music lyrics. (See Figure 3.1.)

**Tree diagram.**   A tree diagram resembles a cluster, but the branches tend to be more linear and hierarchical. Each main branch of Bill Chen's diagram became a "chunk" or section in his paper on possible uses of virtual reality. (See Figure 3.2.)

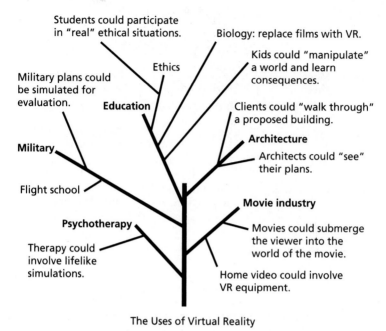

The Uses of Virtual Reality

**FIGURE 3.2** A simple tree diagram

Start with your topic as the trunk. Create main branches for central points and smaller branches for related ideas. Then "revise" your diagram into a working plan or outline for the paragraphs or sections of your project.

**Time sequences.** If your project involves chronology, use a **time sequence.** For example, in planning a self-guided tour of a museum exhibit, James Cole drew a time sequence detailing Andy Warhol's artistic life. When you build a time sequence, frame each event along a line, noting dates, ages, or other time markers. If you wish, add thick connecting lines to mark pivotal events that led to or caused other events and thin lines to show simple time links.

**Problem-solution grid.** Position papers, business reports, and other persuasive pieces often follow a problem-solution sequence, outlining a problem, offering workable solutions, or advocating one solution rather than another. Paula Masek used a problem-solution grid to plan her editorial exploring temporary solutions to the problem of feeding the homeless. Later she discussed each boxed item in a separate section or paragraph of her draft. (See Figure 3.3 on page 14.) To create a problem-solution grid, first state the problem. Underneath, in boxes or columns,

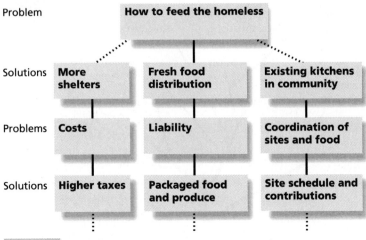

Problem  **How to feed the homeless**

Solutions  **More shelters**  **Fresh food distribution**  **Existing kitchens in community**

Problems  **Costs**  **Liability**  **Coordination of sites and food**

Solutions  **Higher taxes**  **Packaged food and produce**  **Site schedule and contributions**

**FIGURE 3.3**  A problem-solution grid

identify possible solutions. Below these, identify problems each solution might create and then their solutions. Generate as many layers as you wish.

**Outline.** The best-known planning technique is the trusty outline, complete with Roman numerals. The traditional outline may help you to label or arrange ideas but doesn't do much to help *generate* them. A **working outline**, however, can help you generate information or identify missing pieces. As you arrange ideas in an outline (or outline a draft to check its logic, see 6a), consider whether your higher-level generalizations, interpretations, or conclusions are followed by enough supporting details and specifics to inform or persuade a reader. If you spot gaps or unbalanced coverage, consider breaking up a large topic, combining smaller points, expanding ideas, or adding more details or examples.

With a simple topic as your main heading, commit yourself to three second-level headings by writing *A, B,* and *C* underneath. (Leave a lot of space in between.) Then fill in the subheadings. Now develop third-level headings by writing *1, 2,* and *3* beneath *each* letter. Fill them in, too.

Mitch Weber used a working outline to plan a brief history of the non-profit organization where he had a summer internship.

CREATION OF THE FAMILY HEALTH CENTER
A. Founding Work of Susan and Roger Ramstadt
   1. The "vision"
   2. Finding the money
   3. Support from the Crimp Foundation

```
B. The Early Years
   1. Building momentum
   2. The great financial disaster
   3. Rebirth
C. Toward Maturity
   1. Fund-raising after 2000
   2. State recognition and the big award
   3. The new vision: health and sustenance
```

Whatever your planning strategies, use all available tools.

---

**STRATEGY**   **Use electronic planning to expand your options.**

- Use your computer for planning so that you can easily reorganize and develop your ideas into a draft.
- Try interactive questions or prompts from your software, the Web, or the campus computer lab or tutoring center.
- Use a search engine to browse for Web sites on your topic.
- Skim links, gathering possible ideas from varied sites.

---

# 4   Defining Your Purpose, Thesis, and Audience

Think about what writing or speaking on the job, in school, and in civic groups actually *does*. It helps communicate ideas, produce commodities, provide services, or make things work. It can sell, buy, or negotiate things. It can be coolly informative or passionately persuasive. It can do public good or make private profit. And it can produce knowledge that will delight and entertain, lead to personal wisdom, or save lives.

## 4a   Analyzing your purpose

Given all that writing *can* do, one of your early steps is to decide just what a particular piece of writing *needs* to do.

### 1 Define the focus of your task or assignment

In many writing situations, someone hands you a task or assignment, and it's your job to produce effective writing. First think about what focus that assignment or task requires. Then concentrate on how to narrow your focus until you find the kernel or core that will lie at the center of your paper. Meg Satterfield began this process by underlining a key noun phrase in her assignment.

> Most of us have volunteered at some time—helping family or friends  or joining a service-learning project. Tell your audience (our class) about <u>some unexpected outcome of your experience as a volunteer.</u>

Meg decided that her assignment left the topic open but valued something ("an unexpected outcome") that would surprise or engage readers.

**Target your topic.** On your assignment sheet or job description, underline any nouns or noun phrases; use them to invent and narrow possibilities (see 3a).

## 2 Define the purpose of your task or assignment

Focusing on a topic—a noun—gives you a clear sense of what your writing is *about*. But nouns don't act, and your writing needs to *do* something, too. Its **purpose** usually takes the form of an action statement—a verb or verb phrase like these two in Cory Meta's assignment.

> Find a magazine ad that catches your attention. <u>Analyze the ad for its hid-</u><u>den cultural assumptions</u>, being sure to <u>describe exactly what is happen-</u><u>ing in the ad.</u> Note techniques such as camera angle, coloration, and focus.

**Pinpoint what you need to do.** On your assignment sheet or job description, underline any verbs or verb phrases that tell you what to *do*. (See the chart on p. 18 for a list of verbs frequently used in academic writing situations.) Then use planning strategies to generate material related to these verbs (see 3a).

## 3 Rough out a purpose structure

State briefly the purpose of each section of your writing. In planning a student housing guide, Carol Stotsky specified her purposes by developing a tentative order for her section on housing options.

BEGINNING      Show students why housing options are important
                        for them.

MIDDLE           Explore advantages and disadvantages of each in detail.

ENDING           Recommend that traditional students move gradually from
                        security (home or dorm) to independence (off campus).

A sequence such as "1-2-3-4" or "beginning-middle-ending" can help you decide what each part should do. Use verbs that clarify your purpose: *show, explain, claim, counter, build up to.*

## 4b Creating a thesis

Just as readers may look for an executive summary with a report or an abstract before an article, they may expect you to clarify your point right away in a college paper, too. For this reason, a thesis statement often ends the first paragraph. The **thesis**, generally expressed in a single sentence, is the controlling idea that you then explore, support, or illustrate using specific examples or arguments. You may draft a paper with a clear thesis in mind, discover your thesis later on and revise accordingly, or modify your thesis as you look for evidence or ideas to back up your assertions.

To begin defining a thesis, first narrow the topic to some specific angle or perspective. Then begin turning the topic from a noun (a "thing") into a statement that contains a verb. Notice how Lynn Tarelli developed a thesis for her brochure for a parenting group.

**VAGUE TOPIC**      Ritalin

**STILL A TOPIC**    Ritalin for kids with attention-deficit disorder (ADD)

**STILL A TOPIC**    The problem of Ritalin use for kids with ADD

**ROUGH THESIS**     Parents should be careful about using medicines such as Ritalin for kids with ADD.

Lynn progressively sharpened the topic and brought the fourth version to life by expressing an assertion about it, seeing it from a specific perspective.

## 1 Complicate, qualify, or extend your rough thesis

Lynn's thesis still didn't make a clear suggestion to parents about Ritalin: Should it not be used for kids with ADD? Should it be used judiciously?

**FINAL THESIS**     Although Ritalin is widely used to treat children with ADD, parents should not rely too heavily on such drugs until they have explored both their child's problem and all treatment options.

Lynn *complicated* her rough thesis by accepting Ritalin as a legitimate treatment for ADD; her cautions about overreliance and other options *qualified* and *extended* it to create a clearer, more complex statement.

## KEY VERBS USED TO SPECIFY WRITING PURPOSES

**Analyze: Divide or break something into constituent parts so you can observe, describe, and study their relationships.**

Analyze the relationships between form and color, light and shadow, and foreground and background in one of Titian's paintings.

**Argue: Prove a point, or persuade a reader to accept or entertain a position.**

In a letter to the College Senate, argue your position on a campuswide smoking ban.

**Compare and contrast: Show similarities and differences for two or more things.**

Compare and contrast costs at local hospitals for ten surgical procedures.

**Describe: Show how something is experienced through sight, sound, taste, touch, or smell.**

Describe obstacles encountered in local historic homes by visitors in wheel-chairs.

**Discuss: Provide an intelligent, focused commentary about a topic.**

Discuss current transit needs in the metropolitan region.

**Evaluate: Reach conclusions about something's value or worth, using substantiating evidence based on observation and analysis.**

Evaluate the effectiveness of camera technique in Hitchcock's *The Birds.*

**Extend: Apply an idea or concept more fully.**

Extend last year's production figures to take into account the April work slowdown.

**Inform: Present facts, views, phenomena, or events to enlighten your reader.**

Inform homeowners about the hazards of lead paint.

**Show: Demonstrate or provide evidence to explain something.**

Show how Pip, in his later years, is influenced by Joe's working-class values in Dickens's *Great Expectations.*

**Synthesize: Combine separate elements into a single or unified entity.**

Synthesize this list of facts about energy consumption.

**Trace: Map out a history, chronology, or explanation of origins.**

Trace the development of Stalinism.

**Use: Focus on the designated material, selecting specifics from it to explain and illustrate your broader points.**

Use the three assigned poems to illustrate contemporary responses to death.

## 2 Shape an appropriate thesis

You may also refine your thesis to suit your purpose or readers. (See also 9d and 15c.)

**Argumentative thesis.** Readers will expect you to indicate your opinion on an issue and perhaps to acknowledge other views.

> Although bioengineered crops may pose some dangers, their potential for combating worldwide hunger and disease justifies their careful use in farming.

**General thesis.** Readers will expect to learn your conclusions or special perspectives and perhaps understand their importance as well.

> Sooner or later, teenagers stop listening to parents and turn to each other for advice, sometimes with disastrous results.

**Academic thesis.** Readers will expect to learn both your specific conclusion and your plan to support it, using terms appropriate to the field.

> My survey of wedding announcements in local newspapers from 1960 to 2000 indicates that religious background and ethnicity have decreased in importance in mate selection but education and social background remain significant factors.

**Informative thesis.** Readers will expect to learn why information is interesting or useful and how you'll organize or synthesize it.

> When you search for online advice about financial aid, you will find help on three very different kinds of Web sites.

## 3 Develop and modify your thesis

As your ideas evolve, be ready to modify or change your thesis. After outlining his contribution to a library publication on computer literacy, Joel Kitze modified his thesis to give readers more to consider.

THESIS    In spite of expanding technology, computers will never replace books as the chief medium of written literacy.

SUPPORTING IDEA 1    Books are more democratic, since not everyone can afford a personal computer.

SUPPORTING IDEA 2    Books can be enjoyed anywhere--on a bus or beach, in bed.

SUPPORTING IDEA 3    Children enjoy the physical comfort of reading with adults, a comfort harder to achieve with computers.

**MODIFIED THESIS**  `Although computer technology allows masses of information to be stored and conveyed electronically, it will never replace the bound book as the most affordable, convenient, and magical medium for print.`

---

**STRATEGY**  **Develop your thesis.**

Help your reader anticipate and organize information in your writing, fitting separate chunks—paragraphs and sections—into your larger purpose. Use planning strategies (see Chapter 3) or research (see Part 24) to create a series of points that support, expand, or illustrate your thesis. Then extend and modify your thesis by asking why, how, and for what reason.

## 4c Considering your readers

Like an oral presentation, a written text addresses a specific **audience** that includes your actual or implied readers. (See Figure 4.1.)

### 1 Analyze your readers

Begin your audience analysis by asking, "Who are my readers?"

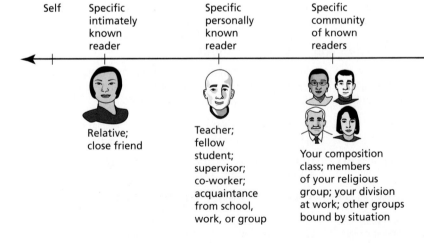

| Self | Specific intimately known reader | Specific personally known reader | Specific community of known readers |

Relative; close friend

Teacher; fellow student; supervisor; co-worker; acquaintance from school, work, or group

Your composition class; members of your religious group; your division at work; other groups bound by situation

**FIGURE 4.1**  The audience continuum

**STRATEGY**    Characterize your readers.

- **Size and familiarity.** How large is your audience? How close to you? Use the audience continuum to define levels of familiarity and formality.
- **Community.** Which expectations of readers are typical of the community in which you are writing? Which are specialized or local? What roles in the community do your readers play or expect you to play?
- **Knowledge.** What do readers already know about your topic? Are they novices or experts?
- **Social context.** What characterizes your readers socially, culturally, and educationally? How do they spend their time?
- **Intellectual disposition.** How do your readers think? Are they conservative? radical? apathetic?
- **Conditions of reading.** Under what conditions will they read?
- **Power.** What is your status relative to readers? Are they peers or superiors? Do you expect them, or do they expect you, to do something?

## 2  Adapt to your readers

Because academic, work, and public communities are broad groups, also ask, "Exactly what do my readers expect?"

- **Select the genre readers expect.** The type of text you choose to write—the **genre**—depends on your purpose and readers. If you request funds for a volunteer project, readers will expect a grant proposal, not a poem.

| Specific publicly known reader | Specific unknown reader | Specific community of unknown readers | General community of unknown readers |
|---|---|---|---|
|  |  |  |  |
| Senator Kennedy; Whoopi Goldberg; president of your college; editor of your local newspaper | Personnel director at Inland Chemicals; editor of the *Journal of Economics*; chair of the university committee on using animals in research; others known by name and affiliation | Board of directors at Inland Chemicals; members of the local PTA; the choir's electronic mailing list; readers of *Hunting Magazine;* other groups with shared interests | Democrats; educated Americans; readers of popular fiction; concerned citizens; working parents |

- **Shape your content to the context.** If you're explaining how to remove mildew for a neighborhood newsletter, skip the history of mildew unless it's relevant to the remedies.
- **Adjust your structure to the situation.** In a letter to your investment firm's client whose stock has tumbled, you might lead up to this news with the circumstances of the loss. A lab report, however, should move directly to the conventional sections.
- **Anticipate possible responses of readers.** Will readers expect you to be clinical and detached, informal and chatty, or in between? How might they react if you're emotional, hostile, or legalistic?

## ESL ADVICE: APPROPRIATE FORMALITY

Spoken English, even in the classroom and the office, may be quite informal. Written English may vary in formality, but readers other than friends and relatives generally expect it to be more formal than spoken language. If you're uncertain about what is appropriate, look at comparable writing done by others, or ask your teacher or supervisor for advice.

# 5    Drafting

If planning resembles storyboarding a movie, then drafting begins the filming, even though you may retake entire scenes and cut lots of footage. **Drafting** is the challenging process of stringing words together into sentences and paragraphs that make sense to a reader.

## 5a Moving from planning to drafting

Although all your planning (see Chapters 3 and 4) prepares you for drafting, you may not know how and where to begin writing. As Amy Burns reviewed a cluster she drew for her paper on superstition, she began jotting notes on "rabbit's foot," one of her "cases of superstition." Using these notes, she began drafting simply with a series of phrases.

> Rabbit's foot—common lucky charm. Omen of good fortune. Brasch says thumping noise from hind paws = communication. Thought to have magical powers. Newborns brushed to chase evil spirits.

Using a simple three-part scheme, Amy then developed a preliminary structure for grouping her ideas on superstition.

INTRODUCTION    `Fear, people who believe, origins`

BODY    `Examples (black cat, #13, ladder, rabbit's foot, etc.)`

CONCLUSION    `Truth and falsity, mystery of superstitions`

Amy used her plan as a way to start, writing an introduction about how superstitions originate in a fear of the unknown.

**Group your ideas.** Use your planning material to place ideas, topics, or terms into one of three categories: introduction, body, and conclusion. If your project has a required or expected structure, use it to define your groups. If you have made a rough outline of your paper, assign chunks of your outline to these parts. You might set up separate computer files so that you can work on these parts one section at a time. Later you can cut and paste the files into a single text.

As you draft, consider whether you're achieving your general purposes (persuading someone or explaining something) or your more specific purposes for different parts (enlivening a paragraph or illustrating a point). Given her specific purpose, to "grab my readers' attention and interest them in superstition," Amy added to her informative but dull opening.

> `Do you knock on wood after making a prediction? shiver when`
> `a black cat crosses your path? consider 13 unlucky? If so, you`
> `have already been swept into the world of superstitions. Many`
> `people practice some of the bizarre rituals of superstition, but`
> `few know why.`

What readers expect first, second, and third may help you determine how to organize to achieve your purpose. You'd probably arrange a local history of a ballpark chronologically but organize an argument for its preservation logically, using your paragraphs to support your assertions.

**Write about your writing.** Begin not by writing your paper but by writing *about* it. What concerns you most? What do you hope to do? How might you start? As you jot notes, you'll be less anxious about starting—after all, you *have* started.

Once you begin drafting, don't worry about choosing perfect words or crafting perfect sentences and paragraphs. Just write as much as you can quickly so that you develop momentum. When momentum develops, keep going.

**Try semidrafting.** Write full sentences until you're about to stall out. Then simply write *etc.* in place of the full text, and continue with your next point. Or add directions to yourself in brackets, noting what to do next. For documented projects or research papers, use semidrafting to note what you need to integrate from sources as Kavita Kamal did when writing about "wild children" (supposedly raised by animals in the woods).

> The first case was that of Victor, the "Wild Boy of Aveyron."
> Victor first appeared in a village in southern France in January
> 1800. His age was estimated at eleven or twelve years. [Explain
> his adoption by Itard and Guerin and their subsequent studies.]
> People assumed that he was a mute because he did not speak. [Now
> go into the stuff from Shattuck about no malformation of the
> tongue, mouth, etc.]

---

### ESL ADVICE:   SEMIDRAFTING AND PHRASING

If you find composing in English difficult, type *XXX*, draw a circle, or make a note in your first language where you need to rework your phrasing. Continue semidrafting so that you get your main ideas down on paper, and fill in the small points later.

## 5b Drafting collaboratively

Try involving others in the process of writing.

### STRATEGY   Find a community sounding board.

- Try talking or emailing about your writing with someone in your writing community. Explaining what you're trying to do may alleviate tension, suggest solutions, or draw ideas from your listener that will help you get started again.
- You might also try *imagining* the most sympathetic listener you can. Then tell him or her all about your project. Focus on this interested friend, and banish that critical reader who peers over your shoulder.

When you write with a work team or a civic or academic group, look for collaborative strategies that suit the group and the context.

- Organize **parallel drafting**, dividing up the project, perhaps by group members' specialties, so that each is responsible for drafting a particular section. You can exchange drafts as you revise and edit, but one person may need to act as editor, integrating the drafts.
- Try **team drafting** when writers share similar ideas and approaches, assigning two writers for each section. The first drafts until he or she gets stuck, and then the second begins where the first stopped. Recirculate the drafts when revising and editing.

- Consider **intensive drafting** when working with a close friend or colleague. Assemble materials in a space where you can work undisturbed. Decide where each will begin drafting, and exchange sections at a certain time or as you finish segments. Continue exchanging drafts, or vary your pattern by having one person compose aloud as the other types.

# 6 Revising

Because so much of what we read is in final, published form, we forget the hours the author has spent **revising**—reconsidering content and structure in terms of community expectations, redrafting whole sections, and struggling to find just the right words. Revision is more than fine-tuning style, grammar, and sentence problems (**editing**) or searching for missing apostrophes and typographical errors (**proofreading**), important though these activities may be (see Chapter 8). Instead, revision means *reading* your draft critically and *reworking* it to make effective changes. It means stepping outside the draft to assess its strengths and weaknesses and then deciding what to expand, clarify, reword, restructure—or just plain cut.

| REVISING, EDITING, AND PROOFREADING | |
|---|---|
| **Major revision** | Focus on sections and chunks as part of the whole. Redraft, reorganize, add, and delete. |
| **Minor revision** | Focus on passages and paragraphs. Revise for sense, style, and economy. |
| **Editing** | Focus on paragraphs, sentences, and words. Edit for correctness and conventions (grammar, sentences, wording, punctuation, mechanics). Edit for clarity, style, and economy. |
| **Proofreading** | Focus on details and final appearance. Proofread for spelling, punctuation, typographical errors, and missing words. |

## 6a Making major revisions

Concentrate first on **major revision**, large-scale changes that make your draft as a whole more effective. For example, if your report seems too informal for your work community, you may decide to redraft its introduction, delete an anecdote, or add more alternative solutions. Think critically about content, structure, tone, style, appeals to audience, and purpose.

## 1 Redraft workable material

Rework ineffective parts, as Jessica White did with her opening.

ORIGINAL DRAFT  I was a cheerleading captain and I loved basketball. I put a lot of work into my cheerleading season. We had great team spirit between the cheerleaders and the teammates. We led our crowd to great enthusiasm and spirit.

WRITER'S ASSESSMENT: **I want people to feel what it was like after the state quarter-finals. This doesn't even say where I was or what was happening.**

REVISED DRAFT  There we were, a bunch of cheerleaders packed into Rebecca's car. Everyone's spirits were soaring; we had won the quarter-final game of the state basketball championship. It was a bitterly cold night, but we laughed, joked, and endlessly replayed the highlights of the game.

Let your draft sit for a few hours or days, and then read it (preferably aloud). Place a question mark next to any ineffective section. After you finish reading, go back to each question mark, and bracket the passage where the writing loses vitality or meaning. Ask yourself what you want to accomplish there, take out a new page (or open a new file), and say it again.

## 2 Reorganize paragraphs or sections

An early draft may reflect your process of discovery instead of the best order for your readers or subject. Keyshawn Williams drafted a memo from a committee looking for ways to cut company expenses. He originally opened with the committee's conclusions, but the group revised the memo to give readers more context—concise background on the committee's task, a clear statement of the problem, and then the recommendations.

> **STRATEGY**  Summarize your paragraphs.
>
> Number the paragraphs in your draft, and write a phrase or sentence to sum up the main point of each. Use this list to spot paragraphs that you could combine or reorganize to create a clearer flow of ideas. Consider whether points at the end belong at the beginning. (See 3b and 7f.)

## 3 Add new material

An addition can develop a paragraph (see 7f), enliven a dull passage, clarify or extend a point, or supply missing detail. When Gina Giacomo revised her Web page explaining the transfer to a new email system, she added material to clarify the transition for readers.

> Your new email address is listed below. It should be easy to remember because it consists of the first six letters of your name. You may send your new address to people or groups that send you messages, but you don't need to. Our server will automatically forward any mail directed to your old address.

Highlight the first and last sentence in each paragraph. Read through these highlighted sentences, identifying any gaps where a paragraph doesn't connect clearly to the one before or after it or where information or detail is missing within the paragraph. (See 7d.)

## 4 Delete unnecessary material

Don't be afraid to slash away large chunks if they're unnecessary, illogical, or redundant, as Brian Corby did in his letter to the zoning board.

> With eighteen stories, Regency Towers will cast a long, wide shadow over Piedmont Park. ~~The building will be quite tall and very wide.~~ For several hours a day, the toddler play area will be darkened. On summer afternoons, the shadow will cut across the baseball diamond. ~~This could be dangerous.~~

Imagine that your draft will be published if you trim at least 10 percent of the fat. Mark sentences where you can cut or paragraphs where you might merge the essentials. (See 33b.)

## 6b Making minor revisions

**Minor revisions** are fairly small changes, mostly refining and polishing passages for three reasons: *sense, style,* and *economy.*

### 1 Revise for sense

When you're immersed in your writing, you may forget what your reader *doesn't* know or think, leading to illogical or puzzling statements. Read your draft carefully to see whether each passage *makes sense* in the context of the whole project. Try to look at the text as your readers might, not in your own way. If possible, ask peer readers to place question marks next to anything confusing.

Paul Tichey asked his peer group to read his draft on Nevada's environ-
mentally threatened wild mustangs. Paul revised the draft after his readers
pointed out that they couldn't tell whether the Air Force was helping or harming the animals.

> , which                 demise
> The Air Force was partly responsible for the reduction in the
>        the                      , has now
> number of wild mustangs on the Tonopah missile range. The Air
> joined forces with
> Force is part of a team that also includes the Bureau of Land
>
> Management and a group of wild-horse preservationists. All three
>                          save      from dehydration and
> groups have banded together to help the wild mustangs in this
> death during the duration of the drought.
> period of drought and dehydration.

## 2 Revise for style

Consider how your prose "sounds"—its rhythm and complexity. In any
rough paragraph, place a +, √, −, or ? next to each sentence to indicate whether
you feel positive, neutral, negative, or uncertain about it. Rewrite what you
don't like; try to get readers' advice on questionable sentences. When in doubt,
try an alternative. (See 32b and 34b.)

Paul placed a minus sign next to the sentence below. He decided that too
many words began with *d*, and *during the duration* seemed redundant.

> The Air Force, which was partly responsible for the demise of
>
> the wild mustangs on the Tonopah missile range, has now joined
>
> forces with the Bureau of Land Management and a group of wild-
>                                             fatal
> horse preservationists to help save the mustangs from
>             while the drought persists.
> dehydration and death during the duration of the drought.

## 3 Revise for economy

Cut what you can without losing sense or coherence. Paul reduced
seventy-eight words to thirty-six—a cut of over 50 percent!

**SECOND
DRAFT**
> A serious problem confronting groups who want to manage
> wild mustangs on military sites in Nevada is the relative
> inaccessibility of the sites, since many require security
> passes or are fenced off, and environmentalists can't come
> and go as they please, as they can on public or even some

private land. It's simply harder to study or help horses on restricted military installations. Open rangeland has easier access, and inspectors can simply move in and out at will.

**THIRD DRAFT (REVISED FOR ECONOMY)** Restricted access to Nevada military sites presents a serious obstacle to successful horse management. Unlike open rangeland, where inspectors can come and go as they please, military sites are often fenced off and require security clearance.

## STRATEGY  Count your words.

Count the words in a passage that lacks economy. Then start cutting. See what percentage you can trim without changing meaning. (See 33b.)

## 6c  Revising collaboratively

Ask at least one person you respect to give you honest feedback. In return, promise to read drafts for your reader.

### 1 Respond helpfully

When you act as a peer reader—or ask someone to read for you—begin by establishing the writer's purpose, audience, and concerns.

- What sort of project is it? What is the writer trying to do?
- For what community is it intended? What do readers expect?
- What does the writer want to learn from a reader?

Jot notes that balance praise with helpful criticism. Don't simply say, "It was really good," or give directions like "Move this to page 2." Instead, offer diplomatic advice: "What would happen if you moved this to page 2?"

### 2 Turn to your readers for their responses

Accept constructive comments from an honest reader gracefully. If you are defensive, your reader is unlikely to give you more feedback. But if a reader questions something you like, remember that you have the final say.

- Give your readers a list of your specific concerns about the draft.
- Minimize apologies. Everyone feels anxious about sharing a draft.
- If time is limited, consider taping reactions, meeting briefly to take notes on responses, emailing, or exchanging comments jotted on the drafts.

- Use responses to plan how to revise. If readers didn't like a section, do you want to change it, delete it, or write it another way?
- Recirculate a collaborative draft, or meet again to revise.

---

**ESL ADVICE: PEER READERS**

You may worry about editing grammar or spelling before you share a draft. Review these details quickly, and look for a peer reader who is willing to ignore the small points in a rough draft. Ask this reader to focus on specific issues (such as the order of ideas) or on common problems (such as weak first paragraphs). Consider sharing your draft with several readers, including native and nonnative speakers of English, for a range of responses.

# 7 Shaping Paragraphs

Every time you indent to begin a new paragraph, you give readers a signal: watch for a shift in topic, another perspective, or a special emphasis. Whether you are writing a history paper, a letter to the editor, or a memo at work, readers will expect your paragraphs to guide them. Revising paragraphs to increase *focus*, *coherence*, and *development* helps readers figure out what's important, how ideas and details logically connect, and what's coming up.

## 7a Recognizing unfocused paragraphs

When you concentrate on a main idea throughout, you create a paragraph that is **focused** because it doesn't stray into unrelated details. A paragraph is **unified** when all its sentences directly relate to its point. Ask questions to help recognize unfocused paragraphs.

- What is the main point (or topic) in this paragraph?
- How many different topics does this paragraph cover?
- Is the focus announced to readers? Where? How?
- Does the paragraph elaborate on the point? Do details fit the topic?

Jeanne Brown used questions to analyze a paragraph on color analysis.

**UNFOCUSED**

A color to look at is the color red. Red is often considered a very fast and sporty color for cars. Porsches that are red are likely to be chosen over blue ones. Red ties are often called "power ties." Red can also be a very daring color to wear. A woman who wears a long red dress and has painted fingernails to match is not a shy woman. She is going to be noticed and will revel in the attention.

WRITER'S REACTION: *My main point?* I want to talk about the strong effects red can have on people. I don't think that the focus on red's power is clear. *Focus announced to readers?* Not really. I need to say that I am discussing the effects red has, not simply that it is a color worth looking at. *Elaboration on the point?* No, not very much. I need to help readers understand how each example explains my view of red's effect on moods and attitudes.

**REVISED**

Red is a color that can affect how people feel and react. Red makes heads turn, and the person associated with the color often ends up feeling important and influential. A red Porsche draws more attention than a blue one. A red tie, or "power tie," can be bold and assertive. Worn with a blue or gray suit, the touch of red makes the wearer stand out in a crowd and builds self-confidence. A woman wearing a long red dress with nails painted to match is probably not shy. She is going to be noticed and will revel in the attention because it reinforces her positive self-image.

## 7b Revising for paragraph focus

Help your readers recognize a paragraph's focus by stating your topic and your main idea or perspective in a **topic sentence**. Begin with this sentence when you want readers to grasp the point right away.

<u>When writing jokes, it's a good idea to avoid vague generalizations.</u> Don't just talk about "fruit" when you can talk about "an apple." Strong writing creates a single image for everyone in the crowd, each person imagining a very similar thing. But when you say "fruit," people are either imagining several different kinds of fruit or they aren't really thinking of anything in particular, and both things can significantly reduce their emotional investment in the joke. But when you say "an apple," everyone has *a clear picture,* and thus a feeling.

—JAY SANKEY, *Zen and the Art of Stand-Up Comedy*

Experiment with other topic sentence options: placing it at the end of the paragraph, repeating it at the end from a different perspective, implying it if your point is unmistakably clear, or adding a limiting or clarifying sentence to narrow your point. Supplement your topic sentences with section headings if readers expect them in a report or proposal.

**STRATEGY**   **Highlight topic sentences.**

Skim your draft, using a highlighter (or bold type) to mark each topic sentence. When you note that one is missing or inadequate, read critically to decide whether to revise the topic sentence or refocus the paragraph. Skim your topic sentences again, tracing your explanation or argument through the draft as a whole.

**ESL ADVICE:   PARAGRAPH CONVENTIONS**

In English, readers expect a paragraph to have a specific focus and often look to a topic sentence for guidance. In Hindi, however, paragraphs may lack a sharply defined topic and may contain loosely related ideas. In some languages, a topic sentence does not begin a paragraph or is not stated directly. As you write in a second language, adjust your paragraphs so they do what readers in that language expect.

## 7c Recognizing incoherent paragraphs

A paragraph is **coherent** if each sentence clearly leads a reader to the next or if the sentences form a recognizable, easy-to-understand arrangement. Paragraphs may lack coherence if sentences are out of logical order or change topic so abruptly that readers must struggle to follow the thought.

Use these questions to check paragraph coherence.

• What words name the topic and main points? Are they repeated?
• What transitions alert readers to relationships among sentences?
• What parallel words and structures highlight similar or related ideas?
• Does the arrangement of ideas and details clarify their relationships?

**LACKS COHERENCE**

Captain James Cook discovered the island of Hawaii in 1779. Mauna Kea, on Hawaii, is the tallest mountain in the Pacific. Cook might have noticed the many mountains on the island as he sailed into Kealakekua Bay. The island also has five major volcanoes. Mauna Loa, another mountain on the island, is a dormant volcano that last erupted in 1984. Kilauea is the most active volcano on earth. It continues to enlarge the land that makes up this largest island in the Hawaiian chain. The volcano sends forth lava continuously.

**READER'S REACTION: This paragraph provides lots of information, but it's hard to follow because it jumps from sentence to sentence.**

**REVISED**

In 1779, Captain James Cook sailed into Kealakekua Bay and discovered the island of Hawaii. As he entered the bay, did Cook **notice** the many **mountains** on the island? Perhaps he **noticed** Mauna Kea, the tallest **mountain** in the Pacific. Perhaps he **spotted** one or more of the five major **volcanoes**. **One of these**, Mauna Loa, is a dormant **volcano** that last erupted in 1984. **Another**, Kilauea, is the most active **volcano** on earth. It sends forth lava continuously. **In addition**, it keeps adding to the landmass of what is already the largest island in the Hawaiian chain.

## 7d Revising for paragraph coherence

By repeating key words, phrases, synonyms, and related words that refer to your topic and main point, you keep readers aware of your focus.

According to recent research, **people married for a long time** often develop similar **facial features**. The **faces** of **younger couples** show only chance resemblances. As **they** share emotions for many years, however, most **older couples** develop similar **expressions**.

Place key words prominently, beginning or ending sentences. Avoid burying them in the middle of sentences.

**Transitional expressions** like *in addition*, *therefore*, and *on the other hand* also alert readers to relationships among sentences.

Many people still consider your college choice your most important career decision. These days, **however**, graduate school is the most important choice **because** the competition for jobs has grown fiercer. **For example**, business positions at the entry level often go to people with MBAs and law degrees. **In addition**, many good jobs require advanced training and skills. **Moreover**, employers pay attention **not only** to the presence of an advanced degree on your résumé **but also** to the program of study **and** the quality of the school.

**Patterns of arrangement** also build coherence by emphasizing how details are related. A **spatial** organization guides readers through the details of a scene, a work of art, or a mechanism in an easy-to-follow order such as left to right or top to bottom. Presenting events in time sequence, first to last, is the clearest **chronological** arrangement. Signal simple rearrangements, such as flashbacks or simultaneous events, with wording like *at the same time*, *next*, and *earlier*. A **question-answer** or **problem-solution** sequence alerts readers to a **logical order**. In a **general-to-specific** pattern, you offer broader generalizations first and then move to more specific details. In a **specific-to-general** pattern, you reverse the order, moving from specific examples and details toward

---

**USEFUL TRANSITIONS FOR SHOWING RELATIONSHIPS**

| | |
|---|---|
| **Time and Sequence** | next, later, after, while, meanwhile, immediately, earlier, first, second, shortly, in the future, subsequently, as long as, soon, since, finally, last, at that time, as soon as |
| **Comparison** | likewise, similarly, also, too, again, in the same manner, in comparison, equally |
| **Contrast** | in contrast, on the one hand . . . on the other hand, however, although, even though, still, yet, but, nevertheless, conversely, at the same time, despite, regardless |
| **Examples** | for example, for instance, such as, specifically, thus, to illustrate, namely, in fact |
| **Cause and Effect** | as a result, consequently, accordingly, if . . . then, is due to this, for this reason, because, as a consequence of, thus |
| **Place** | next to, above, behind, beyond, near, here, across from, to the right, there, in front, in the background, in between, opposite |
| **Addition** | and, too, moreover, in addition, besides, furthermore, next, also, finally, again |
| **Concession** | of course, naturally, it may be the case that, granted, it is true that, certainly, though |
| **Conclusion** | in conclusion, in short, as a result, as the data show, finally, therefore |
| **Repetition** | to repeat, in other words, once again, as I said earlier |
| **Summary** | on the whole, to summarize, to sum up, in short, therefore, in brief |

---

a generalization. You can also link elements by using **parallelism**—repeating the same grammatical structures to highlight similar or related ideas (see 30b).

## 7e Recognizing poorly developed paragraphs

**Paragraph development** provides the examples, facts, concrete details, explanations, or supporting arguments that make a paragraph informative enough to support your ideas, opinions, and conclusions. Short paragraphs are not always underdeveloped, nor are long paragraphs always adequate—yet length can be an important cue. More than two sentences are generally necessary for a paragraph to explore a topic and support a generalization.

**UNDERDEVELOPED**

Recycling is always a good idea—or *almost* always. Recycling some products, even newsprint and other paper goods, may require more energy from fossil fuels and more valuable natural resources than making them over again.

**READER'S REACTION: I'd like to know more before I agree with this. What are these products? How much energy does it take to recycle them? What natural resources do they consume?**

Readers from different fields and communities favor different kinds of supporting information. The detail expected in a lab report obviously differs from that expected in a job application or a grant proposal, but the success of all three depends on clear and powerful supporting detail.

**STRATEGY**    **Check your paragraph development.**
- Does the paragraph present enough material to *inform* readers?
- Does the paragraph adequately *support* any generalizations?

## 7f   Revising for paragraph development

**Examples**, whether brief or extended, help clarify a concept, explain a generalization, or provide reasons to support your position. They help a reader see an idea in action and its consequences.

**BRIEF EXAMPLES**

All kinds of products have been included in the fast-track recalls. For example, a major manufacturer recently recalled tens of thousands of humidifiers that could potentially overheat or catch fire. A leading manufacturer of children's products recalled tens of thousands of baby monitors that could smoke and flame. A prominent clothing retailer recalled more than 100,000 children's jackets with zipper pulls containing unacceptable levels of lead. A well-known company recalled tens of thousands of gas grills because a defective hose could leak gas or cause fires.     —"Fast-Track Recalls," *Consumer Product Safety Review*

**EXTENDED EXAMPLE**

One day in 1957, the songwriter Johnny Mercer received a letter from Sadie Vimerstedt, a widowed grandmother who worked behind a cosmetics counter in Youngstown, Ohio. Mrs. Vimerstedt suggested Mercer write a song called "I Want to Be Around to Pick Up the Pieces When

Somebody Breaks Your Heart." Five years later, Mercer got in touch to say he'd written the song and that Tony Bennett would record it. Today, if you look at the label on any recording of "I Wanna Be Around," you'll notice that the credits for words and music are shared by Johnny Mercer and Sadie Vimerstedt. The royalties were split fifty-fifty, too, thanks to which Mrs. Vimerstedt and her heirs have earned more than $100,000. In my opinion, Mercer's generosity was a class act.

—JOHN BERENDT, "Class Acts"

**STRATEGY**  **Add details and specifics to develop paragraph content.**

- **Examples.** Use brief or extended illustrations.
- **Concrete detail.** Recreate sights, sounds, tastes, smells, movements, and sensations of touch.
- **Facts and statistics.** Offer precise data from your fieldwork or authoritative sources, perhaps in numerical form.
- **Supporting statements.** Explain your own interpretations, or quote people or sources that readers will trust.
- **Summaries.** Present other people's opinions, conclusions, or explanations in compressed form (see 14b), showing how your conclusions agree with, disagree with, or supplement theirs.

**Patterns of development** help you accomplish familiar tasks so that readers can readily recognize the purpose and arrangement of a paragraph or a cluster of paragraphs. How you organize and develop a particular paragraph depends on what you want it to accomplish. In addition, how you arrange a series of paragraphs within an essay depends on what you want that sequence of paragraphs to accomplish and the kinds of explanation, illustration, or other elaboration that readers will find persuasive.

**Narrating.** Turn to **narration** to recount past or present events, recreate an experience, tell an anecdote, or envision the future.

Suddenly the ground thundered, and, as if called, a train caught up with Uncle Clark. It slowed only a little, but not enough to be caught, even by my uncle, strong and sleek as he was. Undaunted, Uncle Clark let out a piercing whistle. Out of the black square shadow of one boxcar shot a long arm. In a flash my uncle grabbed it and was hoisted inside the wide door. We never saw the other hobos; we only heard them laughing at the show they'd given us townies.

—BRENDA PETERSON, "Vaster Than Empires and More Slow"

**Describing.** You can create images of a place, an object, or a feeling or sketch a person's character through **description**, emphasizing emotional impact (**subjective description**) or physical details (**objective description**).

---

**PATTERNS FOR PARAGRAPH DEVELOPMENT**

| TASK | DEVELOPMENT STRATEGY |
|---|---|
| Tell a story; recreate events; present an anecdote | Narrating |
| Provide detail about a scene or object; portray someone's character; evoke a feeling | Describing |
| Explore similarities or differences; evaluate alternatives | Comparing and contrasting |
| Provide directions; explain the operation of a mechanism, procedure, or natural process | Explaining a process |
| Separate a subject into parts; explore the relationships among parts | Dividing |
| Sort things or people into groups; explain the relationships among the groups | Classifying |
| Explain the meaning of a term or concept; explore and illustrate the meaning of a complicated concept or phenomenon | Defining |
| Consider why something did happen (or might); explore possible causes and results | Analyzing causes and effects |

---

With its shed roof sloping north, the cabin sits low and compact in the snow, a pair of moose antlers nailed above a window in the high south wall. There are four dog houses to the rear of it, each of them roofed with a poke of snow-covered hay. A meat rack stands to one side, built high between two stout spruces, and a ladder made of dry poles leans against a tree next to it. A hindquarter of moose hangs from the rack; it is frozen rock hard and well wrapped with canvas to keep it from birds. Just the same, I see that camp-robbers have pecked at it and torn a hole in the canvas. Nothing else can reach it there seven feet above the ground.   —JOHN HAINES, "Three Days"

**Comparing and contrasting.** Paragraphs that **compare** and **contrast** can evaluate alternative policies or products, examine pros and cons, or compare qualities and explanations. A **point-by-point organization** examines each comparable feature for first one subject and then the next.

Topic sentence    But biology has a funny way of confounding expecta-
                  tions. Rather than disappear, the evidence for innate sexual dif-
Feature 1         ferences only began to mount. In medicine, researchers docu-
                  mented that heart disease strikes men at a younger age than it
Feature 2         does women and that women have a more moderate physiolog-
Feature 3         ical response to stress. Researchers found subtle neurological
                  differences between the sexes both in the brain's structure and
Feature 4         in its functioning. In addition, another generation of parents
                  discovered that, despite their best efforts to give baseballs to
                  their daughters and sewing kits to their sons, girls still flocked
                  to dollhouses while boys clambered into tree forts. Perhaps na-
                  ture is more important than nurture after all.
                  —CHRISTINE GORMAN, "Sizing Up the Sexes"

A **subject-by-subject organization** considers each subject in its en-
tirety, within a paragraph or a series of paragraphs.

                  For everyone, home is a place to be offstage. But the com-
Topic sentence    fort of home can have opposite and incompatible meanings for
Subject 1         women and men. For many men, the comfort of home means
                  freedom from having to prove themselves and impress through
                  verbal display. At last, they are in a situation where talk is not
Subject 2         required. They are free to remain silent. But for women, home
                  is a place where they are free to talk, and where they feel the
                  greatest need for talk, with those they are closest to. For them,
                  the comfort of home means the freedom to talk without worry-
                  ing about how their talk will be judged.
                  —DEBORAH TANNEN, "Put Down That Paper and Talk to Me!"

**Explaining a process.** To give directions, show how a mechanism or procedure works, or explain other processes, label the steps or stages clearly. Arrange
them logically, usually chronologically. Devote a paragraph to each part of the
process if you wish to emphasize its stages.

Stage One sleep is very light—just the other side of wakefulness. Stage
Two (which makes up about half our total slumber time) is a transitional phase into either slow-wave or REM sleep, while stages Three
and Four are slow-wave sleep. In slow-wave, or deep, sleep, brain
activity slows to a crawl. In REM, or dreaming sleep, on the other
hand, the brain bursts into high activity virtually identical to being
awake—though the muscles are temporarily paralyzed from the neck
down.                                    —ROYCE FLIPPIN, "Tossing and Turning"

**Dividing and classifying.** When you divide a subject, you split it into parts,
explaining it and the relationships of its parts.

**DIVISION**

Sunglasses should be more than cheap plastic frames with dark lenses. A good pair has three important features: it protects, adds a touch of style, and costs a lot more than $1.99. Eye-damaging ultra-violet rays make protection essential. Your sunglasses should guard against both UV-A rays and the shorter, more damaging UV-B rays. The racks of sunglasses, many sporting designer names, offer styles from wraparound to wire frames, from amber tints in red rims to gray on gray. You can create almost any impression: debonair, retro, sexy, athletic, Hollywood, even owlish and scholarly. Yet trendy appearance and effective protection come at a price. Be ready to pay at least $20 for a pair of sunglasses coated to protect from all the harmful rays and ten times as much (or more) for designer styles from this year's collection.

—MEGHAN TUBRIDY, College Student

To classify, you sort several subjects into groups, exploring similarities *within* groups and differences and relationships *between* groups.

**CLASSIFICATION**

Men all have different styles of chopping wood, all of which are deemed by their practitioners as the only proper method. Often when I'm chopping wood in my own inept style, a neighbor will come over and "offer help." He'll bust up a few logs in his own manner, advising me as to the proper swing and means of analyzing the grain of the wood. There are "over the head" types and "swing from the shoulder" types, and guys who lay the logs down horizontally on the ground and still others who balance them on end, atop of stumps. I have one neighbor who uses what he calls "vector analysis." Using the right vectors, he says, the wood will practically *split itself.*

—JAMES FINNEY BOYLAN, "The Bean Curd Method"

**Defining.** When you introduce a term or concept to your readers, you may need to stipulate the meaning it will carry in your writing or want to contrast its definition with others.

When they hear the word *crystal*, many people think of a mineral dug from the ground. But the lead crystal used to make beautiful plates, glasses, and vases does not come from this source. The crystal in these objects—artworks, actually—is glass with a high lead content. The glass is made from a mixture of sand and other ingredients like potash (potassium) or soda that help the mixture melt. The various minerals also affect the color and clarity of the glass. Lead crystal must contain at least 30 percent to 35 percent lead oxide (by weight) in its ingredients. The resulting material is easier for artists to work with as they grind intricate facets into the surface to create designs that sparkle and intrigue like a finely cut diamond.

—ANDREA HERRMANN, College Student

**Analyzing causes and effects.** You may explain why something has occurred (causes), explore consequences (effects), or combine both.

> Of all the habits I have, there is one my friends simply cannot understand. I always set my clock ahead fourteen minutes. "What for?" everyone asks when they notice that my clock is running so far ahead. The habit started in my first year of high school. I was so nervous about being late for the first day of "real" school that I moved the clock hands ahead—fourteen minutes ahead. When I got into bed, I had a secure feeling that everything would work out fine. Since then, I feel rushed and hurried every time I set my clock to regular time, but relaxed and secure when I set it to my time, fourteen minutes fast.
>
> —Kris Lundell, College Student

## 7g Using special-purpose paragraphs

Paragraphs help begin, end, and link the parts of a text.

**Introductory paragraphs.** Your opening builds your relationship with readers, motivating them to continue reading. It can establish the tone, approach, and degree of formality expected by readers in a given community. It should answer questions like the following.

- What is the main idea or purpose of this writing project?
- What precise topic, problem, or issue will this text address?
- Why should readers be interested in this topic?

This anecdote, for example, introduces the environmental threat posed by Las Vegas.

> It was advertised as the biggest non-nuclear explosion in Nevada history. On October 27, 1993, Steve Wynn, the State's official "god of hospitality," flashed his trademark smile and pushed the detonator button. As 200,000 Las Vegans cheered, the 18-story Dunes sign, once the tallest neon structure in the world, crumbled to the desert floor.
>
> —Mike Davis, "House of Cards"

**Concluding paragraphs.** Your ending may remind readers of key ideas and encourage them to think about information presented or actions proposed.

> So if it's any consolation to those of us who just don't manage to fit enough sleep into our packed days, being chronically tired probably won't do us any permanent harm. And if things get desperate enough,

we just might have to schedule a nap somewhere on our busy calendars. —DANIEL GOLEMAN, "Too Little, Too Late"

---

**CREATING INTRODUCTORY PARAGRAPHS**

Provide background, context, or history.

Tell an anecdote or story, or recall an event.

Explain an issue.

Supply a definition.

Present the sides in a controversy.

Ask a question.

Use an extended example.

Offer an intriguing analogy.

Quote from an authority.

Quote someone's opinion.

Compare another situation, time period, or issue.

Provide statistics to define the issue or problem.

Describe a mysterious or interesting phenomenon.

Cite pertinent or little-known facts.

Avoid obvious generalizations, shopworn phrases, apologies, and references to your own title.

---

**CREATING CONCLUDING PARAGRAPHS**

Summarize main points briefly.

Use a quotation.

Restate the thesis, or repeat proposed recommendations.

Offer a striking example, anecdote, or image.

Echo the introduction.

Predict future events or speculate.

Avoid apologies, overstatements, new ideas, and simply rewording your thesis statement.

---

**Linking paragraphs.** Paragraphs work together to form a coherent whole. Add links to clarify their relationships within a cluster or section. Key words and transitional expressions (see 7d) identify connections between paragraphs just as they do between sentences. Specific sentences and paragraphs also can connect sections in a paper—supplying previews, bridges, and summaries.

**STRATEGY** Connect your paragraphs to guide readers.

- Announce your purpose to help readers anticipate your reasoning.
- Provide a **boundary statement**—a sentence beginning one paragraph but acting as a bridge from the paragraph before. Remind the reader of material covered earlier as you present the topic sentence.

- Add a short **planning paragraph** to help readers anticipate the arrangement of the upcoming discussion.
- Create a **signal paragraph** to alert readers to a major change in direction or the beginning of a new section.
- Use a brief **summary paragraph** to mark the end of a discussion or to review main points for readers.

# 8 Editing and Proofreading

After revising your writing (see Chapter 6), especially your paragraphs (see Chapter 7), you're ready to edit and proofread. **Editing** means adjusting sentences and words for clarity, style, economy, and correctness. A final polish, **proofreading**, eliminates distractions such as misspelled words and typographical errors.

## 8a Writing correctly

Writing correctly means recognizing and using the **conventions**—the options for grammar, sentence structure and style, word choice, punctuation, and mechanics—that readers expect you to use. Some conventions don't vary much across communities, such as using complete sentences or standard spelling in formal prose. In these cases, most writers try to avoid challenging readers' strongly held expectations. After all, a reader irritated by errors isn't likely to give you a high grade, promote you, join your civic crusade, or view you as an attentive writer.

Other conventions, however, vary with the context. For example, newspaper readers wouldn't be surprised to find only one comma in this sentence: *The suspect jumped from the car, evaded the officers and ran into the motel.* But many academic readers would expect a second comma to follow *officers,* perhaps citing the well-known guides of the Modern Language Association (MLA) and the American Psychological Association (APA) as authorities on this comma issue (see Chapters 16–17). Likewise, a chemist would use numerals (such as *12* or *84*) in a lab report, while an art historian might spell out *twelve* and *eighty-four* in an interpretive paper. Effective writers learn how to recognize and edit flexible conventions to meet readers' expectations.

## 8b Editing your own writing

You can improve your editing skills each time you prepare a college paper, a work project, or a public communication. Allow plenty of time to read carefully, and shift your attention from content (what's said) to form (how it's said). Noticing readers' reactions during class or meetings can alert you to their individual and community sensitivities. Check your writing for both the problems readers identify and the features they admire.

As you edit, focus on one issue at a time—commas, perhaps, or wordiness—while you scour your text for specific cases. Then repeat the process for the next issue. Read your text several times to avoid being overloaded by too many problems at once. Edit in your computer file if you are using searches to hunt for words, repetitions, or sentence features that you want to correct or improve, such as overuse of *really* or confusion of *its* and *it's*. After a break, print your paper, and read it again, this time with a red pen or a highlighter in your hand. Check especially carefully for any pattern of errors—repeated mistakes—that instructors, classmates, friends, or other readers have helped you recognize.

### 1 Edit for clarity, style, and economy

Most writing profits from final cosmetic surgery. If your grant proposal, oral presentation, letter to the editor, or other writing project has a length limit, edit ruthlessly to meet this expectation. Ask these questions as you edit:

- **Are my sentences clear and easy to read?** Try reading out loud. Whenever you stumble over the wording, rephrase or restructure.
- **Do I repeat some sentence structures too often?** If too many sentences begin with nouns or *I*, start some with prepositional phrases (see 19b-1) or subordinate clauses (see 19c and 31b–c).
- **Do any words seem odd or inappropriate?** If so, reword. Turn to a dictionary or thesaurus for help. (See 34b, 36b.)
- **If I had to cut ten words per page, which could I drop?** Cut, but avoid new problems (such as short, choppy sentences). (See 32b.)

DRAFT     The aligned pulleys are lined up so that they are located up above the center core of the machine.

READER'S REACTION: **This seems repetitive and boring.**

EDITED     The aligned pulleys are ~~lined up so that they are located~~ **positioned** ~~up~~ above ~~the center core of~~ **the machine's core**.

### 2 Edit for grammatical problems

Editing for grammatical problems challenges you first to *recognize* the problem and then to *edit* to repair or eliminate it. The chart on the back cover

**SERIOUS**
**ERROR**

lists ten errors identified by academic readers as likely to irritate readers and call into question a writer's skills. The sections that discuss these errors are marked by an icon as seen in the margin here. In addition, this handbook's editing advice uses the read-recognize-revise pattern to help you identify errors and select a useful editing strategy.

Check your paper carefully to find potential errors.

- Read your paper from start to finish, circling or marking any errors in grammar, punctuation, and sentence logic. If you can quickly correct an error, do so. Otherwise, finish identifying problems, and then look up the relevant advice in this handbook or other references.
- Read your paper again, this time marking all suspected problems in your text. Follow your instincts if you feel that a sentence is weak or flawed. Then look up the pertinent advice, and edit the errors or flaws. Stick to the possible errors unless you want to improve an awkward or wordy sentence. Ask a teacher, tutor, peer editor, colleague, or friend for advice as needed.

Paragraphs from Jim Tollefson's newsletter for his local nature conservancy show his circled errors and his edited version.

**DRAFT WITH**
**ERRORS**
**MARKED**

Critics of the ⓔndangered Ⓢpecies ⓐct think it is too br⌀ad. Bⓔcause some ⓢpecie'ⓢ may be less vital to environmental balance than others. ⓣhey want to protect species selectiveⓛy, hⓞwever, scientists do not know which species are more important.

*caps*
*fragment*
*apostrophe*
*who?*
*comma splice*

**EDITED**

Critics of the Endangered Species Act think it is too broad because some species may be less vital to environmental balance than others. Our critics want to protect species selectively. However, scientists do not know which species are more important.

Look for patterns—repeated errors—that you recognize or that readers point out. Then you can make many corrections simply by identifying and repairing a specific type of error.

- Analyze your papers, keeping track of your repeated errors.
- Ask a teacher or expert writer to identify your *patterns* of error.
- Use the strategies in this book or create your own for *recognizing* and *editing* your errors. Collect them in a personal editing checklist.
- Use your checklist; replace items you master with new ones.

After editing her report on the effects of loud music, Carrie Brehe added this item to her editing checklist.

```
A lot sounds like one word but is actually two. Think of its
opposite, a little. From the noise paper: "Alot of teenagers do
not know how their hearing works." Strategy: Search for alot.
```

## 8c Editing collaboratively

When you edit collaboratively, you identify and talk about specific problems with "consulting readers," usually friends, peers, or colleagues who help you improve a particular writing project while you learn to identify and repair errors on your own.

**GUIDELINES FOR WRITERS**

- Revise content and organization first to prepare your draft for editing. (If necessary, ask your reader for feedback on larger revisions instead. See 6c.)
- Supply a clean draft; don't waste your reader's time on sloppiness.
- Share your requirements or writing concerns with your reader.

**GUIDELINES FOR READERS**

- Use familiar labels and symbols for comments. (The terms in this handbook are generally accepted in academic, work, and public communities. See the list of symbols on page 395.)
- Just note possible errors. Let the writer use a dictionary, a style guide, or this handbook to identify and repair each problem.
- Be specific; *awkward* or *unclear* may not tell the writer exactly what's wrong. Briefly tell why something does or doesn't work.
- Identify outright errors, but don't "take over" the draft. Rewriting sentences and paragraphs is the writer's job.
- Look for patterns of error, noting repetition of the same mistakes.

## 8d Editing on the computer

Many computer programs claim to offer shortcuts for editors. Some can identify features like verbs in the passive voice or calculate the average length of sentences. Despite their claims, most are no match for human readers and editors. Besides taking time to run, they may question correct sentences while they skip errors (such as typing *the* for *they* because both words are spelled correctly). They also can't help you adjust to different community expectations or readers.

## 8e Proofreading

After you've edited as thoughtfully as possible, it's time for **proofreading**, your last chance to make sure that errors in presentation don't annoy your reader or undermine your ideas and credibility as a writer. If mistakes accumulate in a college paper or project at work, these errors can lead to a poor assessment or hinder your advancement.

- Read out loud or even backwards from the last sentence to the first.
- Look for missing words, incorrect prepositions, missing punctuation marks (especially half of a pair of commas or parentheses), and accidental duplicates.
- Consciously fix your eyes on each word to be sure it doesn't contain transposed letters, typographical errors, and the like.

Your careful editing and proofreading will help insure that your final version is clear, concise, and consistent.

# PART 2

# Using Research Strategies: Reading and Writing Within a Research Community

 **TAKING IT ONLINE**

**SEVEN STEPS TO EFFECTIVE LIBRARY RESEARCH**
http://www.library.cornell.edu/okuref/research/tutorial.html
This hypertext guide to library research offers advice on how to develop research topics, locate background material, and find and evaluate books, periodical articles, recordings, and Internet resources.

**INTERNET TUTORIALS**
http://library.albany.edu/internet
This helpful site can improve your search skills whether you need to pick a search engine, select search terms, or evaluate what you find.

**SINK OR SWIM: INTERNET SEARCH TOOLS AND TECHNIQUES**
http://www.ouc.bc.ca/libr/connect96/search.htm
Probably the most accessible search engine tutorial on the Web, this site presents a full workshop on doing electronic research with ease.

**INTERNET SEARCH STRATEGIES**
http://www.rice.edu/fondren/etext/howto/search.html
Try this page for a quick look at types of search engines, search engine evaluations, search techniques, and source evaluation.

**COMMUNITY INFORMATION BY ZIP CODE**
http://library.csun.edu/mfinley/zipstats.html
When you're conducting research on your own community, visit this site for sources of local information, accessible by zip code.

**TYPES OF SURVEYS**
http://trochim.human.cornell.edu/kb/survtype.htm
This Web site clearly explains the various types of surveys you might use if you do field research.

# PART 2

# Using Research Strategies: Reading and Writing Within a Research Community

# 9 Getting Started: Researching and Writing

Research can take many forms, and it can play many roles in your writing. Put simply, **research** means systematic inquiry into a subject. Your research may lead you to written sources (print or electronic), to fieldwork (interviews, surveys, ethnographic observations), or even to a systematic examination of your own experience. Along the way, you are likely to encounter **research conversations,** exchanges among writers, readers, and speakers investigating certain aspects of a subject. Their shared focus on these aspects or elements of the subject makes it a particular matter of interest—a **research topic.**

You can use the depth of information, ideas, and insights you develop through research for a number of purposes. You might create an **informative** essay, report, or brochure.

> "Everybody's Wheezin': My Generation's Collective Journey with Asthma"
> (informative essay on rising incidence of the affliction)

> "Unions versus Tobacco Growers in Mid-Twentieth Century America"
> (academic paper)

You might create an **argumentative** paper taking a stand on an issue or a **proposal** supporting a particular course of action.

> "Bring the Gray Wolf Back"
> (essay or editorial)

Or you might explain and support an **interpretation** or **analysis.**

> "Rebuilding America: Images of National Identity in Contemporary Popular Song"
> (interpretation of contemporary song lyrics and music videos)

## 9a Beginning your research

Research is a careful, sustained inquiry into a question, phenomenon, or topic—guided by **research questions** that set goals for gathering and examining information. Managing the process of identifying resources, evaluating them, and integrating them with your own ideas and insights requires considerable attention and detailed recordkeeping. The process usually begins simply enough, however, either with your own experiences and reading or in an assignment in class or at work.

## 1 Choosing a topic

Your research can grow from a personal interest, an assignment, a strong feeling or point of view, a pressing issue or problem, or the interests and needs of potential readers.

**Respond to your assignment.** Begin by reading your assignment carefully, underlining key terms. Then respond to the assignment in these ways.

- If a word or phrase immediately suggests a topic, write it down, followed by a list of synonyms or alternate terms.
- If you can't identify a topic right away, take key words and phrases, write them down, and brainstorm related words and phrases, along with the topics they suggest.
- Consider asking the person or people who gave the assignment what they think of a potential topic—and for further topic suggestions. Consider asking potential readers for their reactions.

In an intermediate composition course, Jennifer Figliozzi and Summer Arrigo-Nelson underlined important words in their assignment to "investigate the psychological or social dimensions of a local or campus problem." They then listed some campus problems.

| | | | |
|---|---|---|---|
| canceled classes | student fees | date rape | parking |
| library hours | role of sports | student alcohol use | crime |

They chose "student alcohol use" because the topic sounded interesting, with sources readily available and the field research manageable.

Try to balance your interests with readers' expectations. For example, Jennifer and Summer knew that their audience wanted an academic report using print and electronic sources with field research on a problem. They also considered likely questions and expectations of their audience—the local campus community—as they planned.

**AUDIENCE**   What discoveries or information about student alcohol use might
**QUESTIONS**   benefit the campus community?

**RESPONSE**   Our conclusion about local student drinking behavior could help
      the campus program to reduce student alcohol use.

**Recognize your interests.** Perhaps you have an interest, a passion, a job you like (or hate), a sport or recreation activity, a curiosity, or some other involvement that is part of your life and might be intriguing to readers. You don't need to start with a precise opinion or conclusion—a strong feeling or interest will do. It will help you identify a specific issue or subject worth further study. Here is how two students turned their interests and feelings into research projects.

| INTEREST | TITLE OF FINAL PAPER |
|---|---|
| Curiosity: Why do so many workers in fast food restaurants seem to be recent immigrants? | Easy to Hire, Easy to Fire: Recent Immigrants and the Fast Food Industry |
| Job: I have been working as an EMT, but I'll bet most people don't know anything about the job. | You Won't Meet Us Until You Need Us: What EMTs Do |

**Read for an issue or problem.** So much has been written about topics such as global warming, political bias in the media, or the influence of television violence on behavior that these topics easily exceed the scope of even the most ambitious research paper. A quick bit of browsing, however, can lead you to more focused issues, problems, and topics. Where can you do this browsing? Glance quickly through one or two issues of a magazine or newspaper, scan the entries in a database, or consult informational Web sites. Look for words, phrases, and titles that suggest possible topics, especially questions that are unanswered and issues that (for most people at least) remain unresolved.

**STRATEGY** Consult academic databases.

Turn to academic databases such as EBSCO, PsychLIT, First Search, ScienceDirect, and MEDLINE, choosing a database that covers a field that interests you. Then type in a subject (such as *breast cancer*) and terms that researchers often use to identify questions worth investigating (e.g., *recent issues, controversies, discoveries, risks, new developments,* or *alternatives*).

**Draw on your experience.** Research can begin with your personal or professional interest in a subject, a question or problem, a puzzling phenomenon, or a community's need for information. For example, if you begin sneezing every time you walk past the perfume area in a department store, you might try informal experiments, perhaps seeing how close you can get without sneezing. You might also seek advice from a Web site such as the Health and Environmental Resource Center at http://www.herc.org. Once you begin searching for an explanation, you're asking a research question: What is the relationship between perfume and sneezing?

Even a few words can spark an interest, as Jenny Latimer describes.

After I had stuffed a couple of red licorice sticks into my mouth in front of my co-worker Julie, she picked up the wrapper and said, "I didn't realize they had hydrogenated oils in them. I'll never eat them again!" I started wondering about hydrogenated oils. What are they, and why do they seem to be in everything we eat? When did this start? What do they do to you? Do we need to worry or do something about them?

Your own emotions and attitudes can suggest topics as well.

| EMOTION | POSSIBLE TOPIC | TITLE OF FINAL PAPER |
|---------|----------------|----------------------|
| Fear | I've never seen a tornado, but I've always feared them. I'd like to explore the dangers (real or exaggerated) that they pose. | Seven Good Reasons for Fearing Tornados |
| Sadness | Other students often say, "I'm depressed." I'd like to know whether depression is really a serious problem for college students. | Depression and College Students: How Often and How Serious? |
| Anger | I lose my temper easily. Friends say I'm just hot-tempered, but I worry I'm out of control. What causes anger to boil up so easily? | Two Views of Anger: Letting Off Steam or Losing Control? |

**Pay attention to your audience**   The interests and expectations of your audience can help guide your choice of a topic. The chart on page 51 can help you identify your potential readers' likely concerns and perspectives.

## 2 Narrowing a topic

Think of a **subject** as a broad field, filled with clusters of information, ideas, and written interchanges—clusters that are often only loosely related to each other even though they fall within the same subject area. A **topic** is a single cluster of ideas and information within a broader subject. The term is appropriate because writers interested in questions surrounding the cluster of ideas and information often "speak" to each other through their writing, creating an ongoing **conversation** you can enter through your own writing.

| AUDIENCE EXPECTATIONS FOR RESEARCH WRITING | | | |
|---|---|---|---|
| **AUDIENCE** | **ACADEMIC** | **PUBLIC** | **WORK** |
| **GOALS** | Explain or prove, offer well-supported interpretations or conclusions, analyze or synthesize information for use in other settings | Support arguments for policy or course of action, inform or advise for the public good | Document problems, propose a project or course of action, compare information, improve performance |
| **TYPICAL QUESTIONS** | What does it mean? What happened? How does it occur? How might it be modified? | How can this policy be made better? What do people need or want to know? | What is the problem? How can we solve it? What course of action will help us achieve our goals? |
| **TYPICAL FORMS** | Interpretive (thesis) paper, informative paper, research report, grant report | Position paper, editorial, proposal, informative article, pamphlet, guidelines | Proposal, report, feasibility study, memorandum |
| **AUDIENCE EXPECTATIONS** | Detailed evidence from varied sources including quotations, paraphrases, and summaries; documented sources that acknowledge scholarship | Accessible, fair, and persuasive information with evidence; informal documentation | Clear, direct, and precise information; appropriate detail; less formal documentation |

By limiting your attention to a particular topic, you take an important step toward making your research project manageable. But how can you identify potential topics (or subtopics) that are limited enough to provide a real focus for your writing yet are the subject of enough discussion to provide adequate resources for your work? Pay attention to issues, disagreements, points of discussion, new discoveries, and intriguing ideas or interpretations as you do preliminary research on a subject. These focal points in what others have to say about the subject can suggest ways to narrow your topic choice.

As you browse print and online sources, review your assignment, or talk with an authority on the subject, take note of key words and phrases they use to identify topics of discussion. Pay attention, as well, to questions they raise to identify directions for inquiry and argument. Then respond with statements or questions of your own that focus and narrow potential topics to reasonable limits.

Here are some notes Tou Yang made from articles on the topic *athletic dietary supplements* he located in the database Academic Search Premier.

**NOTES**

"Eat Powder? Build Muscle! Burn Calories!"—creatine monohydrate; lots of athletes swear by it and claim it has only good effects

"Creatine Monohydrate Supplementation Enhances High-Intensity Exercise Performance in Males and Females"—controversy over whether creatine works or not; they claim it does

"From Ephedra to Creatine: Using Theory to Respond to Dietary Supplement Use in Young Athletes"—understanding why athletes use dietary supplements even though they are probably not effective

**RESPONSES**

Some disagreement over whether creatine works or at least over how well it works—take a position on this?

Or explain how it works and what it seems to add to sports performance?

## 3 Identifying keywords

**Keywords**—words or phrases identifying important ideas and clusters of information—are often used in library catalogs and by Web or database search engines (10d, 10f, 11b) to link discussions of a subject. As you examine print or electronic sources, make a list of all the keywords, names, or phrases that might refer to your topic. Note synonyms, such as *maturation* for *growth*. Initially, your keywords can help you define your topic. Later, they can help you develop research questions (9c) and guide your research (10a-3).

## 9b Recognizing different kinds of research writing

No matter what subject you investigate, the specific steps you take will be heavily influenced by your answer to this question: Will I use my research to *inform* or to *persuade?*

An **informative** research paper, report, or Web site focuses on your subject: the phenomenon, discovery, process, controversy, question, person, or performance you are exploring. Your research and writing will focus on discovering information and ideas and sharing them with readers. Your efforts will be subject-driven.

Taking this approach does not mean that your writing will be a dull recitation of facts. On the contrary, you'll use your understanding, insights, and conclusions to organize information from sources to help readers understand, answer potential questions, and reach substantiated conclusions about the topic.

A **persuasive** research project focuses on your **thesis** (see 4b) or conclusion. You'll concentrate on evidence and explanatory details that logically

| RESEARCH WRITING: INFORMATIVE AND ARGUMENTATIVE | | | |
|---|---|---|---|
| **PURPOSE FOR WRITING** | **POSSIBLE FORM** | **POSSIBLE TITLE** | **POSSIBLE FOCUS** |
| Informative | Documented essay | "Everybody's Wheezin': My Generation's Collective Journey with Asthma" | Exploration of rising incidence of the affliction |
| Informative | Report | "'Buy U.S. Bonds': How Posters Helped Shape Public Opinion During World War II" | Historical examination of the ways the government employed posters |
| Informative | Brochure or pamphlet | "What Linux Can (and Can't) Do for Your Computers" | Investigation of both strengths and limitations |
| Informative | Academic research paper | "Unions versus Tobacco Growers in Mid-Twentieth Century America" | Analysis of conflicts during a specific time period |
| Argumentative | Documented essay or editorial | "Bring the Gray Wolf Back" | Presentation and support of stand with reasons and evidence |
| Argumentative | Position paper or *PowerPoint* presentation | "Meeting Objections to Gray Wolf Reintroduction in the Adirondack Region of New York" | Advocacy of position with recognition of alternate views |
| Argumentative | Proposal | "A Three-Step Process for Reintroducing Gray Wolves to Adirondack State Park" | Presentation and support of proposed actions |
| Argumentative (interpretation) | Academic essay | "Dream Interpretation: Three Current Approaches" | Explanation and application of three interpretive approaches to one of the writer's dreams |
| Argumentative (interpretation) | Report on field research | "Diversity on Campus: What Do Western College Students *Really* Think?" | Analysis and interpretation of data gathered on student views |
| Argumentative (interpretation) | Thesis-and-support essay | "Rebuilding America: Images of National Identity in Contemporary Popular Song" | Interpretation of contemporary song lyrics and music videos |

support your point of view, persuade readers, and explain issues or problems. You'll need to do more than just support your conclusions, however. To convince readers, an argument needs to offer detailed information about the issue or problem and the viewpoints involved. It needs to develop, refine, and support your thesis, your proposal, or your interpretation.

## 9c Developing a research question

Research writing, especially informative writing, aims to answer questions, both those raised by specialized research and those likely to interest readers. By developing one or more **research questions**—simple questions about your subject—and by doing this early in the research process, you can set goals for gathering and examining possible sources.

**STRATEGY** **State your research questions.**

Work toward one or two questions early in your research process. Relate your questions to your general and specific goals for writing. Design questions to enlighten both yourself and your readers.

For example, Summer Arrigo-Nelson and Jennifer Figliozzi developed the following questions for their academic research project on the relationship of parental behaviors to college student drinking.

- Will students with permission to drink at home show different drinking behaviors at college than those without permission to drink at home?
- Do the students feel that a correlation exists between drinking behaviors at home and at college?

Research questions can take several forms, depending on your individual preferences and your purposes for writing. Some writers prefer questions that focus on factual or informational matters: *who, what, where, when, why,* and *how.* Other writers prefer questions suggesting both a purpose and an organizational pattern for writing. Jennifer Latimer, for example, arrived at her research questions this way:

I looked at the red licorice sticks package, the fruit-flavored candy package, the wheat crackers box, even the pudding pack—all contained hydrogenated oils. I did some preliminary research and developed two questions for my research and my readers:
What effects do hydrogenated oils have on us?
Should I (and we) ever again eat delicious treats containing them?

## 9d Developing a preliminary thesis

Research essays, reports, and even Web sites generally use a **thesis statement** (see 4b) to guide readers' attention and state the writer's key idea or theme. Your thesis should grow from and reflect your research questions, of course (see 9c). Creating a preliminary thesis early on helps you focus and shape your search strategy (see 10a). Later, complicating, qualifying, and extending your thesis in response to your research will help you review or revise the direction of your work.

Thesis statements in research writing help indicate your purpose for writing (inform or persuade, see 9c). They often follow one of these patterns.

- **Issue.** What is the issue, and what is my stand on it?
- **Problem.** What is the problem, and what solution am I proposing?
- **Public question.** What is the situation we are facing, and how should we respond?
- **Academic question.** What is the phenomenon, and what is my analysis and interpretation of it?

## 9e Creating a research file and a timeline

In a **research file,** you can record and systematically store your activities throughout the research and writing process. It is a good place to accumulate materials and keep them ready for later use. You can build a portable research file in a notebook, in a folder, on note cards, or in a word processing file in your desktop, laptop, or handheld computer.

### 1 Building your research file

- Identify your topic, research questions, or rough thesis (see 4b).
- Create a research plan, listing possible resources and assembling a working bibliography (see 10a).
- Divide your file into sections for your main research and writing stages, and keep it with you as you work.
- Take notes, recording relevant ideas and information from sources (see 9f), including summaries, paraphrases, and quotations (see 9f, g).
- Copy or record passages or images with their sources, ready for possible inclusion.
- Document sources (see Chapters 16–17) of all materials in your file.
- Add reactions, chunks, drafts, and revisions integrating your insights with ideas and information from your sources (see 14a).

Besides creating a research file for material, you need to stick to a schedule so that you finish on time. Because college research projects require sustained effort over several weeks or months, by planning carefully and using your time efficiently, you can avoid the stress of a looming deadline and the fear of turning in an incomplete or substandard paper.

### 2 Constructing a timeline

- Use a printed calendar or your computer to record your plans.
- Divide up the work, noting likely activities and due dates.

- Allow several days or a week for activities such as choosing your topic, stating your research questions and rough thesis, beginning your working bibliography, reviewing your notes and revising your plans, finishing your research, planning or outlining your paper, drafting the paper and source list, getting feedback from peer readers, revising, editing, and proofreading.
- Work backward from the final deadline, scheduling each stage.
- Keep your timeline in your research file, and check it regularly.

## 9f Reading and notetaking

A research project calls for two types of reading—analytical and critical. When you read *analytically*, you try to understand the ideas and information presented in a source. When you read *critically*, you interact with the source, assessing its strengths, limitations, and biases; analyzing its relationships to other texts produced by a research community; and identifying questions or issues it leaves unaddressed.

Analytical reading leads to the summaries, paraphrases, syntheses, quotations, and details you develop into much of the content of a research report or paper. Critical reading leads to many of the insights you contribute to an understanding of the topic.

| ANALYTICAL READING | CRITICAL READING |
|---|---|
| What does it say? | What does it mean or imply? |
| (literal) | (interpretive) |
| —summary | —interpretation |
| —paraphrase | —position of author |
| —synthesis | —nature of publication |
| —quotations | —use in one's own ideas |
| —details | —reception of audience |

### 1 Taking notes

Because analytical reading concentrates on understanding information, **analytical notes** record facts, details, concepts, interpretations, and quotations from your sources, focusing on what's relevant to your research questions. **Critical notes** often accompany them, adding your comments, interpretations, or assessments of a source in relation to your research questions.

### 2 Recording notes

Here are three formats for notetaking. (See also 10a-4.)

**Note cards.** Some writers prefer portable, convenient index cards, generally 4" × 6" or 5" × 7". If you identify the card's topic clearly at the top and restrict each card to one kind of note (quotation, summary, paraphrase, synthesis), you can group, add, or rearrange cards as you plan or write.

**Research journal.** A research journal (usually a notebook) provides space to record information, reflect on new knowledge, and begin assembling your project. Add headings or marginal comments to identify the topics of the notes. Store photocopies or printouts in any pockets or in a folder.

**Electronic notes.** You can use software designed for note taking or set up word-processing files like a research journal or set of note cards (one page = one card). If you specify a subtopic or research question for each entry, you can use these labels to sort, reorganize, or retrieve material.

**STRATEGY**  Link your notes.

- **Link notes to your keywords or research questions.** At the top of each card, page, or entry, use your keywords, research questions, or subtopics to identify how material relates to your topic.
- **Link notes to sources.** Clearly note the source on each card, page, or entry. Use the author's last name or a short version of the title to connect each note to its corresponding working bibliography entry (see 10a-4).
- **Link notes to exact locations.** Include the page numbers of the source, especially for any material quoted or paraphrased. If an electronic source uses paragraph numbers instead of page numbers, note them.

### 3  Recording quotations

When you're using actual books and journals, not photocopies or downloads, be *absolutely certain* that you copy quotations word for word and record the exact page number where each quotation appears. If a quotation runs on to a second page in the source, note both numbers and the place where the page changes. (After all, you don't know what you might finally quote.)

## 9g  Summarizing, paraphrasing, and synthesizing

Analytical reading and notetaking require careful, critical thinking as you draw information and ideas from a source and put them into forms useful in your own writing: quotations, summaries, paraphrases, and syntheses. In a **summary,** you present the essential information in a text without interpreting it. In a **paraphrase,** you restate an author's ideas in your own words, retaining the content and sense of the original but providing your own expression. A **synthesis** brings together summaries of several sources and points out the relationships among the ideas and information.

## 1 Summarizing

A summary helps you understand the key ideas and content in an article, part of a book, a Web site, or a cluster of paragraphs. You can also create summaries as a concise way of presenting ideas and information from a source in your own writing. In an **objective summary,** you focus on presenting the content of the source in compressed form and avoid speculating on the source's line of reasoning. In an **evaluative summary,** you add your opinions, evaluating or commenting on the original passage.

To prepare a summary of information relating to your topic, follow this process.

- **Read** the selection, looking for the most important ideas, evidence, and information. Underline, highlight, or make note of key points and information that you think should be mentioned in your summary.
- **Scan** (reread quickly) the selection to decide which of the ideas and bits of information you noted during your first reading are the *most* important. Try also to decide on the writer's main purpose in the selection and to identify the major sections of the discussion.
- **Summarize** *each section* of the source (each step in the argument, each stage in the explanation) in a *single sentence* that mentions the key ideas and information.
- **Encapsulate** the *entire passage* in a *single sentence* that captures its main point or conclusion.
- **Combine** your section summaries with your overall summary to produce a draft summary of the main point, other important points, and the most important information.
- **Revise** to make sure your summary is logical and easy to read. Check against the source for accuracy.
- **Document** clearly the source of your summary using a standard style of documentation (see Chapters 16–17).

In a summary, you can present the key ideas from a source without including unnecessary detail that might distract readers. Summer Arrigo-Nelson and Jennifer Figliozzi used two one-sentence summaries of research to help introduce one of the questions for their academic research paper.

First, research has shown that adolescents who have open and close relationships with their parents use alcohol less often than do those with conflictual relationships (Sieving). For example, a survey given to students in seventh through twelfth grades reported that approximately 35 percent of adolescent drinkers were under parental supervision while drinking (Department of Education). Based on this research, we are interested in determining if students who were given permission to drink while living with their parents would possess different drinking patterns, upon reaching college, than those who did not previously have permission to drink.

## 2 Paraphrasing

A good paraphrase doesn't add to or detract from the original but often helps you understand a difficult work. When you want to incorporate the detailed ideas and information from a passage into your own writing but don't want to quote your source because the wording is too dense or confusing, then a paraphrase can be the answer.

To paraphrase part of a source, put the information in your own words, retaining the content and ideas of the original as well as the sequence of presentation. (Many paraphrases contain sentences that correspond with the original except for changes in wording and sentence structure.)

- **Read** the selection carefully so that you understand the wording as well as the content.
- **Write** a draft of your paraphrase, using your own words and phrases in place of the original. Rely on synonyms and equivalent expressions. You can retain names, proper nouns, and the like from the original, of course.
- **Revise** for smooth reading and clarity. Change sentence structures and phrasing to make sure your version is easier to understand than your source.
- **Document** clearly the source of your paraphrase using a standard style of documentation (see Chapters 16–17).

As part of her research about alcohol abuse on her campus, Jennifer Figliozzi encountered the following passage in Leo Reisberg's article "Colleges Step-Up Efforts to Combat Alcohol Abuse" in the June 12, 1998, *Chronicle of Higher Education.*

> The university also now notifies parents when their sons or daughters violate the alcohol policy or any other aspect of the student code of conduct. "We were hoping that the support of parents would help change students' behavior, and we believe it has," says Timothy F. Brooks, an assistant vice-president and the dean of students at the University of Delaware.

Because she wanted to avoid long quotations and instead integrate the information smoothly into her discussion, Jennifer paraphrased part of the passage.

*Officials at the University of Delaware thought that letting parents know when students violate regulations on alcohol use would change students' drinking habits, and one administrator now says, "We believe it has" (Reisberg A42).*

## 3 Synthesizing

By bringing together summaries of several sources and pointing out their relationships in a synthesis, you can use your sources in some special ways: to provide background information, to explore causes and effects, to look at contrasting explanations or arguments, or to bring together ideas and information in support of a thesis.

To create a synthesis of your source materials, use the following strategy:

- **Identify** the role a synthesis will play in your explanation or argument as well as the kind of information and ideas you wish to share with readers.
- **Gather** the sources you plan to synthesize.
- **Read** your sources, and summarize each of them (see 9g-1).
- **Focus** on the purpose of your synthesis, and draft a sentence summing up your conclusion about the relationships of the sources.
- **Arrange** the order in which you will present your sources in the synthesis.
- **Write** a draft of your synthesis, presenting summaries of your sources and offering your conclusion about the relationship(s).
- **Revise** so that your synthesis is easy to read. Make sure readers can easily identify the sources of the ideas and information.
- **Document** clearly the sources for your synthesis using a standard style of documentation (see Chapters 16–17).

Many academic papers begin with a summary of prior research designed to identify a need for further research and to provide justification for the research questions. The opening section of Summer Arrigo-Nelson and Jennifer Figliozzi's academic research paper uses synthesis for this purpose.

> Research dealing with student alcohol use most often focuses on children's perceptions of their parents' actions and on the relationship between child and parent. Studies conducted with high school students have supported the hypothesis that positive family relationships are more likely to be associated with less frequent alcohol use among adolescents than are negative relationships. Adolescents model the limited substance use of their parents where there is a good or moderate parent-adolescent relationship (Andrews, Hops, and Duncan). Other factors the studies found to be associated with positive family relationships, along with substance use, were academic achievement, family structure, place of residence, self-esteem, and emotional tone (Martsh and Miller; Weschler, Dowdall, Davenport, and Castillo).

Work and public writing often use synthesis in a similar fashion to identify a problem that needs to be addressed or a policy that needs to be examined or reconsidered.

# 10 Using Library Resources and Research Databases

A good **search strategy** is a plan for locating the resources you need to answer your research question or support your thesis. It will help you to consult a variety of sources providing different kinds of information. It will also direct you to the conversation about your subject—the network of articles, books, conference presentations, online discussions, and electronic resources addressing various aspects of your topic and often offering varied opinions. Finally, a good search strategy directs you to less obvious but perhaps more valuable resources as well as easily accessible ones—to scholarly journals and interviews as well as Web sites, for example.

## 10a Developing a search strategy and working bibliography

A search strategy has five elements: resources, search tools, keywords, working bibliography, and timeline. Keeping these detailed elements in mind as you research is, for most of us, difficult, if not impossible. Put them in writing so you can easily consult them as you work; then review, revise, and add to them as you learn about your topic and discover new resources.

### 1 List your resources

Your search strategy should include a list of the kinds of resources you plan to use—printed books, scholarly journals, newspapers, Web sites, interviews, and surveys, for example. Draw on your preliminary research (9a–d) to create your initial resource list, and update it as you discover other potential resources. If you have specific titles, Web sites, or people in mind as sources, list them here, too, and update your list periodically.

### 2 Identify your search tools

The most obvious search tools come readily to mind when you begin researching: your library's online catalog and Web search engines such as *Google*. These are adequate starting points, but more specialized research tools can lead you to information and ideas new and worthwhile to both you and your readers. Here are some kinds of specialized research tools.

- Indexes of magazine and periodical articles: *Readers' Guide to Periodical Literature, InfoTrac, New York Times Index, Wall Street Journal Index*
- Indexes of articles in scholarly journals in professional publications in fields such as business, public health, law, or engineering: *Social Sciences Index, Applied Science and Technology Index, MLA International Bibliography, Humanities Index, Education Index*
- Academic and professional databases with built-in search engines: *EBSCO, LexisNexis, OCLC First Search;* specialized Web search engines and indexed databases, *Search Questia, AltaVista, Cata List, Metacrawler, Dogpile*

## 3 Use keywords

Many people begin searching for sources using general terms to identify their topic, only to discover that these are not the terms used in an index or search engine. Indexes, databases, library catalogs (10d–f, 11b), and many other reference sources are arranged (or searched) by keywords (see also 9a). If you can identify the keywords or phrases for printed or electronic indexes, you can usually locate all the resources you need. Of course, you may not know which terms and phrases are preferred until you begin your search. Sometimes it helps to have two or three alternative keywords or phrases so that, if a particular database or other resource yields little under one, you can try the others before moving to another resource.

## 4 Compile references for a working bibliography

Your search strategy should make provision for recording information that will help you or your readers locate a source. A list of sources you have examined and may decide to draw on as you write is called a **working bibliography.** In a working bibliography, you should record the types of information you will need to provide in your final paper in a list of works cited, references list, list of works consulted, or footnotes (see Chapters 16–17).

When you are doing research, keep a copy of your working bibliography close at hand so you can make notes about entries to add or delete. (If it is in electronic form, you may be able to make changes right away.)

**Organizing your working bibliography.** You can organize the entries in a working bibliography in several ways.

- Alphabetically, the way they will eventually appear in a list of works cited or references page. This strategy can save time and effort when you are preparing your final text.

## INFORMATION FOR A WORKING BIBLIOGRAPHY

When you examine a source, record the following kinds of information to include in your working bibliography and to use, eventually, in compiling the list of sources for your final paper.

### PRINTED BOOKS

- Author(s) or editor(s)
- Title
- Publication information: place of publication, name of publisher, date of publication
- Volume or edition numbers, if any
- Call number (to help locate the book in library stacks)

### PRINTED ARTICLES

- Author(s) or editor(s)
- Title
- Name of journal, magazine, newspaper, or collection of articles
- Publication information
  - Article in a periodical: volume number, issue number, month or day of publication, page numbers of article (inclusive)
  - Article in a collection: title of collection and editor's name, place of publication, name of publisher, date of publication, page numbers of article (inclusive)

### ELECTRONIC OR ONLINE WORK

- Author(s), editor(s), or group(s) responsible for the document
- Title or name of Web site
- Information about any corresponding print publication (as above)
- Electronic publication information: date of electronic publication or latest update, date you accessed the document, and complete URL; (for online journal) volume and issue number, publication date; (for databases or CD-ROM) document access number or version number; (for email or post to a discussion list) name of sender, subject line, date of posting, name of list, and date of access.

- In categories reflecting the parts of your subject or the kinds of evidence they provide for your argument. This strategy can help you identify at a glance areas covered well and those needing further investigation.
- According to the plan for your paper. This strategy can help you gather your resources efficiently as you write.

## 5 Revise and update your timeline

Your timeline should be part of your search plan (see 9e). Revise and update it to reflect changes in direction or emphasis that arise from discoveries or new ideas that emerge from your research. Revision is particularly easy if you monitor the timeline in electronic form.

## 10b Searching library resources and databases

Your specific search strategy for library resources and research databases should reflect both the advantages and disadvantages of these forms of research, especially in comparison to the readily available resources on Web sites.

**Advantages.** Many important resources are available *at* a library (printed books and articles, microforms, CD-ROM databases, for example) or *through* a library (online databases available only through a library's Web site or on library terminals). Scholarly publications, technical and specialized reports, and government publications are more likely to be available at libraries than on Web sites.

Reference librarians can provide considerable help and advice—and are glad to do so. Libraries often provide Internet and Web access so you can follow a strand of research at *one* location, whether it takes you to printed sources, databases, the Web—or back and forth among them.

**Disadvantages.** Library research may require a substantial time commitment; library schedules may not correspond with your schedule. Library resources can also be difficult to navigate, especially if you are not familiar with the organization of research libraries.

## 1 Examine different kinds of library resources

In general, library resources fall into three categories, each with its own system for locating specific sources.

- Books, pamphlets, and miscellaneous resources including photographs, films, and recordings: Use **online catalogs.**
- Articles in magazines, scholarly journals, and other periodicals: Use **electronic and print indexes,** some of which may be accessed through a library's Web site.
- Databases of articles and information: Use **search engines** embedded in the databases; these also may be available on a library's Web site.

## 2 Move from general to specific resources

Your research will often move from general, less-detailed sources to more specific and detailed ones as you narrow your topic and begin adding depth of detail and specific evidence to your writing. The distinction between general and specific treatment of a topic holds true for online and field resources also, but it is especially sharp for library resources. Often some sections of a library are dedicated to general reference works and others to field- or topic-specific texts.

Another important distinction to bear in mind is that between **primary sources,** consisting of information and ideas in original or close-to-original form (such as historical records, literary works, raw statistics, and actual documents), and **secondary sources,** consisting of works that analyze, summarize, interpret, or explain primary sources.

## 10c Using general resources

You can use general resources to gain a broad overview of a topic, including background information and a sense of relationships to other subjects. General references can also provide names, keywords, and phrases useful for tracing a topic, as well as bibliographies of potential resources. Commercial Internet services like America Online offer access to online reference works, databases, references services, and collections of resources.

**General encyclopedias, ready references, maps, and dictionaries.** These provide very basic information on a wide range of topics. They are good places to start to conduct research for an overview of your topic, but they don't usually provide in-depth information.

*New Encyclopaedia Britannica, Columbia Encyclopedia, Microsoft Encarta, World Almanac and Book of Facts, Canadian Almanac and Directory, Statistical Abstract of the United States, National Geographic Atlas of the World, The American Heritage Dictionary of the English Language, Oxford English Dictionary*

**Specialized encyclopedias and dictionaries.** These provide more in-depth coverage of a specific topic or area. Such works can be easily located in a library's catalog or by searching online. The range of resources is wide.

*Dictionary of the Social Sciences, Dictionary of American Biography, Current Biography, Who's Who in America, McGraw-Hill Encyclopedia of Science and Technology, Encyclopedia of World Art, International Encyclopedia of Business and Management, Encyclopedia of Advertising, International Encyclopedia of Film, International Television Almanac, Encyclopedia of Computer Science, Encyclopedia of Educational Research, Dictionary of Anthropology, Encyclopedia of Psychology, Encyclopedia of the Environment, New Grove Dictionary of*

*Music and Musicians, Encyclopedia of Nursing Research, Encyclopedia of Religion, Encyclopedia of Sociology, Women's Studies Encyclopedia*

**Bibliographies.** These provide organized lists of books and articles on specific topics within a field of study or interest.

*Bibliographic Index: A Cumulative Bibliography of Bibliographies, MLA Bibliography of Books and Articles on the Modern Languages and Literatures, International Bibliography of the Social Sciences, Foreign Affairs Bibliography, Film Research: A Critical Bibliography with Annotations and Essays*

## 10d Consulting books and online catalogs

Library catalogs give you access to books and to many other resources, including periodicals, recordings, government documents, films, historical archives, and collections of photographs. Your library's catalog is most likely an **online catalog**, although **card catalogs** are still occasionally in use in small libraries. You can search under the *author's name,* the *title of a work,* the *subject area,* the title of a *series or periodical containing the work,* and, in some libraries, *words in the title or in a work's description.* Some catalogs list works not only in their home library but also in other libraries in a region or in a consortium, such as a group of college libraries.

Rachel Torres discovered that her library belonged to just such a group when she began her search for resources, especially printed books, on her topic, Afro-Cuban music. She began by typing her topic into the search screen for "words in title or description," and the catalog returned a number of possible sources (see Figure 10.1).

Rachel chose the third item on the list, and moved to the next catalog screen, which provided detailed information about the book along with a list of copies available in the cooperating libraries (see Figure 10.2 on p. 68).

## 10e Examining periodicals, print or electronic indexes, and government documents

**Periodicals** are publications that appear at intervals and contain articles by different authors. **General-interest magazines** appear once a month or weekly, with each issue paginated separately. **Scholarly journals** generally appear less frequently than magazines, perhaps four times a year, with the page numbering running continuously throughout the separate issues that make up an annual volume. **Newspapers** generally appear daily or weekly and frequently consist of separately numbered sections. Most scholarly journals are still available primarily in printed form, although recently many colleges and universities have begun subscribing to journals in electronic form, with current and

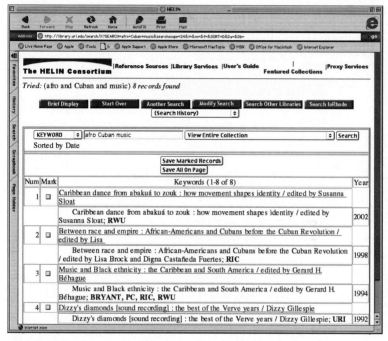

**FIGURE 10.1**   Sample search results for keywords *Afro-Cuban music*

back issues available online, either through terminals in the library or through the library's Web site. Many general-interest magazines and newspapers are now also available in electronic as well as printed form.

## 1 Indexes

You can locate articles in print (and in electronic form) by consulting some of the many print and online **indexes.**

**General and newspaper indexes.** These give you a way to search for topics in the news and in magazines and other periodicals intended for the general public as well as some intended for more specialized audiences. They include *Academic Index, Readers' Guide to Periodical Literature, Wall Street Journal Index, Washington Post Index, InfoTrac, Editorials on File,* and *OCLC/World Catalog.*

**Specialized indexes.** These provide ways to search for publications offering more specialized, technical, or academic resources. Among these are *Anthropological Literature, Humanities Index, Music Index, BIZZ (Business Index), EconLit, Education*

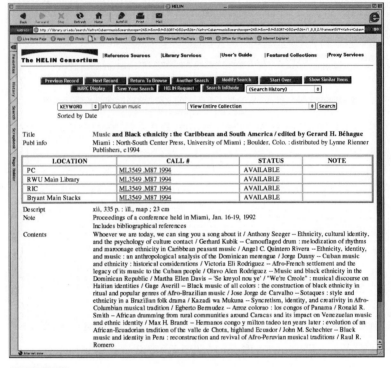

**FIGURE 10.2**  Detailed information for one entry

*Index, ERIC Current Index to Journals in Education, Index to Legal Periodicals, Social Sciences Index, Applied Science and Technology Index,* and *Medline.*

**Abstracts.** Collections of abstracts provide brief summaries of articles in specialized fields. They include *Abstracts of English Studies, Biological Abstracts, Dissertation Abstracts International, Historical Abstracts, Newspaper Abstracts, Psychological Abstracts,* and *Sociological Abstracts.*

## 2 Government documents

**Government documents** include reports of information and research, records of hearings, pamphlets, public information publications, and regulations issued by Congress, federal agencies, and state and local governments. These rich sources of information, both general and technical, are sometimes housed in separate collections in a library.

To access government documents published after 1976, search the *Catalog of U.S. Government Publications* at <http://www.access.gpo.gov/su_docs/locators/ cgp/index.html>. Many government documents are available electronically. For

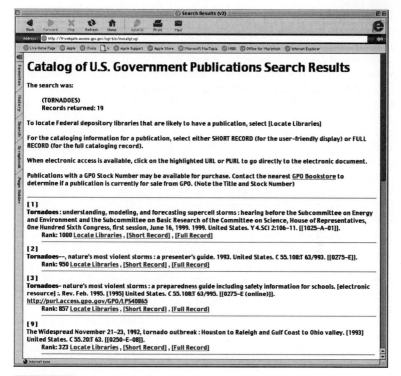

**FIGURE 10.3** Search results in U.S. *Catalog of Government Publications* for keyword *tornadoes*

government documents published before 1976, consult the printed *Monthly Catalog of United States Government Publications.*

After reading several magazine and newspaper articles about tornadoes, Michael Micchie noticed that some of the writers cited government documents and government-sponsored research. He decided to see if any government publications addressed the subject. His search of the *Catalog of United States Government Publications* using the keyword *tornadoes* returned sixteen citations, each with a link to a full description of the document and a link to a list of libraries likely to have a copy of it. Figure 10.3 shows part of the response he received.

## 10f Using online databases

In recent years, researchers (both student and professional) have come to rely on electronic databases for all kinds of information, especially for texts of scholarly and technical articles and for general-interest periodical articles.

College, university, and public libraries have greatly increased the number of on-line databases they make available and will probably continue doing so in the future. The range and number of texts available through databases are growing rapidly and the variety of subjects covered by these services has grown to the point that they are almost an essential element of careful research on any subject.

**Online databases** are simply files of information available through the Internet or Web or, occasionally, on CD-ROMs. Most databases focus on specialized or technical fields. As a result, they are likely to be consulted primarily by researchers with a special interest in a field. This limited number of users stands in contrast to the large numbers of people who access general-interest sites and search engines on the Web. At the same time, specialized databases are expensive to construct and maintain. They index hundreds of thousands of documents and must be continuously updated to serve the needs of researchers who require access to the latest information, ideas, and results of experiments or inquiry. Consequently, most databases restrict access to paying customers, but access does include students and faculty at most universities whose fees are paid by the library making the database available.

Most databases are quite specialized, but also useful and interesting to people interested in the topic areas they cover. Here, for example, is a description of one such reference database, the Family Index, which covers a range of topics most people would consider well worth learning about.

> *Family Index.* Indexes articles on the family from approximately 1,500 interdisciplinary journals. Family-related articles include family history and trends; education; economics, public policy and the law; health care; gerontology; religion; diverse families; marriage; parenthood and child development; sexuality; abuse and neglect; and other family problems.

This typical description of a reference database highlights characteristics typical of others as well. It has a specific focus but provides a wealth of material within that focus. It provides information about articles from a large number of journals, more than would be indexed by a Web search engine (11b). It is updated on a regular basis so that its contents are current. Its focus is up-to-date and contemporary as well, containing references to documents only from 1995 on. If you wish to access earlier publications, this resource will not be helpful. But if you wish to know about the latest work in the field, this may be the best choice for you.

Databases come in several kinds, varying according to the kinds of information they provide: *full-text databases, databases abstracts,* and *indexing or bibliographic databases.* Other kinds of databases (resource databases) include those providing research aids and those housing various kinds of information. Databases also differ according to field of study or interest and to the number and range of resources they contain.

Databases are generally searchable by author, title, and keyword, or by special categories reflecting the scope and emphasis of the particular materials included in a collection.

## 1 Full-text databases

**Full-text databases** list articles and other documents and provide brief summaries of the contents of each item. In addition, they provide the entire texts of all or most of the items indexed. As a result, they can save you time and effort in locating texts of potential sources. In coverage, full-text databases range from extensive collections of scholarly or general-interest articles like *Academic Search Premier* or *Academic Universe* to highly focused collections like *Health Reference Center Academic.*

Some of the most useful full-text databases are listed below.

- **General**
  *Academic Search Premier (EBSCO)*
  Provides full texts of more than 3,180 scholarly publications in social sciences, humanities, education, computer sciences, engineering, language and linguistics, arts and literature, medical sciences, and ethnic studies and similar academic fields.

  *Academic Universe (LexisNexis)*
  Provides news, law, and business information drawing from national and international newspapers and periodicals. Full texts of the articles.

  *National Newspapers*
  Offers indexing, abstracts, and full text of the *New York Times*, the *Wall Street Journal*, the *Washington Post*, and the *Christian Science Monitor.*

  *InfoTrac OneFile (InfoTrac)*
  Contains news and periodical articles. Subjects covered include business, computers, current events, economics, education, environmental issues, health care, humanities, law, politics, science, social science, and sports.

- **Specialized**
  *CQ Researcher*
  Collection of weekly reports each exploring a single, controversial issue. Each report discusses pros and cons, offers comments from experts, includes charts and graphs, offers a timeline of events, and provides lengthy bibliographies.

  *National Environmental Publications Internet Site*
  Database of over 6,000 full-text EPA documents.

  *Health Reference Center Academic (InfoTrac)*
  Contains articles on fitness, pregnancy, medicine, nutrition, diseases, public health, occupational health and safety, alcohol and drug abuse, HMOs, prescription drugs, and similar subjects.

Jenny Latimer was looking for detailed information to use for her paper about the presence of hydrogenated oils in snack foods, especially candy. She knew her research would involve technical information, but she didn't know which field of study would be most likely to provide the information she needed: food science and nutrition, health sciences, chemistry, or biology. She also thought that fields like psychology, sociology, and anthropology might help her explain why we prefer certain kinds of foods over others. In addition, she was worried about finding herself limited to sources that were too technical for her to understand or explain to readers. As a result, she decided to consult a database covering general-interest as well as academic publications and to use one that provided both abstracts and full texts. She hoped that by being able to sample the available sources online, she would be able to decide if they were appropriate for her project or too technical to be useful.

Here are some of the steps she followed. First she entered her search terms into the query screen of the database using the terms *hydrogenated oils* and *candy,* but the search engine was unable to identify any sources using these terms. She then broadened the search using the terms *hydrogenated oils* and *food* connected by AND to search for documents with both (see 11b-2). This search identified eight sources, some of which seemed promising (see Figure 10.4).

Jenny looked at all the articles in abstract and full-text form and took notes on several, including one that provided specific examples she felt might be important for her paper (see Figure 10.5).

After reading and taking notes, Jenny decided that the areas of study most likely to provide her with the kinds of information and insights she needed for her paper were nutrition studies and health sciences.

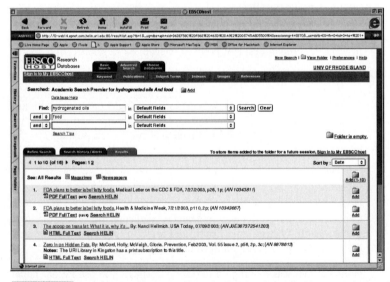

**FIGURE 10.4** Sample database search results for the terms *hydrogenated oils* and *food.*

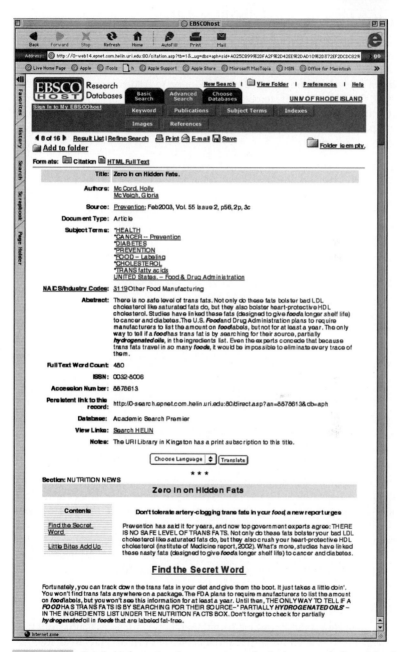

## 2 Databases containing abstracts

A large number of databases, especially those focusing on academic or technical fields, provide abstracts (brief summaries of a document's content) and sometimes full texts of selected items. A new feature of some of these databases is a link to a library's online subscription to academic and technical journals. This allows readers to obtain a full text of an article in a journal for which the library has an online subscription. This feature is likely to become more widespread as libraries shift to more online rather than print subscriptions to scholarly journals.

*PsycINFO*
Indexing and abstracts of journal articles and books in psychology.
*CINAHL (OVID)*
Indexing and abstracts of journal articles and other materials in nursing and allied health.
*Sociological Abstracts (CSA)*
Abstracts and indexing in sociology and related disciplines.
*Biological Abstracts*
Indexing and abstracts of journals in the life sciences.
*America: History and Life (ABC-CLIO)*
Indexing and abstracts of journal articles and materials on U.S. and Canadian history.
*MLA Bibliography (FirstSearch)*
Indexing and abstracts of journals, books, and other materials in language and literature.
*ComAbstracts*
Abstracts of articles published in the field of communication.
*MEDLINE (FirstSearch)*
Indexing and abstracts of journals in medicine.
*ERIC (FirstSearch)*
Indexing and abstracts of journals and other materials in education.

Jenny Latimer's search for information on the presence and effects of hydrogenated oils in foods, especially snack foods and candy, led her to research in nutrition and health sciences and to the database *Health Reference Center—Academic*, which provides abstracts of scholarly articles and conference presentations. In this database she found two abstracts that added breadth and complexity to her research because they suggested that the dangers of hydrogenated oils are not as clear as many people claim (see Figure 10.6).

## 3 Indexing or bibliographic databases

Many databases provide titles and publication (or access) information for articles and documents in a specialized field. They can be quite useful for identifying and locating potential sources. You will generally need to locate the texts

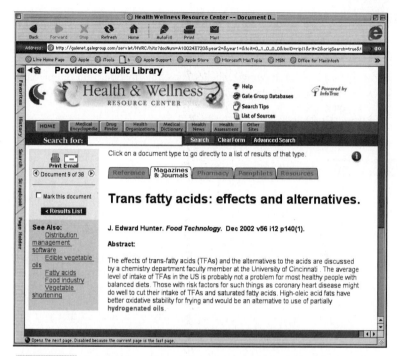

**FIGURE 10.6**   Sample of an abstract from the database *Health Reference Center—Academic*

of these sources through some other means, although some databases may provide a link to a library's online subscription to a scholarly journal.

*Art Index (FirstSearch)*
Indexes over 400 publications in the arts.
*GEOBASE (FirstSearch)*
Indexes articles on geology, geography, and ecology.

## 4  Resource databases

**Resource databases** provide access to information, images, and documents arranged in the form of an electronic reference work, or they offer tools for researchers. Several of the databases you might find helpful in conducting research and in writing your research paper or report are listed below.

*Web of Science (ISI)*
Web access to databases (*Science Citation Index, Social Sciences Citation Index, and Arts & Humanities Citation Index*) of citations in research journals.

Citation indexes allow you to identify the sources used by researchers in their work and to track the strands of a research "conversation."

*RefWorks (CSA)*
Web-based, bibliographic management service you can use to create a list of sources by drawing bibliographical information from online databases and automatically creating entries in a variety of documentation styles.

*WorldCat (FirstSearch)*
Catalog of library holdings and Internet resources worldwide.

**STRATEGY**    **Consult online databases.**

1. Use the descriptions of databases in this section only as a *starting point*. Be alert for databases that are even better suited to your needs.
2. Most libraries prepare handouts describing the online databases to which they subscribe. These generally contain detailed, practical advice. The number of available databases and their sophistication are increasing rapidly. These handouts will provide you with up-to-date information on the availability and features of the library's databases and tell you about the latest additions to the collection.
3. Unless your research is in a relatively advanced state so that you can focus on specific issues or kinds of information, move from general databases to more specialized ones.
4. Keep detailed records of the databases you have consulted, the possible sources you have identified, and any abstracts or full texts you have located. Download or print out copies, and include them in your research file if you can.
5. Pay attention to links and alternative search paths suggested by a database. They may lead you to unexpected and worthwhile resources. They may also lead you astray, so keep a record of the screens you have viewed in case you need to retrace your path.
6. If the full text of an article is not available online, check your library's catalog to see if it is available. (Many libraries provide links to their catalogs as part of their database programs.)
7. If a database provides only an abstract or a bibliographical reference to an article, check to see if the database will email you the full text of articles you find potentially useful. Some databases charge for this service; others will provide texts for free.

## 10g Evaluating library sources

Library sources—books from reputable publishers, articles from scholarly or well-known periodicals, government documents—often have been reviewed by experts and produced with editorial checks. Even so, once you locate these sources, you'll need to decide whether they are appropriate for your research community and your questions and whether they support or deepen your thesis.

---

**STRATEGY**    Use questions to evaluate your sources.

- Does the publisher, journal, or sponsoring organization have a reputation for balance and accuracy? Is it an advocate whose views require caution?
- Is the author's reputation clear? What do other sources think of the author's trustworthiness, fairness, and importance?
- How accurate is your source, especially if it presents facts as truth? Can you spot obvious errors? Which points are well documented?
- How does the writer support generalizations? Do they go beyond the facts? Are they consistent with your knowledge?
- Are the ideas generally consistent with those in your other sources? If different, do they seem insightful or misleading and eccentric?
- Does the source meet the expectations of your research community?
- Does the source appropriately document information, quotations, and ideas or clearly attribute them to the author?
- Has the source appeared without an editorial or review process? Does it apply only to a specific setting? Is its information outdated? Does it cite experts who have political or financial interests? Does it try to obscure its own bias? If so, consider it questionable; use it with caution.

---

# 11  Using Web and Internet Resources

Many writers begin their research on the World Wide Web or the Internet. They do so because of accessibility and the wide range of current resources available. Email, discussion groups, and, above all, Web sites provide varied interpretations, opinions, and information, ranging from text to data to visuals and audio. To access a Web site, you simply need a **browser,** such as *Internet Explorer* or *Netscape,* and an electronic address, known as a **URL** (uniform resource locator). Or you can follow links embedded in an online document (usually marked by an icon or highlighted line).

Web and Internet resources are rich and varied, but they have limitations, too. The texts are often shorter, less detailed, and provide less developed explanations or arguments than do print texts. The electronic texts have not necessarily been reviewed and edited carefully in the ways many print texts have. And the absence of systematic cataloging and indexing on the Web and Internet makes search tools and an efficient search strategy very important.

## 11a Developing a Web and Internet search strategy

In creating your Web and Internet search strategy, emphasize diversity. Go beyond Web sites to electronic versions of printed texts (books, magazines, scholarly and professional journals, and newspapers); electronic databases and collections of documents (including government publications); discussion groups and newsgroups; visual and audio resources; synchronous devices including Webcams; and the links embedded in Web texts.

**STRATEGY** **Make a checklist.**

Turn your plan for Web and Internet research into a checklist you have at hand while you are working online. Include in your checklist reminders to examine a variety of resources, including the following.

| | | |
|---|---|---|
| Web sites and Web pages | Online versions of printed texts | Online databases (see 10f) |
| Synchronous devices | Discussion groups and newsgroups | Visual and audio documents |
| Embedded links | Collections of documents | Online periodicals |

## 11b Using search engines

To locate Web and Internet resources, use a **search engine,** an electronic tool that identifies and gathers data about Web pages and Internet sites such as discussion groups. The sites a search engine identifies, the information it gathers, and the way it selects and organizes information depend on two things: (1) the principles on which it operates and (2) the questions you ask of it.

### 1 General search engines

General search engines typically search for resources according to keywords or phrases you type into a search box. Results from different search engines may both overlap and differ because each search engine indexes only a selection of the sites on the Web or Internet. Each also uses its own principles of selection and arrangement, identifying different sites and providing different information about them (see Figure 11.1). Using several search engines is worth-

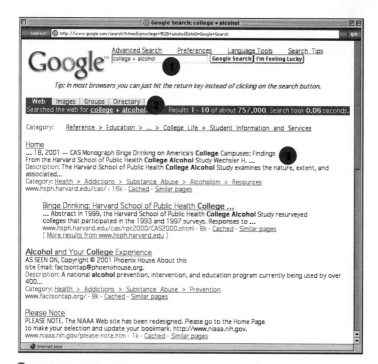

1. Keywords used in search
2. Results of search
3. One source with annotation

**FIGURE 11.1** Results of a *Google* search using the keywords *alcohol* and *college*

while, although each search may turn up many irrelevant, dated, or untrustworthy sites for every one that is relevant.

---

## GENERAL SEARCH ENGINES

*Google* <http://www.google.com>

*AltaVista* <http://altavista.com>

*Yahoo!* <http://www.yahoo.com>

*AllTheWeb* <http://alltheweb.com/>

*Wisenut* <http://wisenut.com>

*Lycos* <http://www.lycos.com>

*Teoma* <http://www.teoma.com>

*HotBot* <http://hotbot.com/>

Sometimes a search returns disappointing or confusing results. Perhaps the keywords or phrases in your query are not the ones used by some sites, so the search engine passes them by. Your query may be fine, but the results may be disappointing because the search engine finds the parts of a phrase or name rather than the whole.

Rashelle Jackson was working on a project guided by this research question: "What techniques used in hip hop performance make it different from other kinds of music?" She typed the words *hip hop techniques* into several search engines, and each responded with lists of resources including a site with the title "The Phonograph Turntable and Performance Practice in Hip Hop." The descriptions she encountered using the first three search engines were uninformative, incomplete, and even misleading. Only the fourth gave her a good idea of the site's contents and its relevance to her search (see Figure 11.2).

---

The Phonograph Turntable and Performance Practice in **Hip Hop** ...
... This transformation has been concurrent with the invention by the
**Hip Hop** DJ of a ... sliding lever which allows the performer to effect
certain **techniques** on a ...


The **Phonograph Turntable** and Performance Practice in **Hip Hop** Music
The **Phonograph Turntable** and Performance Practice in **Hip Hop** Music
Miles White ... globalization of **Hip Hop** music and culture ... invention by
the **Hip Hop** DJ of a new technical ... capabilities of...


The **Phonograph Turntable** and Performance Practice in **Hip Hop** Music
White. Introduction...


The **Phonograph Turntable** and Performance Practice in **Hip Hop** Music
The **Phonograph Turntable** and Performance Practice in **Hip Hop** Music
Miles White ... globalization of **Hip Hop** music and culture ... invention by
the **Hip Hop** DJ of a new technical ... capabilities of the **phonograph**, a
process which ... Description: The popularization and globalization of **Hip
Hop** music and culture over the past twenty or so years has provided new
and refreshing areas of inquiry and research across a number of academic
disciplines and critical approaches. The scholarly work...

---

**FIGURE 11.2**   Search engine results for the keywords *hip hop techniques*

## 2 Advanced searches

If your results for a search seem uneven or unhelpful—too many items, too few items, or mostly irrelevant items—click on the advanced search advice available on most search engines. Find out how to search most productively, using specific words, math signs (+, -), symbols (* to look for all variations using part of a word), or automatic default combinations.

Word your query to combine, rule out, or treat terms as alternatives. Use the principles of Boolean logic to focus on what you actually want to know.

| | |
|---|---|
| OR (expands) | Search for either term (documents referring to either X OR Y) |
| AND (restricts) | Search for both terms (documents referring to both X AND Y, but not to either alone) |
| NOT (excludes) | Search for X unless X includes the term Y (documents referring to X, but not those referring also to Y; X NOT Y) |

## 3 Metasearch sites

A **metasearch** site enables you to conduct your search using several search engines simultaneously—and then to compare the results. Conducted early in your research, a metasearch can help you identify which search engines are most likely to be useful for your task. Metasearches can also suggest interesting new directions for your inquiry.

| | |
|---|---|
| *Dogpile* | <http://dogpile.com> |
| *Momma* | <http://www.momma.com> |
| *Metacrawler* | <http://metacrawler.com> |
| *Profusion* | <http://www.profusion.com> |

*Profusion.com* helps locate focused search sites. Figure 11.3 on page 82 shows a partial listing of search areas from the *Profusion* meta site.

## 4 Focused and question-oriented sites

Some search sites focus on specific disciplines, fields of inquiry, or content areas. As you narrow your search or look for more complex information or the results of academic studies, these focused search sites will become more useful.

Other search tools allow you to ask questions rather than use keywords, for example, *Ask Jeeves* at <http://ask.com>. Or they may link keyword queries to what (sometimes) are related, relevant resources as does *WebReference* at <http://WebReference.com>.

**FIGURE 11.3** Partial listing of search areas on the focused *Profusion* metasearch site

## 11c Consulting Web sites and Internet resources

To identify and use appropriate resources on the World Wide Web and the Internet, you should recognize some important kinds of Web sites and Internet sites, their content and purposes, and the uses you can make of them.

### 1 Individual Web sites

Individual Web sites are not necessarily *about* individuals, although they may be, as is the case with *home pages* created by individuals to share events in their lives or to broadcast their opinions. Individuals may share accounts of experiences: white water rafting, service on a United Nations peacekeeping force, or work on an oil rig in Northern Alaska. Home pages maintained by researchers often contain links to their research articles, both those that have appeared in print and those in progress.

**Blogs** are Web sites offering daily or weekly accounts of a person's activity and thoughts. They can be fascinating sources of information from people in war zones, in dangerous parts of the world, or in important jobs. Others can be just plain boring. The search engine *Lycos* at <http://lycos.com> maintains a focus area on blogs under the title *Tripod Blog Builder* that includes these topics: "Create and Edit Your Blog," "What Is a Blog?" "Recently Updated Blogs" (examples of ongoing Blogs), and a "Blog Directory."

## 2 Sponsored Web sites

All kinds of organizations—public, private, corporate, academic, governmental, religious, and social—sponsor Web sites. The suffixes on the electronic addresses often indicate what kind of organization the sponsor is.

| | |
|---|---|
| *edu* | educational institution |
| *gov* | government agency |
| *org* | nonprofit or service organization |
| *com* | business organization (commercial) |
| *net* | network organization |

A sponsored Web site may be little more than a billboard or marketing device, yet sponsored Web sites can also be excellent sources of up-to-date information and articulate, fair advocates for a cause. The usefulness and the integrity of a sponsored Web site generally depend on the character of the sponsoring organization and the resources devoted to creating and maintaining it.

## 3 Advocacy Web sites

Advocacy Web sites explain or defend an organization's actions and beliefs and argue for specific policies (see Figure 11.4 on p. 84). Although they are biased in favor of the organization's position—after all, they *advocate* for the point of view—many are of high quality: explaining positions, answering critics, and providing detailed supporting evidence and documentation along with lists of readings on the topic or issue. Some even provide links to Web sites with opposing points of view as a way of stimulating open discussion.

## 4 Informational Web sites

Carefully organized informational Web sites provide tables of data, historical background, reports of research, answers to frequently asked questions

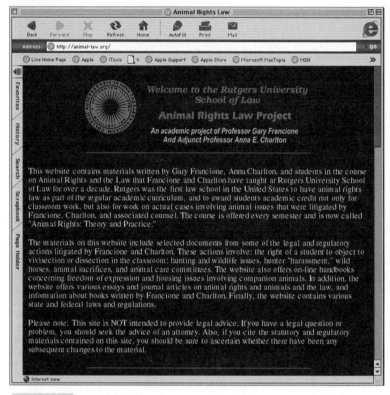

FIGURE 11.4   Home page of an advocacy Web site

(FAQs), links, and lists of references. Large Web sites may also provide site maps and allow for keyword searches.

Be aware, however, that many informational Web sites are poorly organized, unevenly developed, and even untrustworthy. Look on the Web site for information about the sponsoring organization, the way the information for the Web site is gathered and maintained, and the date of the last update.

Informational Web sites may focus on a particular subject such as sleep research, horror movies, or poetry from the Beat Generation of the 1950s, or an activity such as an environmental project or steps to developing a healthy lifestyle. Or they may focus on the sponsoring institution itself, providing information about its activities, ongoing research projects, and research results.

## 5  Research-oriented Web sites

Research-oriented Web sites are informational in a broad sense, but they are more narrowly focused than most informational Web sites and are arranged in different ways. Research-oriented Web sites typically contain one or more of the following.

1. Full texts of research reports (sometimes twenty-five or more pages)
2. Summaries of completed or ongoing research projects
3. Electronic texts of research articles that appeared in print journals or book-length collections
4. Extensive data frequently presented in the form of downloadable tables, graphs, and charts or available as texts of field notes and discussions of statistics
5. Reviews of current research
6. Texts of unpublished conference papers and other presentations
7. Announcements of grants, conferences, and forthcoming publications
8. Addresses or phone numbers for researchers
9. Bibliographies of books and articles; links to related Web sites
10. Artistic performances and creations (see Figure 11.5)

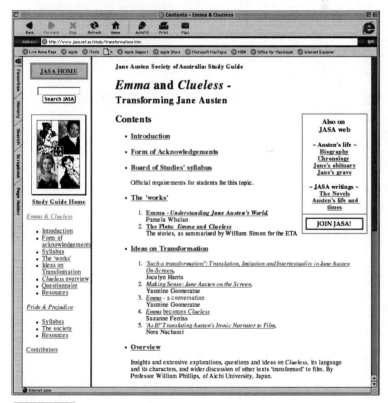

**FIGURE 11.5** Web site devoted to Jane Austen weaves literary history with information on film performances

Universities, research institutes, and professional organizations often maintain research-oriented Web sites, as is the case with the Web site maintained by the American Psychological Association (see Figure 11.6).

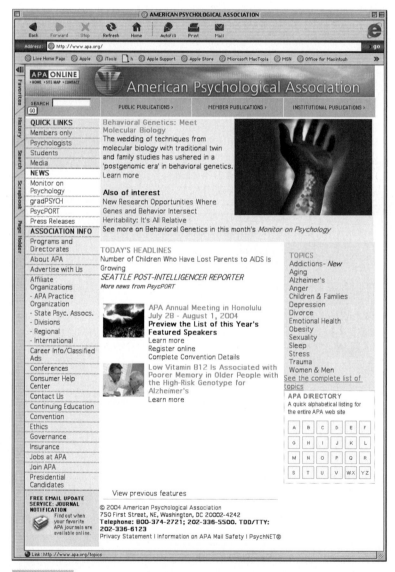

**FIGURE 11.6** Opening page for the American Psychological Association Web site

## 6 Online periodicals and books; electronic versions of print publications

Online magazines, newspapers, and scholarly journals are similar to print publications in many ways. Indeed, many appear in both online and print versions.

*Los Angeles Times*    <http://www.latimes.com>
*Newsweek*    <http://www.newsweek.com>
*Business Week*    <http://www.businessweek.com>
*Weekly Standard*    <http://www.weeklystandard.com>
*The Nation*    <http://www.thenation.com>
*Dallas Star-Telegram*    <http://www.dfw.com>

Many online sites go one step further and make back issues or selected articles available, as is the case with publications like the following.

*Scientific American*    <http://www.sciam.com> (general-interest magazine of science and technology)
*Social Text*    <http://www.nyu.edu/pubs/socialtext> (academic journal of social and political analysis)
*Salon*    <http://www.salon.com> (general-interest magazine of social and cultural commentary)
*Journal of Mundane Behavior*    <http://www.mundanebehavior.org> (academic articles on popular culture)

## 7 Electronic lists and discussion groups

The Internet and the Web play host to many discussion groups, some focusing on highly specialized topics like beekeeping, small countries in Eastern Europe or Africa, and poetry slams. The postings to such lists vary in quality, from inquiries by novices to discussions and responses from nationally recognized experts. It can be difficult to judge the quality of contributions because the writers may identify themselves only by screen names.

An **electronic list** posts messages from members of a mailing list to all other members and gives them a chance to respond. **Newsgroups** or **bulletin boards** are open sites where you can post messages or questions of your own and read postings from other people. Both kinds of sites are good places to gather opinions, possible sources, and an understanding of readers' expectations about a topic. Many search engines will help you locate postings shown in Figure 11.7 on page 88.

## 8 Government publications sites

Government publications on an astonishing range of topics are available in print form in most college and university libraries. In addition, many

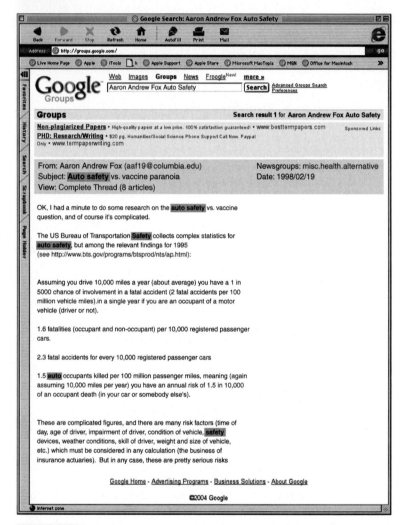

**FIGURE 11.7** Newsgroup message from *Google* requesting research help

government agencies have spent considerable effort developing Web sites for access to their reports and documents. Use the following sites to identify government publications relevant to your research.

*FirstGov*   <http://www.firstgov.gov>
*Catalog of U.S. Government Publications*   <http://www.access.gpo.gov/su_docs/locators/cgp>
*FedStats*   <http://www.fedstats.gov/search.html>
*FedWord*   <http://www.fedword.gov>

## **11d** Evaluating Web and Internet sources

Web and Internet sources often have not been edited or reviewed by outside readers, so you can't assume that they are credible or reliable. The following sites offer help in examining Web sources critically.

"The Good, the Bad and the Ugly: or, Why It's a Good Idea to
    Evaluate Web Sources"
    <http://lib.nmsu.edu/instruction/eval.html>
"Thinking Critically about World Wide Web Resources"
    <http://www.library.ucla.edu/libraries/college/help/critical/index.htm>
"Evaluating Web Resources" (with links to checklists and examples)
    <http://www2.widener.edu/Wolfgram-Memorial-Library/
    webevaluation/webeval.htm>

### 1 Examine Web materials critically

Examine Web sources carefully and ask questions appropriate to the kinds of information and ideas being presented.

- Is the material documentary (films, sounds, images, surveys)? If so, consider authenticity, biases, and relevance to your research questions.
- Is the resource textual (essays, narratives, studies, articles)? If so, consider its authorship, construction, level of detail, support for reasoning, complexity, fairness, sources, and documentation.
- Is the resource peculiar to the Web (personal, educational, corporate, organizational sites)? If so, consider its genre, affiliation, reputation, possible motivation, construction, design, and value in terms of content.
- Is the resource conversational? If so, analyze it as primary material (see 11d-3).

### 2 Ask critical questions about Web materials

To evaluate the strengths, weaknesses, and credibility of Web resources such as personal pages and organizational sites, ask the following questions developed by Paula Mathieu and Ken McAllister at the University of Illinois at Chicago as part of the *Critical Resources in Teaching with Technology* (CRITT) project.

**Who benefits? What difference does that make?** The Web pages at <http://www.whymilk.com>, for example, seem dedicated entirely to the reader's health, as Figure 11.8 on page 90 illustrates. But because this site promotes drinking milk every day, critical readers can easily see that milk producers and distributors will also benefit from these milk sales.

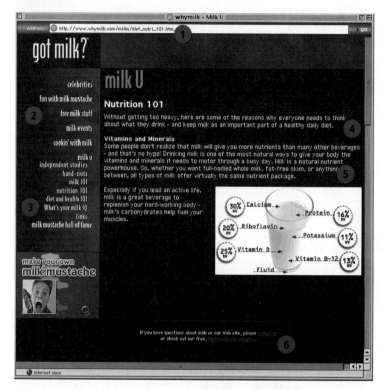

① Commercial site

② Includes features designed to appeal to readers

③ Offers personal analysis of diet and exercise

④ Advocates drinking milk

⑤ Uses graphics to convey information

⑥ Offers more information

READER'S REACTION: **Why are you sharing all this? How do you benefit? How do I know this is accurate, complete information?**

**FIGURE 11.8**    Web page sponsored by the milk industry

**Who's talking? What difference does that make?** The "speaker" responsible for all the site's positive facts about milk is identified as "us" in the invitation to request more information. The site's privacy statement, however, identifies the site owner as the California Fluid Milk Processor Advisory Board. What might be the point of view of this group? Will all the "facts" appear on the pages, especially any that might question milk's goodness?

① Organizational site

② Uses title to introduce position

③ Uses graphics to highlight point of view

④ Uses statistics

⑤ Cites authority

READER'S REACTION: **Given the number of milk drinkers, how serious is this risk? Isn't this view a bit extreme?**

**FIGURE 11.9**   Web page sponsored by an advocacy group

In contrast, the Web page at <http://liberator.enviroweb.org/fall94/ milk.html> links milk drinking to disease (see Figure 11.9). This article was published in *AnimaLife,* founded by an advocacy group, Cornell Students for the Ethical Treatment of Animals (CSETA). The author doesn't supply his background, leaving readers to judge his evidence and reasoning. He does seem to provide scientific support, but readers may find the reasoning strained and the tone impassioned.

Yet another perspective is offered by "Lactose Intolerance" at <http://www.niddk.nih.gov/health/digest/pubs/lactose/lactose.htm> (see Figure 11.10). Sponsored by the National Digestive Diseases Information Clearinghouse, part

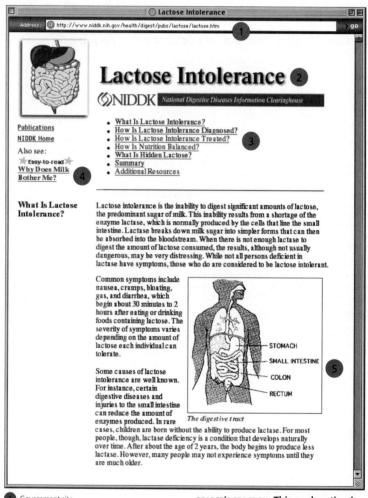

① Government site
② Identifies topic in title
③ Uses questions and answers to explain
④ Supplies link to consumer information
⑤ Adds informative graphics

READER'S REACTION: **This explanation is very clear. The sponsor is identified, too.**

**FIGURE 11.10** Web page sponsored by a government agency

of the National Institutes of Health, this site presents impartial information about lactose intolerance, an inability to digest milk sugar that affects millions of people. The "speaker," an authoritative government agency, clearly answers questions about dairy products. The page appeals to health-oriented readers with direct language, visuals, and specifics. Elsewhere on the site, the agency supplies a technical discussion as well.

**What's missing? What difference does that make?** The *Why Milk?* site is a commercial venture promoting cow's milk. Naturally, it ignores soy, goat, and other milk (and nonmilk) options. In contrast, "Milk . . . Help Yourself," published by an animal rights group, omits data on milk's safety and health benefits. On the other hand, "Lactose Intolerance" does not promote or attack dairy products; instead, it aims to inform, giving the public reliable advice and ignoring commercial or organizational interests. Each of these—like every resource—has a point of view that guides its selection and presentation of information. Examining who benefits, who speaks, and what is omitted can help you critically evaluate this point of view.

### 3 Evaluate conversational resources

Electronic mailing lists, newsgroups, or Web-based forums can provide you with instant access to firsthand information. However, you need extra vigilance to distinguish authoritative comments, backed by genuine expertise, from unsupported opinions. One strategy is to treat conversational materials as primary resources, data which you need to analyze and interpret for your readers. Ask critical questions: What do you know about the author's expertise, credibility, fairness, logical reasoning, or supporting evidence? Do other resources substantiate the author's claims? How does the author's view relate to your research thread? How would your research community react to the material?

## 12 Doing Fieldwork

**Field research** is firsthand research, gathering material directly from people you interview or survey or from events and places you observe. Your fieldwork addresses your research questions with original, even surprising, findings that are the product of your own investigation, not somebody else's research. Because you may find that your results vary or are more complex than you expected, it's important to plan your field research with an open mind or a "neutral" perspective on what you're investigating. This perspective will help you to avoid leading questionnaires, biased notes during an observation, or data-gathering methods that skew your results, such as interviewing only one social group about food in the student union.

Good field research also involves interpretation. Give the data you collect the same critical "reading" and analysis you give to all other sources. Secondary sources from your research may suggest how to present your findings and what to conclude from your data. Of course, your fieldwork goals and methods depend on your task and research community.

**Academic.** Field research in sociology, psychology, business, education, or urban planning often means studying people's behaviors or outlooks to find patterns, causes, or effects. In chemistry, engineering, or pharmacy, it inquires into how substances, organisms, objects, or machines work. When you plan your fieldwork, find out about any institutional approval needed for research involving other people (see 12d).

**Work.** Field research in businesses and organizations often looks at how customers (or staff) act and interact, how problems might be solved, or how quality or efficiency might be improved. Market researchers gauge interest in a product or recruit consumers for taste tests or "focus groups" that respond to products or marketing strategies.

**Public.** Field research in public settings often gathers (and measures) people's opinions on issues or policies. Government research in the public interest can profoundly affect laws and regulations. Researchers for the Environmental Protection Agency, for instance, sample soil, water, and air across the country to test levels of pollutants or contaminants.

> **STRATEGY** **Prepare for your fieldwork.**
>
> Do background research, and plan your fieldwork carefully. To identify worthwhile questions or problems, look over research already conducted. Use the methods of others as models for your own.

## 12a Conducting an interview

Talk with experts or people with pertinent experiences or opinions to test or supplement your other sources. An interview can be structured or open-ended. As you plan, think about your goals, and shape the interview questions accordingly.

---

**STRATEGY**  **Organize a productive interview.**

- List potential interviewees and possible questions. Consider whether you will need a lengthy conversation or just a few short answers.
- Write out your questions, arranging them logically. Avoid any that could be answered by *yes* or *no* or that are unclear or leading.
- Use your questions, but don't be shackled by them. In the interview, follow up on new information and ideas that serve your purpose.
- If you wish to tape-record instead of take notes, always ask permission. Bring extra tapes and batteries as well as backup paper and pen.
- After an interview, send a thank-you note—both to be polite and in case you need a follow-up interview.

## **12b** Using a survey, poll, or questionnaire

Surveys, polls, and questionnaires gather opinions or information about specific behaviors and possible future actions. They can be administered orally (asking questions in a mall or on the phone), on paper (filling out a survey in a restaurant), or, increasingly, in electronic form (responding in a file on the Web). In any case, you'll need to think through your questions carefully and test your instrument before you administer it for your study.

### 1 Use surveys and polls

**Surveys** and **polls** collect short answers, often in *yes/no* form, providing statistics for charts, comparisons, or support. All can provide basic information, but what they supply in simplicity and speed, they lack in depth and complexity.

**STRATEGY**  **Prepare for a survey or poll.**

- Decide which people you want to survey or poll. How many do you need to contact? Of what gender, age, or occupation?
- Always draft, test, and revise your questions in advance.
- Select your location; it may determine who answers your questions.

Shane Hand marked answers to his recycling questions on a tally sheet.

```
Do you . . .
Use coffee mugs instead of polystyrene cups?      Yes    No
Reuse plastic wrap, foil, and plastic bags?       Yes    No
Recycle newspapers and/or magazines?              Yes    No

Are you willing to . . .
Take your own bags to the store?                  Yes    No
```

## 2 Use questionnaires

Usually mailed, **questionnaires** can gather in-depth information from many people but need careful preparation for clarity. (See the sample questionnaire at the end of the research paper in 17c.)

---

**STRATEGY** | **Design your questionnaire.**

- Consider your purpose (what you want to find out and why), the selection of your participants (the characteristics of the people you will question), and your expectations (possible problems).
- Decide whether to group questions in sections and whether to ask multiple-choice or yes-no questions that supply numerical data, open-ended questions that supply narrative detail, or a combination of these.
- Figure out what respondents might be willing to do (writing, checking, circling, or marking answers) and how you will analyze answers.
- Draft your questions, and test them on several people. Ask your testers to identify where they were confused or lacked information.
- Revise the questionnaire, and prepare it for distribution. Try to fit your questions on one page (front and back), but leave room for comments.

---

## 12c Conducting an ethnographic study

You can use **ethnographic research** to interpret practices, behaviors, language, and attitudes of groups connected by interests or ways of understanding and acting. Because an **ethnography**—the written report of this cultural analysis—aims for in-depth understanding, you may use several methods to gather detailed information about your subject, including observations of people, events, and settings; conversations or interviews with **informants** (people who provide information about the group to which they belong); and collection of **artifacts** (characteristic material objects).

Focus your fieldwork on a specific setting, activity, person, or group. Conduct **structured observations** in which you objectively watch a situation, behavior, or relationship in order to understand its elements and processes. For instance, to study how preschoolers use language during play, you might conduct a series of structured observations at a day-care center.

---

**STRATEGY** | **Plan a structured observation.**

- Choose the site; if necessary, get permission to observe.
- Decide how to situate yourself (in one spot or moving) and how to explain your presence to those observed.
- Decide what information or artifacts you want to gather and why. Try to anticipate how you will use this material in your report.

- Consider what equipment you will use to record information: tape recorder, camera, notepad, or video camera.
- Anticipate problems, and plan strategies for dealing with them.

The following notes were transcribed from an audiotape for an anthropology study of a person with an unusual occupation.

> Dave Glovsky—Palace Playland: Dave's Guessing Stand
> (Sound of game, the Striker: hammer swings in background)
> [First interchange between Brian Schwegler and Dave Glovsky is inaudible because of background noise.]
> *BS:* So, Dave, can you tell me a little something about how you guess? Can you tell me how you guess?
> *DG:* Ages? I read the lower lids. I read the lower lid. It deteriorates as we get older. The more it gets darker, they get older. Even children of sixteen can fool me with the deterioration under the eyes. They can have beautiful skin, but I don't check the skin. I check the lower lid of their eyes.
> [The interview continues until a customer arrives.]
> *DG:* Hey, come on in, have fun. What do you want me to guess?
> *Female cust:* My age.
> *DG:* All right, that's a dollar. (Holds up one dollar bill.) A hundred dollar bill. Step into the office here. (Points to a patch of pavement.)

When you report ethnographic data, be precise. Offer interpretations that go beyond simply presenting details.

First Draft: Dave the Guesser
by Brian Schwegler

"Come on in, have some fun with the famous guesser of Old Orchard," says Dave "The Guesser" Glovsky. Relying on his voice and personality to attract customers, he seems out of place in this mechanized wonderland. Hand-painted signs covered with cramped writing are his advertisement. . . .

As I stand in front of his stand and read his signs, a young woman approaches Dave.

"Hey, come on in, have fun. What do you want me to guess?" Dave asks.

"My age," says the young woman.

"All right, that's a dollar." Holding up the dollar bill that the woman gives him, Dave examines it the way a jeweler examines a precious stone. "A hundred dollar bill." Pointing to a space on the pavement, Dave says, "Step into the office here." Dave checks her out from all angles, looking for the clue that will let him know her age within two years, his margin of error. . . .

## 12d Obtaining consent and approval for research on human subjects

Whenever you conduct research on human subjects, even when administering a short questionnaire, you need to abide by certain ethical and legal principles to avoid injuring your subjects. (This is also true of animal research.) "Injury" doesn't just mean physical harm, such as testing a product known to cause cancer. It also refers to psychological injury, such as interviewing children about traumatic events in their lives. Furthermore, participants are protected by privacy laws; although most people know when they become uncomfortable answering questions, they may not always be aware of how the law protects them. Consult with a teacher or a human subjects board member on your campus to ensure that your research meets the proper standards.

Most campuses have a committee, board, or administrative unit that provides information about using human subjects in research. Such groups are responsible for approving research plans after considering their legal and ethical implications as well as the kinds of information that the researcher proposes to gather. The group can approve, disapprove, or return a proposal for revision.

Gaining approval to conduct human subject research is required on most campuses—and has the benefit of protecting the researcher as well as the people who participate. However, whether you need approval for field research involving people will depend on various factors. In some cases, an entire class can receive general approval to conduct surveys, polls, or questionnaires; in other cases, no approval may be necessary. Be sure that you and your instructor know the practices on your campus, and follow the requirements accordingly.

**STRATEGY** Follow conventions for informed consent.

Besides meeting institutional guidelines and regulations, ethical field research involves some commonsense principles.

- Explain your research to participants. You may need to keep the explanation general so that you don't influence their responses, but you should not conceal the purpose and nature of your study.
- Make clear to participants what will happen with the data you gather. Who will see it? How long will it be kept? (Human subject committees have requirements for the collection, use, storage, and disposal of data, and you should follow those requirements.)
- Explain whether you will preserve anonymity or offer an option of anonymity. If you need to use names, will you use pseudonyms?
- Give your subjects the option of seeing the results of your research.

# 13 Avoiding Plagiarism

Consider the following cases. (1) After procrastinating for weeks, Kim can't imagine finishing her research paper on time. Following a friend's advice, she uses her credit card to buy a paper for $50 from an Internet paper mill, puts her name on it, and hands it in. (2) Paul realizes that a research paper he wrote the previous semester also fits the assignment in his spring class. He makes some minor changes and hands it in without mentioning that he originally wrote it for another course. (3) In her research paper, Tisha quotes a paragraph from an excellent source, dutifully citing it in her text and her references. A paragraph later, she adds more from the source, but forgets to put quotation marks around the text or include an in-text citation.

Which of these cases is plagiarism? Which falls under "academic dishonesty"? Are they of equal severity? If someone like Tisha just makes an honest mistake while writing a paper, should she be guilty of plagiarism and suffer the (increasingly harsh) consequences?

## 13a Recognizing plagiarism

**Plagiarism,** which comes from a Latin word for "kidnapping," generally refers to the theft of another person's ideas or words. However, plagiarism is a cultural concept, part of a system of beliefs and regulations that govern the ways we write and the way we use people's words. Although plagiarism exists in all communities, the standards for acknowledging and citing sources vary with the context. In college, you are in a setting where the rules about plagiarism are strict and apply to almost any kind of work you do for a course. Not learning and following those rules can lead to a failing grade for either a paper or an entire course, a special plagiarism notation on your transcript, or expulsion from your college or university. Very serious plagiarism, especially at higher levels of research and scholarship, can result in lawsuits and can ruin a career.

According to the Council of Writing Program Administrators (WPA), plagiarism in an academic setting "occurs when a writer deliberately uses someone else's language, ideas, or original (not common-knowledge) material without acknowledging its source" (<www.wpacouncil.org>). Thus, turning in someone else's paper as your own, taking someone's original idea from a book as your own, and copying passages or even sentences into your paper without noting their source all represent plagiarism. Technically, turning in your own earlier

| GENERAL ATTITUDES ABOUT PLAGIARISM IN THREE COMMUNITIES | | | |
|---|---|---|---|
| | **ACADEMIC** | **WORK** | **PUBLIC** |
| **BELIEFS ABOUT PLAGIARISM** | Strongly believes in individual ownership of ideas, texts, inventions, and other products of research and scholarship | Vigorously protects slogans, icons, language, and organizational representations from general use or appropriation by competitors | Remains relatively unconcerned about the ownership of words produced for wide public or civic circulation, not for profit |
| **BELIEFS ABOUT WRITTEN MATERIALS** | Views writing as intellectual property of writer (but sometimes owned by institution) | Views written materials as part of mission, products, or services, often owned by organization (not writer) | May view materials as part of group identity or mission, but sees public benefit or advocacy, not ownership, as goal |
| **ATTITUDES ABOUT TEAMWORK** | Generally accepts teamwork and team credits (with disciplinary differences) | Relies on internal work teams, all expected to defend organization's territory | May expect collaboration to facilitate consensus and efficiency within and among groups |
| **EXPECTATIONS OF WRITERS** | Expects writers to credit original author of almost any written source and to distinguish the writer's words and ideas from the source's | Expects careful protection of organizational materials, but accepts unattributed use of "boilerplate" language of unclear origin or value | Expects writers to share generously, freely adapting and circulating materials, but to credit local or national authorities who substantiate values, claims, and advocacy |
| **REGULATORY MECHANISMS** | Codifies and enforces strict plagiarism rules that can lead to paper, course, or status penalties | Turns to lawsuits to challenge theft of corporate identity, products, services, or intellectual property | Generally accepts shared materials such as flyers, bylaws, and brochures, but could resort to legal protection of group identity or integrity |

work isn't plagiarism, but it's generally not allowed by teachers. Furthermore, if you don't substantially revise the original paper, you're denying yourself the chance to learn.

## 13b The problem of intention

Some cases of plagiarism are conscious and deliberate: the writers know exactly what they're doing, they know it's wrong, and they take the risk. In other cases, the writers are trying to work honestly but haven't learned appropriate documentation practices or they come from a culture with different norms. Even so, for many readers and teachers, your naiveté makes no difference at all. If the result still *looks* like plagiarism you may still be found guilty of academic misconduct. In writing classes, however, you have an opportunity to learn good source work and the conventions of attribution, so that you won't find yourself in a position of defending yourself to begin with.

Figure 13.1 represents plagiarism from the perspective of both the writer and a reader or teacher. At the top of the figure are cases of deliberate and conscious plagiarism. For most honest writers, the problem of plagiarism begins somewhere at the bottom of the figure, as they try to acknowledge sources but do so clumsily or incorrectly.

If you choose to plagiarize consciously and deceptively, remember that plagiarism hurts everyone—including you: it cheats you out of your own learning opportunity, it robs others (parents, taxpayers) who may be funding your education; it subverts and complicates the work of teachers who are trying to help you learn; it slows social progress by undermining the achievement of higher standards of education and work; and it damages those who put time and energy into producing the work you're now stealing. But we can help you learn how to cite sources carefully and responsibly, so you don't find yourself in situations represented by the bottom part of Figure 13.1.

## **13c** Recognizing when to document sources

In general, you need to document the words, ideas, and information you draw from another person's work. Keep in mind the three most important reasons for documenting sources:

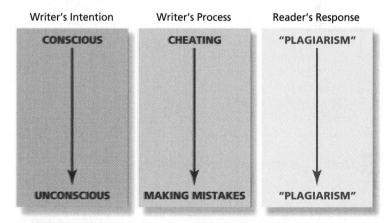

| Writer's Intention | Writer's Process | Reader's Response |
| --- | --- | --- |
| CONSCIOUS | CHEATING | "PLAGIARISM" |
| UNCONSCIOUS | MAKING MISTAKES | "PLAGIARISM" |

**FIGURE 13.1** Representation of plagiarism from the perspective of the writer and of a reader or teacher

1. To add support to your conclusions and credibility to your explanations by showing that they are based on careful research
2. To give credit to others for their original work
3. To show your readers where they can obtain the materials you cite (and from there, perhaps others)

Decisions on what needs documenting may vary from audience to audience. If you're writing to a general audience, readers may expect you to cite sources for your discussion of subatomic particles. If you're writing for a physics professor or an audience of physicists, you might assume that such matters are common knowledge. However, in some college classrooms, your teacher may want to know all the works you have consulted in order to see the evidence of your explorations.

**YOU MUST DOCUMENT**

- Word-for-word (direct) quotations taken from someone else's work
- Paraphrases or summaries of someone else's work, whether published or presented more informally in an interview or email message
- Ideas, opinions, and interpretations that others have developed and presented, even if they are based on common knowledge
- Facts or data that someone else has gathered or identified if the information is not widely enough known to be considered common knowledge
- Information that is not widely accepted or that is disputed
- Illustrations, charts, graphs, photographs, recordings, original software, performances, interviews, and the like
- Anything from the Internet that you can reasonably cite, including emails from listservs, text from blogs and chatrooms, and so forth

**BUT DO NOT DOCUMENT**

- Ideas, opinions, and interpretations that are your own
- Widely known ideas and information—the sort you can locate in common reference works or that people writing or speaking on a topic usually present as common knowledge
- Commonly used quotations ("To be, or not to be")

## 13d Working with common knowledge

In every field, researchers share certain kinds of knowledge. Everyone in biological fields, for example, knows what a "double helix" is and would not need to cite a source for such information, which is called **common knowledge.** When your topic or discipline is unfamiliar to you, however, you may not know what counts as common knowledge.

**Test whether information is common knowledge.**

- Consider whether information seems to be widely accepted and frequently repeated in sources or generally shared by educated readers. If it's not, *cite the source.*
- Consider your composition teacher—who wants to know that you have learned from your sources—as your primary reader. To show your learning, cite what might be regarded as common knowledge in a specialized field.
- Ask several people whether they know a particular fact that might be considered common knowledge. Or ask yourself. If the answer is "no," cite it.
- When in doubt, *cite.* It's easier to cut an unnecessary reference when you revise than to have to find it again in your research file.

## 13e Citing sources responsibly

When you include quotations, paraphrases, and summaries in your writing, you *must* acknowledge their sources. If you don't, you're treating someone else's work as your own.

- Be sure you enclose someone else's exact words in quotation marks.
- Make sure that paraphrases and summaries are in your own words.
- Be sure to cite the source of any ideas or information that you quote, paraphrase, or summarize.

The following paraphrase is too close to the original to be presented without quotation marks and would be considered plagiarized, even if you had done so without knowing better.

**ORIGINAL PASSAGE**

Malnutrition was a widespread and increasingly severe problem throughout the least developed parts of the world in the 1970s, and would continue to be serious, occasionally reaching famine conditions, as the millennium approached. Among the cells of the human body most dependent upon a steady source of nutrients are those of the immune system, most of which live, even under ideal conditions, for only days at a time. (From Laurie Garrett, *The Coming Plague,* New York: Penguin, 1994, p. 199)

**POORLY PARAPHRASED VERSION**

Garrett points out that malnutrition can give microbes an advantage as they spread through the population. Malnutrition continues to be a severe problem throughout the least developed parts of the world. The human immune system contains cells that are dependent upon a steady source of nutrients. These cells may live, even under ideal conditions, for only days at a time.

The writer of the poorly paraphrased version made only minor changes in some phrases and "lifted" others verbatim. It's difficult, therefore, to tell which words or ideas are Garrett's and which are the writer's.

**APPROPRIATE PARAPHRASE**

Garrett points out that malnutrition can give microbes an advantage as they spread through the population. The human body contains immune cells that help to fight off various diseases. When the body is deprived of nutrients, these immune cells will weaken (Garrett 199).

Because this writer's paper focused on the general threat of global disease, he also could have simply summarized the passage. (See 9g-1, 14b-3.)

**APPROPRIATE SUMMARY**

It has been suggested that malnutrition can weaken the immune system and make people more susceptible to diseases they would otherwise fight off (Garrett 199).

Inadvertent plagiarism—really a kind of sloppiness in your writing process—often happens when you are working between your source material and your developing paper. You *think* you're using your own words, but the words of your source are so fresh in your mind that they creep in and "become" yours.

**STRATEGY**   Avoid inadvertent plagiarism.

Keep your distance whenever you paraphrase or summarize a source.

- Be sure to look back at the source and compare your words with those of the source.
- If any phrases or sentences are too close to the original, either quote the material directly and exactly (using quotation marks), or revise your summary or paraphrase so that you're not using the author's words as your own.

## 13f Learning how to cite sources in context

Academic research usually acknowledges and draws on the work of previous scholars and researchers. Most academic writers indicate where they fit in the tradition of research on a topic and explain any agreements and disagreements with earlier work. As they present their explanations, arguments, and evidence, they also supply precise, formal documentation in the style favored by their academic field. For four common styles used to cite sources as they are mentioned in the text and then listed at the end of the paper, see Chapters 16 and 17 on MLA and APA documentation. If your instructor does not specify a documentation style, ask what is expected, and follow directions carefully.

The following excerpt from Summer Arrigo-Nelson and Jennifer Figliozzi's research report shows their careful integration (and critique) of a research study, cited in MLA style.

> First, although both questions 1 and 4 looked to determine student alcohol use within the home, a discrepancy appeared between the percentage of people who replied that they were offered alcohol at home and those who said that their parents believed alcohol was only for those over twenty-one years of age. This discrepancy could have arisen if the students in the sample were not thorough in their evaluation of their parents' views, in which case, correlations drawn from this data should not be relied upon (Aas, Jakobsen, and Anderssen).

When you read academic research, you'll find that many of the conventions for citation and quoting material will be relevant to your own papers, which will most often assume a similar academic orientation. Material from other settings, however, may follow somewhat different conventions. Work audiences will expect concise treatment of things they already know and extended summaries, tables, graphs, and illustrations—all carefully documented with a recognizable citation system (see Chapters 16–17). Material designed for general public consumption may cite sources in a somewhat informal fashion; texts with many footnotes or academic-sounding references can confuse or put off some public audiences.

The following paragraph is excerpted from a publication of the "Exxon Valdez Oil Spill Trustee Council" <http://www.oilspill.state.ak.us> which contains documents of public interest with special focus on the Exxon Valdez cleanup effort and that spill's impact on the Alaskan shoreline environment. The excerpt comes from a report of research investigating the recovery of the harlequin duck from the effects of the oil spill. Notice how the writer condenses several important and scientifically complex studies into a research synthesis that is readily understandable by a reasonably educated public audience but does not overwhelm the reader with complex references, preferring to provide alternative ways, at the Web site, to access the actual research studies.

> Winter surveys from 1995–1998 found that adult female survival was lower in oiled versus unoiled areas, and a similar survival scenario is suggested from data collected in 2000 to 2002. Oil remained in the subsurface of the intertidal zone through 2001, including under some mussel beds where harlequin ducks could be feeding. Biopsies from harlequin and Barrow's goldeneye ducks continue to show differences in an enzyme indicative of exposure to hydrocarbons between birds from oiled versus unoiled parts of the sound. These differences are consistent with the possibility of continued exposure to spill-derived hydrocarbons in the western sound. The biological effect of this possible exposure has not been established, but the declining trend of female survivability in the oiled areas may be continuing. Although this result cannot be attributed unequivocally to oil exposure, there is reason for concern about possible oil exposure and reduced survival for harlequin ducks in the western sound.

If you cite such work in your own papers or projects, you may wish to "unpack" the general references into specific citations. In more informal and less research-oriented public writing, be sure that you check any quotations or material that appear to be from a source other than the public document itself. If you encounter an unreferenced quotation, try contacting the organization or author of the document to get the full citation for the source.

In contrast, consider an excerpt from a document at the same oil spill site that is clearly intended for other researchers and scholars with technical backgrounds, such as academics in marine biology departments at research universities or members of the Environmental Protection Agency who monitor coastal pollution (<http://www.oilspill.state.ak.us>). Notice especially how careful the authors are to cite the sources of their information. Notice, too, how specialized their language and terminology are and how they rely on established studies (dating back two decades) to provide their background information.

> The composition, distribution, abundance, and productivity of plant and animal plankton communities in the GOA have been reviewed by Sambrotto and Lorenzen (1986); Cooney (1986); Miller (1993); and Mackas and Frost (1993). In general, dramatic differences are observed between pelagic communities over the deep ocean, and those found in shelf, coastal, and protected inside waters (sounds, fjords, and estuaries). Specifically, the euphotic zone seaward of the shelf edge is dominated year round by very small phytoplankters—tiny diatoms, naked flagellates, and cyanobacteria (Booth 1988). Most are smaller than 10 microns in size, and their combined standing stocks (measured as chlorophyll concentration) occur at very low and seasonally stable levels. It was orig-

inally hypothesized that a small group of large oceanic copepods (*Neocalanus spp.* and *Eucalanus bungii*) limited plant numbers and open ocean production by efficiently controlling the plant stocks through grazing (Heinrich 1962). More recent evidence, however, indicates the predominant grazers on the oceanic flora are not the large calanoids (Dagg 1993), but instead abundant populations of ciliate protozoans and heterotrophic microflagellates (Miller et al. 1991a, 1991b; Frost 1993).

# 14 Integrating Sources

No doubt you've had the experience of being surrounded by photocopied pages from books and articles, note cards or slips of paper with quotations on them, and ideas scribbled on a note pad along with references to various sources. Now you're facing the daunting task of weaving all this information into your own words as you create a research paper.

## 14a Choosing purposes for your sources

Your research paper is an original contribution to a subject area—something *you* create through your thorough sleuthing for information and your way of pulling all that information together and presenting it for others. Yet it's also about *other people's* work. It's your way of representing what a community of scholars and researchers and commentators has said about a topic, or how this community has tried to answer a question. Weaving other people's words and ideas into your own paper can accomplish many specific purposes. The way you integrate outside material into your writing often depends on what you're trying to *do* with the source.

**STRATEGY**   Consider what the goal of your paper is.

- As you gather and read your source material, take notes about the possible purposes it might serve in your paper.
- As you write the paper (see Chapter 15), refer to your notes to make strategic decisions about what to incorporate at different points in the paper.

- Avoid trying to "force" a quotation to fit a purpose it doesn't serve; for example, if an author has objectively cited a controversial position, it would misrepresent that author to imply that he or she holds that position as well.
- Be willing to scrap a source or citation if it serves no purpose in your paper.
- Avoid the "display for teacher" syndrome—putting in quotations and referencing sources just to show your instructor that you have collected some information.

## 1 Introducing a topic and providing background

Especially at the beginning of your paper, you may want to use some of your sources to explain a context, introduce your topic, or provide a history or background. Be careful not to rely too much on outside sources, however, because you need to establish your own voice and explain what you will do in the paper.

In his paper on conspiracy theories, Sam Roles decided to use one of his sources to provide background on why conspiracy theories are hard to refute. Material from Sam's paper shows that he has followed the MLA style in documenting his sources (see Chapter 16).

> Conspiracy theories arise, according to scholars, for a
> number of reasons: political fragmentation and suspicion of
> difference (Pipes); something to occupy the imagination of
> a bored subculture (Fenster); and fear of more powerful
> groups (Johnson). For example, in the 1950s and 1960s,
> communism provided a . . .

## 2 Summarizing prior research

In some cases, your research paper may be exploring a topic or relationship many others have written about. Instead of trying to provide lots of references, you can use some of your sources selectively to give a brief summary of others' work.

To introduce his paper about conspiracy theories, for example, Sam Roles summarized the different categories of research on the topic, selecting representative references in each category.

> Conspiracy theories are studied within several disciplines.
> Psychologists, for example, consider the relationship
> between conspiracy theories and disorders such as paranoia

(Edmunds). Sociologists examine the formation and spread
of conspiracy theories within a culture or group, and its
underlying causes (Haskins). Political scientists focus on
the way that political ideologies can lead to the creation
of beliefs about leaders' motives (Argyle). And experts in
anthropology consider the cultural bases of myth creation,
fear of persecution, or the construction of alternative
realities (Lizaro). In my . . .

## 3 Providing examples and cases

If you begin with generalizations about your topic or question, you will
want to provide specific examples to illustrate your points. In the following
paragraph, Sam Roles's generalization (in black) is illustrated by three examples
(in blue). Notice how each example comes from a different source.

Many conspiracy theories surround political figures or
political events. The Apollo moon missions, for example,
are now questioned by conspiracy theorists as having been
staged by the government in a studio (Adams). For decades,
it has been thought that Jack the Ripper was actually
Prince Albert Victor Christian Edward ("Prince Eddy"), the
Duke of Clarence (Evans and Skinner). And theories of who
assassinated President John F. Kennedy abound (Posner).

## 4 Showing evidence or support

When you make a point or state part of your argument, the words of experts can help you support your ideas. To present both sides of the debate over
whether a UFO was found in New Mexico in the 1940s and the discovery covered up by the government, Sam Roles incorporated a quotation from a book
taking one side of the issue.

But were these sightings really UFOs? As Berlitz and Moore
have pointed out, New Mexico in the late 1940s was "the
site of the major portion of America's postwar defense
efforts in atomic research, rocketry, aircraft and missile

development, and radar-electronics experimentation" (18).
Such activity, such as flashes of light in the sky, could
have been mistaken for the presence of UFOs.

In his notes on his sources, Sam had written the following, indicating a specific purpose for the quotation, related to the broader plan for his paper.

*Use to begin showing disagreement with UFO claim.*

## 5 Expanding an idea

As you develop ideas, use your sources to help extend, refine, or elaborate on them. This approach is especially useful when you make a transition from one part of your paper to the next. Short quotations, summaries, and paraphrases can serve this purpose when woven together with your words and ideas. Occasionally, a block quotation may be effective, as in the following example.

Joltes (1995) points out how difficult it is to change the
views of conspiracy theorists even when there is
overwhelming evidence and rational explanation to account
for a phenomenon:

> Likewise, when the US Air Force discloses the
> existence of a weather balloon experiment that
> offers a rational explanation for the "Roswell
> incident," a conspiracy buff will claim that
> records were faked, witnesses bought off or
> silenced, or whatever else was necessary to
> conceal evidence of alien contact. The aliens
> really do exist, but all the evidence has been
> suppressed, destroyed, or altered; therefore, the
> conspiracy theorist has had to work diligently to
> reconstruct what really happened, often producing
> "evidence" that is obviously contrived and
> illogical. But this matters not as long as it fits
> the theory.

## 6 Taking issue with a claim

You may want to argue against what someone else has said or what some group (of scholars or others) believes. After clearly explaining and citing sources for the opinion or belief, you can refute or "answer" the claim by drawing on other sources. Your artful use of sources can show weaknesses in a line of reasoning, or it can advance your own point of view on a topic, as in the following example.

```
In summarizing his report of a carefully coordinated 1994
investigation of the Roswell incident, Col. Richard M.
Weaver says that "the Air Force research did not locate or
develop any information that the 'Roswell Incident' was a
UFO event" (1). Records did indicate, however, that the
government was engaged in a "top secret balloon project,
designed to attempt to monitor Soviet nuclear tests, known
as Project Mogul" (1). Tests of these balloons are the only
plausible explanation of numerous UFO sightings and of the
desert debris assumed to be an alien spacecraft.
```

## 14b Summarizing, paraphrasing, and synthesizing

You can integrate sources into your paper in several ways: as quotations, paraphrases, or summaries. Furthermore, not all sources will appear in words; for example, you might want to include charts of facts, details, and statistics, or other visuals such as pictures, graphs, and screen shots.

### 1 Integrating quotations

Quoting someone's words means putting them into your paper or oral presentation in the *exact* way that they appeared in the original text (an obvious reason why it's so important for you to be accurate when taking notes during the research stage of your project). Avoid stringing quotations together or using many long quotations set off in blocks (which may look like padding). Instead, use direct quotations for these purposes.

- To show that you're accurately representing ideas that you want to challenge, modify, or extend
- To preserve an especially stylish, persuasive, or concise way of saying something

- To show vividly and dramatically what other people think
- To provide a jumping-off point for your thoughts or a change of pace

You can set off the exact words of a source with quotation marks as you blend them into your discussion. For example, you can quote entire sentences, interpreting them or linking them to your point.

> Yet alcohol awareness campaigns have seen only moderate
> success. "Although heavy drinking and monthly and daily
> alcohol use among high school seniors have declined since
> the 1980s, the decline is less among college-bound seniors,
> and binge drinking is a widespread problem on college
> campuses" (Bradley and Miller 1).

Or you can use an **embedded quotation,** weaving in key wording if it is less than a line or two.

**EFFECTIVE**　Yet a 1994 government investigation of the Roswell inci-
dent "located no records at existing Air Force offices
that indicated any 'cover-up' by the USAF or any indica-
tion of such a recovery" of alien debris (Weaver 1).

Here are some general guidelines for short quotations.

- Follow your introductory line with a colon only if that line is a complete sentence. Use commas to set off a tag such as "X says" that introduces or interrupts a quotation; vary *says* with other verbs (*claims, explains, shows*).
- When you work a quotation into your own sentence, use the context to decide whether it should be separated with a comma.
- If you leave out words or add to a quotation, use ellipses (see 42d) or brackets (see 42b) to identify your changes.
- Position these punctuation marks *inside* concluding single or double quotation marks: commas, periods, and question or exclamation marks that apply to the quoted material.
- Position these punctuation marks *outside* concluding single or double quotation marks: semicolons, colons, and question or exclamation marks that apply to the whole sentence.

## 2 Using block quotations

A **block quotation** is a longer passage from a source, set off from your own prose because of length. Remember that readers expect you to *do* something with block quotations, not just insert them.

If you quote a passage longer than four lines typed (MLA style) or forty words or more (APA style), set it off from your prose. Begin on the line after your introduction. Indent one inch or ten spaces (MLA style) or five spaces (APA style). Double-space the quotation; do not use quotation marks (unless they appear in the source).

**MLA STYLE**

Some psychologists believe that conspiracy theories have their origins in the public's trust in authority. If that "authority" is not fully credentialed but appears to be, the public may formulate beliefs that are not supported by evidence, a point made by Robyn M. Dawes in an analysis of why people believe in epidemic cases of child sexual abuse and the presence of satanic cults:

> Asking people to doubt the conclusions concerning widespread childhood sexual abuse and satanic cults is asking them not only to reject the usual bases of authority and consensus for establishing reality, but in addition to accept principles that violate foundations of everyday functioning. Now in point of fact we do ask people to accept such principles, and they do. Few people, for example, believe that the world is flat, even though it appears to be, or believe that cigarettes and alcohol are good for them, even though both may have very pleasant effects. We return once more to the efficacy of authority. People who have no direct experience of the curvature of the earth believe that it is not flat, and even the greatest devotees of tobacco and alcohol believe that these drugs are harming them. We accept what we have been told by "reputable authorities." (We even accept what has

been communicated by very minor authority figures,

such as the person who draws a map that shows the

Suez Canal to be longer than the Panama Canal.)

(Dawes 3)

**APA STYLE**

Perez (1998) anticipates profound shifts in staff training.

The greatest challenge for most school districts is to

earmark sufficient funds for training personnel, not for

purchasing or upgrading hardware and software. The

technological revolution in the average classroom will

depend to a large degree on innovation in professional

development. (p. 64)

Begin the first line without further indentation if you are quoting from one paragraph. Otherwise, indent all paragraphs 1/4" or three spaces (MLA style) or any additional paragraphs 1/2" or five spaces (APA style).

Also present four or more lines of poetry in a double-spaced block quotation. On the line after your introduction, indent ten spaces or an inch from the left margin (MLA style). Do not use any quotation marks unless the verse contains them.

**MLA STYLE**

Donald Hall also varies line length and rhythm, as "The Black-

Faced Sheep" illustrates.

My grandfather spent all day searching the valley

and edges of Ragged Mountain,

calling "Ke-<u>day</u>!" as if he brought you salt,

"Ke-<u>day</u>! Ke-<u>day</u>!" (lines 9-12)

## 3 Paraphrasing and summarizing

To make your writing smoother and more sophisticated, be selective in using quotations. Usually you can summarize, even combining several sources, or paraphrase rather than quoting sources directly.

Yet at first, government officials denied they had any tests

underway in New Mexico. Many officials were as baffled as

the general public, including Captain Tom Brown, AAF

information officer, who told reporters that he and his colleagues were as mystified as everyone else about the phenomena. (Rotondo A1)

## 4 Integrating facts, details, and statistics

You can build entire paragraphs around facts, details, and statistics drawn from your sources as long as you indicate clearly the sources of your information. You may retain some of the emphasis of your source in using these materials; more likely, you'll end up integrating these details into prose that reflects your own purposes.

## 5 Using visuals

**Visuals** (drawings, photos, graphs, and the like) can sometimes present or emphasize data better than words. If you copy a visual from print or download it from an electronic resource, you'll need to cite the source, and you may need permission to use it. Whether you create a visual yourself or draw it from your research, make sure it adds to the written text and doesn't simply substitute for it. Visuals that add to a written explanation or extend it imaginatively can increase the credibility and effectiveness of your writing.

> **STRATEGY** For emphasis, or an imaginative approach, integrate visuals for your readers.
>
> - Put the visual as near to the relevant written text as you can without disrupting the flow of the text or distorting the visual.
> - Don't interrupt the writing in ways that make it hard to read.
> - Make sure your visuals are of good quality and of appropriate size for the page.
> - Ask one or more readers whether your visuals are easy to understand and whether they add to the text's ideas and effect.
> - Label each visual (*Figure 1, Figure 2 . . . ; Table 1, Table 2 . . .*) in a form appropriate to the documentation style you are using (see Chapters 16–17).

# 15 Writing, Revising, and Presenting Your Research

How do you know when to begin *writing* your research paper? Actually, there's no set time. If you've been recording your responses as a critical reader and assembling material as answers to your research questions, you've already begun drafting. Think strategically about your task as you move toward a more complete text.

## 15a Reviewing your research questions

You began with a clear research question (see 9c) or rough thesis (see 9d) and developed it as you consulted sources, took notes, and built your research file. Now, however, is the time for decisions and any second thoughts. Do you still want to *explain* and present detailed information, or is your goal now to *persuade* readers to share the strong opinions you have developed? Are your original research questions still worthwhile, or have you arrived at a new set to answer for readers? Has your research changed your outlook and your thesis, too?

> **STRATEGY**   Let your research questions guide your draft.
>
> Arrange your research questions in a logical sequence, adding any others that you now think you ought to address. Answer the questions, and use them to determine the tentative order of material in your draft.

## 15b Reviewing your purpose

Review your readers' expectations, values, questions, and likely reactions to your project (see 4c and see the chart on p. 51). Try to respond with clear explanations, arguments, and supporting evidence. Also consider the goals that your research questions reflect (see 9c).

I'm going to tell readers about the three kinds of depression that may afflict college students—"the blues," common depression, and clinical depression.
(informative paper)

I want readers to agree with me that hunting is an acceptable activity when not excessive.
(persuasive paper)

I have a three-step solution to the problem of people downloading music without paying for it.
(persuasive problem-solution paper)

You also began with a plan, perhaps a formal outline, a set of notes, or a **purpose structure,** a series of statements briefly describing what you intend to do in each section of your paper, like this one for a paper on the problem of sleep deficits among high school students.

Beginning: Explain what sleep deficits are and how studies show that most high school students' schoolwork suffers because of them. Argue that the solution to the problem is to begin the school day later.

First Middle: Explain the problem that high school students need more sleep than most people think; the early beginning of the high school day robs them of sleep they need.

Second Middle: Explain that the high school day begins early because the buses have to be used by elementary, middle, and high school students; most districts can't afford more buses. Show that most school administrators believe it's ok for high school students to get up early.

Third Middle: Argue that changing starting times is important despite the difficulties. Tell how high schools that have changed their start times show improved student performance linked to overcoming sleep deficits. Explain that they claim the change has been worth the cost.

Fourth Middle: Outline the cost-effective strategies used by districts with later start times. Argue that these strategies should be adopted by almost all districts to help solve the problem.

End: Summarize solution; urge readers to take action in their districts.

## 15c Building from a thesis to a draft

Begin with a thesis statement (see 4b) based on your research questions. Modify it as you draft, perhaps breaking it into several sentences, or organize around its parts, repeated at key points. Instead of a detailed traditional outline, try a working outline, blocking out the general sequence and relating the segments (see 3b). Pull together the materials that belong in each part using whatever method of grouping suits your resources and notes.

> **STRATEGY**  **Group your materials in sequence.**
>
> • Arrange your cards or notes in relation to one another. As patterns emerge, you may see how other material fits.
> • Prepare pieces of paper describing available information—major points from sources, paraphrases, summaries, or ideas to include. Arrange these in relation to each other until you find a workable grouping (see Chapter 14 on integrating sources).
> • Photocopy your research journal if you've written on both sides of the pages or don't want to cut it up. Then cut out the separate entries, arrange them in a sequence, and draft transitions to connect them.
> • Use your word processing program to cut and paste relevant electronic notes into a new file wherever they seem to fit.

Once you have chunks of related materials, move from the largest units to the smaller sections, interweaving notes, source materials, and additions. Write transitions between the chunks, explaining how they fit together. Use your research questions to focus your introduction and conclusion, but direct these key parts to your readers as you draft.

> **STRATEGY**  **Design an introduction and a conclusion for readers.**
>
> For the introduction, ask, "How can I make readers want to read on?" For the conclusion, ask, "How can I keep readers thinking about my topic?" Try several versions of each, experimenting with style and content.

## 1 Organize an informative research paper

It's true that an informative research paper follows the shape of its subject. But it also needs to take into account your readers' expectations, knowledge, and values in addition to your desire to make sure that readers understand your insights and conclusions. If you don't have an overall plan in mind, however, consider building your writing around one or more of these familiar informative plans.

• Describe a surprising or puzzling phenomenon, then explain it.
• Outline a challenging task or goal and the ways to accomplish it.
• Explain a common view; then suggest a new perspective.
• Focus on relationships, events, or objects that people consider unimportant. Explain why, to the contrary, they are very important.
• Compare the customs, values, or beliefs of one social or cultural group to those of another. Or explain them to people unfamiliar or (initially, at least) unsympathetic to these customs or beliefs.
• Start with a phenomenon that people have explained differently and generally unsatisfactorily. Then offer your detailed explanation, indicating why you think it is more satisfactory.

- Concentrate on your own insights, explanations, and conclusions. Organize around *your* selection and arrangement of information.

## 2 Organize a persuasive research paper

A persuasive research essay advances, supports, and defends a thesis. The thesis may be a stand on an issue (an argumentative proposition), a proposed policy or solution to a problem, or an interpretation of a subject. What sets persuasive research writing apart is the acknowledgement of alternative opinions, policies, or interpretations. Thus, your plan needs to account not only for reasons and evidence to support your thesis but also for grounds for preferring it to the alternatives.

- Explain the issue, problem, or object of interpretation—the focal point of differing opinions or interpretations.
- State your thesis, and add other indications of your opinion, proposition, solution, or interpretation.
- Acknowledge and summarize other points of view, and demonstrate why yours is preferable.

Organize logically, perhaps following one of these arrangements.

- *Present alternatives.* Begin by discussing the issue or problem. Then discuss the alternatives in detail, indicating why each is lacking in whole or part. End with the presentation of your own perspective, which may incorporate parts of the alternatives. This strategy is useful when your research has identified extensive arguments in favor of other opinions or solutions.
- *Summarize the scholarship.* Begin with a detailed analysis of other interpretations, solutions, or policies. Indicate why this prior work is limited, flawed, or inadequate. Then offer your own solution or interpretation that addresses the weaknesses.
- *Find a middle ground.* Begin by outlining other views, interpretations, or solutions that take unsatisfactory, even extreme, positions. Then present your own reasonable middle perspective.

## 15d Revising and editing

Allow time to revise what you've written based on your audience's needs, the community for which you're writing, your research questions, and your purposes (see 6a–b). Ask others to respond to your draft (see 6c). Carefully edit (see 8b–c), proofread (see 8e), and design your document. Make sure that any quotations are accurate and that page numbers and authors are cited correctly (see 14b). Double-check your documentation form (see Chapters 16–17).

## 15e  Presenting your research

Be certain, especially for academic readers, that you supply your paper in exactly the print form or electronic format expected. For a print paper following an academic style such as MLA or APA, be sure to lay out the paper precisely as that style requires. For examples, see the sample MLA (Chapter 16) and APA (Chapter 17) papers. If your document can be submitted electronically, use any required software, and submit the file on a disk or as an attachment. If approved by your instructor or expected by your workplace or public audience, you may want to use a presentation program like *PowerPoint* that encourages the combination of text and graphics.

If you are expected to prepare a Web document in HTML or a similar language, readers will be able to move around at will and follow links to related documents or sources. A multimedia presentation using a program such as Macromedia *Dreamweaver* enables you to incorporate text, audio, still visuals, and action video. The result can be similar to a television documentary with the option of combining extensive text with detailed information, references, and documentation. Check with your instructor, supervisor, civic colleagues, or others involved to be certain that a particular electronic format will meet their expectations.

If your project is collaborative, organize these tasks as a group.

### STRATEGY   Research collaboratively within your community.

- Work together to define your topic or issue, identify keywords, and state your research questions.
- Organize as your teacher, supervisor, or group expects.
- Divide responsibilities for building a working bibliography, capitalizing on individual strengths, background, and expertise.
- Meet regularly to stay on track, assessing what you've found and what you need to find. Come to meetings ready to compare, connect, supplement, exchange, and critique.
- Try strategies for collaborative drafting (see 5b), revising (see 6c), and editing (see 8c). Organize and rehearse together for any oral presentation.

# Documenting Sources: MLA Style

## ▼ TAKING IT ONLINE

**MLA STYLE**

http://www.mla.org/style/style_main.htm

For reliable information on MLA documentation style and for sample
citations that will complement what you'll find in the upcoming section,
visit the official site of the Modern Language Association (MLA), an
organization that encourages the study of English, American, and other
literatures and languages. Click on "MLA Style," and then visit the FAQ
page for advice on specific issues such as documenting Web sources.

For more advice on using MLA style, check the home page of your
library or tutoring center, or go to one of the sites below. Be certain
that any site you use is updated to reflect the most current MLA style.

**MLA CITATION STYLE**

http://www.lie.edu/cwis/cwp/library/workshop/citmis.htm

If you appreciate visual learning cues, try this color-coded guide to sample
MLA entries for a list of works cited.

**MLA CITATION EXAMPLES WRITTEN BY HCC LIBRARY**

http://www.hcc.hawaii.edu/education/hcc/library/mlahcc.html

This site, sponsored by the Honolulu Community College Library,
provides general formats and typical examples for entries for an MLA
list of works cited.

**USING MODERN LANGUAGE ASSOCIATION (MLA) FORMAT**

http://owl.english.purdue.edu/handouts/research/r_mla.html

One of the many useful documents supplied by the Purdue University
Online Writing Lab, this page explains how to lay out your paper, prepare
Works Cited entries, and present long and short quotations in MLA style.

# PART 3

# Documenting Sources: MLA Style

## Guide to MLA Formats for In-Text (Parenthetical) Citations

## Guide to MLA Formats for List of Works Cited

# 16 Using MLA Documentation Style

The MLA (Modern Language Association) documentation style offers a convenient system for acknowledging and directing readers to your sources for ideas, information, and quotations. It consists of an in-text citation (generally in parentheses) that leads a reader to the corresponding entry in a list of works cited (at the end of the text).

**STRATEGY**  Use MLA style in the humanities to emphasize exact sources.

**ACADEMIC SETTINGS**
When readers expect MLA style or simple parenthetical documentation

**WORK AND PUBLIC SETTINGS**
When your subject and readers would be well served by a simple documentation style that seldom uses footnotes or endnotes
When you need an easy way to identify exact sources of quotations, paraphrases, or summaries
When other writers or publications in your setting use MLA, modified MLA, or a similar informal style

For more on MLA style, see the *MLA Handbook for Writers of Research Papers* (6th ed., New York: MLA, 2003), the *MLA Style Manual and Guide to Scholarly Publishing* (2nd ed., New York: MLA, 1998), or updates posted on the MLA Web site at <http://www.mla.org/style/style_main.htm>.

**IN-TEXT CITATION**

Although the average Haitian peasant calls himself a Catholic and views himself as such, he generally continues to call on his African ancestors' gods, or <u>loa</u>, for spiritual and emotional support. As one peasant put it, "One must be Catholic to serve the loa" (Metraux 59).

—Fredza Léger, College Student

**ENTRY IN THE LIST OF WORKS CITED**

Metraux, Alfred. <u>Haiti: Black Peasants and Their Religion.</u> London: Harrap, 1960.

## 16a Using MLA in-text (parenthetical) citations

The MLA documentation style uses a citation in the text (usually an author's name) to identify a source. Readers can easily locate this source, described in full, in the list of works cited that ends the paper. In-text citations follow standard patterns, and many note the exact page in the source where readers can find the particular information mentioned.

**DRAFT**    Even costumes convey the film's theme (Dell, p. 134).

**READER'S REACTION: Why does a comma follow the author's name? Why is *p.* used before the page number?**

**EDITED**    Even costumes convey the film's theme (Dell 134).

### 1. Author's Name in Parentheses

You can provide the author's name in parentheses. For a quotation or specific detail, give the page number in the source.

**IN PARENTHESES**    When people marry now "there is an important sense in which they don't know what they are doing" (Giddens 46).

### 2. Author's Name in Discussion

You can include the author's name (or other information) in your discussion, clarifying which observations are your source's.

**IN DISCUSSION**    Giddens claims that when people marry now "there is an important sense in which they don't know what they are doing" (46).

## 3. General Reference

A **general reference** refers to a source as a whole, to its main ideas, or to information throughout; it needs no page number.

**IN PARENTHESES**    Many species of animals have complex systems of communication (Bright).

**IN DISCUSSION**    As Michael Bright observes, many species of animals have complex systems of communication.

## 4. Specific Reference

A **specific reference** documents words, ideas, or facts from a particular place in a source, such as the page for a quotation or paraphrase.

**QUOTATION**    Dolphins can perceive clicking sounds "made up of 700 units of sound per second" (Bright 52).

**PARAPHRASE + FACTS**    Bright reports that dolphins recognize patterns consisting of seven hundred clicks each second (52).

## 5. One Author

Provide the author's last name in parentheses, or integrate either the full name or last name alone into the discussion.

According to Maureen Honey, government posters during World War II often portrayed homemakers "as vital defenders of the nation's homes" (135).

## 6. Two or Three Authors

Name all the authors in parentheses or in the discussion.

The item is noted in a partial list of Francis Bacon's debts from 1603 on (Jardine and Stewart 275).

For three authors, do the same: (Norman, Fraser, and Jenko 209).

## 7. More Than Three Authors

Within parentheses, name the first author and add *et al.* ("and others"). Within your discussion, use a phrase like "Chen and his colleagues point out . . ."

or something similar. If you name all the authors in the works cited list rather than using *et al.*, do the same in the text citation (see Entry 3 on p. 128).

```
More funding would encourage creative research on complementary

medicine (Chen et al. 82).
```

## 8. Corporate or Group Author

When an organization is the author, name it in the text or the citation, but shorten or abbreviate a cumbersome name.

```
The consortium gathers journalists at "a critical moment" (Comm.

of Concerned Journalists 187).
```

## 9. No Author Given

When no author is named, use the title instead. Shorten a long title as in this version of *Baedeker's Czech/Slovak Republics*.

```
In 1993, Czechoslovakia split into the Czech Republic and the

Slovak Republic (Baedeker's 67).
```

## 10. More Than One Work by the Same Author

When the list of works cited includes more than one work by an author, add a shortened form of the title to your citation.

```
One writer claims that "quaintness glorifies the unassuming

industriousness" in these social classes (Harris, Cute 46).
```

## 11. Authors with the Same Name

When authors have the same last name, identify each by first initial (or entire first name, if necessary for clarity).

```
Despite improved health information systems (J. Adams 308),

medical errors continue to increase (D. Adams 1).
```

## 12. Indirect Source

Use *qtd. in* ("quoted in") to indicate when your source provides you with a quotation (or paraphrase) taken from yet another source. Here, Feuch is the source of the quotation from Vitz.

```
For Vitz, "art, especially great art, must engage all or almost

all of the major capacities of the nervous system" (qtd. in Feuch

65).
```

### 13. Multivolume Work

To cite a whole volume, add a comma after the author's name and *vol.* before the number (Cao, vol. 4). To specify one of several volumes that you cite, add volume and page numbers (Cao 4: 177).

In 1888, Lewis Carroll let two students call their school
paper Jabberwock, a made-up word from Alice's Adventures in
Wonderland (Cohen 2: 695).

### 14. Literary Work

After the page number in your edition, add the chapter (*ch.*), part (*pt.*), or section (*sec.*) number to help readers find the passage in any edition.

In Huckleberry Finn, Mark Twain ridicules an actor who "would
squeeze his hand on his forehead and stagger back and kind of
moan" (178; ch. 21).

Identify a part as in (386; pt. 3, ch. 2) or, for a play, the act, scene, and line numbers, as in (Ham. 1.2.76). For poems, give line numbers (lines 55–57) or (55–57) after the first case; if needed, give both part and line numbers (4.220–23).

### 15. Bible

Place a period between the chapter and verse numbers (Mark 2.3–4). In parenthetical citations, abbreviate names with five or more letters, as in the case of Deuteronomy (Deut. 16.21–22).

### 16. Two or More Sources in a Citation

Separate sources within a citation with a semicolon.

Differences in the ways men and women use language can
often be traced to who has power (Tanner 83-86; Tavris
297-301).

### 17. Selection in Anthology

For an essay, story, poem, or other work in an anthology, cite the work's author (not the anthology's editor), but give page numbers in the anthology.

According to Corry, the battle for Internet censorship has
crossed party lines (112).

## 18. Electronic or Other Nonprint Source

After identifying the author or title, add numbers for the page, paragraph (*par.*, *pars.*), section (*sec.*), or screen (*screen*) if given. Otherwise, no number is needed.

Offspringmag.com summarizes current research on adolescent

behavior (Boynton 2).

The heroine's mother in the film Clueless died as the result of

an accident during liposuction.

---

### PLACEMENT AND PUNCTUATION OF PARENTHETICAL CITATIONS

Put parenthetical citations close to the quotation, information, paraphrase, or summary you are documenting.

- At the end of a sentence before the final punctuation

  Wayland Hand reports on a folk belief that going to sleep on a

  rug made of bearskin can relieve backache (183).

- After the part of the sentence to which the citation applies, at a natural pause in the sentence so that you do not disrupt it, or after the last of several quotations in a paragraph, all from one page of the same source

  The folk belief that "sleeping on a bear rug will cure

  backache" (Hand 183) illustrates the magic of external objects

  producing results inside the body.

- At the end of a long quotation set off as a block (see 14b), after the end punctuation with a space before the parentheses

  Many baseball players are superstitious, especially pitchers.

  > Some pitchers refuse to walk anywhere on the day of
  >
  > the game in the belief that every little exertion
  >
  > subtracts from their playing strength. One pitcher
  >
  > would never put on his cap until the game started and
  >
  > would not wear it at all on the days he did not
  >
  > pitch. (Gmelch 280)

### 19. Informative Footnote or Endnote

Use a note when you wish to comment on a source, provide background details, or supply lengthy information of use to only a few readers. Place a superscript number (raised slightly above the line of text) at a suitable point in your paper. Label the note itself with a corresponding number, and provide it as a footnote at the bottom of the page or as an endnote at the end of the paper, before the list of works cited, on a page titled "Notes."

[1] Before changing your eating habits or beginning an exercise program, check with your doctor.

## 16b Creating an MLA list of works cited

Provide readers with full detail about your sources in an alphabetical list following the last page of your text.

- **Page format.** Use the heading "Works Cited" (or "Works Consulted," for all sources used) centered one inch below the top edge of a new page. Continue the page numbering from the body of the paper.
- **Indentation.** Do not indent the first line of each entry. Indent additional lines one-half inch or five spaces.
- **Spacing.** Double-space all lines within and between the entries. Leave a single space (or two spaces, if you wish) after a period within an entry. Keep your spacing consistent throughout all entries.
- **Alphabetizing.** Alphabetize by last names of authors (or first names for authors with the same last name); then alphabetize by title multiple works by the same author. For sources without an author, use the first word in the title (other than *A*, *An*, or *The*).

DRAFT    Fem. and Polit. Theory, by C. Sunstein. UCP, 1990.

READER'S REACTION: **Entries that follow the MLA pattern are easy to understand. Are these notes?**

EDITED    Sunstein, Cass R. Feminism and Political Theory.

Chicago: U of Chicago P, 1990.

## STRATEGY  Find and match the MLA models.

- Take bibliographic notes as you use a source (see 10a–4).
- Figure out what type of source you've used—book, article, online document, or other form. Use the Guide on the Part 3 divider to find the sample entry for that type. Prepare your entry following this pattern.
- Identify how many authors or other features your source has. Find the patterns for these, and rework your entry as needed.
- Check the details in each entry for the sequence of information, capitalization, punctuation, and abbreviations.

## Books and Works Treated as Books

**MODEL FORMAT FOR BOOKS AND WORKS TREATED AS BOOKS**

period + space    period + space    colon + space
↓             ↓            ↓
Author(s). Title of Work. Place of Publication:

Publisher, Year Published.
↑         ↑       ↑
indent ½″    comma + space    period
or five spaces

- **Author.** Give the last name first, followed by a comma, and then the first name and any middle name or initial. End with a period.
- **Title.** Underline the title (and any subtitle), and capitalize the main words (see 43b). End with a period (unless the title concludes with a dash or a question or exclamation mark).
- **Publication information.** Begin with city of publication, a colon, and a space. Give the publisher's name in shortened form (*U of Chicago P* for *University of Chicago Press* or *McGraw* for *McGraw-Hill, Inc.*) followed by a comma, the year of publication, and a period.

### 1. One Author

Hockney, David. Secret Knowledge: Recovering the Lost Techniques
   of the Old Masters. New York: Viking Studio, 2001.

### 2. Two or Three Authors

Begin with the first author's last name. Add other names in regular order, separated by commas with *and* before the final name.

Kress, Gunther, and Theo van Leeuwen. Reading Images: The Grammar
   of Graphic Design. London: Routledge, 1996.

### 3. Four or More Authors

After the first name, add *et al.* ("and others"). You may give all the names; if so, list them in the text citations too (see Entry 7 on p. 123).

Bellah, Robert N., et al. Habits of the Heart: Individualism and
   Commitment in American Life. Berkeley: U of California P,
   1985.

Bellah, Robert N., Richard Madsen, William M. Sullivan, Ann
   Swidler, and Steven M. Tipton. Habits of the Heart:

Individualism and Commitment in American Life. Berkeley:

U of California P, 1985.

### 4. Corporate or Group Author

Alphabetize by the first main word of the group's name. If this body is also the publisher, repeat its name, abbreviated if appropriate.

Nemours Children's Clinic. Diabetes and Me. Wilmington, DE:

Nemours, 2001.

### 5. No Author Given

Alphabetize by the first main word of the title.

Guide for Authors. Oxford: Blackwell, 1985.

### 6. More Than One Work by the Same Author

List multiple works by an author alphabetically by the first main word of each title. For the first entry, include the name of the author. For additional entries, use three hyphens instead of the name, ending with a period. If the author or authors are not *exactly* the same for each work, include the names in full.

Tannen, Deborah. The Argument Culture: Moving from Debate to

Dialogue. New York: Random, 1998.

- - -. You Just Don't Understand: Women and Men in Conversation.

New York: Ballantine, 1991.

### 7. One or More Editors

Begin with the editor's name followed by *ed.* (or *eds.*).

Achebe, Chinua, and C. L. Innes, eds. African Short Stories.

London: Heinemann, 1985.

### 8. Author and Editor

Begin with either the author's or the editor's name depending on whether you are using the text itself or the editor's contributions.

Wardlow, Gayle Dean. Chasin' That Devil Music: Searching

for the Blues. Ed. Edward Komara. San Francisco: Miller,

1998.

**9. Translator**

Begin with the author unless you emphasize the translator's work.

Baudrillard, Jean. <u>Cool Memories II: 1978-1990</u>. Trans. Chris

Turner. Durham: Duke UP, 1996.

**10. Edition Following the First**

Note the edition (*Rev. ed.*, *1998 ed.*, *2nd ed.*) after the title.

Coe, Michael D. <u>The Maya</u>. 6th ed. New York: Thames, 1999.

**11. Reprint**

Supply the original publication date after the title; follow with the publication information from the version you are using.

Ishiguro, Kazuo. <u>A Pale View of Hills</u>. 1982. New York: Vintage

Intl., 1990.

**12. Multivolume Work**

Indicate the total number of volumes after the title (or after the editor's or translator's name).

Tsao, Hsueh-chin. <u>The Story of the Stone</u>. Trans. David Hawkes.

5 vols. Harmondsworth, Eng.: Penguin, 1983-86.

If you cite only a specific volume, supply that volume number and publication information. End with the total number or the full range of dates, if you wish.

Tsao, Hsueh-chin. <u>The Story of the Stone</u>. Trans. David Hawkes.

Vol. 1. Harmondsworth, Eng.: Penguin, 1983. 5 vols.

**13. Work in a Series**

Add the series (*Ser.*) name and any item number after the title.

Hess, Gary R. <u>Vietnam and the United States: Origins and Legacy</u>

<u>of War</u>. Intl. Hist. Ser. 7. Boston: Twayne, 1990.

**14. Book Pre-1900**

The publisher's name is optional; when omitted, add a comma after place of publication.

Darwin, Charles. <u>Descent of Man and Selection in Relation to Sex</u>.

New York, 1896.

## 15. Book with Publisher's Imprint

Give the imprint name, a hyphen, and the publisher's name.

Sikes, Gini. *8 Ball Chicks: A Year in the Violent World of Girl*

Gangs. New York: Anchor-Doubleday, 1997.

## 16. Anthology or Collection of Articles

Supply the editor's name, with *ed.*, and then the title of the collection. (To cite a selection, see Entry 34 on p. 135.)

Wu, Duncan, ed. *Romantic Women Poets: An Anthology*. Oxford:

Blackwell, 1997.

## 17. Conference Proceedings

Begin with the title unless an editor is named. Follow with details about the conference, including name and date.

*Childhood Obesity: Causes and Prevention*. Symposium Proc., 27

Oct. 1998. Washington: Center for Nutrition Policy and

Promotion, 1999.

## 18. Title Within a Title

Within a book title, don't underline another book's title, but underline a title normally in quotation marks.

Weick, Carl F. *Refiguring* Huckleberry Finn. Athens: U of Georgia

P, 2000.

Golden, Catherine, ed. *The Captive Imagination: A Casebook on*

"The Yellow Wallpaper." New York: Feminist, 1992.

## 19. Pamphlet

Use the same form for a pamphlet as for a book.

Vareika, William. *John La Farge: An American Master (1835-1910)*.

Newport: Gallery of American Art, 1989.

## 20. Dissertation (Published)

When published, a doctoral dissertation is treated as a book. Add *Diss.*, the school, and the date of the degree.

Said, Edward W. *Joseph Conrad and the Fiction of Autobiography*.

Diss. Harvard U, 1964. Cambridge: Harvard UP, 1966.

### 21. Dissertation (Unpublished)

Use quotation marks for the title; add *Diss.*, the school, and the date.

> Swope, Catherine Theodora. "Redesigning Downtown: The Fabrication
> of German-Themed Villages in Small-Town America." Diss. U of
> Washington, 2003.

### 22. Government Document

Begin with the name of the government and agency, the independent agency, or the author, if any. Start with *United States* for a report from a federal agency or for congressional documents, adding *Cong.* (*Congress*), the branch (*Senate* or *House*), and the number and session (*101st Cong., 1st sess.*). Include the titles of both the document and any book in which it is printed. Use *GPO* for the federal Government Printing Office.

> Sheppard, David I., and Shay Bilchick, comps. Promising
> Strategies to Reduce Gun Violence Report. US Dept. of
> Justice. Office of Juvenile Justice and Delinquency
> Prevention. Washington: GPO, 1999.

> United States. Cong. House. Anti-Spamming Act of 2001. 107th
> Cong., 1st sess. Washington: GPO, 2001.

### Articles from Periodicals and Selections from Books

**MODEL FORMAT FOR ARTICLES AND SELECTIONS**

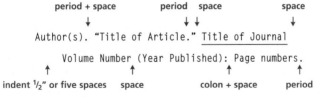

- **Author.** Give the last name first, followed by a comma. Add the first name and any middle name or initial. End with a period.
- **Article title.** Give the full title in quotation marks, with the main words capitalized. Conclude with a period inside the quotation marks (unless the title ends in a question mark or an exclamation point).
- **Publication information.** Underline the journal or book title. Supply volume number (and sometimes issue number), year of publication, and page numbers. The volume number appears on the publication's title page or cover; use Arabic numerals even if the periodical uses Roman numerals. Introduce page numbers with a colon except for selections

from books and in a few other situations shown in entries that follow. For page ranges, limit the second number to its two final numerals (14–21, 162–79) unless unclear (1498–1524).

**23. Article in Journal Paginated by Volume**

When each volume consists of several issues paginated continuously, give the volume number right after the journal's title.

> Rockwood, Bruce L. "Law, Literature, and Science Fiction: New
>
> Possibilities." <u>Legal Studies Forum</u> 23 (1999): 267-80.

**24. Article in Journal Paginated by Issue**

When the issues making up a volume are paginated separately, follow the volume number with a period and the issue number.

> Adams, Jessica. "Local Color: The Southern Plantation in Popular
>
> Culture." <u>Cultural Critique</u> 42.1 (1999): 171-87.

**25. Article in Weekly Magazine**

Note the day, month (abbreviated except for May, June, and July), and year followed by a colon. Give the sequence of page numbers (27–38). If the pages are not consecutive, give the first page with a plus sign (23+).

> Conlin, Michelle. "Unmarried America." <u>Business Week</u> 20 Oct.
>
> 2003: 106+.

**26. Article in Monthly Magazine**

> Jacobson, Doranne. "Doing Lunch." <u>Natural History</u> Mar. 2000: 66-69.

**27. Article with No Author Given**

Alphabetize by title, excluding *A, An,* and *The.*

> "The Obesity Industry." <u>Economist</u> 27 Sept. 2003: 64+.

**28. Article in Newspaper**

Cite pages as you would for a magazine (see Entry 25), but add any section number or letter. Omit *The, A,* or *An* beginning a newspaper's name. For a local paper, add the city in brackets after the title unless it's named there.

> Willis, Ellen. "Steal This Myth: Why We Still Try to Re-create
>
> the Rush of the 60's." <u>New York Times</u> 20 Aug. 2000: AR1+.

### 29. Editorial

Start with the author or, if none, with the title.

"A False Choice." Editorial. <u>Charlotte Observer</u> 16 Aug. 1998: 2C.

### 30. Letter to the Editor

Larson, Dea. Letter. <u>Wall Street Journal</u> 28 Oct. 2003: A17.

### 31. Interview (Published)

Identify the person interviewed, not the interviewer, first. For untitled interviews, supply *Interview* (without underlining or quotation marks) in place of a title.

Stewart, Martha. "I Do Have a Brain." Interview with Kevin Kelly.

    <u>Wired</u> Aug. 1998: 114.

### 32. Review

Begin with the name of the reviewer or the title for an unsigned review. For an untitled review, follow the reviewer's name with *Rev. of* ("Review of"), the work's title, *by*, and the work's author.

Muñoz, José Esteban. "Citizens and Superheroes." Rev. of <u>The</u>

    <u>Queen of America Goes to Washington City</u>, by Lauren Berlant.

    <u>American Quarterly</u> 52 (2000): 397-404.

Hadjor, Kofi Buenor. Rev. of <u>The Silent War: Imperialism and the</u>

    <u>Changing Perception of Race</u>, by Frank Furendi. <u>Journal of</u>

    <u>Black Studies</u> 30 (1999): 133-35.

### 33. Article in Encyclopedia or Reference Work

Begin with the author's name or an unsigned article's title. Note only the edition and date for a common reference work or series. If entries appear alphabetically, you may leave out the volume or page.

Oliver, Paul, and Barry Kernfeld. "Blues." <u>The New Grove</u>

    <u>Dictionary of Jazz</u>. Ed. Barry Kernfeld. New York: St.

    Martin's, 1994.

"The History of Western Theatre." <u>The New Encyclopaedia</u>

    <u>Britannica: Macropedia</u>. 15th ed. 1987. Vol. 28.

## 34. Chapter in Edited Book or Selection in Anthology

List the author of the selection or chapter, then its title (in quotation marks, but underline titles of novels, plays, and so on; see 40b, 44a). Next, provide the underlined title of the book containing the selection or chapter. If the book is edited, follow with *Ed.* and the names of the editors. Add publication information and page numbers for the selection.

```
Atwood, Margaret. "Bluebeard's Egg." "Bluebeard's Egg" and Other
     Stories. New York: Fawcett-Random, 1987. 131-64.
```

For a reprinted selection, you may add the original source. Use *Rpt. in* ("Reprinted in") to introduce a subsequent reprint.

```
Atwood, Margaret. "Bluebeard's Egg." "Bluebeard's Egg" and Other
     Stories. New York: Fawcett-Random, 1987. 131-64. Rpt. in
     Don't Bet on the Prince: Contemporary Feminist Fairy Tales
     in North America and England. Ed. Jack Zipes. New York:
     Methuen, 1986. 160-82.
```

## 35. More Than One Selection from Anthology or Collection

Include an entry for the collection. Use its author's name for cross-references from individual selections.

```
Goldberg, Jonathan. "Speculation: Macbeth and Source." Howard and
     O'Connor 242-64.
Howard, Jean E., and Marion F. O'Connor, eds. Shakespeare
     Reproduced: The Text in History and Ideology. New York:
     Methuen, 1987.
```

## 36. Preface, Foreword, Introduction, or Afterword

Identify the section as a preface, foreword, introduction, or afterword. Add the title of the work and its author, following *By*.

```
Tomlin, Janice. Foreword. The Complete Guide to Foreign Adoption.
     By Barbara Brooke Bascom and Carole A. McKelvey. New York:
     Pocket, 1997.
```

## 37. Letter (Published)

Name the letter writer as the author. Include the letter's date or any collection number.

Garland, Hamlin. "To Fred Lewis Pattee." 30 Dec. 1914.

Letter 206 of Selected Letters of Hamlin Garland.

Ed. Keith Newlin and Joseph B. McCullough. Lincoln:

U of Nebraska P, 1998.

## 38. Dissertation Abstract

For an abstract in *Dissertation Abstracts International (DAI)* or *Dissertation Abstracts (DA)*, include *Diss.* ("Dissertation"), the institution's name, and the date of the degree. Add publication information for that volume of abstracts.

Hawkins, Joanne Berning. "Horror Cinema and the Avant-Garde."

Diss. U of California, Berkeley, 1993. DAI 55 (1995): 1712A.

### Field and Media Resources

## 39. Interview (Unpublished)

First identify the person interviewed and the type of interview: *Personal interview* (you conducted it in person), *Telephone interview* (you talked to the person over the telephone), or *Interview* (someone else conducted the interview, perhaps on radio or television). If the interview has a title, use it to replace *Interview*. Give the date of the interview or other detail.

Schutt, Robin. E-mail interview. 7 Oct. 2001.

Coppola, Francis Ford. Interview with James Lipton. Inside the

Actors Studio. Bravo, New York. 10 July 2001.

## 40. Survey or Questionnaire

MLA does not specify a form for these field resources. When citing your own research, you may wish to use this format.

Figliozzi, Jennifer Emily, and Summer J. Arrigo-Nelson.

Questionnaire on Student Alcohol Use and Parental

Values. U of Rhode Island, Kingston. 15-20

Apr. 2004.

## 41. Observation

Because MLA does not specify a form, you may wish to cite your field notes in this way.

Ba, Ed. Ski Run Observation. Vail, CO. 26 Jan. 2004.

## 42. Letter or Memo (Unpublished)

Give the author's name, a brief description (*Memo to Jane Cote* or, for a letter to you, *Letter to the author*), and the date. For letters between other people, identify any library holding the letter in its collection.

Hall, Donald. Letter to the author. 24 Jan. 1990.

## 43. Oral Presentation

Identify the speaker, title or type of presentation, and meeting details, including sponsor, place, and date.

Johnson, Sylvia. "Test Fairness: An Oxymoron? The Challenge

of Measuring Well in a High Stakes Climate." Amer.

Educ. Research Assn. Sheraton Hotel, New Orleans.

27 Apr. 2000.

## 44. Performance

Following the title of the play, opera, dance, or other performance, note the composer, director, writer, theater or location, city, and date. (Include actors when relevant.)

Cabaret. By Joe Masteroff. Dir. Sam Mendes. Studio 54, New York.

2 July 2001.

## 45. Videotape or Film

Alphabetize by title, and generally name the director. Name others important for identifying the work or for your discussion. Identify the distributor, date, and other relevant information.

Rosencrantz and Guildenstern Are Dead. Dir. Tom Stoppard. Perf.

Gary Oldman, Tim Roth, and Richard Dreyfuss. Videocassette.

Buena Vista Home Video, 1990.

Rosencrantz and Guildenstern Are Dead. Dir. Tom Stoppard. Perf.

Gary Oldman, Tim Roth, and Richard Dreyfuss. Cinecom

Entertainment, 1990.

## 46. Television or Radio Program

"The Tour." I Love Lucy. Dir. William Asher. Nickelodeon. 2 July

2001.

### 47. Recording

Identify the form of the recording unless it is a compact disc.

The Goo-Goo Dolls. <u>Dizzy Up the Girl</u>. Warner, 1998.

Mozart, Wolfgang Amadeus. Symphony no. 40 in G minor. Vienna

  Philharmonic. Cond. Leonard Bernstein. Audiocassette.

  Deutsche Grammophon, 1984.

### 48. Artwork or Photograph

Leonardo da Vinci. <u>Mona Lisa</u>. Louvre, Paris.

Larimer Street, Denver. Personal photograph by author. 5 May

  2004.

### 49. Map or Chart

<u>Arkansas</u>. Map. Comfort, TX: Gousha, 1996.

### 50. Comic Strip or Cartoon

Provide the cartoonist's name, any title, and *Cartoon* or *Comic strip.*

Cochran, Tony. "Agnes." Comic Strip. <u>Denver Post</u> 9 May 2004,

  Comics sec.:4.

### 51. Advertisement

First, name the product or organization advertised.

Toyota. Advertisement. <u>GQ</u> July 2001: 8.

### Online and Electronic Resources

**MODEL FORMAT FOR ONLINE BOOK OR DOCUMENT**

period + space          period  space          colon + space
↓                          ↓ ↓                    ↓
Author(s). "Title of Page or Document." Place of Publication:

      comma + space     period + space
          ↓                 ↓
      Publisher, Year Published. [for print book, if available]

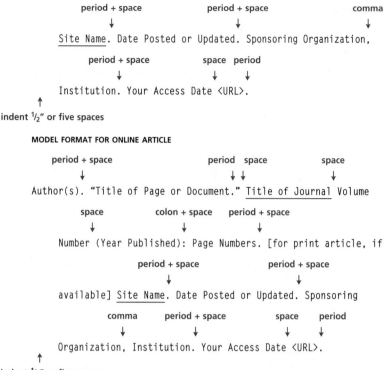

period + space          period + space          comma
↓                       ↓                       ↓
Site Name. Date Posted or Updated. Sponsoring Organization,

period + space          space period
↓                       ↓    ↓
Institution. Your Access Date <URL>.
↑
indent ½″ or five spaces

**MODEL FORMAT FOR ONLINE ARTICLE**

period + space                    period  space          space
↓                                 ↓   ↓                   ↓
Author(s). "Title of Page or Document." Title of Journal Volume

space           colon + space   period + space
↓               ↓               ↓
Number (Year Published): Page Numbers. [for print article, if

period + space                    period + space
↓                                 ↓
available] Site Name. Date Posted or Updated. Sponsoring

comma           period + space          space   period
↓               ↓                       ↓       ↓
Organization, Institution. Your Access Date <URL>.
↑
indent ½″ or five spaces

- **Author, title, and publication information.** Supply available information like that for a print source so a reader could identify or find the item.
- **Dates.** Give the date the material was posted, revised, or updated and then, just before the URL, the date you accessed the source.
- **Uniform resource locator (URL).** Enclose the complete URL (beginning with *http, gopher, telnet,* or *ftp*) in angle brackets (< >). Include the search page, path, links, or file name needed to reach the page or frame you used, especially to avoid an unwieldy URL. Split the URL only after a slash; do not add a hyphen.
- **Page numbering.** Include any page, paragraph (*par., pars.*), section (*sec.*), or screen numbers provided.

## 52. Professional Web Site

History of the American West, 1860-1920. 25 July 2000. Denver

    Public Lib. 16 Oct. 2001 <http://memory.loc.gov/

ammem/award97/codhtml>.

### 53. Academic Home Page

Note the creator, title or description such as *Home page*, and sponsor.

Baron, Dennis. Home page. 16 Aug. 2000. Dept. of English,

    U of Illinois, Urbana-Champaign. 10 Oct. 2003

    <http://www2.english.uiuc.edu/baron/Default.htm>.

### 54. Online Book

Add any available information about print publication.

London, Jack. The Iron Heel. New York: Macmillan, 1908. The Jack

    London Collection. 10 Dec. 1999. Berkeley Digital Library

    SunSITE. 15 July 2001 <http://sunsite.berkeley.edu/

    London/Writing/IronHeel/>.

### 55. Selection from Online Book

Muir, John. "The City of the Saints." Steep Trails. 1918. 17 July

    2001 <http://encyclopediaindex.com/b/sttrl10.htm>.

### 56. Online Journal Article

Dugdale, Timothy. "The Fan and (Auto)Biography: Writing the Self

    in the Stars." Journal of Mundane Behavior 1.2 (2000). 19

    Sept. 2000 <http://www.mundanebehavior.org/issues/v1n2/

    dugdale.htm>.

### 57. Online Magazine Article

Wright, Laura. "My, What Big Eyes . . ." Discover 27 Oct. 2003.

    4 Apr. 2004 <http://www.discover.com/web-exclusives-archive/

    big-eyed-trilobite1027/>.

### 58. Online Newspaper Article

Mulvihill, Kim. "Childhood Obesity." San Francisco Chronicle

    12 July 2001. 15 July 2001 <http://www.sfgate.com/

    search>.

## 59. Online Government Document

United States. Dept. of Commerce. Bureau of the Census. Census
Brief: Disabilities Affect One-Fifth of All Americans. Dec.
1997. 18 July 2001 <http://www.census.gov/prod/3/97pubs/
cenbr975.pdf>.

## 60. Online Editorial

"Mall Mania/A Measure of India's Success." Editorial.
startribune.com Minneapolis-St.Paul. 31 Oct. 2003. 14 Nov.
2003 <http://www.startribune.com/stories/1519/4185511.html>.

## 61. Online Letter to the Editor

Hadjiargyrou, Michael. "Stem Cells and Delicate Questions."
Letter. New York Times on the Web 17 July 2001. 18 July 2001
<http://www.nytimes.com/2001/07/18/opinion/L18STEM.html>.

## 62. Online Interview

Rikker, David. Interview with Victor Payan. San Diego
Latino Film Festival. 1999. 20 Jan. 2002 <http://
www.sdlatinofilm.com/video.html#Anchor-David-64709>.

## 63. Online Review

Chaudhury, Parama. Rev. of Kandahar, dir. Mohsen Makhmalbaf. Film
Monthly 3.4 (2002). 19 Jan. 2002 <http://www.filmmonthly.com/
Playing/Articles/Kandahar/Kandahar.html>.

## 64. Online Abstract

Prelow, Hazel, and Charles A. Guarnaccia. "Ethnic and Racial
Differences in Life Stress among High School Adolescents."
Journal of Counseling & Development 75.6 (1997). Abstract.
6 Apr. 1998 <http://www.counseling.org/journals/
jcdjul197.htm#Prelow>.

### 65. Online Database: General Entry

For entries from online databases to which libraries subscribe (through services such as EBSCO or LexisNexis), begin with the details of print publication, if any. Name the database, the service, the library, and your date of access. Then give the URL. If it is too long, give the URL of the search page for the site. Should the service give only the first page number of the printed text, follow it with a hyphen, space, and period, as in 223-.

> Kallis, Giorgos, and Henri L. F. De Groot. "Shifting
>
> Perspectives on Urban Water Policy in Europe." European
>
> Planning Studies 11 (2003): 223-28. Academic Search
>
> Premier. EBSCO. Auraria Lib., Denver, CO. 19 Dec. 2003
>
> <http://0-web12.epnet.com.skyline.cudenver.edu>.

### 66. Online Database: Journal Article

> Stillman, Todd. "McDonald's in Question: The Limits of the Mass
>
> Market." American Behavioral Scientist 47 (2003): 107-18.
>
> Academic Search Premier. EBSCO. U of Rhode Island Lib. 15
>
> Nov. 2003 <http://0-ejournals.ebsco.com>.

### 67. Online Database: Article Abstract

> Lewis, David A., and Roger P. Rose. "The President, the Press,
>
> and the War-Making Power: An Analysis of Media Coverage
>
> Prior to the Persian Gulf War." Presidential Studies
>
> Quarterly 32 (2002): 559-71. Abstract. America: History and
>
> Life. ABC/CLIO. U of Rhode Island Lib. 1 Nov. 2003
>
> <http://0-serials.abc-clio.com>.

### 68. Online Database: Magazine Article

> Barrett, Jennifer. "Fast Food Need Not Be Fat Food."
>
> Newsweek 13 Oct. 2003: 73-74. Academic Search Premier.
>
> EBSCO. U of Rhode Island Lib. 31 Oct. 2003
>
> <http://0-ejournals.ebsco.com>.

## 69. Online Database: Newspaper Article

Lee, R. "Class with the 'Ph.D. Diva.'" <u>New York Times</u> 18 Oct.

2003: B7. <u>InfoTrac OneFile</u>. InfoTrac. Providence Public

Lib., RI 31 Oct. 2003 <http://infotrac.galegroup.com/menu>.

## 70. Online Database: Summary of Research

ERIC Clearing House on Higher Education. "ERIC Digest: Early

Decision Programs." <u>ERIC Digests</u>. ERIC, the Educational

Resources Information Center. ED470540. 2002. U of Rhode

Island Lib. 7 Nov. 2003 <http://www.ericfacility.net/

ericdigests/ed470540.html>.

## 71. Online Database: Collection of Documents

"Combating Plagiarism." <u>The CQ Researcher</u> 9 Sept. 2003.

CQ Press. U of Rhode Island Lib. 12 Nov. 2003

<http://0-library.cqpress.com.helin.uri.edu:80/

cqresearcher/>.

## 72. Online Database: Personal Subscription Service

Include your access route (introduced by *Keyword* or *Path*).

"Native American Food Guide." <u>Health Finder</u>. 16 July 2001.

America Online. 16 July 2001. Keyword: Health.

## 73. Online Videotape or Film

Coppola, Francis Ford, dir. <u>Apocalypse Now</u>. 1979.

<u>Film.com</u>. 17 July 2001 <http://ramhurl.film.com/

smildemohurl.ram?file=screen/2001/clips/apoca.smi>.

## 74. Online Television or Radio Program

Edwards, Bob. "Adoption: Redefining Family." <u>Morning Edition</u>.

Natl. Public Radio. 28-29 June 2001. 17 July 2001

<http://www.npr.org/programs/morning/features/2001/

jun/010628.cfoa.html>.

### 75. Online Recording

Malcolm X. "The Definition of Black Power." 8 Mar. 1964. <u>Great</u>
<u>Speeches</u>. 2000. 18 July 2001 <http://www.chicago-law.net/
speeches/speech.html#1m>.

### 76. Online Artwork

<u>Elamite Goddess</u>. 2100 BC (?). Louvre, Paris. 16 July 2001
<http://www.louvre.fr/louvrea.htm/search>.

### 77. Online Map or Chart

"Beirut [Beyrout] 1912." Map. <u>Perry-Castañeda Library Map</u>
<u>Collection</u>. 16 July 2000. <http://www.lib.utexas.edu/
maps/historical/beirut2_1912.jpg>.

### 78. Online Comic Strip or Cartoon

Auth, Tony. "Spending Goals." Cartoon. <u>Slate</u> 7 Sept. 2001. 16
Oct. 2001 <http://cagle.slate.msn.com/politicalcartoons/
pccartoons/archives/auth.asp>.

### 79. Online Advertisement

Mazda Miata. Advertisement. 16 July 2001 <http://
www.mazdausa.com/miata/>.

### 80. Other Online Sources

When citing a source not shown here (such as a photo, painting, or recording), adapt the nonelectronic MLA model.

NASA/JPL. "Martian Meteorite." <u>Views of the Solar System:</u>
<u>Meteoroids and Meteorites</u>. Ed. Calvin J. Hamilton.
1999. 13 June 1999 <http://spaceart.com/solar/eng/
meteor.htm#views>.

## 81. FTP, Telnet, or Gopher Site

Treat a source obtained through FTP (file transfer protocol), telnet, or gopher as you would a similar Web source.

Clinton, William Jefferson. "Radio Address of the President to

the Nation." 10 May 1997. 29 June 1999

<ftp://OMA.EOP.GOV.US/1997/5/10/1.TEXT.1>.

## 82. Email

Give the writer's name, message title or type, and date. Be sure to hyphenate *e-mail* in MLA style.

Trimbur, John. E-mail to the author. 17 Sept. 2000.

## 83. Online Posting

Aid readers (if you can) by citing an archived version.

Brock, Stephen E. "School Crisis." Online posting. 27 Apr. 2001.

Special Events Chat Transcripts. Lycos Communities. 18 July

2001 <http://clubs.lycos.com/live/Events/transcripts/

school_crisis_tscript.asp>.

## 84. Synchronous Communication

When citing material from a MUD, a MOO, or another form of synchronous communication, identify the speaker, the event, its date, its forum (such as *CollegeTownMOO*), and your access date. End with *telnet* and the address. Cite an archived version if possible.

Finch, Jeremy. Online debate "Can Proust Save Your Life?"

3 Apr. 1998. CollegeTownMOO. 3 Apr. 1998

<telnet://next.cs.bvc.edu.7777>.

## 85. CD-ROM, Diskette, or Magnetic Tape

Note the medium (*CD-ROM*, *Diskette*, *Magnetic tape*), the name of the vendor, and the publication date.

Shakespeare, William. All's Well That Ends Well. William

Shakespeare: The Complete Works on CD-ROM. CD-ROM. Abingdon,

Eng.: Andromeda Interactive, 1994.

**86. CD-ROM Abstract**

Add information for any parallel printed source. Identify the database and medium (*CD-ROM*, *Diskette*), vendor, and publication date.

```
Straus, Stephen. Interview with Claudia Dreifus. "Separating

    Remedies from Snake Oil." New York Times 3 Apr. 2001: D5+.

    Abstract. CD-ROM. InfoTrac. 19 July 2001.
```

## 16c Sample MLA paper

The *MLA Handbook* recommends beginning a research paper with the first page of the text, using the format shown on page 147. Refer to the features of Jenny Latimer's paper, noted in the margins, as you prepare your paper.

**1" from top of page**

Jenny Latimer

Professor Schwegler

Writing 101

7 November 2003

**Heading format without title page**

**Double-spaced heading and paper**

**1"
margin
on each
side**

**¶
indented
5 spaces or
½"**

**Anecdote
introduces
purpose of
research**

**Field
research
confirms
anecdote**

No, Thanks, I'll Pass on That

1    One night at work my friend Kate turned down my offer
of a red licorice stick after quickly checking the
ingredients on the bag. I asked her to explain why, and
she replied that they contained hydrogenated oils, which
are, accordng to research articles she had read, "silent
killers." She went on briefly to describe the horrors they
do to your body, the various foods that contain them, as
well as the effort she makes to avoid hydrogenated oils. I
was shocked and intrigued by this news and decided to
explore the reality of what she'd said.

2    A day or two later, while browsing through the
shelves at the supermarket, I started checking
ingredients. To my astonishment I couldn't seem to find a
snack without these words on the back. Whether followed
by the word "coconut," "cottonseed," or "soy bean," there
it was lurking amidst the other ingredients--hydrogenated
oil. I was horrified! Thinking these scary oils couldn't
be everywhere, I continued my search. A box of toaster
tarts, again yes. A can of soup, there it was. I picked
up a bag of pretzels, tossed it back on the shelf, and
left the store in frustration, needless to say without
buying a snack. Returning home I realized I needed to know
the truth; I set out to find the answers to my questions.

**1" margin at bottom**

Latimer 2

**First research question**

3    My first question was this: what exactly does it
mean to hydrogenate an oil? This is where things get a
little technical: to hydrogenate is to add hydrogen.
During the hydrogenation process the hydrogen atoms of a
fatty acid are moved to the opposite side of the double
bond of its molecular structure (Roberts). According to

**Page number omitted when not available**

Lewis Harrison, author of <u>The Complete Fats and Oils
Book</u>, this changed fatty acid molecule can actually be
toxic to the body. It can cause oxidative stress and
damage the body in the same way as cigarette smoke and
chemical toxins. It can alter the normal transport of
minerals and nutrients across cell membranes. As a
result, foreign invaders may pass the cell membrane

**Paragraph synthesizes several sources**

unchallenged; also supplies and information important to
the cell may not be allowed in. Good fats that the body
uses for many functions are not allowed to pass through
the membrane while these fatty acids build up unused

**Citation from book inludes page number**

outside the cell, making us fat (Armstrong; Rudin and
Felix 21).

4    To formulate hydrogenated oils, gas is fused into
the oils using a metal catalyst (such as aluminum,
cobalt, and nickel). These metals are needed to fuse the
hydrogen into the oils. After hydrogenation these fatty
acids are called trans-fatty acids or hydrogenated oils

**Process summarized**

(Harrison 93). As a result, my licorice snacks were
making me fat--which was a given--but not only that. They
were actually disrupting the normal functions of my

**Second research question**

cells. What was this doing to me in the long run?

Latimer 3

5     After production companies started using hydrogenated

oils, which were first introduced in 1914 and fully part of

the food production market in the mid-fifties, substantial

increases in several diseases occurred rapidly within the

span of a few years. According to information available

from the National Institutes of Health, during 1973 to 1994

there was a 22% increase from 364 cancers of assorted types

to 462 cancers for every 100,000 people. And from 1973 to

1992, those 364 cancers rose to 530 for every 100,000

people. This 31% increase was an additional 9% increase

from the previous years (Dewey).

6     Dr. Andrew Weil, one of the nation's leading advocates

of holistic medicine, claims that hydrogenated oils are

"one of the most toxic substances Americans consume" (qtd.

in Alter). Another article compared hydrogenated oils to

inhaling cigarette smoke: "They will kill you--slowly over

time, but surely as you breathe" (Armstrong). The Food and

Drug Administration and the American Heart Association

agree that trans-fatty acids raise LDL ("bad") cholesterol

levels and lower HDL ("good") cholesterol levels, therefore

increasing the risk of coronary disease--a leading cause of

death in the United States. The Institute of Medicine

reported this year that trans fats may raise levels of

lipoprotein, higher levels of which have been associated

with a greater risk of heart and blood vessel disease

(Roberts). Trans fats also have artery-clogging qualities

(McCord and McVeigh).

Historical
background
supplied

Discussion
of risk
continues

Indirect source
(with
quotation
from someone
else) identified

Group
authors cited
in sentence

Latimer 4

**Specific risks identified**

7   Hydrogenated oils have also been shown to increase the risks of breast cancer. According to research by the Cancer Research Foundation of America, women with the highest levels of trans fatty acids were 40% more likely to develop breast cancer than those with lower levels (Cancer Research Foundation; Cancer Web Project). Some have speculated that hydrogenated oils are the cause of what is called non-insulin-dependent diabetes type II, wherein a person produces enough insulin, but it does not reduce the sugar levels in the blood. It is unknown what causes the insulin to be resistant (Dewey).

**Opposing views acknowledged**

8   On the other hand, according to James R. Marshall in an article for Nutrition Reviews, there is no conclusive evidence that trans fatty acids specifically are a cause of cancer; fats in general are known to cause cancer, but trans fatty acids are not directly responsible. Marshall maintains that "Any effort to lower the risks of heart diseases should be focused on decreasing total fat intake, and not on consuming less trans fat or saturated fat." Bruce Watkins, in an article for Food Technology, says that foods "should be evaluated based on their impact on overall health. For instance, total fat and not trans fat or saturated fat alone, is correlated with obesity and cancer."

**Cause of situation discussed**

9   So in today's health-conscious America, why do over 40% of our foods still contain hydrogenated oils? The answer is money. The process of hydrogenation increases the volume of the oil, thus making more oil available

Latimer 5

to sell. Hydrogenating creates a product that can exist
at room temperature as either a solid or a liquid;
therefore, any desired consistency is possible (Byers).
Hydrogenated oils also give food products a rich flavor
and texture at cheaper costs.

10    But most importantly for manufacturers, hydrogenated
oils act as a preservative, which means a longer shelf
life for products and fewer returns of spoiled products
(Dewey). By using hydrogenated oils rather than other
less health-threatening oils, food companies are saving
money (Dewey). Juan Menjivar, vice president of global
research and development at Rich Products, estimates that
it will cost a few pennies more per pound of ingredients
to eliminate trans fats (Haarlander). Research alone for
a replacement for trans fats will cost companies tens of
millions of dollars (Dwyer). Up until now, companies have
relied on the ignorance or lack of concern of the public,
along with keeping their prices lower than those of
healthier foods, to stay in business.

11    This situation, however, is changing. By January 1,
2006, the US Food and Drug Administration will require that
the amount of trans fatty acids in the product be listed on
the label directly under the line for saturated fats. This
requirement is encouraging companies to use healthier oils so
as not to scare away consumers (Haarlander). The entire food
industry is researching options for different oils and for
ways of preparing new products, said Stephanie Childs of the
Grocery Manufacturers of America (Dwyer).

**Future
situation
identified**

**12**   The reason the FDA is giving food companies three
years is because this is such a large change, and companies
need time to adjust. Because there will be a need for new
products, these products need time to grow. Food doesn't
grow overnight. Many countries have recognized the health
issues of hydrogenated oils for some time. In Denmark, the
country with the lowest diagnosed rates of heart disease,
cancers, and diabetes, hydrogenated oils have been banned
for over forty years. Many other countries have limitations
on the amounts of hydrogenated oils in foods (Dewey).

**13**   So, until 2006, how can one avoid trans fats? Although
trans fats do occur naturally in tiny amounts in some dairy
products and meats, the majority of trans fats come from
processed foods. In addition to the many health food stores
full of hydrogenated-free foods, most supermarkets stock
them in special sections. Although the greater part of what
you will find in your snack food, frozen food, and ready-
bake aisles will contain hydrogenated oils, some producers
have already made the switch from trans fats: Frito-Lay
Doritos®, Jolly Time® Pop Corn, Tostitos® and Cheetos®, Take
Control® Spread, I Can't Believe It's Not Butter® products,
some Kraft food products, and products from Jaret
International, which makes Sour Patch Kids® and Swedish
Fish®.

**14**   There are also ways to find the amount of trans fatty
acids that are in a food. Where the words "hydrogenated
oil" appear on the list of ingredients is a clue; the higher
up on the list, the greater the content in the product.

Advice
for
readers

Latimer 7

Take the amount of total fat listed on the label, and
subtract all the other fats listed; chances are the
remaining number is trans fat. The highest levels of trans
fats are found in the foods that you might expect: French
fries, doughnuts, cookies, cakes, margarine, single-
serving soups such as ramen noodles, grilled foods,
pizza, waffles, breaded fish sticks, pot pies, and many
frozen convenience items ("Think"). As an alternative,
try making things from scratch, using canned veggies and
soups, having butter instead of margarine, going for
broiled or baked over grilled or fried, and if you're
craving a snack, choosing jelly beans or gummy bears over
chocolate and cookies.

15  So I return to the supermarket, and as I walk in, I
am surrounded by processed-hydrogenated food, rows upon
rows of cookies and candies, boxes and bags of
tantalizing treats. But now that I've found the answers
to my questions and know what is in the things I have
been eating, I find it easy to resist temptation. Instead
I walk to the small health-food section toward the back.
More expensive--but worth it. Actually, I feel great. If
giving up licorice sticks is what it takes to keep my
body in good health, then that's a price I'm willing to
pay.

*Article without author cited by title*

*Anecdote concludes with outcomes of research*

| | |
|---|---|
| Page numbers continue | ↕ 1″ from top of page    ↕ ½″ from top  Latimer 8 |

Works Cited   Heading centered

Sources from paper listed alphabetically

Alter, Alexandra. "Alarms Raised Over Partially

   Hydrogenated Oil." <u>Columbia News Service</u> 21 May 2003.

All lines double-spaced

   26 Oct. 2003 <http://naturalhealthchiropractic.com/

   know_that.html#fats>.

First line of each entry not indented

American Heart Association. "Hydrogenated Fats."

   2002. 26 Oct. 2003 <http://www.amhrt.org/

   presenter.jhtml?identifier=4662>.

Armstrong, Eric. "What's Wrong with Partially Hydrogenated

   Oils?" <u>Treelight Health.com</u>. 2001. 30 Sept. 2003

Additional lines indented 5 spaces (½″)

   <http://www.treelight.com/health/

   PartiallyHydrogenatedOils.html>.

Byers, Tim. "Hardened Fats, Hardened Arteries?" <u>New

   England Journal of Medicine</u> 337 (1997): 1554.

   Abstract. <u>Academic Search Premier</u>. EBSCO. U of Rhode

   Island Lib. 26 Oct. 2003 <http://0-web20.epnet.com>.

Cancer Research Foundation of America. "Trans Fatty Acids

   Linked to Breast Cancer Risk." Aug. 1998. 10 Sept.

   2003 <www.dldewey.com/columns/breast2.htm>.

Cancer WEB Project. 1997-2003. Dept. of Medical Oncology:

   U of Newcastle upon Tyne. 10 Sept. 2003

   <http://cancerweb.ncl.ac.uk/cgi-bin/

   omd?query=hydrogenation&action=Search+OMD>.

Dewey, David Lawrence. "Food for Thought: Hydrogenated

   Oils Are Silent Killers." 18 Sept. 1998. 30 Sept.

   2003 <http:www.dldewey.com/hydroil.htm>.

Dwyer, Kelly Pate. "Frito-Lay Removes Trans Fats from

   Chips." <u>Knight Ridder/Tribune Business News</u> 28 Sept.

↕ 1″ margin at bottom

2003. InfoTrac OneFile. Providence Public Lib. 26

Oct. 2003 <http://web4galegroup.com>.

Haarlander, Lisa. "Nutrition: Getting the Fat Out."

News Business Reporter 1 Sept. 2003. 24 Oct. 2003

<http://www.buffalo.com>.

Harrison, Lewis. The Complete Fat and Oils Book. New

York: Avery-Penguin, 1996.

Marshall, James R. "Trans Fatty Acids in Cancer."

Nutrition Reviews May 1996. Abstract. Health and

Wellness Resource Center. Gale. U of Rhode Island

Lib. 26 Oct. 2003 <http://galenet.galegroup.com>.

McCord, Holly, and Gloria McVeigh. "Smart Bites."

Prevention Dec. 2001. Academic Search Premier.

EBSCO. U of Rhode Island Lib. 26 Oct. 2003

<http://0-web20.epnet.com>.

Roberts, Shauna S. "IOM Takes Aims at Trans Fats."

Diabetes Forecast 56 (2003): 17-18. Academic Search

Premier. EBSCO. U of Rhode Island Lib. 26 Oct. 2003

<http://0-web20.epnet.com>.

Rudin, Donald, and Clara Felix. The Omega-3 Phenomenon.

New York: Rawson Assoc., 1987.

"Think Before You Eat: Trans Fats Lurking in Many Popular

Foods." Knight Ridder/Tribune News Service 8 Sept.

2003. InfoTrac OneFile. Providence Public Lib., 26

Oct. 2003 <http://web4.infotrac.galegroup.com>.

United States Food and Drug Administration. "What Every

Consumer Should Know About Trans Fatty Acids." 9 July

Latimer 10

2003. 23 Oct. 2003 <http://www.fda.gov/oc/initiatives/

transfat/q_a.html>.

Watkins, Bruce A. "Trans Fatty Acids: A Health Paradox?"

Food Technology 152 (1998): 120. Abstract. Health

and Wellness Resource Center. Gale. U of Rhode Island

Lib. 26 Oct. 2003 <http://galenet.galegroup.com>.

# Documenting Sources: APA Style

## ▼ *TAKING IT ONLINE*

### APA STYLE
**http://www.apastyle.org**
Visit this official Web site of the American Psychological Association for current, accurate information about APA style. For special issues, click on topics such as electronic references or style tips, including an archive of previous Tips of the Week. Changes and updates in APA style are announced here as well.

For further advice on using APA style, check the home page of your library or tutoring center or other academic sites such as the one below. Be certain that any site you use has been revised and updated to reflect the most current APA style.

### USING AMERICAN PSYCHOLOGICAL ASSOCIATION (APA) FORMAT
**http://owl.english.purdue.edu/handouts/research/r_apa.html**
Sponsored by the Purdue University Online Writing Lab, this page explains how to lay out a paper, present quotations, and prepare entries for a reference list following APA style.

### APA CITATION STYLE
**http://www.liu.edu/cwis/cwp/library/workshop/citapa.htm**
This color-coded guide makes it easy to see what's needed for entries in an APA reference list.

### CITATION STYLE GUIDES
**http://www.libraries.wright.edu/quicklinks/references/citing.html**
This page offers links to help you with the style guides for several fields, including the *WSU Writing Center Mini-Manual for Using APA Style in Research Papers.*

# PART 4

# Documenting Sources: APA Style

# 17 Using APA Documentation Style

The documentation style developed by the APA (American Psychological Association) identifies a source by providing its author's name and its date of publication within parentheses. For this reason, the APA style is often called a name-and-date style. The information in the parenthetical citation (Kitwana, 2002) will guide readers to more detail about the source in a reference list at the end of the paper or report.

    Kitwana, B. (2002). The hip hop generation: Young blacks and the

        crisis in African American Culture. New York: Basic Civitas.

**STRATEGY** Use APA style in the social sciences to emphasize current sources.

**ACADEMIC SETTINGS**

When readers expect APA or a name-and-date style

**WORK AND PUBLIC SETTINGS**

When business or professional readers prefer a name-and-date system or want to see at once how current your sources are

When you need a simple way to identify sources and dates

When other writers or publications in your setting use APA style, modified APA style, or a similar informal system

For more on this documentation style, consult the *Publication Manual of the American Psychological Association* (5th ed., Washington, DC: APA, 2001). Updates are posted on the APA Web site at <http://www.apastyle.org>.

## 17a Using APA in-text citations

The APA system provides in-text parenthetical citations for quotations, paraphrases, summaries, and other specific information from a source. (For advice on what to document, see 13c–f.) APA style makes the year of publication part of an in-text citation which refers to a reference list.

DRAFT    The current argumentative climate impedes exchanges among

those with differing ideas (Tannen).

READER'S REACTION: **Is this source up to date?**

EDITED    The current argumentative climate impedes exchanges among

those with differing ideas (Tannen, 1998).

### 1. Author's Name in Parentheses

When you include both the author's name and the year of publication in parentheses, separate them with a comma. To specify the location of a quotation, paraphrase, summary, or other information, add a comma, *p.* or *pp.*, and the page number(s) on which the material appears in the source.

One recent study examines the emotional intensity of "the fan's

link to the star" (Gitlin, 2001, p. 129).

### 2. Author's Name in Discussion

When you include an author's name in your discussion, give the date of the source in parentheses after the name. Provide the page number in the source following any quotation or paraphrase.

For Gitlin (2001), emotion is the basis of "the fan's link to the

star" (p. 129).

### 3. Specific Reference

Indicate what you are citing: *p.* ("page"), *chap.* ("chapter"), *figure, para.* or ¶ (paragraphs) in electronic sources. Spell potentially confusing words. For classical works always indicate the part (chap. 5), not the page.

Teenagers who survive suicide attempts experience distinct stages

of recovery (Mauk & Weber, 1991, Table 1).

### 4. One Author

You can vary your in-text citations as you present both the name and date in parentheses, both in the text, or the name in the text.

```
Dell's 2002 study of charter schools confirmed issues identified
earlier (James, 1996) and also updated Rau's (1998) school
classification.
```

### 5. Two Authors

In a parenthetical citation, separate the names with an ampersand (&); in your text, use the word *and*.

```
Given evidence that married men earn more than unmarried men
(Chun & Lee, 2001), Nakosteen and Zimmer (2001) investigate how
earnings affect spousal selection.
```

### 6. Three to Five Authors

Include all the names, separated by commas, in the first citation. In parenthetical citations, use an ampersand (&) rather than *and*.

```
Sadeh, Raviv, and Gruber (2000) related "sleep problems and
neuropsychological functioning in children" (p. 292).
```

In any following references, give only the first author's name and *et al.* ("and others"): Sadeh et al. (2000) reported their findings.

### 7. Six or More Authors

In all text citations, follow the first author with *et al.*: (Berg et al., 1998). For your reference list, see Entry 2 on page 162.

### 8. Corporate or Group Author

Spell out the name of the organization, corporation, or agency in the first citation. Follow any cumbersome name with an abbreviation in brackets, and use the shorter form in later citations.

FIRST CITATION
```
Besides instilling fear, hate crimes limit where women
live and work (National Organization of Women [NOW],
2001).
```

LATER CITATION
```
Pending legislation would strengthen the statutes on
bias-motivated crimes (NOW, 2001).
```

### 9. No Author Given

Give the title or the first few words of a long title.

> These photographs represent people from all walks of life
> (*Friendship*, 2001).

Full title: *Friendship: Celebration of humanity.*

## 10. Work Cited More Than Once

When you cite the same source more than once in a paragraph, repeat the source as necessary to clarify a page reference or specify one of several sources. If a second reference is clear, don't repeat the date.

> Much of the increase in personal debt can be linked to
> unrestrained use of credit cards (Schor, 1998, p. 73). In fact,
> according to Schor, roughly a third of consumers "describe
> themselves as either heavily or moderately in financial debt"
> (p. 72).

## 11. Authors with the Same Name

When your references include works by two authors who share the same last name, provide the author's initials for each in-text citation.

> Scholars have examined the development of African American
> culture during slavery and reconstruction (E. Foner, 1988),
> including the role of Frederick Douglass in this process
> (P. Foner, 1950).

## 12. Personal Communications, Including Interviews and Email

In your text, cite letters, interviews, memos, email, telephone calls, and so on using the name of the person, the expression *personal communication*, and the full date. Readers have no access to such sources, so you can omit them from your reference list.

> According to J. M. Hostos, the state no longer funds services
> duplicated by county agencies (personal communication, October
> 7, 2003).

## 13. Two or More Sources in a Citation

If you sum up information from several sources, include them all in your citation. Separate the authors and years with commas; separate the sources with semicolons. List the sources alphabetically, then oldest to most recent for several by the same author.

Several studies have related job satisfaction with performance
(Faire, 2002; Hall, 1996, 1999).

**14. Two or More Works by the Same Author in the Same Year**

If you use works published in the same year by the same author or author team, alphabetize the works, and add letters after the year to distinguish them.

Gould (1987a, p. 73) makes a similar point.

**15. Content Footnote**

You may use a content footnote to expand material in the text. Place a superscript number above the related line of text; number the notes consecutively. On a separate page at the end, below the centered heading "Footnotes," present the notes in numerical order. Begin each with its superscript number. Indent five to seven spaces for the first line only of each note, and double-space all notes.

**TEXT**  I tape-recorded and transcribed all interviews.[1]

**NOTE**  [1]Although background noise obscured some parts of
the tapes, these gaps did not substantially affect the
material studied.

## **17b** Creating an APA reference list

On a separate page at the end of your text (before notes or appendixes), provide a list of references to the sources you've cited.

- **Page format.** Allow a one-inch margin, and center the heading "References" without underlining or quotation marks.
- **Alphabetizing.** List the works alphabetically by author or by the first main word of the title if there is no author. Arrange two or more works by the same author from oldest to most recent, by year of publication.
- **Spacing.** Double-space within and between all entries.
- **Indentation.** Do not indent the first line, but indent all additional lines like paragraphs, consistently a half inch or five to seven spaces.

**DRAFT**  Carlson, NR., and Buskist, Wm. (1997), *Psychology: The
Science of Behavior.* Boston, Allyn & Bacon.
**READER'S REACTION: This writer seems very careless about detail. I
wonder if the research is this sloppy, too.**

**EDITED**  Carlson, N. R., & Buskist, W. (1997). *Psychology: The
science of behavior* (5th ed.). Boston: Allyn &
Bacon.

## Books and Works Treated as Books

MODEL FORMAT FOR BOOKS AND WORKS TREATED AS BOOKS

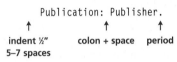

```
Author(s). (Date). Title of work. Place of
        Publication: Publisher.
```

indent ½"      colon + space      period
5–7 spaces

- **Author.** Give the author's last name followed by a comma and the *initials only* of the first and middle names. Use the same inverted order for all the names of co-authors. Separate the names of co-authors with commas, and use an ampersand (&) before the name of the last author.
- **Date.** Put the year of publication in parentheses followed by a period.
- **Title.** Italicize the title, but capitalize only proper names and the first word of the main title and any subtitle.
- **Publication information.** Name the city (and the country or the state's postal abbreviation except for major cities) followed by a colon and a space. Supply the publisher's name without words such as *Inc.* or *Publishers.*

### 1. One Author

```
Wilson, W. J. (1996). When work disappears: The world of the new
    urban poor. New York: Knopf.
```

### 2. Two or More Authors

List up to six authors; add *et al.* to indicate any others.

```
Biber, D., Conrad, S., & Reppen, R. (1998). Corpus linguistics:
    Investigating language structure and use. Cambridge,
    England: Cambridge University Press.
```

### 3. Corporate or Group Author

Treat the group as an author. When author and publisher are the same, give the word *Author* after the place instead of repeating the name.

```
Amnesty International. (2001). Annual report 2001 [Brochure].
    London: Author.
```

## 4. No Author Given

*Boas anniversary volume: Anthropological papers written in honor of Franz Boas.* (1906). New York: Stechert.

## 5. More Than One Work by the Same Author

List works chronologically with the author's name in each entry.

Aronowitz, S. (1993). *Roll over Beethoven: The return of cultural strife.* Hanover, NH: Wesleyan University Press.

Aronowitz, S. (2000). *From the ashes of the old: American labor and America's future.* New York: Basic Books.

## 6. More Than One Work by the Same Author in the Same Year

If works by the same author appear in the same year, list them alphabetically based on the first main word in the title. Add lowercase letters after the dates to distinguish them in text citations: (Gould, 1987b).

Gould, S. J. (1987a). *Time's arrow, time's cycle: Myth and metaphor in the discovery of geological time.* Cambridge, MA: Harvard University Press.

Gould, S. J. (1987b). *An urchin in the storm: Essays about books and ideas.* New York: Norton.

## 7. One or More Editors

Include (*Ed.*) or (*Eds.*) after the names of the editor or editors.

Bowe, J., Bowe, M., & Streeter, S. C. (Eds.). (2001). *Gig: Americans talk about their jobs.* New York: Three Rivers Press.

## 8. Translator

Bourdieu, P. (1990). *In other words: Essays towards a reflexive sociology.* (M. Adamson, Trans.). Stanford, CA: Stanford University Press.

## 9. Edition Following the First

Identify the edition in parentheses after the title (for example, *3rd ed.* or *Rev. ed.* for "revised edition").

> Groth-Marnat, G. (1996). *Handbook of psychological assessment*
>
> (3rd ed.). New York: Wiley.

## 10. Reprint

> Butler, J. (1999). *Gender trouble*. New York: Routledge. (Original
>
> work published 1990)

## 11. Multivolume Work

> Strachey, J., Freud, A., Strachey, A., & Tyson, A. (Eds.).
>
> (1966-1974). *The standard edition of the complete*
>
> *psychological works of Sigmund Freud* (J. Strachey et al.,
>
> Trans.) (Vols. 3-5). London: Hogarth Press and the Institute
>
> of Psycho-Analysis.

## 12. Anthology or Collection of Articles

> Appadurai, A. (Ed.). (2001). *Globalization*. Durham: Duke
>
> University Press.

## 13. Encyclopedia or Reference Work

> Winn, P. (Ed.). (2001). *Dictionary of biological psychology*.
>
> London: Routledge.

## 14. *Diagnostic and Statistical Manual of Mental Disorders*

After an initial full in-text citation, you may use standard abbreviations: *DSM-III* (1980), *DSM-III-R* (1987), *DSM-IV* (1994), or *DSM-IV-TR* (2000).

> American Psychiatric Association. (1994). *Diagnostic and*
>
> *statistical manual of mental disorders* (4th ed.).
>
> Washington, DC: Author.

## 15. Dissertation (Unpublished)

Gomes, C. S. (2001). *Selection and treatment effects in managed care.* Unpublished doctoral dissertation, Boston University.

## 16. Government Document

Select Committee on Aging, Subcommittee on Human Services, House of Representatives. (1991). *Grandparents' rights: Preserving generational bonds* (Com. Rep. No. 102-833). Washington, DC: U.S. Government Printing Office.

## 17. Report

Begin with the individual, group, or agency that has written the report. If the same body publishes the report, use *Author* in the publication information. If the report has a number, put it in parentheses after the title but before the period.

Dossey, J. A. (1988). *Mathematics: Are we measuring up?* (Report No. 17-M-02). Princeton, NJ: Educational Testing Service. (ERIC Document Reproduction Service No. ED300207)

### Articles from Periodicals and Selections from Books

#### MODEL FORMAT FOR ARTICLES

period +    period +                period +
space       space                   space
↓           ↓                       ↓
Author(s). (Date). Title of article. *Title of Periodical,*
*Volume Number,* Page numbers.
↑           ↑       ↑               ↑
indent ½"   number  comma           period
5–7 spaces  italicized  italicized

- **Author.** Follow the author's last name and initials with a period.
- **Date.** Supply the date in parentheses followed by a period.
- **Title of article.** Capitalize only proper names and the first word of the title and any subtitle. Do not use quotation marks or italics. End with a period.
- **Title of journal, periodical, or book.** Italicize the journal title, with all main words capitalized, and the volume number. Follow with page numbers. Capitalize a book title like an article title, but italicize it.

### 18. Article in Journal Paginated by Volume

Omit the issue number when the page numbers run continuously throughout the different issues making up a volume.

Klein, R. D. (2003). Audience reactions to local TV news. *American Behavioral Scientist, 46,* 1661-1672.

### 19. Article in Journal Paginated by Issue

When page 1 begins each issue, include the issue number in parentheses, but not italicized, directly after the volume number.

Sadeh, A., Raviv, A., & Gruber, R. (2000). Sleep patterns and sleep disruptions in school-age children. *Developmental Psychology, 36*(3), 291-301.

### 20. Special Issue of Journal

Begin with the special issue's editor (if other than the regular editor). If no editor is indicated, begin with the title.

Balk, D. E. (Ed.). (1991). Death and adolescent bereavement [Special issue]. *Journal of Adolescent Research, 6*(1).

### 21. Article in Weekly Magazine

Adler, J. (1995, July 31). The rise of the overclass. *Newsweek, 126,* 33-34, 39-40, 43, 45-46.

### 22. Article in Monthly Magazine

Dold, C. (1998, September). Needles and nerves. *Discover, 19,* 59-62.

### 23. Article with No Author Given

True tales of false memories. (1993, July/August). *Psychology Today, 26,* 11-12.

### 24. Article in Newspaper

Use *p.* or *pp.* to introduce the article's page numbers.

Murtaugh, P. (1998, August 10). Finding a brand's real essence. *Advertising Age,* p. 12.

## 25. Editorial or Letter to the Editor

Ellis, S. (2001, September 7). Adults are problem with youth
sports [Letter to the editor]. *USA Today*, p. 14A.

## 26. Interview (Published)

Although APA does not specify a form for published interviews, you may wish to employ the following form.

Dess, N. K. (2001). The new body-mind connection (John T.
Cacioppo) [Interview]. *Psychology Today, 34*(4),
30-31.

## 27. Review with Title

Following the title of the review, describe in brackets the kind of work (*book, film, television program*), and give the work's title.

McMahon, R. J. (2000). The Pentagon's war, the media's
war [Review of the book *Reporting Vietnam: Media and
military at war*]. *Reviews in American History, 28*,
303-308.

## 28. Review Without Title

Derdery, K. (2002). [Review of the book *The politics of
gender after socialism*]. *American Anthropologist, 104*,
354-355.

## 29. Article in Encyclopedia or Reference Work

Chernoff, H. (1978). Decision theory. In *International
encyclopedia of statistics* (Vol. 1, pp. 131-135). New York:
Free Press.

## 30. Chapter in Edited Book or Selection in Anthology

Chisholm, J. S. (1999). Steps to an evolutionary ecology of mind.
In A. L. Hinton (Ed.), *Biocultural approaches to the
emotions* (pp. 117-150). Cambridge, England: Cambridge
University Press.

### 31. Dissertation Abstract

Yamada, H. (1989). American and Japanese topic management

strategies in business conversations. *Dissertation Abstracts*

*International, 50*(09), 2982B.

If you consult the dissertation on microfilm, end with the University Microfilms number in parentheses: (University Microfilms No. AAC–9004751).

### Field and Media Resources

### 32. Unpublished Raw Data

When you use data from field research, briefly describe its topic within brackets, and end with *Unpublished raw data.*

Hernandez, J. (2003). [Survey of attitudes on unemployment

benefits]. Unpublished raw data.

### 33. Interview (Unpublished)

If you have conducted an interview, cite it only in the text: (R. Gelles, personal communication, November 20, 2003).

### 34. Personal Communications (Including Email)

Cite letters, email, phone calls, and other communications unavailable to readers only in your text (see Entry 12 on p. 160).

### 35. Paper Presented at a Meeting

Nelson, J. S. (1993, August). *Political argument in political*

*science: A meditation on the disappointment of political*

*theory.* Paper presented at the annual meeting of the

American Political Science Association, Chicago.

### 36. Videotape or Film

Musen, K. (Producer/Writer), & Zimbardo, P. (Writer). (1990).

*Quiet rage: The Stanford prison study* [Motion picture].

(Available from Insight Media, New York)

### 37. Television or Radio Program

Siceloff, J. L. (Executive Producer). (2002). *Now with Bill*

*Moyers* [Television series]. New York: WNET.

## 38. Recording

Begin with the name of the writer and the copyright date.

Freeman, R. (1994). Porscha [Recorded by R. Freeman & The
Rippingtons]. On *Sahara* [CD]. New York: GRP Records.

### Online and Electronic Resources

## 39. Web Site

Brown, D. K. (1998, April 1). *The children's literature Web
guide.* Calgary: Author. Retrieved August 23, 1998, from
http://www.acs.UCalgary.ca/~dkbrown/

## 40. Online Book or Document

If you can't pinpoint a date of publication, use *n.d.* ("no date").

Frary, R. B. (n.d.). *A brief guide to questionnaire development.*
Retrieved August 8, 1998, from http://ericae.net/ft/tamu/
upiques3.htm

## 41. Selection from Online Book or Document

Lasswell, H. D. (1971). Professional training. In *A pre-view of
policy sciences* (chap. 8). Retrieved May 4, 2002, from
http://www.policysciences.org/spsresources.htm

## 42. Online Journal Article

Sheridan, J., & McAuley, J. D. (1998). Rhythm as a cognitive
skill: Temporal processing deficits in autism. *Noetica,
3*(8). Retrieved December 31, 1998, from http://www.cs
.indiana.edu/Noetica/OpenForumIssue8/McAuley.html

## 43. Online Article Identical to Print Version

If online and print articles are identical, you may use the print format
but identify the online version you used.

Epstein, R. (2001). Physiologist Laura [Electronic version].
*Psychology Today, 34*(4), 5.

If the online article differs in format or content, add your retrieval date with the URL.

**44. Online Newsletter Article**

> Cashel, J. (2001, July 16). Top ten trends for online
>
> communities. *Online Community Report.* Retrieved October 18,
>
> 2001, from http://www.onlinecommunityreport.com/features/10/

**45. Online Newspaper Article**

> Phillips, D. (1999, June 13). 21 days, 18 flights. *Washington*
>
> *Post Online.* Retrieved June 13, 1999, from
>
> http://www.washingtonpost.com/wp-srv/business/
>
> daily/june99/odyssey13.htm

**46. Online Organization or Agency Document**

> Arizona Public Health Association. (n.d.). *Indigenous health*
>
> *section.* Retrieved September 6, 2001, from http://
>
> www.geocities.com/native_health_az/AzPHA.htm

**47. Online Government Document**

> U.S. Department of Labor, Women's Bureau. (2001). *Women's jobs*
>
> *1964-1999: More than 30 years of progress.* Retrieved
>
> September 7, 2001, from http://www.dol.gov/dol/
>
> wb/public/jobs6497.htm

**48. Online Document from Academic Site**

> Cultural Studies Program. (n.d.). Retrieved September 9, 2001,
>
> from Drake University, Cultural Studies Web site:
>
> http://www.multimedia.drake.edu/cs/

**49. Online Report**

> Amnesty International. (1998). *The death penalty in Texas: Lethal*
>
> *injustice.* Retrieved September 7, 2001, from
>
> http://www.web.amnesty.org/ai.nsf/index/AMR510101998

**50. Online Report from Academic Site**

Use "Available from" rather than "Retrieved from" if the URL will take your reader to access information rather than the source itself.

Vandell, D. L., & Wolfe, B. (2000). *Child care quality: Does it matter and does it need to be improved?* (Special Report No. 78). Available from University of Wisconsin, Institute for Research on Poverty Web site: http://www.ssc.wisc.edu/ irp/sr/sr78.pdf

**51. Online Abstract**

Include the source of the original work.

National Bureau of Economic Research. (1998). Tax incentives for higher education. *Tax Policy and the Economy, 12,* 49-81. Abstract retrieved August 24, 1998, from http://www-mitpress.mit.edu/journal-editor .tcl?ISSN=08928649

**52. Online Database: Journal Article**

Piko, B. (2001). Gender differences and similarities in adolescents' ways of coping. *The Psychological Record, 51*(2), 223-236. Retrieved August 31, 2001, from InfoTrac Expanded Academic database.

**53. Online Database: Newspaper Article**

Sappenfield, M. (2002, June 24). New laws curb teen sports drugs. *The Christian Science Monitor.* Retrieved June 26, 2002, from America Online: News Publications database.

**54. Presentation from Virtual Conference**

Brown, D. J., Stewart, D. S., & Wilson, J. R. (1995). *Ethical pathways to virtual learning.* Paper presented at the Center on Disabilities 1995 virtual conference. Retrieved September 7, 2001, from http://www.csun.edu/ cod/95virt/0010.html

### 55. Email

Cite email only in your text. (See Entry 12, p. 160.)

### 56. Online Posting

Treat these as personal communications (see Entry 12, p. 160) unless they are archived and accessible.

> Lanbehn, K. (2001, May 9). Effective rural outreach. Message
>
> posted to State Independent Living Council Discussion
>
> Newsgroup, archived at http://www.acils.com/silc/

### 57. Computer Program

Begin with the name of an author who owns rights to a program or with its title (without italics).

> Family Tree Maker (Version 9.0) [Computer software]. (2001).
>
> Fremont, CA: Learning Company.

### 58. CD-ROM Database

> Hall, Edward T. (1998). In *Current biography: 1940-1997*.
>
> Retrieved March 14, 1999, from Wilson database.

## 17c Sample APA paper

The APA manual recommends beginning a paper with a separate title page, as illustrated on page 173. The student also included an abstract before the paper and her questionnaire in the appendix following it.

**Number title page and all
others using short title**     Body Esteem     1

**Abbreviate title (50 characters
maximum) for heading**

Running head: BODY ESTEEM

**Center title and all other lines**

Body Esteem in Women and Men

Sharon Salamone

The University of Rhode Island

**Supply names
and
institution**

Professor Robert Schwegler

Writing 233

Section 2

April 30, 2003

**Supply course
information
and date if
requested by
your instructor**

**Begin on new page**

**Center heading**   Body Esteem   2

**Do not indent**   Abstract

Undergraduate students, male and female, were asked to complete a Body Esteem Survey to report attitudes toward their bodies (body images). Responses to the survey provided an answer to the question of whether the men or the women had higher body esteem. The mean responses for women and men indicated a higher level of body esteem among men with a statistically significant difference in the means. Because the sample was limited to college undergraduates and displayed little variety in ethnicity (predominantly White), the findings of the study are limited. Prior research on ethnicity and body image suggests that a more ethnically varied sample might produce different results.

**Summarize paper in one ¶, no more than 120 words**

**Double-space abstract and paper**

[Besides the abstract, typical sections in an APA paper are Introduction, Method, Results, and Discussion.]

↓ 1" from top of new page      Body Esteem    3

Body Esteem in Men and Women

1      The concept of beauty has changed over the years in
Western society, especially for women. In past centuries
the ideal was a voluptuous and curved body; now it is a
more angular and thin shape (McCabe & Monteath, 1997).
Lean, muscular bodies are currently held up as ideals
for men, too. Ideals of physical appearance and
attractiveness play an important role in the lives of
people. Often, people considered attractive are preferred
as working partners, as dating partners, or as job
candidates (Lennon, Lillethun, & Buckland, 1999). Media
images endorse particular body ideals as well; for
example, "media in Western countries have portrayed a
steadily thinning female body ideal" (McCabe & Monteath,
1997, p. 711).

2      Most of us assume that women are quite concerned
about their weight and appearance--their body images--and
that they often lack positive body esteem, perhaps as a
result of media images and other cultural influences
(Polivy & Herman, 1987; Rodin, Silberstein, & Striegel-
Moore, 1984; Wilcox & Laird, 2000). But what about men?
Are they concerned as well? Is their level of body esteem
higher or lower than women's or about the same? In this
paper I report on a study I undertook with a group of
college undergraduates to compare the attitudes of men
and women toward their bodies. In particular, I wanted to
determine whether or not the men had a higher body esteem
than the women had.

↑ 1" margin at bottom

← 1" margin on each side →

Indent ¶s
and
reference list
consistently,
½" or 5 to 7
spaces

Problem
and
background
introduced

Citation
includes
more than
one source

Research
questions
identified

Body Esteem    4

**Center subheading**    Introduction

**3**    Thinness is prized in contemporary society,

**Background
including
prior
studies**

especially for women. In our culture, thinness, a

statistical deviation, has become the norm, leading

millions of women to believe their bodies are

abnormal. Therefore, it is reasonable for women to be

concerned about their appearance and compare themselves

to others on the basis of what they believe to be the

norm (Lennon et al., 1999). As Lennon et al.

point out, "Comparison with such images may be

related to negative outcomes such as low self-esteem

(Freedman, 1984), dissatisfaction with appearance

(Richens, 1991), eating disorders (Peterson, 1987; Stice

et al., 1994), and negative body image (Freedman, 1984)"

(p. 380).

**4**    Body image is basically made up of two important

components: one's perception and one's attitude toward

body image. Social factors can play a large role in

determining both components (McCabe & Monteath, 1997).

**Body image
and women
introduced**

Given the cultural pressures on women to be thin, we

might expect many women to have somewhat negative body

images. As Wilcox and Laird (2000) put it, "To many

observers, the media appear to be unwittingly engaged in

a campaign to make women feel badly about themselves"

(p. 279).

**5**    On the other hand, some researchers suggest that

**Body image
and men
introduced**

"men seem less obsessed with and disturbed by being or

becoming fat: thus, the occurrence of pathogenic values

Body Esteem   5

related to eating and body size is extremely low among
men" (Demarest & Allen, 2000, p. 465). Although there is
some research, "the literature on body image perception
in men is far more limited" than that on women (Pope et
al., 2000, p. 1297). Possible reasons to suspect that men
also suffer from distorted perceptions of body image have
been evident in two recent studies. First, men with
eating disorders believe that they are fatter than men of
normal weight believe. Also, recent studies have shown
that athletes perceive themselves to be small and frail
when they are, in fact, large and muscular (Pope et al.,
2000). Moreover, in one study, men indicated that they
would prefer to have a body with twenty-seven pounds more
muscle than they actually have (Pope et al., 2000). Thus
it seems reasonable to ask whether men and women have
clearly different levels of body esteem.

Method

6    To measure differences between men's and women's
levels of body esteem, I administered a Body Esteem Scale
(BES) (Franzoi & Sheilds, 1984). Participants in my study
were 174 undergraduate college students from a state
university. I approached them and asked them to complete
the BES. I asked each willing participant to read and
sign an informed consent form before participating. This
form states that the participant may stop at any point if
he or she feels uncomfortable answering a particular
question or group of questions and reassures each person
that he or she will remain anonymous.

Procedure
for study
explained

**7**    The majority of the participants, between the ages

**Participants described**

of 18 and 59, were White, making up 81% of the sample.

Blacks and African Americans made up 6.3%; Asian/Pacific

Islanders made up 3.4%; Latino/Latina, mixed race, and

all others made up 2.9% each; and Native Americans made

up .6% of the sample. The sample was equally divided

between men and women.

**8**    The Body Esteem Scale consists of general questions

**Questionnaire described with cross-reference to appendix**

(BES) (see Appendix) followed by three components (BES 1,

BES 2, and BES 3). BES 1 makes up the Physical/Sexual

Attractiveness part of the scale, focusing primarily on

elements of the body; BES 3 consists of the Physical

Condition component of the scale, covering such matters

as stamina, physical condition, and strength. BES 1 and

BES 3 have different forms and questions for women and

men. For BES 2, the women's questionnaire constitutes the

Weight Concern component of the scale while the men's

questionnaire constitutes the Upper Body Strength

component of the scale.

Results

**9**    I recorded the results from the questionnaires into

**Findings explained**

an Excel spreadsheet. In order to determine whether women

or men had higher levels of body esteem as measured by

the BES, I calculated the average score for each group

(statistical mean). The mean for women was lower than for

men: for women, $M$ = 3.2304; for men, $M$ = 3.6514. From

this I arrived at my preliminary conclusion that for this

Body Esteem    7

particular sample of college students, the men had
clearly higher body esteem than did the women, by .4211,
or approximately .4 on a scale of 1-5.

10    I realized, however, that results can occur by chance
and that there are statistical procedures for determining
the likelihood that chance was responsible for the
difference between the two groups. To determine whether
the results were statistically significant (not occurring
by chance), I had the spreadsheet program calculate an
ANOVA (univariate analysis of variance) to compare the two
body esteem indexes. The results indicated that the
differences were significant, $F (1.172) = 28.05$, $p < .05$.

11    I conducted this study in order to determine whether
men had higher, lower, or similar levels of body esteem
compared with the levels women had, at least for the
group of people (university undergraduates) I was
studying. For this group, it is clear that men had higher
levels of body esteem.

Main
conclusion
stated

### Discussion

12    Comparing men's and women's body esteem is not as
simple as this study might seem to suggest, however. The
body esteem scales for men and women are certainly
comparable, but they do not measure exactly the same
things. According to Franzoi and Shields (1984), body
esteem for women appears to consist of three primary
components: sexual attractiveness, weight concern,  and
physical condition. The sexual attractiveness subscale
consists of physical attributes that cannot generally be

Findings
qualified

Body Esteem    8

changed through exercise, but only through cosmetics. The
physical appearance subscale includes body parts that can
be altered through exercise of the control of food
intake. The third subscale pertains to qualities such as
stamina, agility, and strength. For men, the first
subscale measures facial features and some aspects of the
physique. The second subscale is composed of upper body
parts and functions that can be altered through
exercising. The third subscale is similar to the woman's
physical subscale, consisting of stamina, agility, and
strength.

**Possibilities
for future
research
suggested**

13    As social attitudes and values change, perhaps men's
and women's versions of the BES may need to change too.
As sports and physical strength become more important to
women, parts of the BES may possibly need to be revised
to be more parallel to the men's. Right now, however, the
BES seems to provide some understanding of the different
levels of bodily self-esteem held by women and men.

**Findings
analyzed**

14    The great pressure on women in our society to be
thin and physically attractive according to standards
that do not represent a normal range of body types and
sizes probably accounts for the difference between the
women's and men's results. Franzoi and Shields (1984)
make a comment that helps explain the higher body esteem
of the males: "It appears that men associate these body
parts and functions, not with how they and others assess
them as static objects, but with how they will help or
hinder physical activity" (p. 178).

**15**    My results are consistent with other research. For example, "In studies of body-shape perception, men typically have more positive body images than women do, regardless of their weight" (Demarest & Langer, 1996, p. 569). Overall, men are generally satisfied with their body sizes, although they misjudge what women think to be attractive (Demarest & Allen).

**16**    Gender is not the only factor that influences body image. Ethnicity is also very important, especially among women. In interviews conducted by Lopez, Blix, and Blix (1995) and by Rosen and Gross (1987), Black women seem to have more positive body images and less desire to be thin than White or Hispanic women (Demarest & Allen, 2000). When compared to Black women, White women showed greater body dissatisfaction at lower body weights (Demarest & Allen). It has also been found that Black men were less likely than White men to refuse a date with a woman because she was overweight. According to Demarest and Allen, among the female participants, Black women have a more accurate view of the perception of men, whereas White women have a more distorted perception.

**17**    In my study, the majority of the sample consisted of White participants. This may have affected my results and my conclusions. Because ethnicity is important in a study such as this, a more varied sample would lead to stronger conclusions.

**Begin on
new page**                                  References

Demarest, J., & Allen, R. (2000). Body image: Gender,
    ethnic, and age differences. *Journal of Social
    Psychology, 140,* 465-471.

Demarest, J., & Langer, E. (1996). Perception of body
    shape by underweight, average-weight, and overweight
    men and women. *Perceptual and Motor Skills, 83,*
    569-570.

Franzoi, S. L., & Shields, S. A. (1984). The body esteem
    scale: Multidimensional structure and sex
    differences in a college population. *Journal of
    Personality Assessment, 407,* 173-178.

Lennon, S. J., Lillethun, A., & Buckland, S. S. (1999).
    Attitudes toward social comparison as a function of
    self-esteem: Idealized appearance and body image.
    *Family & Consumer Sciences Research Journal, 27,*
    379-405.

Lopez, E., Blix, G., & Blix., A. G. (1995). Body image of
    Latinas compared to body image of non-Latina white
    women. *Health Values, 19,* 3-10.

McCabe, M. P., & Monteath, S. A. (1997). The influence of
    societal factors on female body image. *Journal of
    Social Psychology, 137,* 708-727.

Polivy, J., & Herman, C. P. (1987). The diagnosis and
    treatment of abnormal eating. *Journal of Consulting
    and Clinical Psychology, 55,* 635-644.

Pope, H. G., Bureau, B., DeCol, C., Gruber, A. J.,
    Hudson, J. I., Jouvent, R., & Mangweth, B. (2000).

Body Esteem    11

Body image perception among men in three countries.
*American Journal of Psychiatry, 157,* 1297-1301.

Rodin, J., Silberstein, L., & Striegel-Moore, R. (1984).
Women and weight: A normative discontent. In T. B.
Sonderegger (Ed.), *Nebraska symposium on motivation:
Psychology and gender* (pp. 267-307). Lincoln:
University of Nebraska Press.

Rosen, J. C., & Gross, J. (1987). Prevalence of weight
reducing and weight gaining in adolescent boys and
girls. *Health Psychology, 6,* 131-147.

Wilcox, K., & Laird, J. D. (2000). The impact of media
images of super-slender women on women's self-
esteem: Identification, social comparison, and self-
perception. *Journal of Research in Personality, 34,*
278-276.

**Begin on
new page**

Appendix

Body Esteem Scale for Adolescents and Adults:

General Questions

Instructions: Indicate how often you agree with the
following statements, ranging from "never" (0) to
"always" (4). Circle the appropriate number beside each
statement.

Never = 0  Seldom = 1  Sometimes = 2  Often = 3  Always = 4

1. I like what I look like in pictures.          0 1 2 3 4

2. Other people consider me good looking.        0 1 2 3 4

3. I'm proud of my body.                         0 1 2 3 4

4. I am preoccupied with trying to change my
   body weight.                                  0 1 2 3 4

5. I think my appearance would help me get
   a job.                                        0 1 2 3 4

6. I like what I see when I look in the mirror. 0 1 2 3 4

7. There are lots of things I'd change about
   my looks if I could.                          0 1 2 3 4

8. I am satisfied with my weight.                0 1 2 3 4

9. I wish I looked better.                        0 1 2 3 4

10. I really like what I weigh.                   0 1 2 3 4

11. I wish I looked like someone else.            0 1 2 3 4

12. People my own age like my looks.             0 1 2 3 4

13. My looks upset me.                            0 1 2 3 4

14. I'm as nice looking as most people.          0 1 2 3 4

15. I'm pretty happy about the way I look.       0 1 2 3 4

16. I feel I weigh the right amount for my
    height.                                      0 1 2 3 4

Body Esteem    13

17. I feel ashamed of how I look.          0 1 2 3 4

18. Weighing myself depresses me.          0 1 2 3 4

19. My weight makes me unhappy.            0 1 2 3 4

20. My looks help me to get dates.         0 1 2 3 4

21. I worry about the way I look.          0 1 2 3 4

22. I think I have a good body.            0 1 2 3 4

23. I'm looking as nice as I'd like to.    0 1 2 3 4

# Editing Grammar:
# Meeting Community Expectations

## ▼ *TAKING IT ONLINE*

### PURDUE ONLINE WRITING LAB (OWL)
**http://owl.english.purdue.edu/**
Visit this site for the most complete list of resources, handouts, and
exercises about grammar and editing collected by any American university.
The site also offers grammar advice for ESL writers.

### THE GOOD GRAMMAR, GOOD STYLE ™ PAGES
**http://www.protrainco.com/info/grammar.htm**
Do you have a grammar question? Check this site's searchable database
and "Articles & Answers" archive.

### INTERACTIVE QUIZZES
**http://webster.commnet.edu/grammar/quiz_list.htm**
This page will lead you to nearly two hundred grammar quizzes, some
written by students, to help you brush up on the topics of your choice.

### WRITING TIPS
**http://faculty.rmwc.edu/jabell/writing.htm**

### THE MARKETING DEPARTMENT'S TOP 10 LIST OF WRITING ERRORS AND THEN SOME
**http://www.csun.edu/~hfbus023/errors.html**
These guidelines from professors will help you recognize and edit common
writing errors.

### DAVE'S ESL CAFÉ HINT OF THE DAY
**http://eslcafe.com/webhints/hints.cgi**
Read the hint of the day, and search the archive for past hints, too.

# PART 5

# Editing Grammar:
# Meeting Community Expectations

# 18 Recognizing Words Working in Sentences

To edit effectively, you need to recognize sentence components and their working relationships. At the simplest level, sentences consist of different types of words, often called *parts of speech:* nouns, pronouns, verbs, adjectives, adverbs, prepositions, conjunctions, and interjections.

## 18a Recognizing nouns and articles

You can recognize a **noun** by looking for a word that names a person, a place, an idea, or a thing. For most nouns, form the **plural** (two or more) by adding *-s* or *-es* to the **singular** (one): *cow + -s = cows; gas + -es = gases.* Some nouns are irregular: *child, children; deer, deer.* Use a noun's **possessive** form to express ownership (see 39a–b on apostrophes).

| SINGULAR | SINGULAR POSSESSIVE (*'S*) | PLURAL | PLURAL POSSESSIVE (*'*) |
|---|---|---|---|
| student | student's | students | students' |

| TYPES OF NOUNS | |
|---|---|
| **Count noun** | Names individual items that can be counted: *four cups, a hundred beans* |
| **Noncount noun (mass noun)** | Names material or abstractions that cannot be counted: *flour, water, steel* |
| **Collective noun** | Names a unit composed of more than one individual or thing (see 22b-2 on agreement): *group, board of directors, flock* |
| **Proper noun** | Names specific people, places, titles, or things (see 43b on capitalizing): *Miss America; Tuscaloosa, Alabama; Microsoft Corporation* |
| **Common noun** | Names nonspecific people, places, or things (see 43b on capitalizing): *children, winner, town, mountain, company, bike* |

A noun often requires an **article:** *the, a* (before a consonant sound), or *an* (before a vowel sound).

An **intern** prepared a **report** for the **doctor** at **Hope Hospital**.

---

## ESL ADVICE: NOUNS AND THE USE OF ARTICLES

Remember that you'll still communicate your meaning even if you choose the wrong article or forget one. Notice as you read how the **indefinite articles** (*a* or *an*) and the **definite article** (*the*) are used.

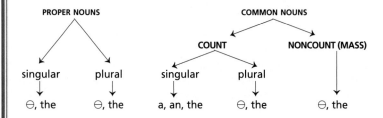

$\ominus$ = no article

**Singular proper nouns** generally use no article, and **plural proper nouns** usually use *the*.

SINGULAR        Rosa Parks helped initiate the civil rights movement.

PLURAL          **The** Everglades have abundant wildlife and plants.

**Singular count nouns** use *a, an,* or *the* and cannot stand alone.

SINGULAR        **The** pig is **an** intelligent animal.

**Plural count nouns** use either no article (to show a generalization) or *the* (to refer to something specific).

GENERALIZATION    Books are the best teachers. [books in general]

SPECIFIC         **The** books on his desk are due Monday. [specific books]

**Noncount (mass) nouns** use either no article or *the,* never *a* or *an*. **General noncount nouns** sometimes stand alone. **Specific noncount nouns,** which have been limited in some way, use *the*.

DRAFT           A laughter is good medicine.

GENERAL    Laughter is good medicine. [laughter in general]

SPECIFIC    **The** laughter of children is good medicine. [specific type of laughter]

Follow these guidelines when you select *a, an,* or *the.*

- Use *a* or *an* when you are not referring to any specific person or thing (using a nonspecific, singular count noun). Use *a* before a consonant sound and *an* before a vowel sound.

I need **a** car to go to work. [unknown, nonspecific car or any car]

- Use *the* when you are referring to an exact, known person or thing (using a specific, singular noun).

I need **the** car to go to work. [specific, known car]

**The** car that she bought is metallic gray. [specific, known car]

- Generally use no articles with plural count and noncount nouns.

COUNT    Airline tickets to Chicago are at half price.

NONCOUNT    Information about flights to Chicago is now available.

- Use *the* when a plural count noun or a noncount noun is followed by a modifier, such as an adjective clause (see 19c-1) or prepositional phrase (see 19c-1), that makes the noun specific.

COUNT    **The** airline tickets that you bought are at half price.

NONCOUNT    **The** information on the flight board has changed.

## 18b Recognizing pronouns

To recognize a **pronoun,** look for a word like *them, she, his,* or *it* that takes the place of a noun and can play the same roles in a sentence. You can use a pronoun to avoid repeating a noun, but the pronoun's meaning depends on a clear relationship to the noun to which it refers—its **antecedent** or **headword.** (See 22d on agreement and 26a on pronoun reference.)

antecedent        pronoun
**Jean** presented **her** proposal to the committee.

You can also use a pronoun to modify a noun or another pronoun.

**This** part has been on order for a month, and **that** one for a week.

A pronoun changes form to show **number** (singular or plural), **gender** (masculine, feminine, or neuter), and role in a sentence—**subject, object,** or **possessive** (see 19a on sentence structure and 21a on pronoun form).

## PRONOUNS AND THEIR FUNCTIONS

| | |
|---|---|
| **Personal pronouns** | Designate persons or things using a form reflecting the pronoun's role in the sentence (see 21a) |
| SINGULAR | *I, me, you, he, him, she, her, it* |
| PLURAL | *we, us, you, they, them* |
| **Possessive pronouns** | Show ownership (see 21a on pronouns and 39a–b on apostrophes) |
| SINGULAR | *my, mine, your, yours, her, hers, his, its* |
| PLURAL | *our, ours, your, yours, their, theirs* |
| **Relative pronouns** | Introduce clauses that modify or add information to a main clause (see 19c and 31b on subordination) |
| | *who, whom, whose, which, that* |
| **Interrogative pronouns** | Introduce questions |
| | *who, which* |
| **Reflexive and intensive pronouns** | End in *-self* or *-selves;* enable the subject or doer also to be the receiver of an action (reflexive); add emphasis (intensive) |
| SINGULAR | *myself, yourself, herself, himself, itself* |
| PLURAL | *ourselves, yourselves, themselves* |
| **Indefinite pronouns** | Refer to people, things, and ideas in general rather than a specific antecedent (see 22c-4) |
| SINGULAR | *anybody, each, every, neither, none, something* |
| PLURAL | *both, few, fewer, many, others, several* |
| VARIABLE | *all, any, enough, more, most, some* |
| **Demonstrative pronouns** | Point out or highlight an antecedent; can refer to a noun or a pronoun or sum up an entire phrase or clause |
| | *this, that, these, those* |
| **Reciprocal pronouns** | Refer to individual parts of a plural antecedent |
| | *one another, each other* |

## 18c  Recognizing verbs

To identify **verbs,** look for words that express actions (*jump, build*), occurrences (*become, happen*), and states of being (*be, seem*). Change a verb's form to reflect person and number (see 22a on agreement) and to signal relationships in time (see 20a–g on **tense**).

PERSON          She **restores** furniture.          They **restore** furniture.

NUMBER          The copier **makes** noise.          The copiers **make** noise.

TENSE           They **prepare** the invoices.       They **prepared** the invoices.

Other forms show voice (see 20i and 32b-3) and mood (see 20h).

ACTIVE VOICE      The pump **cleans** the water.

PASSIVE VOICE     The water **is cleaned** by the pump.

INDICATIVE MOOD   The report **was** on the desk.

SUBJUNCTIVE MOOD  If the report **were** on the desk, I would have found it.

You can use a main verb alone or with one or more **helping (auxiliary) verbs,** which include the forms of *be, do,* and *have.* A helping verb and a main verb form a **verb phrase.** You can also use **modal auxiliary verbs** as helping verbs but never as main verbs. They include *will/would, can/could, shall/should, may/might, must,* and *ought.* (See 20d.)

MAIN VERB       The city **welcomes** tourists all year round.

HELPING + MAIN  The tourist agency **is planning** a video.

MODAL + MAIN    They **might decide** to include the Old Courthouse.

Use **action verbs** to show an action or activity: *swim, analyze, dig, turn.* Use **linking verbs** (or **state-of-being verbs**) to express a state of being or an occurrence: *is, seems, becomes, grows.* These verbs link a subject with a **complement** that renames or describes it (see 19a-2).

ACTION          The company and the union **negotiated** a contract.

LINKING         The flowers **smelled** musky.

**Phrasal verbs** include a verb plus a closely associated word that seems like a preposition but is known as a **particle,** as in *run down* ("exhaust"). Unlike verb-plus-preposition combinations, whose meanings are the sums of their parts (*run* = action + *by* = direction), phrasal verbs have meanings that differ from those of the separate words. For example, *clear out* means "depart" and *run by* means "consult."

|                phrasal verb | verb + preposition |
| I **ran** the idea **by** the committee. | I **ran by** the house. |

## 18d Recognizing adjectives

To identify **adjectives,** look for words that modify nouns, pronouns, or word groups acting as nouns. They answer questions like "How many?" "Which one?" or "What kind?" (see 23a on adjective features).

HOW MANY?   The **two** reports reached different conclusions.

WHICH ONE?   Our report is the **last** one.

WHAT KIND?   Reusing the filter was **dangerous**.

Adjectives come in three degrees of comparison: *high, higher, highest; crooked, more crooked, most crooked* (see 23a).

---

### ESL ADVICE:  ADJECTIVE FORMS

Adjectives in English never use a plural form.

DRAFT   Santo Domingo is renowned for beautifuls beaches.

EDITED   Santo Domingo is renowned for beautiful beaches.

---

## 18e Recognizing adverbs

To identify **adverbs,** look for words that modify verbs, adjectives, other adverbs, or entire sentences. They answer such questions as "When?" "Where?" "Why?" "How often?" "Which direction?" "What conditions?" and "What degree?" (see 23a).

WHEN?   Our committee met **yesterday.** [modifies verb *met*]

WHAT DEGREE?   We had a **very** long meeting. [modifies adjective *long*]

HOW OFTEN?   I attend board meetings **quite** frequently. [modifies adverb *frequently*, which modifies verb *attend*]

Many adverbs consist of an adjective plus *-ly* (*quickly, blindly, frequently*) although some adjectives also end in *-ly* (*neighborly, lovely*). Other common adverbs include *very, too, tomorrow, not, never, sometimes,* and *well.* Adverbs come in three degrees of comparison: *frequently, more* (or *less*) *frequently, most* (or *least*) *frequently* (see 23a).

You can use **conjunctive adverbs** such as *however, moreover, thus,* and *therefore* to indicate logical relationships. (See 31a for a list.)

They opposed the policy; **nevertheless,** they implemented it.

## 18f Recognizing prepositions

To recognize a **preposition,** look for a word like *in* or *at* followed by a noun or pronoun, forming a **prepositional phrase** (see 19b-1). The phrase adds precise, detailed information to a sentence.

The office in **this region** sells homes priced above **$150,000.**

| COMMON PREPOSITIONS | | | | |
|---|---|---|---|---|
| about | at | despite | near | to |
| above | before | down | of | toward |
| across | behind | during | off | under |
| after | below | except | on | until |
| against | beneath | for | out | up |
| along | between | from | outside | upon |
| among | beyond | in | over | with |
| around | by | into | past | within |
| as | concerning | like | through | without |

### ESL ADVICE: PREPOSITIONS

PREPOSITIONS OF PLACE: AT, ON, IN, AND NO PREPOSITION

| AT | ON | IN | NO PREPOSITION |
|---|---|---|---|
| the mall* | the bed* | (the) bed* | downstairs |
| home | the ceiling | the kitchen | downtown |
| the library* | the floor | the car | inside |
| the office | the horse | (the) class* | outside |
| school* | the plane | the library* | upstairs |
| work | the train | school* | uptown |

*You may sometimes use different prepositions for these locations.

PREPOSITIONS OF TIME: *AT, ON,* AND *IN*
- Use *at* for a specific time.
- Use *on* for days and dates.
- Use *in* for nonspecific times during a day, month, season, or year.

Brandon was born **at** 11:11 a.m. **on** a Monday **in** 1991.

PREPOSITIONS OF PLACE: *AT, ON,* AND *IN*
- Use *at* for specific addresses.
- Use *on* for names of streets, avenues, and boulevards.
- Use *in* for names of areas of land—states, countries, continents.

She works **at** 99 Tinker Street **in** Dayton.

The White House is **on** Pennsylvania Avenue **in** Washington, DC.

In general, use prepositional phrases in this order: place, then time.

place + time

The runners will start **in the park** on Saturday.

### TO OR NO PREPOSITION TO EXPRESS GOING TO A PLACE

- When you express the idea of going to a place, use the preposition *to*.

I am going **to** work.　　I am going **to** the office.

- In the following cases, use no preposition.

I am going home.　　I am going downstairs (downtown, inside).

### FOR AND *SINCE* IN TIME EXPRESSIONS

- Use *for* with an amount of time (minutes, hours, days, months, years) and *since* with a specific date or time.

The housing program has operated **for** many years.

The housing program has operated **since** 1971.

### PREPOSITIONS WITH NOUNS, VERBS, AND ADJECTIVES

- Nouns, verbs, and adjectives may appear with certain prepositions.

**NOUN + PREPOSITION**　He has an <u>understanding</u> **of** global politics.

**VERB + PREPOSITION**　Managers <u>worry</u> **about** many things.

**ADJECTIVE + PREPOSITION**　Life in your country is <u>similar</u> **to** life in mine.

### NOUN + PREPOSITION COMBINATIONS

| | | | |
|---|---|---|---|
| approval of | confusion about | hope for | participation in |
| awareness of | desire for | interest in | reason for |
| belief in | grasp of | love of | respect for |
| concern for | hatred of | need for | understanding of |

### VERB + PREPOSITION COMBINATIONS

| | | | |
|---|---|---|---|
| ask about | differ from | pay for | study for |
| ask for | grow into | prepare for | think about |
| belong to | look at | refer to | trust in |
| care for | participate in | step into | work for |

### ADJECTIVE + PREPOSITION COMBINATIONS

| | | | |
|---|---|---|---|
| afraid of | careless about | interested in | similar to |
| angry at | familiar with | made of | sorry for |
| aware of | fond of | married to | sure of |
| capable of | happy about | proud of | tired of |

## 18g Recognizing conjunctions

To recognize **conjunctions,** look for words that join other words and word groups, signaling their relationships.

**Coordinating conjunctions.** You can use *and, but, or, nor, for, yet,* and *so* to link grammatically equal elements (see 31a).

WORDS            analyze **and** discuss, compare **or** contrast

PHRASES          over past sales **yet** under current goals

CLAUSES          They petitioned the board, **but** they lost their appeal.

**Subordinating conjunctions.** Use words such as *because* or *if* to create a **subordinate** (or **dependent**) **clause.**

        main clause                    subordinate clause
    Li spoke persuasively, **though** the crowd favored her opponent.

Such a clause cannot stand on its own as a sentence; you need to attach it to a **main** (or **independent**) **clause** that it qualifies or limits. (See 31b for a list of conjunctions.)

**Correlative conjunctions.** These pairs include *not only . . . but also, either . . . or, both . . . and,* and similar combinations. They join sentence elements that are grammatically equal. (See 30b on parallelism.)

## 18h Recognizing interjections

To recognize **interjections,** look for expressions that convey a strong re-action or emotion, such as surprise (*Hey!*) or disappointment (*Oh, no!*). They may stand alone or be loosely related to the rest of a sentence.

# 19 Recognizing Sentence Parts and Patterns

Careful editing depends on your ability to recognize the different parts of sentences so that you can change their relationships or choose among alternative patterns. See also Chapter 18, which reviews the functions of the words combined to form phrases, clauses, and sentences.

## 19a  Recognizing subjects and predicates

The essential parts of a sentence are a **subject** and a **predicate.**

### 1  Look for sentence subjects

To recognize a **simple subject,** look for one or more nouns (or pronouns) naming the doer or the topic. To identify a **complete subject,** find the simple subject *plus* all its modifying words.

SIMPLE SUBJECT     **Email** has changed business communication.

COMPLETE SUBJECT   **All the sales staff on this floor** left early.

A subject may be singular, plural, or compound (linked by *and* or *or*).

SINGULAR SUBJECT   **She** put the monitor on the desk.

PLURAL SUBJECT     **These pills** are difficult to swallow.

COMPOUND SUBJECT   **John and Chifume** are medical students.

In most sentences, the subject comes before the verb. An **expletive construction** (*there is/are* or *here is/are*) allows you to delay the subject until after the verb (see 32b-2).

USUAL ORDER        **Homeless people** camped here.

EXPLETIVE          There were **homeless people** camping here.

For emphasis, you can reverse (invert) the subject and verb.

INVERTED           In this tiny house was born **a leader.**

Questions often place the subject between helping and main verbs.

QUESTION           Did **the board** approve the light-rail proposal?

In an **imperative** sentence expressing a request or command, the subject *you* generally is implied but not stated (see 19d).

IMPERATIVE         [**You**] Put the insulation around the door frame.

## 2 Look for sentence predicates

The **predicate** indicates an action or relationship expressed in a sentence. It may specify consequences or conditions. A **simple predicate** includes only a verb (see 18a) or verb phrase (see 20d).

**VERB** The bus **stopped.**     **VERB PHRASE** The bus **might stop.**

The verb may be single or compound (linked by *and* or *or*).

**SINGLE** The client **slipped.**     **COMPOUND** The client **slipped and fell.**

To recognize a **complete predicate,** look for a verb or verb phrase *plus* modifiers and other words that receive the action or complete the verb.

**COMPLETE PREDICATE**     The lab tech **gave me the printout.**

**Object patterns.** With a **transitive verb,** you will often include a **direct object** in the predicate, telling *who* or *what* receives the action.

predicate
subject     verb (direct object)
The bank officer **approved** the loan.

A sentence with a transitive verb can also include an **indirect object,** a noun or pronoun telling readers *to whom* or *for whom* the action is undertaken.

direct
subject     verb     indirect object     object
The Marine Corps Reserve **gives** needy children toys.

You can add information to a predicate with an **object complement,** a noun or adjective that renames or describes the direct object.

**NOUN**     His co-workers elected **Jim** project leader.

**ADJECTIVE**     Critics judged **the movie** inferior.

**Subject complement patterns.** With a **linking verb,** such as *is, seems,* or *feels* (see 18c), you can include a **subject complement,** "completing" the subject by describing or renaming it.

subject
subject     verb     complement
The grant proposal **is** too complicated.

**Intransitive verb patterns.** An **intransitive verb** doesn't take an object or a complement; neither is needed to complete the meaning.

Our team **lost.**     Last week, the ferryboat **sank.**

---

### FIVE BASIC PREDICATE STRUCTURES

1. **Subject + intransitive verb**
   The bus crashed.
2. **Subject + transitive verb + direct object**
   A passenger called the police.
3. **Subject + transitive verb + indirect object + direct object**
   The paramedic gave everyone a blanket.
4. **Subject + transitive verb + direct object + object complement**
   Officials found the driver negligent.
5. **Subject + linking verb + subject complement**
   The quick-thinking passenger was a hero.

---

## 19b Recognizing phrases

A **sentence** is a word group with a subject and a predicate that can stand alone (see 19d). In contrast, a **phrase** is a word group that lacks a subject, a predicate, or both. A phrase cannot stand alone and must be integrated within a freestanding sentence. If you capitalize and punctuate a phrase like a sentence, you create a fragment (see 24a).

### 1 Look for prepositional phrases

To recognize a **prepositional phrase,** look first for a **preposition**—a word like *at, for, under,* or *except* (see the list in 18f ). Then identify the **object of the preposition**—the noun, pronoun, or word group that follows the preposition.

| **to** the beach | **near** her | **after** a falling out | **inside** the case |

A prepositional phrase can act as an adjective (almost always following the noun or pronoun it modifies) or as an adverb (placed next to the verb modified or elsewhere in the sentence). (See also 33b on conciseness.)

AS ADJECTIVE    The coupons **in the newspaper** offer savings **on groceries.**

AS ADVERB    Her watch started beeping **during the meeting.**

**During the meeting,** her watch started beeping.

## 2 Look for absolute phrases

An **absolute phrase** includes (1) a noun, pronoun, or word group acting as a noun and (2) a present or past participle and any modifiers (*the deadline approaching quickly*). You can use the phrase to modify a sentence as a whole rather than a word or element within the sentence.

They fought the fire, **the dense smoke slowing their efforts.**

## 3 Look for appositive phrases

To recognize an **appositive,** look for information added by renaming a noun or pronoun. An **appositive phrase** consists of an appositive (generally a noun) along with its modifiers. (See also 37e.)

Ken Choi, **my classmate,** won an award for his design.

He used natural materials, **berry dyes,** for example.

## 4 Look for verbal phrases

You can build phrases around verb parts, known as **verbals:** participles, gerunds, and infinitives. These can function as nouns, adjectives, or adverbs—but they can never stand alone as verbs. A **verbal phrase** consists of a verbal plus its modifiers, object, or complements.

**Participial phrases.** Look for **participial phrases** with *-ing* (present participle) or *-ed/-en* (past participle) forms of a verbal, using them as adjectives to modify a noun or pronoun.

Few neighbors **attending the meeting** owned dogs.

They signed a petition **addressed to the health department.**

**Gerund phrases.** To recognize a **gerund phrase,** look for the *-ing* form of a verbal (present participle) used as a noun in a subject, object, or subject complement.

sentence subject                   object of preposition
**Closing the landfill** may keep it from **polluting the bay.**

## ESL ADVICE: GERUNDS

You can use only a gerund, not an infinitive, after some verbs.

GERUND    Children enjoy **reading** fairy tales.

**COMMON VERBS TAKING GERUNDS**

| | | | |
|---|---|---|---|
| admit | consider | finish | postpone |
| anticipate | delay | imagine | practice |
| appreciate | deny | keep | quit |
| avoid | discuss | mind | recommend |
| can't help | enjoy | miss | suggest |

You must use gerunds with some idiomatic expressions.

- After *go* (any tense): I **go** swimming.    I **went** kayaking.
- After *spend time*: Volunteers **spend** a lot of **time** helping others.
- After *have* + noun: Pilots **have difficulty** flying in bad weather.
- After a preposition: Midwives are trained **in** assisting at childbirth.

In each of the following examples, *to* is not part of an infinitive. *To* acts like a preposition and must be followed by a gerund ending in *-ing*.

I look **forward** to working at the museum.

He is **accustomed** to designing exhibits.

Patrons are **used** to viewing complex displays.

**Infinitive phrases.** To recognize an **infinitive phrase,** look for the *to* form of a verbal used as an adjective, adverb, or noun.

**ADVERB**        He used organic methods **to raise his garden.**

**NOUN (SUBJECT)**    **To live in the mountains** was his goal.

## ESL ADVICE: INFINITIVES

Some verbs take only an infinitive, not a gerund.

**INFINITIVE**        Some students **need** to work part time.

**COMMON VERBS TAKING INFINITIVES**

| | | | |
|---|---|---|---|
| agree | expect | need | refuse |
| ask | fail | offer | seem |
| choose | hope | plan | venture |
| claim | intend | pretend | want |
| decide | manage | promise | wish |

Use an object-infinitive pattern after some verbs.

subject   +   verb   +   object   +   infinitive
Doctors often **advise** their patients to eat well.

**COMMON VERBS TAKING AN OBJECT + INFINITIVE**

| | | | |
|---|---|---|---|
| advise | encourage | need | teach |
| allow | expect | permit | tell |
| ask | force | persuade | urge |
| convince | help | require | want |

When *make, let,* and *have* suggest "caused" or "forced," they follow a different model using the infinitive without *to* (the base form).

She **made/let/had** me clean my room.

Use infinitives after certain adjectives.

| I | **am** | <u>delighted</u> | <u>to meet</u> you. |
|---|---|---|---|
| The report | **is** | <u>easy</u> | <u>to understand</u>. |
| The volunteers | **are** | <u>pleased</u> | <u>to help</u>. |

**Gerund or infinitive phrases.** You can follow some verbs with either a gerund (the *-ing* form used as a noun) or an infinitive.

## ESL ADVICE: GERUNDS OR INFINITIVES

The meaning stays the same when you use most verbs that can be followed by either a gerund or an infinitive.

GERUND    Developers prefer **working** with local contractors.

INFINITIVE    Developers prefer **to work** with local contractors.

**COMMON VERBS TAKING EITHER GERUNDS OR INFINITIVES**

| | | | |
|---|---|---|---|
| begin | hate | like | start |
| can't stand | intend | love | stop |
| continue | learn | prefer | try |

*Remember, forget, regret,* and *stop* change meaning with a gerund or an infinitive.

GERUND    I **remembered** <u>meeting</u> Mark. [I recall an event in the past.]

INFINITIVE    I **remembered** <u>to meet</u> Mark. [I did not forget to do this in the past.]

GERUND    I will never **forget** <u>visiting</u> Texas. [I recall a past event.]

INFINITIVE    I never **forget** <u>to study</u> for exams. [I remember to do something.]

GERUND    I **regret** <u>telling</u> you about her. [I'm sorry I told you in the past.]

| INFINITIVE | I **regret** to tell you that you were not hired. [I'm sorry to tell you now.] |
| GERUND | I **stopped** smoking. [I do not smoke anymore.] |
| INFINITIVE | I **stopped** to smoke. [I paused to smoke.] |

## 19c Recognizing subordinate clauses

A **main clause** is a word group that includes a subject and a verb and can act as a complete sentence. (A main clause is sometimes called an **independent clause.**)

| MAIN CLAUSE | I had many appointments last Friday. |

In contrast, a **subordinate clause** contains both a subject and a predicate yet cannot stand on its own as a sentence. It begins with a subordinating word such as *if, although,* or *that.* This subordinating word prevents the clause from acting like a sentence on its own. (See the list of subordinating words in 31b.)

| SUBORDINATE CLAUSE | **because** I was busy |
| CONNECTED TO SENTENCE | **Because I was busy,** I didn't call. |

Subordinate clauses are also called **dependent clauses** because they "depend" on the main clause to which they are attached. Don't punctuate a subordinate clause as a sentence. If you do, you create a fragment (see 24a).

### 1 Look for subordinate clauses as adjectives

If you begin a subordinate clause with a word like *who, which, that, whom,* or *whose* (**relative pronouns**) or with *when* or *where* (**relative adverbs**), you can use the clause as an adjective to modify a noun or pronoun. Generally, you put the modifying clause right after the noun or pronoun it modifies.

Many people **who live in Erie** came to the meeting.

They opposed the road **that the county plans to approve.**

*Who, whom, whose,* and *that* modify people. *Which, whose,* and *that* modify animals, places, and things. In spoken English *whom* generally is optional, but it is used in formal writing, especially in the academic community.

| STRATEGY | Use adjective clauses to combine short sentences. |
| CHOPPY | I have an aunt. Her book is on the best-seller list. |
| COMBINED | I have an aunt **whose** book is on the best-seller list. |

## ESL ADVICE: ADJECTIVE CLAUSES

You may include or drop a relative pronoun if it is not the subject of the clause. Either way is correct.

**INCLUDED**    The Web site **that** we designed was very popular.

**OMITTED**    The Web site we designed was very popular.

When a relative pronoun is the subject of an adjective clause, the clause can be changed to an **adjective phrase.** To make this change in a clause with a *be* verb, omit the relative pronoun and the *be* verb.

                              X   X
**CLAUSE (WITH *BE*)**    He is the man **who is studying German.**

**PHRASE**    He is the man **studying German.**

With another verb, omit the relative pronoun, and change the verb to a present participle. (See 19b-4 on participial phrases.)

                        X
**CLAUSE (NOT *BE*)**    He is the man **who wants to study German.**

**PHRASE**    He is the man **wanting to study German.**


## 2 Look for subordinate clauses as adverbs

If you begin a clause with a subordinating conjunction such as *because, although, since,* or *while* (see list in 31b), you can use the subordinating clause as an adverb (modifying verbs, adjectives, or adverbs).

**WHY?**    She volunteered **because she supports the zoo.**

**WHEN?**    **As the rally continued,** Jean joined the picket line.


## ESL ADVICE: ADVERB CLAUSES

Adverb clauses explain time, reason, contrast, and condition.

**TIME**    **When** the weather changes, the malls stock winter clothes.

**REASON**    It is difficult to buy shorts **because** winter has started.

**CONTRAST**    **Although** some shoppers turn to catalogs, others do not.

**CONDITION**    Our online customers may do the same **unless** we expand our inventory.

**SOME WORDS TO INTRODUCE ADVERB CLAUSES**

| TIME | REASON | CONTRAST | CONDITION |
|------|--------|----------|-----------|
| after | as | although | as long as |
| as, while | because | even though | even if |
| before | now that | though | if |
| once | since | while | only if |
| since | whereas | | provided that |
| until | | | unless |
| when | | | |

## 3 Look for subordinate clauses as nouns

**Noun clauses** begin with *who, whom, whose, whoever, whomever, what, whatever, when, where, why, whether,* or *how.* Look for them in the roles of nouns: subject, object, object of a preposition, or complement.

**SENTENCE SUBJECT** **What she said** is interesting.

**DIRECT OBJECT** You should pack **what you need for the trip.**

## ESL ADVICE:  NOUN CLAUSES

When you form a complex sentence by combining a noun clause with other sentence parts, the clause acts like a noun in the sentence.

*THAT* **CLAUSE** I believe **that** life exists in other solar systems.

*YES/NO* **QUESTION**
**CLAUSE** I wonder **if** life exists in other solar systems.

I wonder **whether** life exists in other solar systems.

*WH-* **QUESTION**
**CLAUSE** I wonder **where** signs of other life may be found.

The third type above is formed by a question embedded into the sentence as a statement. It is introduced by a *wh-* question word such as *who, whom, what, where, when, which, why, how, how much,* or *how many.* When the noun clause follows an introductory clause, the noun clause uses question word order.

**QUESTION** Who discovered the fire?

**NOUN CLAUSE** Do you know **who discovered the fire**? [question word order]

Change to statement order when the question includes a form of *be* and a subject complement, a modal, or the auxiliary *do, does, did, have, has,* or *had.* Also use statement word order with *if* and *whether* clauses.

**QUESTION** Who **are** your friends?

| | |
|---|---|
| NOUN CLAUSE | I wonder who your friends **are.** [statement word order] |
| QUESTION | How **can** I meet them? |
| NOUN CLAUSE | Please tell me how I **can** meet them. [statement word order] |

## 19d Recognizing different sentence types

Consider using various sentence structures and purposes.

### 1 Look for sentence structures

Try to vary the kind and number of clauses you include.

**Simple sentence.** A sentence with one main (independent) clause and no subordinate (dependent) clauses is a **simple sentence.**

The mayor proposed an expansion of city hall.

**Compound sentence.** A sentence with two or more main (independent) clauses and no subordinate (dependent) clauses is a **compound sentence.** (See 31a on coordination.)

main clause        main clause
**Most people praised the plans,** yet **some found them dull.**

**Complex sentence.** A sentence with one main (independent) clause and one or more subordinate (dependent) clauses is a **complex sentence.** (See 31b on subordination.)

subordinate clause       main clause
Because people objected, **the architect revised the plans.**

**Compound-complex sentence.** A sentence with two or more main (independent) clauses and one or more subordinate (dependent) clauses is a **compound-complex sentence.**

subordinate clause       subordinate clause
Because he wanted to make sure that the expansion did not damage

main clause
the existing building, **the architect examined the frame of the older**

main clause
**structure,** and **he asked the contractor to test the soil stability.**

### 2 Look for sentence purposes

You can also vary sentences according to the relationship you want to establish with readers. A **declarative sentence** makes a statement. An **interrogative sentence** poses a question. An **imperative sentence** requests or commands. An **exclamatory sentence** exclaims.

| | |
|---|---|
| DECLARATIVE | The motor is making a rattling noise. |
| INTERROGATIVE | Have you checked it for overheating? |
| IMPERATIVE | Check it again. |
| EXCLAMATORY | It's on fire! |

# 20 Using Verbs

In casual speech, many different verb forms may be acceptable to listeners, especially those within your own dialect community.

| | |
|---|---|
| CASUAL SPEECH | My daddy **be pushin'** me to do good in school. |
| | Jimmy **should'a went** with them. |
| | We **were fixin'** to eat dinner. |
| | You **might could carpool** to work with Don. |

LISTENER'S REACTION: **What sounds fine when we talk might not be correct in a paper.**

In your writing, however, nonstandard verb forms may distract readers who expect you to write fluently in standard English. Some readers may even assume that you are uneducated or careless if you don't edit the verb forms in your final drafts. Adjust to the expectations of your readers. After all, the formal language of the academic community is as inappropriate on the street corner as casual language is in a history paper or marketing report.

## 20a Recognizing simple present and past tense verbs

When you use a simple verb in a sentence, you put that verb into the **present tense** for action occurring now or the **past tense** for action that has already occurred. Most verbs form the past tense by adding -ed to the present tense form, also called the **base form.** Depending on the verb, this addition may be pronounced as -t (*baked*), -d (*called*), or -ed (*defended*).

---

**ESL ADVICE:  SIMPLE PRESENT AND SIMPLE PAST**

Only these two tenses stand alone with no helping verbs. (See 20d.)

| | |
|---|---|
| **SIMPLE PRESENT** | They **live** in the new dormitory. |
| **SIMPLE PAST** | They **lived** in an apartment last semester. |
| **DRAFT** | The chef **cooking** in the kitchen yesterday. [present participle without any helping verb] |
| **EDITED** | The chef **was cooking** in the kitchen yesterday. |

---

## 20b Editing present tense verbs

You need no special ending to mark the present tense *except* in the third person singular form (with *he, she,* or *it* or a singular noun). Use -s or -es for the third person singular.

The cafeteria **opens** at eight o'clock.

For plurals in the third person (*I, you, we, they* or a plural noun), you do not use -s or -es. This can be confusing because plural nouns often end in -s or -es but the verb should not (*customers + wait*).

The customers **wait** in line until the cafeteria **opens.**

**Present tense in academic settings.** In the academic community, readers may expect special uses of the present tense. When writing for your humanities courses, use the present tense to discuss a piece of literature, a film, an essay, a painting, or a similar creative production. Treat events, ideas, characters, or statements from such works as if they exist in an ongoing present tense. (See 28g.)

In Erdrich's *Love Medicine,* Albertine **returns** to the reservation.

In the social sciences and sciences, use the present tense to discuss the results and implications of a current study or experiment, but use the past tense to review the findings of earlier researchers.

Although Maxwell (1991) **identified** three crucial classroom interactions, the current survey **suggests** two others as well.

---

**ESL ADVICE:  THE THIRD PERSON -S OR -ES ENDING**

Be sure to add an -s or -es to verbs that are third person singular.

| SUBJECT | VERB | SUBJECT | VERB + -S |
|---|---|---|---|
| I/you/we/they | **write** | he/she/it (animal, thing, concept) | **writes** |

## 20c Editing past tense verbs

When you write the past tense of a regular verb, you usually add -ed to its base form. Sometimes you may leave off the -ed if you don't "hear" it, especially when a word beginning in d or t follows the verb.

DRAFT          The company **use** to provide dental benefits.

EDITED         The company **used** to provide dental benefits.

About sixty **irregular verbs** are exceptions to the "add -ed" rule; most change an internal vowel in the simple past tense (run, ran).

DRAFT          The characters in the movie **sweared** constantly.

EDITED         The characters in the movie **swore** constantly.

### COMMON IRREGULAR VERBS

| PRESENT | PAST | PAST PARTICIPLE |
|---------|------|-----------------|
| arise | arose | arisen |
| am/is/are | was/were | been |
| bear | bore | borne |
| begin | began | begun |
| bite | bit | bitten/bit |
| blow | blew | blown |
| break | broke | broken |
| bring | brought | brought |
| buy | bought | bought |
| catch | caught | caught |
| choose | chose | chosen |
| come | came | come |
| creep | crept | crept |
| dive | dived/dove | dived |
| do | did | done |
| draw | drew | drawn |
| dream | dreamed/dreamt | dreamt |
| drink | drank | drunk |
| drive | drove | driven |
| eat | ate | eaten |
| fall | fell | fallen |
| fight | fought | fought |
| fly | flew | flown |
| forget | forgot | forgotten |
| forgive | forgave | forgiven |

| PRESENT | PAST | PAST PARTICIPLE |
|---|---|---|
| get | got | got/gotten |
| give | gave | given |
| go | went | gone |
| grow | grew | grown |
| hang (person) | hanged/hung | hanged/hung |
| hang (object) | hung | hung |
| hide | hid | hidden |
| know | knew | known |
| lay | laid | laid |
| lead | led | led |
| lie | lay | lain |
| light | lit/lighted | lit |
| lose | lost | lost |
| prove | proved | proved/proven |
| ride | rode | ridden |
| ring | rang | rung |
| rise | rose | risen |
| run | ran | run |
| see | saw | seen |
| seek | sought | sought |
| set | set | set |
| shake | shook | shaken |
| sing | sang/sung | sung |
| sink | sank/sunk | sunk |
| sit | sat | sat |
| speak | spoke | spoken |
| spring | sprang | sprung |
| steal | stole | stolen |
| strike | struck | struck |
| swear | swore | sworn |
| swim | swam | swum |
| take | took | taken |
| tear | tore | torn |
| throw | threw | thrown |
| wake | woke/waked | woken/waked/woke |
| wear | wore | worn |
| write | wrote | written |

## 20d Recognizing complex tenses and helping verbs

To recognize complex tenses, look for a **helping** or **auxiliary verb** (such as *is* or *has*) with a main verb in the form of the **past participle** (the *-ed/-en* form) or the **present participle** (the *-ing* form).

The **present participle** is formed by adding -ing to the base form of the verb (the form with no endings or markers).

|  | helping verb | main verb (present participle) |
|---|---|---|
| He | was/will be/had been | **loading** the truck. |

The **past participle** of most verbs is just like the simple past tense (base form + -ed). Because this form can be irregular, check the chart on irregular verbs (see 20c) or the dictionary if you are uncertain of the form.

|  | helping verb | main verb (past participle) |
|---|---|---|
| REGULAR VERB | Mike has/had | **rented** the truck. |
| IRREGULAR VERB | The copier has/had | **broken** down. |

## ESL ADVICE: PRINCIPAL PARTS OF VERBS AND HELPING VERBS

### PRINCIPAL PARTS OF VERBS IN ENGLISH

| BASE FORM | PAST | PRESENT PARTICIPLE | PAST PARTICIPLE |
|---|---|---|---|
| **REGULAR VERBS** | | | |
| live | lived | living | lived |
| want | wanted | wanting | wanted |
| **IRREGULAR VERBS** | | | |
| eat | ate | eating | eaten |
| run | ran | running | run |

Most verbs combine one or more helping verbs (also called auxiliary verbs) with a main verb to form a **verb phrase.**

| HELPING VERB | I **was walking** to school during the snowstorm. |
|---|---|
| HELPING VERBS | I **have been walking** to school for many years. |

Helping verbs include *am, is, are, will, would, can, could, have, has, had, was, were, should, might, may, must, do, does,* and *did.* These words may be combined, as in *have been, has been, had been, will be, will have,* and *will have been.*

### VERB FORMS AND HELPING VERBS FOR COMMONLY USED VERB TENSES

The past, present, and future progressive use forms of *be.*

#### PROGRESSIVE FORM

| | subject + *was/were* + present participle |
|---|---|
| PAST | I **was** working in my studio yesterday. |

| | subject + *am/is/are* + present participle |
|---|---|
| PRESENT | I **am** working in my studio right now. |

FUTURE
subject + *will* (modal) + *be* + present participle
I **will be** working in my studio tomorrow.

The past, present, and future perfect use forms of *have*.

**PERFECT FORM**

PAST
subject + *had* + past participle
I **had** tried to call you all day yesterday.

PRESENT
subject + *have/has* + past participle
I **have** tried to call you all day today.

FUTURE
subject + *will* (modal) + *have* + past participle
I **will have** called you by midnight tonight.

## **20e** Editing progressive and perfect tenses

When you use the **present, past,** and **future progressive** tenses, you can show an action in progress at some point in time.

PRESENT PROGRESSIVE    The carousel **is turning** quickly.

PAST PROGRESSIVE    The horses **were bobbing** up and down.

FUTURE PROGRESSIVE    The children **will be laughing** from the thrill.

In progressive tenses, the main verb must take the *-ing* ending. In the future progressive tense, the verb must also include *be*.

Use correct, complete forms in writing, even if your spoken dialect omits them.

WORD OMITTED    The interview **starting** five minutes late.

EDITED    The interview **is starting** five minutes late.

WRONG FORM    The employees **was running** for the elevator.

EDITED    The employees **were running** for the elevator.

**Indicating the order of events.** Turn to the three **perfect tenses** to show the order in which events take place.

Use the **past perfect tense** for the first event to indicate that it had already happened before something else took place.

The fire **had burned** for an hour before the brigade arrived.

Avoid substituting simple past tense for the past participle.

MISTAKEN PAST    The band **had forgot** the first tour.

EDITED    The band **had forgotten** the first tour.

Use the **present perfect tense** much like the past perfect, showing action that has happened before without a specific time marker or that you insist has already occurred.

I **have reported** the burglary already.

The present perfect also shows action begun in the past and continuing into the present. It differs from the simple past, which indicates an action already completed or specified in time.

**PRESENT PERFECT**   I **have lived** in St. Louis for three weeks.

**SIMPLE PAST**   I **lived** in St. Louis in 1998.

Select the **future perfect tense** to show that something will have happened by the time something else will be taking place.

The chef **will have baked** all the cakes before noon.

## ESL ADVICE:  SIMPLE PRESENT AND PRESENT PROGRESSIVE TENSES

Use the **simple present** tense to describe factual or habitual activities. These occur in the present but are not necessarily in progress.

**SHOWS FACT**   The planets **revolve** around the sun.

**SHOWS HABIT**   The bus usually **arrives** late.

### COMMON TIME EXPRESSIONS FOR  PRESENT TENSE HABITUAL ACTIVITIES

| | | | |
|---|---|---|---|
| all the time | every holiday | every year | rarely |
| always | every month | frequently | sometimes |
| every class | every semester | most of the time | usually |
| every day | every week | often | never |

Use the **present progressive** tense to describe activities in progress. If you wish, you can add expressions to pinpoint the time of the activity.

am/is/are + present participle
DeVaugh **is testing** the process.

DeVaugh **is testing** the process **this month.**

### COMMON TIME EXPRESSIONS FOR PRESENT TENSE ACTIVITIES IN PROGRESS

| | | | |
|---|---|---|---|
| at the moment | this afternoon | this month | this year |
| right now | this evening | this morning | today |

When you choose between the simple present and present progressive tenses, think about the time of the activity. Is it happening only at the moment (present progressive) or all the time as a fact or habit (simple present)?

**PRESENT (FACT)**            All people communicate in some language.

**PRESENT (HABIT)**          The students speak their own languages at home.

**PRESENT PROGRESSIVE**      Kim is studying Spanish this term.
**(AT THE MOMENT)**

## VERBS THAT ARE TROUBLESOME IN PROGRESSIVE TENSES

| | EXAMPLE | OTHER USAGES AND MEANINGS |
|---|---|---|
| **SENSES** | | |
| see | I **see** the beauty. | I **am seeing** that doctor. (meeting with, visiting, dating) |
| hear | I **hear** the birds. | I **have been hearing** about the problem for a while. (receiving information) |
| smell | The flowers **smell** strong. | I **am smelling** the flowers. (action in progress) |
| taste | The food **tastes** good. | The cook **is tasting** the soup. (action in progress) |
| **POSSESSION** | | |
| have | We **have** many friends. | We **are having** a lot of fun. (experiencing) |
| own | They **own** many cars. | |
| possess | She **possesses** wealth. | |
| belong | The book **belongs** to me. | |
| **STATES OF MIND** | | |
| be | I **am** tired. | |
| know | I **know** the city well. | |
| believe | She **believes** in God. | |
| think | I **think** it is true. (know, believe) | I **am thinking** about moving. (having thoughts about) |
| recognize | She **recognizes** him. (knows) | |
| understand | The professor **understands** the equation. | |
| mean | I **don't mean** to pry. (don't want) | I **have been meaning** to visit. (planning, intending) |
| **WISH OR ATTITUDE** | | |
| want | We **want** peace. | |
| desire | He **desires** freedom. | |

**WISH OR ATTITUDE**

| | | |
|---|---|---|
| need | We **need** rain. | |
| love | Children **love** snow. | I **have been loving** this book. (enjoying) |
| hate | Dan **hates** mowing. | |
| like | Lee **likes** skiing. | |
| dislike | She **dislikes** tests. | |
| seem | They **seem** kind. | |
| appear | He **appears** tired. (seems to be) | He **is appearing** at the theater. (acting, performing) |
| look | He **looks** tired. (seems to be) | We **are looking** at the map. (action of using eyes) |

## 20f Editing troublesome verbs (*lie, lay, sit, set*)

Here are a few verbs confused even by experienced writers.

| VERB | PRESENT | PAST | PARTICIPLE |
|---|---|---|---|
| lie (oneself) | lie | lay | lain |
| lay (an object) | lay | laid | laid |
| sit (oneself) | sit | sat | sat |
| set (an object) | set | set | set |

**DRAFT**    I **laid** down yesterday for a nap. I **have laid** down every afternoon this week.

**EDITED**    I **lay** down yesterday for a nap. I **have lain** down every afternoon this week.

**DRAFT**    First Eric and Lisa **sat** the projector down on the table. Then they **set** down as the meeting began.

**EDITED**    First Eric and Lisa **set** the projector down on the table. Then they **sat** down as the meeting began.

## 20g Recognizing clear tense sequence

Conversation can jump from tense to tense with little warning. In writing, however, readers expect you to stick to one tense or to follow a clear **sequence of tenses** that relates events and ideas in time (see 28b).

             present              past
**LOGICAL**    People **forget** that four candidates **ran** in 1948.

             future            present
**LOGICAL**    I **will accept** your report even if it **is** a bit late.

LOGICAL
> past
> The accountant **destroyed** crucial evidence because no one
> past perfect
> **had asked** him to save the records.

LOGICAL
> past perfect
> None of the crew **had realized** that food stored in cans sealed
> present (for generally true statement)
> with lead solder **is** poisonous.

---

## TENSES OF REGULAR AND IRREGULAR VERBS IN THE ACTIVE VOICE

Once you decide when actions or events occur, use this chart to help you select the appropriate verb tense.

### PRESENT, PAST, AND FUTURE (showing simple actions)

**PRESENT** (action taking place now, including habits and facts)

| I/you/we/they | examine/begin |
| he/she/it | examines/begins |

**PAST** (action that has already taken place at an earlier time)

| I/you/he/she/it/we/they | examined/began |

**FUTURE** (action that will take place at an upcoming time)

| I/you/he/she/it/we/they | will examine/begin |

### PRESENT, PAST, AND FUTURE PERFECT (showing order of events)

**PRESENT PERFECT** (action that has recurred or continued from past to present)

| I/you/we/they | have examined/begun |
| he/she/it | has examined/begun |

**PAST PERFECT** (action completed before something else happened)

| I/you/he/she/it/we/they | had examined/begun |

**FUTURE PERFECT** (action that will have happened before something else happens)

| I/you/he/she/it/we/they | will have examined/begun |

### PRESENT, PAST, AND FUTURE PROGRESSIVE (showing action in progress)

**PRESENT PROGRESSIVE** (action in progress now, at this moment)

| I | am examining/beginning |
| you/we/they | are examining/beginning |
| he/she/it | is examining/beginning |

**PAST PROGRESSIVE** (action that was in progress earlier)

| I/he/she/it | was examining/beginning |
| you/we/they | were examining/beginning |

*(Continued)*

**FUTURE PROGRESSIVE** (action that will be in progress later on)

I/you/he/she/it/we/they        will be examining/beginning

**PRESENT, PAST, AND FUTURE PERFECT PROGRESSIVE**
(showing duration of action in progress)

**PRESENT PERFECT PROGRESSIVE** (action that has been in progress up to now)

I/you/we/they                    have been examining/beginning
he/she/it                        has been examining/beginning

**PAST PERFECT PROGRESSIVE** (action that had already been in progress before something else happened)

I/you/he/she/it/we/they        had been examining/beginning

**FUTURE PERFECT PROGRESSIVE** (action that will have been in progress by the time something else happens)

I/you/he/she/it/we/they        will have been examining/beginning

## 20h Recognizing the subjunctive mood

Sentences can be classified by **mood,** the form of a verb that reflects the speaker's or writer's attitude. Most sentences are in the **indicative** (statements intended as truthful or factual like "The store closed at 10") or the **imperative** (commands like "Stop!"). Occasionally the **subjunctive** expresses uncertainty—supposition, prediction, possibility, desire, or wish.

SUBJUNCTIVE        **Were** the deadline today, our proposal would be late.

The subjunctive has faded from most casual speech and some writing. It is still expected by many readers in formal writing using **conditional statements,** often beginning with *if* and expressing the improbable or hypothetical.

DRAFT (PAST)        If fuel efficiency **was** improved, driving costs would go down.

EDITED
(SUBJUNCTIVE)        If fuel efficiency **were** improved, driving costs would go down.

Don't add *would* to the *had + verb* structure in the conditional clause, even if *would* appropriately appears in the **result clause** that follows the conditional.

EXTRA *WOULD*        If fuel efficiency **would have improved,** driving costs **would have gone** down.

EDITED        If fuel efficiency **had improved,** driving costs **would have gone** down.

Finally, some clauses with *that* require a subjunctive verb when they follow certain verbs that make demands or requests.

| | |
|---|---|
| **DRAFT (PAST)** | The judge <u>asked</u> <u>that</u> the witnesses **be swore** in. |
| **EDITED** | The judge asked that the witnesses **be sworn** in. |

Use the present tense form with *that,* even in the third person singular.

The court ordered that      I/you/he/she/it/we/they      appear.

For the verb *is,* the forms are *be* (present) and *were* (past).

## ESL ADVICE: CONDITIONALS

Three types of **conditional statements** depend on a condition or are imagined. These may be (1) *true* in the present, (2) *untrue* or contrary to fact in the present, or (3) *untrue* or contrary to fact in the past. Each has an *if* clause and a result clause that combine different verb tenses.

### TYPES OF CONDITIONAL STATEMENTS

#### TYPE I: TRUE IN THE PRESENT

| *IF* CLAUSE | RESULT CLAUSE |
|---|---|

• **Generally true in the present as a habit or as a fact**

| *if* + subject + present tense | subject + present tense |
|---|---|
| If I drive to school every day, | I get to class on time. |

• **True in the future as a one-time event**

| *if* + subject + present tense | subject + future tense |
|---|---|
| If I drive to school today, | I will get to class on time. |

• **Possibly true in the future as a one-time event**

| *if* + subject + present tense | subject + modal + base form verb |
|---|---|
| If I drive to school today, | I may/should get to class on time. |

#### TYPE II: UNTRUE IN THE PRESENT

| *IF* CLAUSE | RESULT CLAUSE |
|---|---|
| *if* + subject + past tense | subject + *would/could/might* + base form verb |
| If I drove to school, | I would arrive on time. |
| If I were a car owner, | I could arrive on time. |

With Type II, the form of the verb *be* in the *if* clause is always *were.*

#### TYPE III: UNTRUE IN THE PAST

| *IF* CLAUSE | RESULT CLAUSE |
|---|---|
| *if* + subject + past perfect tense | subject + *would/could/might* + *have* + past participle |
| If I had driven to school, | I would not have been late. |

## 20i Recognizing active and passive voice

To recognize a verb in the **active voice,** look for a sentence in which the agent or doer of an action is the subject of the sentence (see 32b-3).

|  | AGENT (SUBJECT) | ACTION (VERB) | GOAL (OBJECT) |
|---|---|---|---|
| ACTIVE | The car | **hit** | the lamppost. |
| ACTIVE | Dana | **distributed** | the flyers. |

In contrast, when a verb is in the **passive voice,** the goal of the sentence appears in the subject position, and the doer may appear in the object position, after the word *by* (in an optional prepositional phrase). The verb itself adds a form of *be* as a helping verb to the participle form.

|  | GOAL (SUBJECT) | ACTION (BE FORM + VERB) | [AGENT: PREPOSITIONAL PHRASE] |
|---|---|---|---|
| PASSIVE | The lamppost | **was hit** | [by the car]. |
| PASSIVE | The flyers | **were distributed** | [by Dana]. |

The active and passive versions of a sentence create different kinds of emphasis because they use different words as sentence subjects.

| ACTIVE | The city council **banned** smoking in restaurants. |
|---|---|
| PASSIVE | Smoking in restaurants **was banned** by the city council. |
| AGENT OMITTED | Smoking in restaurants **was banned.** |

### ESL ADVICE: THE PASSIVE VOICE

All tenses can appear in the passive voice *except* these progressive forms: present perfect, past perfect, future, future perfect. In the following sentences, the agent or doer of the action is not the subject *food,* but rather *chef.*

#### VERB FORMS IN THE PASSIVE VOICE

| TENSES | SUBJECT + *BE* FORM + PAST PARTICIPLE |
|---|---|
| PRESENT | The food **is prepared** by the chef. |
| PRESENT PROGRESSIVE | The food **is being prepared** by the chef. |
| PAST | The food **was prepared** by the chef. |
| PAST PROGRESSIVE | The food **was being prepared** by the chef. |
| PRESENT PERFECT | The food **has been prepared** by the chef. |
| PAST PERFECT | The food **had been prepared** by the chef. |
| FUTURE | The food **will be prepared** by the chef. |
| FUTURE PERFECT | The food **will have been prepared** by the chef. |

Each passive verb must have a form of *be* and a past participle (ending in *-ed* for regular verbs). Sometimes the *-ed* ending is hard to hear when spoken, so edit carefully for it.

**MISSING *-ED***  The young man was **call** to the conference room.

**EDITED**  The young man was **called** to the conference room.

# 21 Using Pronouns

Readers count on you to use different forms of pronouns to guide them through your sentences. The wrong choices can mislead or irritate them.

**DRAFT**  **Him** and **me** will make a strong management team.

**READER'S REACTION: *Him and me* makes the writer sound careless and uneducated.**

**EDITED**  **He** and **I** will make a strong management team.

Although most pronouns won't give you trouble, at times you may struggle with choices between *we* or *us*, *her* or *she*, and *who* or *whom*.

## 21a Recognizing pronoun forms

A pronoun changes form according to its role in a sentence: subject, object, or possessive, showing possession or ownership. (See also 18b.)

subjective  possessive  objective
**He** and **his** design team created the furniture for **us**.

### 1 Choosing subjective forms

Choose a subjective form if a pronoun acts as the subject of all or part of a sentence or if it renames or restates a subject.

**She** wants to know why the orders have not been filled.

Because **they** were unable to get a loan, the business failed.

Atco will be hiring people **who** are willing to work the night shift.

I attend class more regularly than **he** [does].

---

## FORMS OF PRONOUNS

### PERSONAL PRONOUNS

|  | SUBJECTIVE | | OBJECTIVE | | POSSESSIVE | |
|---|---|---|---|---|---|---|
|  | SINGULAR | PLURAL | SINGULAR | PLURAL | SINGULAR | PLURAL |
| First person | I | we | me | us | my | our |
|  |  |  |  |  | mine | ours |
| Second person | you | you | you | you | your | your |
|  |  |  |  |  | yours | yours |
| Third person | he | | him | | his | |
|  | she | they | her | them | her | their |
|  |  |  |  |  | hers | theirs |
|  | it | | it | | its | |

### RELATIVE AND INTERROGATIVE PRONOUNS

| SUBJECTIVE | OBJECTIVE | POSSESSIVE |
|---|---|---|
| who | whom | whose |
| whoever | whomever | |
| which | which | |
| that | that | |
| what | what | |

### INDEFINITE PRONOUNS

| SUBJECTIVE | OBJECTIVE | POSSESSIVE |
|---|---|---|
| anybody | anybody | anybody's |
| everyone | everyone | everyone's |

---

When you use a pronoun to rename the subject following a form of the verb *be* (*is, am, are, was, were*) you create a **subject complement** (see 19a-2). You choose the subjective form because you are restating the subject.

**SUBJECTIVE FORM**  **The last art majors** to get jobs were Becky and **I.**

In conversation, people may use the objective form. In writing, however, choose the correct form. If it sounds stilted or unnatural, rewrite the sentence.

**CONVERSATION**  The new traffic reporter is **him.**

**STILTED**  The new traffic reporter is **he.**

**REWRITTEN**  **He** is the new traffic reporter.

## 2 Choosing objective forms

When you make a pronoun the direct (or indirect) object of an entire sentence, use the objective form.

indirect object    direct object

The company bought **her an antivirus program.**

In addition, use objective forms for pronouns playing other object roles in a sentence.

---

**STRATEGY**    Choosing objective forms

As you edit, check whether a pronoun is acting as an object within some part of a sentence. Check also whether it renames or restates an object. If it plays either role, choose the word's objective form.

object of preposition
The rest of **them** had to wait several months for the software.

object in relative clause
An accountant <u>**whom** the firm hired</u> helped her out.

object in gerund phrase
Mr. Pederson's research for the report included <u>interviewing **them.**</u>

object in participial phrase
<u>Having interviewed **us,**</u> too, Mr. Pederson had a lot of material to summarize.

The report contained interviews with the two dissatisfied workers,
appositive renames object
**her and him.**

---

You may find pronouns used with infinitives (*to* + a verb) tricky so keep the following example in mind.

OBJECTIVE FORM    Mr. Pederson asked **us** to review the minutes.

*Us* might seem the subject of the phrase *to review the minutes.* It is the direct object of the sentence, however (*Mr. Pederson asked* **us**). The objective form is correct.

## 3 Choosing possessive forms

When you use a pronoun to show possession, choose the possessive form. The particular form you use depends on whether the pronoun appears *before a noun* or *in place of a noun.*

BEFORE NOUN    The Topeka office requested a copy of **her** report.

REPLACING NOUN    **Hers** was the most up-to-date study available.

You should also use the possessive form before gerunds (-*ing* verb forms that act as nouns). Because this use of the possessive is often ignored in speech, you may need to practice writing it until it begins to "sound right" to you.

CONVERSATION    Them requesting the report pleased our supervisor.

EDITED    **Their** requesting the report pleased our supervisor.

English nouns also vary in form to show possession, signaled by an apostrophe ('s or '): *the study/the study's conclusions.* (See 39a–b.) Don't confuse nouns and pronouns by adding an apostrophe to a possessive pronoun.

---

**STRATEGY**    Choosing between *its* and *it's*.

*Its*, not *it's*, is the form of the possessive pronoun. Test which you need by replacing the pronoun with *it is* (the expansion of *it's*). If *it is* fits, keep the apostrophe. If *it is* doesn't fit, omit the apostrophe.

DRAFT    The food pantry gave away (*its/it's*) last can of tuna.

REPLACEMENT TEST    The food pantry gave away **it is** last can of tuna. **It is doesn't make sense.**

USE POSSESSIVE    The food pantry gave away **its** last can of tuna.

---

## 21b Editing common pronoun forms

Many problems with pronoun forms occur at predictable places. Pay attention to the following troublesome constructions.

### 1 Pay attention to compound subjects and objects

When you use a compound subject such as *the committee and* I or *Jim and me,* the rule is simple: Use the same case for the pronoun in the compound that you would use for a single pronoun in the same role.

COMPOUND SUBJECT    Denise or (*he? him?*) should check the inventory.

SUBJECTIVE FORM    Denise or **he** should check the inventory.

COMPOUND OBJECT    The coach selected (*she? her? and he? him?*) as captains.

OBJECTIVE FORM    The coach selected **her and him** as captains.

**STRATEGY** Focus-imagine-choose.

* **Focus** on the pronoun whose form you need to choose.

DRAFT          Anne-Marie and **me** will develop the videotape.
                FOCUS: *I* or *me?*

* **Imagine** each choice for the pronoun as the subject (or object).

#1 (INCORRECT)      **Me** will develop the videotape.

#2 (CORRECT)      **I** will develop the videotape.

* **Choose** the correct form for the compound subject (or object).

EDITED         Anne-Marie and **I** will develop the videotape.

If the appropriate form is not immediately clear to you, see the chart in 34a. Choosing what "sounds right" may not work with compounds.

## 2 Watch for pronouns that rename or are paired with nouns

When you rename a preceding noun or pronoun in an **appositive,** match the form of the word being renamed. If you pair pronouns like *we* or *us* with nouns, identify the role of the noun and match the pronoun form with it—*we, they* (subjective) or *us, them* (objective).

**STRATEGY** Test alternatives.

* For appositives, imagine alternative versions of the sentence without the noun (or pronoun) that was renamed.

SENTENCE        The two book illustrators on the panel, (*she? her?*) and (*I? me?*), discussed questions from the audience.

#1 (INCORRECT)      **Her** and **me** discussed questions from the audience.

#2 (CORRECT)      **She** and **I** discussed questions from the audience.

EDITED         The two book illustrators on the panel, **she** and **I**, discussed questions from the audience.

* For pronoun-noun pairs, imagine alternatives without the noun.

SENTENCE        The teaching evaluation should be conducted by (*us? we?*) students, not by the faculty or administration.

#1 (INCORRECT)      The teaching evaluation should be conducted by **we.** . . .

#2 (CORRECT)      The teaching evaluation should be conducted by **us.** . . .

EDITED         The teaching evaluation should be conducted by **us** students, not by the faculty or administration.

## 3 Align comparisons with *than* or *as*

When creating a comparison with *than* or *as* followed by a pronoun, make sure the pronoun form you choose accurately signals the information left out. A pronoun in the subjective case acts as the subject of the implied statement; a pronoun in the objective case acts as the object.

**SUBJECTIVE**   I gave her sister more help than **she** [did].

**OBJECTIVE**   I gave her sister more help than [I gave] **her.**

If readers may miss the grammatical signals, rewrite the sentence.

**MAY BE
AMBIGUOUS**   I like working with Aisha better than she.

READER'S REACTION: **Does this mean that you prefer to work with Aisha? Or that you like to work with Aisha better than someone else does?**

**REWRITTEN**   She doesn't like working with Aisha as much as I do.

## 4 Choose between *who* and *whom*

You often use the pronouns *who* and *whom, whoever* and *whomever* to begin subordinate clauses known as **relative clauses** or **adjective clauses.** Choose *who* and *whoever* when you use the pronouns as subjects; choose *whom* and *whomever* when you use them as objects.

**SUBJECT**   The boy **who wins the race** should get the prize.

**OBJECT**   Give this delicate assignment to **whomever you trust.**

Choose between *who* and *whom* according to the role the pronoun plays *within the relative clause.* Ignore the role the clause plays *within the sentence.*

**DRAFT**   The fine must be paid by **whomever** holds the deed.

**Although the whole clause is the object of the preposition *by*, within the clause the pronoun acts as a subject, not an object.**

**EDITED**   The fine must be paid by **whoever** holds the deed.

At the beginning of a question, you should use *who* when the pronoun is the subject of the sentence and *whom* when the pronoun is an object.

**SUBJECT**   **Who** is most likely to get the reader's sympathy at this point in the novel, Huck or Jim?

**OBJECT**   **Whom** can Cordelia trust at the end of the scene?

# 22 Making Sentence Parts Agree

Readers get mixed signals when sentence parts are not coordinated.

**INCONSISTENT** The city council and the mayor is known for her skillful responses to civic debate.

READER'S REACTION: **I thought the sentence was about two things—the city council and the mayor—but when I read *is* and *her,* it seemed to be about only one, the mayor.**

**EDITED** The city council and the mayor **are** known for **their** skillful responses to civic debate.

Readers expect you to help them understand how the ideas in a sentence relate by making the parts of a sentence work together grammatically—by showing **agreement** in number, person, and gender.

## 22a Recognizing agreement

Within a sentence, a subject and verb should agree in **number** (singular or plural) and **person** (first, second, or third).

You **know** our client. She **wants** to see the design next week.

In addition, each pronoun should agree with its **antecedent,** the noun or other pronoun to which it refers, in **number** (singular, plural), **person** (first, second, third), and **gender** (masculine, feminine, neuter).

The **crews** riding their snowplows left early; the **airport** needed its runways cleared.

---

**AGREEMENT: NUMBER, PERSON, AND GENDER**

- *Number* shows whether words are singular (one person, animal, idea, or thing) or plural (two or more) in meaning.

  **SINGULAR** This **community** needs its own recreation center.

  **PLURAL** Local **communities** need to share their facilities.

*(Continued)*

---

**AGREEMENT: NUMBER, PERSON, AND GENDER** *(Continued)*

- *Person* indicates the speaker or subject being spoken to or about.

  **First person (speaker):** *I, we*
  **I** <u>operate</u> the compressor.      **We** <u>operate</u> the compressor.

  **Second person (spoken to):** *you*
  **You** <u>operate</u> the forklift.

  **Third person (spoken about):** *he, she, it, they*; nouns naming things, people, animals, ideas

  **He/she/it** <u>operates</u> the drill.      **They** <u>operate</u> the drill.

- *Gender* refers to masculine (*he, him*), feminine (*she, her*), or neuter (*it*) qualities attributed to a noun or pronoun.

  **MASCULINE/FEMININE**
  The future <u>father</u> rushed for **his** car keys, while his <u>wife</u> packed **her** bag.

  **NEUTER**
  Despite **its** recent tune-up, the <u>car</u> stalled near the hospital.

---

## 22b Creating subject-verb agreement (simple)

To make subjects and verbs agree, make sure they are aligned in two ways: **number** (singular or plural) and **person** (first, second, or third). Keeping them aligned helps your sentences convey consistent, clear meaning.

### 1 Check subjects, then verbs

First look for the subject. Identify its number (singular or plural) and person (first, second, or third). Then edit the verb so that it agrees.

DRAFT          The clients is waiting.

BOTH PLURAL    The **clients** <u>are</u> waiting.

BOTH SINGULAR  The **client** <u>is</u> waiting.

### 2 Watch out for plurals

Most plural nouns end in -*s* or -*es*, yet exactly the opposite is the case for present tense verbs.

- **Look for a plural subject:** nouns ending in -*s* or -*es*; plural pronouns such as *they* and *we*.

EXCEPTIONS
- Nouns with irregular plurals (*person/people* or *child/children*)
- Nouns with the same form for singular and plural (*moose/moose*)

SINGULAR    The dam prevent**s** flooding.

PLURAL    The dam**s** prevent flooding.

- **Check for a plural verb:** -*s* or -*es* in present tense.

EXCEPTIONS
- Verbs with irregular forms, including *be* and *have* (see 20c)

- **Check the verb again.** If you find a main verb *plus* a helping verb, re-member this: the helping verb *sometimes* changes form for singular and plural, but the main verb remains the same (see 20d).

|  | HELPING VERB CHANGES FORM | HELPING VERB DOES NOT CHANGE |
|---|---|---|
| SINGULAR | The **park** <u>does seem</u> safer. | The **park** <u>might seem</u> safer. |
| PLURAL | The **parks** <u>do seem</u> safer. | The **parks** <u>might seem</u> safer. |

## ESL ADVICE: SUBJECT-VERB AGREEMENT

Some troublesome verbs change form according to person or tense.    **SERIOUS ERROR**

- **Be verbs** (present and past)
  I **am/was.**    He/She/It **is/was.**    You/We/They **are/were.**

- **Helping verb *be*** (present progressive and past progressive tenses)
  I                **am** talking.      I/He/She/It    **was talking.**
  You/We/They    **are** talking.    We/You/They    **were talking.**
  He/She/It      **is** talking.

- **Have verbs** (present)
  I/You/We/They    **have** a new home.    He/She/It    **has** a new home.

- **Helping verb *have*** (present perfect and present perfect progressive tenses)
  I/You/We/They    **have** lived here      **have** been living
                   for years.              here since May.
  He/She/It        **has** lived here       **has** been living
                   for years.              here since May.

- **Do or does to show emphasis**
  I/You/We/They    **do** want the job.    He/She/It    **does** want it.

- **Doesn't or don't to show the negative**
  I/You/We/They    **don't** exercise      He/She/It    **doesn't** exercise
                   enough.                              enough.

SERIOUS ERROR **22c** **Creating subject-verb agreement (complex)**

Checking for subject-verb agreement sometimes becomes complicated. Try to remember the words and structures that cause problems and be ready to look up the editing strategies below.

### 1 Watch for collective nouns or plural nouns with singular meanings

A **collective noun** is singular in form yet identifies a group of individuals (*audience, mob, crew, troop, tribe,* or *herd*). When the group acts as a single unit, choose a singular verb. When group members act individually, choose a plural verb.

ONE SINGLE UNIT   The **staff** is hardworking and well trained.

INDIVIDUAL MEMBERS   The **staff** have earned the respect of our clients.

**Nouns with plural forms and singular meanings.** Nouns like *politics, physics, statistics, mumps,* and *athletics* have -s endings but are singular.

**Mathematics** is an increasingly popular field of study.

**Titles and names.** When your sentence subject is a book title or company name, choose a singular verb even if the name or title is plural. Think to yourself, "The *company* pays . . ." or "The *book* is. . . ."

Home Helpers **pays** high wages and **has** excellent benefits.

**Numbers.** A measurement or figure (even one ending in -s) may still be singular if it names a quantity or unit as a whole. When it refers to individual elements, treat it as a whole.

**Four years** is the amount of time she spent studying stress.

*The White Roses* **is** second on the best-seller list this month.

STRATEGY   **Use the pronoun test**

Decide which pronoun accurately represents a complicated subject: *he, she,* or *it* (singular) or *they* (plural). Read your sentence aloud using this replacement pronoun; edit the verb to agree.

DRAFT   The **news** about the job market _____ surprisingly good.
   PRONOUN TEST: **I could replace "The news" with "It" and say "It is."**

EDITED   The **news** about the job market **is** surprisingly good.

### 2 Check subjects linked by *and, or,* and *nor*

*And* creates a **compound subject;** *or* and *nor* create **alternative subjects.**

**Compound subjects.** Because *and* or *both . . . and* make the subject plural (even if its parts are singular), you generally need to choose a plural verb.

PLURAL          **Ham and eggs** <u>are</u> ingredients in this casserole.

TWO PEOPLE      **My friend and my co-worker** <u>have</u> paintings in the show.

If the parts should be taken as a unit or if the parts designate a single person, thing, or idea, you need to choose a singular verb.

UNIT (SINGULAR) **Ham and eggs** <u>is</u> still my favorite breakfast.

ONE PERSON      **My friend and co-worker** <u>has</u> paintings in the show.

*Both . . . and* always needs a plural verb, whether the elements joined are singular or plural.

> **Both** the president **and** her advisor <u>are</u> in Tokyo this week.

> **Both** the president **and** her advisors <u>are</u> in Tokyo this week.

**Alternative subjects.** When you use *or* or *nor* (*either . . . or, neither . . . nor*) to connect alternative parts of the subject, the verb agrees with the closer part. Putting the plural element closer to the verb often is less awkward.

PLURAL CLOSE    The auditor or **the accountants** <u>review</u> each report.
TO VERB

SINGULAR CLOSE  False records or **late reporting** <u>weakens</u> the review process.
TO VERB

*Either . . . or, neither . . . nor,* and *not only . . . but also* may take either a singular or a plural verb, depending on the subject closer to the verb.

> **Either** the president **or** her <u>advisor</u> <u>is</u> in Tokyo.

> **Neither** the president **nor** her <u>advisors</u> <u>are</u> in Tokyo.

## 3 Pay attention to separated subjects and verbs

When you insert words between the subject and verb of a sentence, you may be tempted to make the verb agree with one of the intervening words rather than the actual subject.

To find the real subject, imagine the subject without intervening words or phrases. Then check that the subject and verb agree.

DRAFT           The new trolley system, featuring expanded routes and lower fares, are especially popular with senior citizens.

FAULTY          The new **trolley system** . . .
AGREEMENT       **are** especially popular with senior citizens.

**EDITED**   The new **trolley system,** featuring expanded routes and lower fares, is especially popular with senior citizens.

## ESL ADVICE:  SEPARATED SUBJECTS AND VERBS

Check for agreement if phrases or clauses separate subject and verb.

**PHRASE**   A person **with sensitive eyes** has to wear sunglasses.

**CLAUSE**   A person **whose eyes are sensitive** has to wear sunglasses.

When the subject is the same in both the main and subordinate clauses, the verbs must agree.

**SAME SUBJECT**   A **person** who **wants** to protect her eyes **wears** sunglasses.

If you mistake a phrase like *as well as, in addition to, together with,* or *along with* for *and,* you may be tempted to treat a noun following it as the subject.

The **provost,** as well as the deans, has issued new guidelines.

If you mean *and,* use the word itself.

**REWRITTEN**   The provost **and** the deans have issued new guidelines.

**DRAFT**   A regular tune-up, along with frequent oil **changes,** prolong the life of your car.

   **IMAGINE: A regular tune-up . . . prolongs the life of your car.**

**EDITED**   A regular **tune-up,** along with frequent oil changes, prolongs the life of your car.

## 4  Recognize unusual word order

When you alter typical word order to create emphasis or ask a question, make sure the verb still agrees with the subject. The verb and subject should agree even with inverted (reversed) word order.

**QUESTION**   Are **popular comedy and action films** mere escapism?

**EMPHASIS**   After victory comes **overconfidence** for many teams.

***There is, there are.*** Expletive constructions such as *there are* and *it is* invert (reverse) the usual subject-verb sentence order, allowing you to put the subject *after* the verb (see 32b-2). Then the verb agrees with the subject that follows it.

| SINGULAR | There is **opportunity** for people starting service industries. |
|---|---|

| PLURAL | There are many **opportunities** for service industries. |
|---|---|

**Is, appears, feels, and other linking verbs.** When you build a sentence around *is, appears, feels* or another linking verb (see 18c), make sure the verb agrees with the subject. You may be tempted to make it agree with the noun or pronoun renaming the subject (the complement, see 18c), but edit carefully to avoid this problem.

|  | subject      verb      complement |
|---|---|
| DRAFT | The chief **obstacle** to change are the **mayor and her allies.** |

| EDITED | The chief **obstacle** to change is the mayor and her allies. |
|---|---|

## ESL ADVICE:  SUBJECT-VERB AGREEMENT

- Check for agreement with compound verbs (more than one verb) in a simple sentence.

   The clerk **collects, sorts,** and **files** reports.

- Check for subject-verb agreement in a complex sentence (see 19d).

| ADVERB CLAUSE | When the snow **falls,** we enjoy the scenery. |
|---|---|
| ADJECTIVE CLAUSE | The young man that I work with **lives** in town. |
| ADJECTIVE CLAUSE | The young man that **works** with me **lives** in town. |

- Check for correct selection of helping verbs.

| THIRD PERSON DOES | That restaurant **does** give special dinner discounts. |
|---|---|
| MODAL | The president **might** give a speech this evening. |

## 5 Pay attention to troublesome words

Watch for words such as *all, everybody, who, that,* and *each.*

**All, everybody, none.** *All, everybody,* and *none* (and other indefinite pronouns) do not refer to specific ideas, people, or things. Most have clearly singular meanings and require singular verbs.

**Someone** is mailing campaign flyers.

**Everybody** has the duty to vote.

You can treat a few pronouns, such as *all, any, most, none,* and *some,* as either singular or plural according to meaning.

---

### SOME INDEFINITE AND RELATIVE PRONOUNS

| GENERALLY SINGULAR | | PLURAL | EITHER SINGULAR OR PLURAL |
|---|---|---|---|
| another | neither | both | all |
| anybody | nobody | few | any |
| anyone | none | many | enough |
| anything | no one | others | more |
| each | nothing | several | most |
| either | one | | some |
| every | other | | that |
| everybody | somebody | | which |
| everyone | someone | | who |
| everything | something | | whose |
| much | | | |

---

> **STRATEGY**   Ask "Can it be counted?"

- Does the pronoun refer to something that *cannot be counted*? Choose singular.

> **SINGULAR**   **All** of the <u>food</u> **is** for the camping trip next week.
> *food* = **food in general (not countable);** *all* = **singular**

- Does the pronoun refer to two or more elements of something that *can be counted*? Choose plural.

> **PLURAL**   **All** of the <u>supplies</u> **are** for the camping trip next week.
> *supplies* = **many kinds of supplies (countable), such as baking mixes, bottled water, and dried fruit;** *all* = **plural**

***Who, which,*** **and** ***that.*** *Who, which,* and *that* (relative pronouns, see 18b) do not have singular and plural forms, yet the words to which they refer (antecedents) generally do. Choose a singular or plural verb according to the number of the antecedent.

**SINGULAR**   He likes **a film** that **focuses** on the characters.

**PLURAL**   I prefer **films** that **combine** action and romance.

Make a habit of noticing the phrases *one of* and *the only one of.* They can create agreement problems when they come before *who, which,* or *that.*

Dr Tazu is **one** of the engineers who <u>design</u> storage systems.

*Who* refers to the plural *engineers;* the verb, *design,* is plural. There are other engineers like Dr. Tazu.

Dr. Tazu is **the only one** of the engineers who designs storage systems.

*Who* refers to the singular *Dr. Tazu;* the verb, *designs,* is singular. Dr. Tazu is the only one who designs storage systems.

***Each* and *every.*** Your placement of *each* or *every* can create a singular (*each one*) or plural (*they each*) meaning.

*Each* before compound subject + singular verb
**Each** supervisor and manager checks the logs daily.

*Each* after compound subject + plural verb
The supervisors and managers **each** check the logs daily.

## ESL ADVICE: QUANTIFIERS

A **quantifier**—a word like *each, one,* or *many*—indicates the amount or quantity of a subject.

EXPRESSIONS FOLLOWED BY A PLURAL NOUN + A SINGULAR VERB
Each of/Every one of/One of/None of     the **students** lives on campus.

EXPRESSIONS FOLLOWED BY A PLURAL NOUN + A PLURAL VERB
Several of/Many of/Both of         the **students** live off campus.

In some cases, the noun after the expression determines the verb form.

EXPRESSIONS FOLLOWED BY EITHER A SINGULAR OR A PLURAL VERB

                              noncount noun + singular verb
Some of/Most of/All of/A lot of     the **produce** is fresh.

                              plural noun + plural verb
Some of/Most of/All of/A lot of     the **vegetables** are fresh.

*MUCH AND MOST* (NOT *MUCH OF* OR *MOST OF*) WITH NONCOUNT AND PLURAL NOUNS
NONCOUNT NOUN    **Much traffic** occurs during rush hour.

PLURAL NOUN      **Most Americans** live in the cities or suburbs.

*Other, others,* and *another* may act as pronouns or adjectives.

PRONOUNS
***Others* + plural verb:** adds points about a topic; there may be more points.

I enjoy Paris for many reasons. Some reasons are the architecture and gardens; **others are** the wonderful people, culture, and language.

*The others* (plural) **+ plural verb;** *the other* (singular) **+ singular verb:** adds the last point or points about the topic; there are no more.

Some hikers favor Craig's plan; **the others want** to follow Tina's.

**ADJECTIVES**

*Another* **+ singular noun:** adds an idea; there may be more ideas.
*Other* **+ plural noun:** adds more ideas; there may be more ideas.

One strength of our engineering team is our knowledge of the problem. **Another strength** is our experience. **Other strengths** include our communication skills, teamwork, and energy.

*The other* **+ singular or plural noun:** adds the final point or points to be discussed.

Of the two very important sights to see in Paris, one is the Louvre Museum, and **the other one** is the Cathedral of Notre Dame.

One of the major sights in Paris is the Louvre Museum. **The other sights** are the Eiffel Tower, the Champs-Élysées, the Cathedral of Notre Dame, and the Arc de Triomphe.

## 22d  Creating pronoun-antecedent agreement

Agreement between a pronoun and its antecedent (in **number, person,** and **gender**—see 22a) helps readers recognize the link between them.

plural antecedent      pronoun
**Campers** should treat **their** tents with a mildew-preventing spray.

---

**STRATEGY**  **Find the specific word to which a pronoun refers.**

If you are uncertain about which pronoun form to use, circle or mark the specific word (or words) to which it refers. Then edit either the pronoun or the antecedent so that the two elements match.

**INCONSISTENT**    Proposals should address its audience.

**CLEAR**    **Proposals** should address **their audiences.**

**CLEAR**    **A proposal** should address **its audience.**

A **collective noun** such as *team, group, clan, audience, army,* or *tribe* can act as a singular or plural antecedent, depending on whether it refers to the group as a whole or to the members acting separately.

SINGULAR    The **subcommittee** submitted **its** revised report.

PLURAL    The **subcommittee** discussed **their** concerns.

## 1 Check antecedents linked by *and*, *or*, and *nor*

When a pronoun refers to several things (Luis *and* Jennifer, for example), the pronoun form you choose usually depends on the word that links the elements of the antecedent.

**Antecedents joined by *and*.** When you form a **compound antecedent** by joining two or more antecedents with *and*, refer to them with a plural pronoun (such as *they*), even if one or more are singular.

**Luis and Jenni** said that the lab tests they ran were conclusive.

**The other students and I** admit that the tests we ran were not.

This guideline has two exceptions.

- If a compound antecedent refers to a single person, thing, or idea, use a singular pronoun.

  **My colleague and co-author** is someone skilled at lab analysis.

- If you place *each* or *every* before a compound antecedent to single out the individual members of the compound, use a singular pronoun.

  **Each** of the soil and water samples arrives in its own container.

**Antecedents joined by *or* or *nor*.** When you join the parts of an antecedent with *or* or *nor* (or *either . . . or*, *neither . . . nor*), make sure the pronoun agrees with the part closer to it.

**Neither** the manager **nor** the **engineers** wrote their reports on time.

If one part is singular and the other plural, try putting the plural element second or rewriting to avoid an awkward or confusing sentence.

CONFUSING    Either Jim and Al or Dalhat will include the projections in his report.

READER'S REACTION: **Will Jim and Al add to Dalhat's report? Or will the projections go into one of two reports, Dalhat's or Jim and Al's?**

EDITED    Either Dalhat or **Jim** and **Al** will include the projections in their report.

**REWRITTEN**   Either Dalhat will include the projections in his report, or Jim
and Al will include them in theirs.

**REWRITTEN**   Either Dalhat or Jim and Al will include the projections in the
team's report.

## 2 Watch for pronouns that refer to other pronouns

Many words like *somebody* and *each* (indefinite pronouns see 18b-5) are
singular. The pronouns that refer to them should also be singular.

**Somebody** on the team left her racket on the court.

**Each** of the men has his own equipment.

To avoid either sexist language (see 35a) or inconsistency, use *both* a plural pronoun and a plural antecedent, especially when writing for the academic community.

**SEXIST**   **Everybody** included charts in **his** sales **talk.**

**INFORMAL**
**(SPOKEN)**   **Everybody** included charts in **their** sales **talks.**

**WRITTEN**   **All presenters** included charts in **their** sales **talks.**

---

### ESL ADVICE: DEMONSTRATIVE ADJECTIVES OR PRONOUNS

**Demonstrative adjectives** or **pronouns** are either singular (*this, that*)
or plural (*these, those*), depending on the noun being modified. (See 18b.)

**INCONSISTENT**   This crystals of water make snowflakes.

**BOTH PLURAL**   **These crystals** of water make snowflakes.

**INCONSISTENT**   Those snowflake crystal is made of frozen water.

**BOTH SINGULAR**   **That snowflake crystal** is made of frozen water.

# 23 Using Adjectives and Adverbs

If you confuse adjectives and adverbs or use them improperly, many
readers will notice these errors.

**DRAFT**    The new medication acts **quick.**

**READER'S REACTION:** *Quick* **doesn't fit here. Maybe the writer is careless
or doesn't know what to use.**

**EDITED**    The new medication acts **quickly.**

Although academic readers may be especially alert to these differences, use
modifiers carefully in formal contexts, whatever the community.

## 23a Recognizing what adjectives and adverbs do

Adjectives and adverbs modify—add to, qualify, focus, limit, or extend
the meaning of—other words and thus are called **modifiers.**

---

### FEATURES OF ADJECTIVES AND ADVERBS

**ADJECTIVES**
- Modify nouns and pronouns
- Answer "How many?" "What kind?" "Which one (or ones)?" "What
  size, color, or shape?"
- Include words like *blue, complicated, good,* and *frightening*
- Include words created by adding endings like *-able, -ical, -less, -ful,* and
  *-ous* to nouns or verbs (such as *controllable, sociological, seamless,
  careful, nervous*)

**ADVERBS**
- Modify verbs, adjectives, and other adverbs
- Modify phrases (*almost* beyond the building), clauses (*soon after* I added
  the last ingredients), and sentences (*Remarkably,* the mechanism was not
  damaged.)
- Answer "When?" "Where?" "How?" "How often?" "Which direction?"
  "What degree?"
- Consist mostly of words ending in *-ly,* like *quickly* and *carefully*
- Include some common words that do not end in *-ly,* such as *fast, very,
  well, quite,* and *late*

---

You can use most modifiers in three forms, depending on how many things
you compare—no other things, two things, or three or more.

**POSITIVE**    The cab drove **quickly** on the **smooth** road.

**COMPARATIVE (2)**    The cab drove **more quickly** on the **smoother** road.

**SUPERLATIVE (3+)**    The cab drove **most quickly** on the **smoothest** road.

## COMPARATIVE AND SUPERLATIVE FORMS

### ADJECTIVES

**ONE SYLLABLE**
Most add -er and -est (*pink, pinker, pinkest*).

**TWO SYLLABLES**
Many add -er and -est (*happy, happier, happiest*).
Some add either -er and -est or *more* and *most* (*foggy, foggier, foggiest; foggy, more foggy, most foggy*).

**THREE (OR MORE) SYLLABLES**
Add *more* and *most* (*plentiful, more plentiful, most plentiful*).

### ADVERBS

**ONE SYLLABLE**
Most add -er and -est (*quick, quicker, quickest*).

**TWO (OR MORE) SYLLABLES**
Most add *more* and *most* (*carefully, more carefully, most carefully*).

### NEGATIVE COMPARISONS

**ADJECTIVES AND ADVERBS**
Use *less* and *least* (*less agile, least agile; less clearly, least clearly*).

## IRREGULAR COMPARATIVES AND SUPERLATIVES

| ADJECTIVE | COMPARATIVE | SUPERLATIVE |
|---|---|---|
| bad | worse | worst |
| good | better | best |
| ill (harsh, unlucky) | worse | worst |
| a little | less | least |
| many | more | most |
| much | more | most |
| some | more | most |
| well (healthy) | better | best |

| ADVERB | | |
|---|---|---|
| badly | worse | worst |
| ill (badly) | worse | worst |
| well (satisfactorily) | better | best |

When you use two or more adjectives in a series, you need to place them in the appropriate order before the main noun.

---

**ESL ADVICE:** ADJECTIVES IN A SERIES

| DETERMINER | QUALITY | PHYSICAL DESCRIPTION | NATIONALITY | MATERIAL | QUALIFYING NOUN | MAIN NOUN |
|---|---|---|---|---|---|---|
| that | expensive | smooth black | German | fiberglass | racing | car |
| four | little | round white | | plastic | Ping-Pong | balls |
| several | beautiful | young red | Japanese | | maple | trees |

---

## 23b Editing adjectives and adverbs

Because not all adverbs end in -ly and some adjectives do (*friendly, lonely*), you can't always rely on -ly to help you choose a modifier.

### 1 Figure out what a modifier does in a sentence

First try to analyze what the modifier will do in your sentence.

- Do you need an adjective? Adjectives answer the questions "How many?" "What kind?" "Which one (or ones)?" or "What size, color, or shape?"
- Or do you need an adverb? Adverbs answer the questions "When?" "Where?" "How?" "How often?" "Which direction?" or "What degree?"

DRAFT        Write **careful** so that the directions are clear.

QUESTION: **Write how? This word answers an adverb question.**

EDITED       Write **carefully** so that the directions are clear.

The word modified also can tell you whether to use an adverb or adjective.

---

**STRATEGY**    Draw an arrow.

Point to the word that is modified. If this word acts as a noun or pronoun, modify it with an adjective; if it acts as a verb, adjective, or adverb, modify it with an adverb.

DRAFT        The insulation underwent **remarkable** quick deterioration.

CONNECTION: **Remarkable modifies *quick* (and answers the adverb question "How quick?"). *Quick* in turn modifies *deterioration* (and answers the adjective question "What kind of deterioration?") Replace *remarkable* with an adverb.**

EDITED       The insulation underwent **remarkably** quick deterioration.

### 2 Check the sentence pattern

Verbs such as *look, feel,* and *prove* can show both states of being (**linking verbs**) and activities (**action verbs**). The verb *is* always acts as a linking verb. Choose an adjective for a state of being; choose an adverb for an action or activity.

| subject | linking verb | complement (adjective) |
|---|---|---|
| The room | smelled | musty. |

The procedure    proved    unreliable.

**ADJECTIVE (BEING)** The metal cover over the motor <u>turned</u> **hot.**

**ADVERB (ACTION)** The large wheel <u>turned</u> **quickly.**

**ADJECTIVE**        The movement <u>grew</u> **rapid.** [The motion became quick.]

**ADVERB**          The movement <u>grew</u> **rapidly.** [The group spread its ideas.]

## 3 Pay special attention to *real/really, sure/surely, bad/badly,* and *good/well*

Common uses of *real/really, sure/surely, bad/badly,* and *good/well,* may be acceptable in speech but not in other settings.

**INFORMAL SPEECH** I feel **badly** that our group argues so much.

> **READER'S REACTION: Someone who *feels badly* has a poor sense of touch.**

**BAD/BADLY; GOOD/WELL**

- Use *bad* (adjective) with linking verbs such as *is, seems,* or *appears* (see 18c, 19a-2).

  I feel **bad** that our group argues so much. [not *badly*]

- Use *badly* (adverb) with action verbs.

  The new breathing apparatus <u>works</u> **badly.** [not *bad*]

- Use *good* (adjective) with linking verbs.

  The chef's new garlic dressing <u>tastes</u> **good.** [not *well*]

- Use *well* (adverb) with action verbs unless it refers to health.

  The new pump <u>works</u> **well.** [not *good*]

**REAL/REALLY; SURE/SURELY**

- Use *really* (adverb) to modify an adjective like *fast, efficient,* or *hot.*

  Lu Ming is **really** <u>efficient.</u> [not *real*]

  Lu Ming works **really** <u>efficiently.</u> [not *real*]

- Use *surely* (adverb) to modify adjectives like *misleading, outdated,* or *courageous.*

  This diagram is **surely** <u>misleading.</u> [not *sure*]

## 4 Pay attention to comparisons and double negatives

Someone with only two children may say, "She's my oldest." In writing, however, you need to be more precise.

To compare two things, use the **comparative form** (-*er* or *more*); to compare three or more, use the **superlative form** (-*est* or *most*).

INACCURATE   The survey covered four age groups: 20–29, 30–44, 45–59, and 60+. Those in the older group smoked least.

READER'S REACTION: **Does this mean that the people in the older *groups* smoked least or that the people in the *oldest* group smoked least?**

PRECISE   The survey covered four age groups: 20–29, 30–44, 45–59, and 60+. Those in the **oldest group** smoked least.

**Double comparatives.** Most readers will not accept a double comparative (combining the -*er* form and *more*) or a double superlative (combining the -*est* form and *most*).

DRAFT   Jorge is the **most agilest** athlete in the squadron.

EDITED   Jorge is the **most agile** athlete in the squadron.

**Illogical comparatives.** Some adjectives and adverbs such as *unique, impossible, pregnant, dead, gone, perfectly*, and *entirely* cannot logically take comparative or superlative form.

ILLOGICAL   Gottlieb's "Nightscape" is a **most unique** painting.

READER'S REACTION: **How can a thing be *more* or *most* if it is unique—the only one?**

LOGICAL   Gottlieb's "Nightscape" is a **unique** painting.

**Double negatives.** Informal speech and dialects may combine negatives such as *no, none, not, never, hardly, scarcely*, and *haven't* and *don't* (formed with *n't*, abbreviating *not*). In writing, however, readers are likely to feel that two negatives used together—a **double negative**—cancel each other out.

DRAFT   The nurses **can't hardly** manage routine care, much less emergencies.

READER'S REACTION: **This sounds more like a conversation than a staffing report.**

EDITED   The nurses **can hardly** manage routine care, much less emergencies.

# Editing Sentence Problems: Understanding Community Options

 **▼ *TAKING IT ONLINE***

### WHAT IS A SENTENCE FRAGMENT?

http://www.harpercollege.edu/writ_ctr/fragmnt.htm

This Web site includes examples, suggestions, and links to two simple tests for detecting fragments. Its conversational tone makes this site easy to understand and use.

### ALMOST . . . EVERYTHING YOU WANTED TO KNOW ABOUT COMMA SPLICES

http://www.uark.edu/campus-resources/qwrtcntr/resources/handouts/commasp2.html

This site includes definitions, examples, and an exercise on comma splices, fused sentences, and fragments.

### THE MISPLACED MODIFIER, A.K.A. THE SENTENCE DANGLER

http://ace.acadiau.ca/english/grammar/mmodifier.htm

This page identifies one of the "ten most wanted" grammar outlaws and includes quizzes to help you rehabilitate this outlaw.

### SEQUENCE OF VERB TENSES

http://ccc.commnet.edu/grammar/sequence.htm

Take a look at the handy charts on the sequence of tenses for active verbs, infinitives, and participles.

### PARALLELISM

http://www.english.uiuc.edu/cws/wworkshop

Visit "Parallelism" in both the "Grammar Handbook" and "Tips & Techniques" for advice on what parallel structure is and how to use it effectively.

### COORDINATION/SUBORDINATION

http://students.itec.sfsu.edu/ised783/Writing/coord.html

This site can help you use coordination and subordination effectively.

# PART 6

# Editing Sentence Problems: Understanding Community Options

# 24 Editing Sentence Fragments

If you present a group of words as a sentence when they do not form a complete sentence, you are likely to irritate readers and undermine your authority as a writer.

**PARTS MISSING**   The insurance company processing the claim.

   READER'S REACTION: **Something is missing. What did the company *do*?**

**EDITED**   **The insurance company** processing the claim <u>sent</u> a check.

Despite having a capital letter at the beginning and a period at the end, a **sentence fragment** is only part of a sentence, not a complete sentence.

A fragment is considered the most serious sentence-level error by many college instructors as well as workplace and public readers. On occasion, an **intentional fragment** may create emphasis or a change of pace, especially in imaginative writing (see 24c). An unintentional fragment, however, forces readers to do the writer's job, mentally reattaching a word group to a nearby sentence or supplying missing information. If you make readers do your work, they may be too distracted to attend to your ideas and may harshly judge your writing (and you as a writer).

## 24a Recognizing sentence fragments

Before you can edit fragments effectively, you need to be able to distinguish complete sentences from word groups missing a subject or a verb (see 19a) and from clauses detached from sentences to which they belong.

### 1 Look for a subject and a verb

A **complete sentence** contains both a subject and a complete verb, expressed or implied. If a word group lacks either, it's a fragment.

> **STRATEGY**   Ask questions
>
> **Sentence Test 1: Ask *Who* (or *what*) *does*? Or *Who* (or *what*) *is*?**
>
> - Does a word group answer "Who?" or "What?" If not, it *lacks a subject* and is a fragment.

| | |
|---|---|
| **FRAGMENT** | Also needs a family counselor. |
| | READER'S REACTION: **I can't tell *who* (or *what*) needs a counselor.** |
| **EDITED** | **Hope Clinic** also needs a family counselor. |
| **IMPERATIVE** | **[You]** Use the spectrometer to test for the unknown chemical. |

In an imperative sentence (see 19d-2), the subject *you* is understood and needn't be stated.

• Does a word group answer "Does?" or "Is?" If not, it *lacks a verb* and is a fragment.

| | |
|---|---|
| **FRAGMENT** | The new policy to provide health care coverage on the basis of hours worked each week. |
| | READER'S REACTION: **I can't tell what the new policy *does* or *is*.** |
| **EDITED** | The new policy **provides** health care coverage on the basis of hours worked each week. |

**Sentence Test 2:** See if you can turn a word group into a question that can be answered *yes* or *no*. If you can, the word group is a sentence.

| | |
|---|---|
| **WORD GROUP** | They bought a van to carry the equipment. |
| **QUESTION** | Did they buy a van to carry the equipment? |
| **CONCLUSION** | The word group is a sentence. |
| **WORD GROUP** | Bought the building for a warehouse. |
| **QUESTION** | Did _____ buy the building for a warehouse? |
| **CONCLUSION** | The question doesn't have a subject, so the word group is a fragment. |
| **EDITED** | **Johnson Plumbing** bought the building for a warehouse. |
| **WORD GROUP** | The company providing repairs for our computers. |
| **QUESTION** | Does the company **providing** repairs for our computers? |
| | CAUTION: **Do not begin the question with *is, are, has,* or *have,* or you may unintentionally provide a verb for the word group being tested.** |
| **CONCLUSION** | *Providing* can't act as the verb in its current form, so this is a fragment. |
| **EDITED** | The company **is** providing repairs for our computers. |

---

### RECOGNIZING A SENTENCE

A **sentence**—also called a **main** (or **independent**) **clause**—is a word group with a subject and verb that can stand alone.

SENTENCE          **The hungry bears** were hunting food.

SENTENCE          Because spring snows had damaged many plants, **the hungry bears** were hunting food in urban areas.

A **subordinate** (or **dependent**) **clause** has a subject and a predicate, yet it cannot stand on its own as a sentence because it begins with a subordinating word like *because, although, which*, or *that*.

FRAGMENT          Because **spring snows** had damaged many plants.

A **phrase** is a word group that lacks a subject, a predicate, or both. It cannot stand alone.

FRAGMENTS          were hunting      in urban areas      the hungry bears

---

**Confusing verbs and verbals.** In checking for fragments, be careful not to mistake a **verbal** for a verb. Verbals include participles (*testing, tested*), infinitives (*to test*), and gerunds (*testing*) (see 19b–4). A verbal alone can never act as the verb in a sentence. If you add words like *is, has, can,* or *should* (helping verbs, see 20d), you can turn verbals into verbs (*was testing, should test*).

## 2 Look for words like *although, because, that, and since*

Pay attention to word groups containing a subject and a verb but beginning with subordinators such as *although, if, because,* or *that* (see the list in 31c). These words tell readers to regard the clause that follows as part of a larger statement.

Once you have identified a word group beginning with a subordinator or with a relative pronoun (*that, what, which,* or *who*; see 21a), check whether it is attached to a main clause—a cluster of words that can stand on its own as a sentence (see box, above). If the word group is unattached, it is a fragment.

FRAGMENT          Residents love the mild climate. Which **has encouraged outdoor events.**

EDITED            Residents love the mild climate, **which** has encouraged outdoor events.

### 3 Pay attention to *for example* and verbal fragments

Word groups beginning with phrases like *for example, such as,* or *for instance* are sometimes disconnected from sentences and mistakenly made to stand on their own. Often, too, verbal phrases (verbal plus object and modifiers, 19b–4) are detached from related sentences and asked, inappropriately, to stand on their own.

**SERIOUS ERROR** **24b** Editing sentence fragments

You can correct sentence fragments in four ways.

### 1 Supply the missing element

| | |
|---|---|
| FRAGMENT | **The judge allowing adopted children to meet their natural parents**. |
| EDITED (VERB ADDED) | The judge **favors** allowing adopted children to meet their natural parents. |

### 2 Attach the fragment to a nearby main clause. Rewrite if necessary

| | |
|---|---|
| FRAGMENT | Trauma centers give prompt care to heart attack victims. <u>Because</u> **rapid treatment can minimize heart damage**. |
| ATTACHED | Trauma centers give prompt care to heart attack victims **because** rapid treatment can minimize heart damage. |
| FRAGMENT | **Introducing competing varieties of crabs into the same tank**. He did this in order to study aggression. |
| REWRITTEN | He **introduced** competing varieties of crabs into the same tank in order to study aggression. |

### 3 Drop a subordinating word, turning a fragment into a sentence

| | |
|---|---|
| FRAGMENT | **Although** several people argued against the motion. It still passed by a majority. |
| EDITED | Several people argued against the motion. It still passed by a majority. |

### 4. Rewrite a passage to eliminate a fragment

| | |
|---|---|
| FRAGMENT | Some sports attract many participants in their fifties, sixties, and even seventies. **For example**, **tennis and bowling**. |

**EDITED
(ATTACHED)**    Some sports, **such as tennis and bowling**, attract many participants in their fifties, sixties, and even seventies.

**REWRITTEN
(EMPHASIZED)**    Some sports attract many participants in their fifties, sixties, and even seventies. For example, **tennis and bowling appeal to older adults year-round**.

## 24c  Using partial sentences

In magazines, campaign literature, advertisements, and even well-written essays, you may encounter **partial sentences**—sentence fragments used intentionally, effectively, but sparingly. Partial sentences can call attention to details ("Deep rose, not red."), emphasize ideas ("Wilson. For the future."), heighten contrasts ("And in the last lane, my brother."), or add transition ("Next, the results."). Other uses include informal questions and answers ("Where?" "On my desk.") and exclamations ("Too bad!").

- Use partial sentences only when readers are likely to accept them.
- When in doubt, seek a reader's advice, or look at comparable writing.
- Have a clear purpose—describing, emphasizing, or contrasting.
- Be sure readers can supply missing elements or connect word groups.
- Make sure readers won't mistake your partial sentence for a fragment.

## 25  Editing Comma Splices and Fused Sentences

You can easily confuse and annoy readers if you inappropriately join two or more sentences using either a comma only (**comma splice**) or no punctuation at all (**fused sentence**). If you don't clearly mark the parts and boundaries of a sentence, readers may have to puzzle over its meaning.

**COMMA SPLICE**    CBS was founded in 1928 by William S. Paley, his uncle and his father sold him a struggling radio network.

**READER'S REACTION: At first I thought CBS had three founders: Paley, his uncle, and his father. Then I realized that Paley probably bought the network from his relatives.**

**EDITED**    CBS was founded in 1928 by William S. Paley ; his uncle and his father sold him a struggling radio network.

**FUSED SENTENCE** The city had only one swimming pool without an admission fee the pool was poorly maintained.

**READER'S REACTION: I can't decide whether the single pool in town is poorly maintained or the only free pool is in bad shape.**

**EDITED** The city had only one swimming pool **, but** without an admission fee, the pool was poorly maintained.

A **comma splice** links what could be two sentences (two main or independent clauses) by a comma alone. On the other hand, a **fused sentence** (or **run-on sentence**) joins what could be two sentences without any punctuation mark or connecting word to establish clear sentence boundaries. These errors are likely to occur when you draft quickly or when you write sentences with the same subject, related or contrasting ideas, or one illustrating the other.

## 25a Recognizing comma splices

To find comma splices, look for commas scattered between word groups that could stand on their own as sentences. Join these word groups by more than a comma alone.

**COMMA SPLICE** The typical Navajo husband serves as a trustee, the wife and her children own the family's property.

**EDITED** The typical Navajo husband serves as a trustee **, but** the wife and her children own the family's property.

**READER'S REACTION: Until you added *but*, I missed your point about the woman playing a more important role than the man.**

 **SERIOUS ERROR** ## 25b Recognizing fused sentences

Although fused sentences may be any length, look for long sentences with little or no internal punctuation. Such sentences may combine freestanding (main) clauses without signaling their relationships.

If your sentence seems to contain more than one statement, check for appropriate punctuation and connecting words.

**FUSED SENTENCE** The scientists had trouble identifying the fossil skeleton it resembled that of both a bird and a lizard.

**WRITER'S REACTION: I've made two statements here.**

**EDITED** The scientists had trouble identifying the fossil skeleton **because** it resembled that of both a bird and a lizard.

**READER'S REACTION: Adding *because* separates the two main points and makes the ideas easier to understand.**

**25c** Editing comma splices and fused sentences

Here are six strategies for correcting comma splices and fused sentences. As you edit, choose a strategy that brings your ideas into sharper perspective, creates emphasis, and highlights relationships.

### 1 Create separate sentences. (____. ____.)

**COMMA SPLICE**   The sport calls for a total of fourteen people (or twelve people and two dogs) divided into two teams, they throw a disk called a Frisbee up and down a field.

**EDITED**   The sport calls for a total of fourteen people (or twelve people and two dogs) divided into two teams• **T**hey throw a disk called a Frisbee up and down a field.

**FUSED SENTENCE**   Football does not cause the most injuries among student athletes gymnastics is the most dangerous sport.

**EDITED**   Football does not cause the most injuries among student athletes• **G**ymnastics is the most dangerous sport.

### 2 Use a comma plus *and, but, or, for, nor, so,* or *yet.* (____ , and ____.)

When main clauses convey equally important ideas, try linking them with a comma plus a coordinating conjunction telling how they relate.

**COMMA SPLICE**   The finance department has reviewed the plan, the operations department is still analyzing it.

**EDITED**   The finance department has reviewed the plan **,** **but** the operations department is still analyzing it.

**FUSED SENTENCE**   The emergency room is understaffed it still performs well.

**EDITED**   The emergency room is understaffed **,** **yet** it still performs well.

Three or more closely related clauses can be punctuated as a series to emphasize their connection. Especially for the academic community, include both a comma and a coordinating conjunction before the last item (see 37d).

**SERIES OF CLAUSES**   We collected the specimens, we cleaned them **,** **and** we measured them.

### 3 Make one clause subordinate. (*Because* ____, ____.)

Subordinators such as *although, when, because, until, where,* and *unless* (see 43c) can specify a range of relationships between clauses, as can relative pronouns such as *who, which,* or *that.* A **subordinate clause** includes the subordinator plus a subject and a verb; it cannot stand alone as a sentence.

COMMA SPLICE    Automobiles are increasingly complex, skilled mechanics may spend several weeks a year in training.

EDITED    **Because** automobiles are increasingly complex, skilled mechanics may spend several weeks a year in training.

FUSED SENTENCE    Margaret Atwood is best known for her novels her essays and poems are also worth reading.

EDITED    **Although** Margaret Atwood is best known for her novels, her essays and poems are also worth reading.

## 4 Use a semicolon. (___; ___.)

Use a semicolon to join two main clauses and emphasize their similar importance. (See 38a.)

COMMA SPLICE    An autopilot is a device that corrects drift, the system senses and reacts to changes in the aircraft's motion.

EDITED    An autopilot is a device that corrects drift; the system senses and reacts to changes in the aircraft's motion.

FUSED SENTENCE    Most colleges offer alternatives to four years on campus study abroad, exchange programs with other schools, and cooperative programs are common.

EDITED    Most colleges offer alternatives to four years on campus; study abroad, exchange programs with other schools, and cooperative programs are common.

## 5 Use wording like *however, moreover, for example,* and *in contrast* plus a semicolon. (___; however, ___.)

*However, consequently, moreover,* and other **conjunctive adverbs** (see 31a–b) specify relationships between clauses. You can use transitional expressions such as *in contrast* and *in addition* for similar purposes.

COMMA SPLICE    To draw the human body, you must understand it, therefore, art students sometimes dissect cadavers.

EDITED    To draw the human body, you must understand it; **therefore,** art students sometimes dissect cadavers.

FUSED SENTENCE    Chickens reach market size within months the lobster takes six to eight years.

| EDITED | Chickens reach market size within months **;** **in contrast ,** the lobster takes six to eight years. |
|---|---|

Conjunctive adverbs and transitional expressions can begin the second main clause or appear within it. Set them off with a comma or commas; join the clauses with a semicolon (see 38a-1).

| BEGINNING OF CLAUSE | The Great Lakes were once heavily polluted **;** **however ,** recently fish and other wildlife have returned. |
|---|---|
| MIDDLE OF CLAUSE | The Great Lakes were once heavily polluted **;** recently **,** **however ,** fish and other wildlife have returned. |
| END OF CLAUSE | The Great Lakes were once heavily polluted **;** recently fish and other wildlife have returned **,** **however**. |

## 6 Use a colon. ( ___ : ___ .)

When a clause summarizes, illustrates, or restates a preceding clause, you can join them with a colon. (See 38b-3.)

| COMMA SPLICE | Foreign study calls for extensive language preparation, vaccinations and a passport are not enough. |
|---|---|
| EDITED | Foreign study calls for extensive language preparation **:** vaccinations and a passport are not enough. |

### ESL ADVICE: *BECAUSE* AND *BECAUSE OF*

The subordinator *because* introduces a clause with a subject and verb; the preposition *because of* introduces a phrase with its object.

| DRAFT | Because of the pay is low, José must look for another job. |
|---|---|
| EDITED | **Because** the pay is low, José must look for another job. |
| EDITED | **Because of** the low pay, José must look for another job. |

### ESL ADVICE: CONNECTING WORDS WITH THE SAME MEANING

Connecting words may have the same meaning but need different punctuation.

| COORDINATOR | José likes his job **,** **but** it doesn't pay enough. |
|---|---|
| CONJUNCTIVE ADVERB | José likes his job **;** **however ,** it doesn't pay enough. |

---

## ESL ADVICE: SENTENCE VARIETY

American academic and workplace readers tend to prefer short sentences with varied sentence patterns. Native speakers usually avoid comma splices and fused sentences by creating separate sentences, adding a coordinating conjunction with a comma, or creating a subordinate clause. Sophisticated writers sometimes use a semicolon or colon for special effect.

# 26 | Creating Pronoun Reference

Readers expect pronouns to make a sentence less repetitive and easier to understand by taking the place of nouns (or other pronouns). For this substitution to work effectively, your readers must recognize the word to which a pronoun refers so they can tell exactly what the sentence means.

**AMBIGUOUS REFERENCE**
Much of my life with the circus consisted of leading the elephants from the cages and hosing **them** down.

READER'S REACTION: **What got hosed down? elephants? cages? both?**

**EDITED**
Much of my life with the circus consisted of hosing the elephants down after leading **them** from **their** cages.

The word to which the pronoun refers is known as its **antecedent** (or **headword**). When **pronoun reference**—the connection between pronoun and antecedent—isn't clear and specific, readers may be confused. By creating clear pronoun reference, you tie ideas and sentences together, clarify their relationships, and focus readers' attention.

 SERIOUS ERROR **26a** Recognizing unclear pronoun reference

If readers say they "get lost" reading your work or "can't figure out what you are saying," make sure each pronoun refers *clearly* to one specific antecedent, either one word or several words acting as a unit.

### 1 Watch for ambiguous or distant pronoun reference

A pronoun may seem to refer to more than one possible antecedent (**ambiguous reference**) or may be too distant from its antecedent (**remote reference**) for a reader to recognize the connection.

AMBIGUOUS
REFERENCE

Robespierre and Danton disagreed over the path the French Revolution should take. **He** believed that the Revolution was endangered by internal enemies.

READER'S REACTION: **I'm lost. Who's he? Robespierre or Danton?**

EDITED

Robespierre and Danton disagreed over the path the French Revolution should take. **Robespierre** believed that the Revolution was endangered by internal enemies.

## 2 Look for vague or implied pronoun reference

If readers have to guess what a pronoun refers to, you may have referred to the entire idea of an earlier passage (**vague** or **broad pronoun reference**) or to an **implied antecedent**, suggested but not stated.

IMPLIED
ANTECEDENT

A hard frost damaged most of the local citrus groves, but **it** has not yet been determined.

READER'S REACTION: **I'm not sure what *it* means, though I guess it's related to the frost damage.**

STATED

A hard frost damaged most of the local citrus groves, but **the extent of the loss** has not yet been determined.

Certain words—*it, they, you, which, this,* or *that*—are especially likely to refer to vague, implied, or indefinite antecedents. To spot imprecise references, search for these pronouns. In each case, see if you can find an antecedent stated in the passage.

## 26b Editing for clear pronoun reference

Your choices for editing pronoun reference will depend on the particular problem you are trying to correct.

### 1 Correcting ambiguous or distant reference

When a pronoun threatens to confuse readers because it refers to two or more possible antecedents (ambiguous reference), you can correct the problem in two ways.

1. **Replace** the troublesome pronoun with a noun.
2. **Reword** the sentence.

AMBIGUOUS
REFERENCE

Detaching the measuring probe from the glass cylinder is a delicate job because **it** breaks easily.

READER'S REACTION: **Which is so fragile, the probe or the cylinder?**

REPLACED WITH
NOUN

Detaching the measuring probe from the glass cylinder is a delicate job because **the probe** breaks easily.

REWORDED

Because the measuring probe breaks easily, detaching it from the glass cylinder is a delicate job.

If a pronoun is too far away from its antecedent to refer to it clearly, either move the pronoun closer or replace it with a noun.

## 2 Editing vague or implied reference

Keeping pronouns and antecedents together is especially important for word groups beginning with *who, which,* and *that* (relative pronouns). Avoid confusion by placing the pronoun right after its antecedent.

CONFUSING

In my old bedroom, I saw a stale piece of the bubble gum under **the dresser that I loved to chew as a boy**.

EDITED

In my old bedroom, I saw under the dresser a stale piece of **the bubble gum that I loved to chew as a boy.**

Sometimes you need to follow *which, this,* or *that* with an explanation of the pronoun's referent.

VAGUE
REFERENCE

Redfish have suffered from oil pollution and the destruction of their mangrove swamp habitat. **This** has led to a rapid decline in the redfish population.

READER'S REACTION: **Does** *this* **refer to the destruction of habitat, to oil pollution, or to both?**

SPECIFIED

Redfish have suffered from oil pollution and the destruction of their mangrove swamp habitat. **This combination** has led to a rapid decline in the redfish population.

EXPLAINED

Redfish have suffered from oil pollution and the destruction of their mangrove swamp habitat. **That increasingly serious pair of challenges** has led to a rapid decline in the redfish population.

*You* is commonly accepted in letters, emails, and other kinds of writing where it means, "you, the reader" (see 28a). When *you* refers to people and situations in general, however, it may lead to imprecise sentences.

INDEFINITE
ANTECEDENT

In Brazil, **you** pay less for an alcohol-powered car than for a gasoline-powered one.

READER'S REACTION: **Who is** *you***? I'm not likely to buy a car in Brazil.**

REPLACED WITH
NOUN

In Brazil, **consumers** pay less for an alcohol-powered car than for a gasoline-powered one.

REWRITTEN    In Brazil, alcohol-powered cars cost less than gasoline-powered ones.

## 3 Clarifying the antecedent to which the pronoun refers

Many academic readers will consider a possessive noun used as an antecedent an error, although the pattern is common in informal writing. Pair a possessive noun with a possessive pronoun (*Kristen's . . . hers*), or rewrite to eliminate the possessive noun.

UNCLEAR    The **company's** success with a well-known jazz fusion artist led **it** to contracts with other musicians.

EDITED
(POSSESSIVE PAIR)    The **company's** success with a well-known jazz fusion artist led to **its** contracts with other musicians.

EDITED
(NO POSSESSIVE)    Success with a well-known jazz fusion artist led the company to other contracts.

INAPPROPRIATE    In William Faulkner's *The Sound and the Fury*, he begins the story from the point of view of a mentally retarded person.

EDITED    In *The Sound and the Fury*, **William Faulkner** begins the story from the point of view of a mentally retarded person.

## 4 Reworking a passage to create a reference chain

You can guide readers through a passage using a chain of pronouns to connect sentences. A **reference chain** begins with a statement of your topic, which is then linked to pronouns (or nouns) later in the passage.

**UNCLEAR**
Sand paintings were a remarkable form of Pueblo art. An artist would sprinkle dried sand of different colors, ground flower petals, corn pollen, and similar materials onto the floor to create **them**. The sun, moon, and stars as well as animals and objects linked to the spirits were represented in the figures **they** contained. **Their** purpose was to encourage the spirits to send good fortune to humans.
**Because *them* and *they* are buried at the ends of sentences in the middle of the paragraph, readers may lose sight of the topic, sand paintings.**

**EDITED TO CREATE A REFERENCE CHAIN**
Sand paintings were a remarkable form of Pueblo art. To create **them**, an artist would sprinkle dried sand of different colors, ground flower petals, corn pollen, and similar materials onto the floor. **They** contained figures representing the sun, moon, and stars as well as animals and objects linked to the spirits. **Their** purpose was to encourage the spirits to send good fortune to humans.

> **STRATEGY**   Techniques for developing a reference chain
> - State the antecedent clearly in the opening sentence.
> - Link the antecedent to pronouns in sentences that follow.
> - Be sure no other possible antecedents interrupt the links in the chain.
> - Don't interrupt the chain and then try to return to it later.
> - Call attention to the links by giving the pronouns prominent positions (usually beginning sentences); vary their positions only slightly.

# 27   Editing Misplaced, Dangling, and Disruptive Modifiers

Readers sometimes see a sentence like a string of beads. If the silver bead is designed to reflect the red one, they expect to find those beads placed next to each other just as they expect to find related parts of a sentence together.

**MISPLACED MODIFIER**
The wife believes she sees a living figure behind the wallpaper in the story by Charlotte Perkins Gilman, which adds to her sense of entrapment.

READER'S REACTION: **How could a story add to a feeling of entrapment?**

**MODIFIER MOVED**
The wife **in the story by Charlotte Perkins Gilman** believes she sees a living figure behind the wallpaper, which adds to her sense of entrapment.

**MODIFIER MOVED**
**In the story by Charlotte Perkins Gilman**, the wife believes she sees a living figure behind the wallpaper, which adds to her sense of entrapment.

In the draft, the modifier is not positioned to relate clearly to the word it modifies. Once the sentence is rearranged, the wife is "in the story," and the wallpaper "adds to her sense of entrapment." The relationship between a modifier and the word(s) it modifies needs to be clear to readers. If it is unclear, the result will be unanswered questions and confusion.

**SERIOUS ERROR**   ## 27a Recognizing misplaced, dangling, and disruptive modifiers

When a modifier is poorly positioned or illogically related to the word(s) it is supposed to modify (its **headword**), readers are likely to find a sentence vague, illogical, or unintentionally humorous.

## 1 Look for misplaced modifiers

A word or word group that is not close enough to its headword is a **misplaced modifier**. It appears to modify some other word or to modify *both* the word before and the word after.

**CONFUSING** The caterer served food to the directors standing around the room on flimsy paper plates.

READER'S REACTION: **Surely the directors weren't standing on the plates!**

**MODIFIER MOVED** The caterer served food **on flimsy paper plates** to the directors standing around the room.

## 2 Look for dangling modifiers

To find a **dangling modifier**, look for a sentence that begins with a modifier but doesn't name the person, idea, or thing modified. Readers will assume that this modifier refers to the subject of the main clause immediately following. If it doesn't, the modifier dangles.

**DANGLING** Looking for a way to reduce complaints from nonsmokers, a new ventilation fan was installed.

READER'S REACTION: **How could a fan look for anything? The sentence never tells me *who* wants to reduce complaints.**

**SUBJECT ADDED** Looking for a way to reduce complaints from nonsmokers, **the company installed** a new ventilation fan.

## 3 Look for disruptive modifiers

Readers generally expect subjects and verbs to stand close to each other. The same is true for other sentence elements—verbs and their objects or complements, parts of infinitives, and verb phrases. Modifiers that come between such elements may be **disruptive modifiers** if they create long and distracting interruptions.

**DISRUPTIVE** The researcher, **because he had not worked with chimpanzees before and was unaware of their intelligence**, was surprised when they undermined his experiment.

However, a brief, relevant interruption can add variety and suspense.

**CLEAR** The researcher, **unfamiliar with chimpanzees**, was surprised when they undermined his experiment.

How can you tell whether modifiers placed between subject and verb are disruptive? Modifiers that provide information related to both subject and verb are likely to be disruptive because a reader can't tell which they relate to. Modifiers related to the subject alone generally aren't disruptive.

|  |  |
|---|---|
| **DISRUPTIVE** | subject              modifier<br>Work on the building, **due to problems with the construc-**<br>                verb<br>**tion permits,** <u>was completed</u> three months late. |

|  |  |
|---|---|
| **NOT DISRUPTIVE** | subject          modifier         verb<br>The <u>youth center</u> **that opened last month** <u>has drawn</u> crowds. |

---

### ESL ADVICE: POSITION OF MODIFIERS

Some languages clarify the relationship between a modifier and its head-word through the form or ending of the words. Because modifiers in English tend to change location, not form, to show which words they describe, the position of a modifier can drastically change its meaning.

---

## 27b Editing misplaced, dangling, and disruptive modifiers

You can call on a variety of techniques to edit problems with modifiers.

### 1 Editing misplaced modifiers

Try these two techniques for editing misplaced modifiers.

- **Move** the modifier closer to the words it should modify.
- **Rewrite** or **modify** a sentence so that the connection between modifier and words to be modified is clear.

***Who, which, or that.*** For a clear connection, try to put *who, which,* or *that* immediately after its headword to avoid modifying the wrong word.

| | |
|---|---|
| **MISPLACED** | The environmental engineers discovered another tank behind<br>the building that was leaking toxic wastes.<br>READER'S REACTION: **I know a building can leak, but I'll bet the writer meant that the tank was the culprit.** |
| **MOVED AFTER HEADWORD** | Behind the building, the environmental engineers discovered<br>another tank **that** was leaking toxic wastes. |

***Only, hardly, merely,* and similar words.** In most cases, move a word like *only, almost, hardly, just, merely, simply,* and *even* (**limiting modifiers**) directly before the word to which it applies.

**Only** charities for children are maintaining their support.
**They are the sole charities able to maintain support.**

Charities for **only** children are maintaining their support.
**The charities are for children from families with one child.**

Charities for children are **only** maintaining their support.
**They are not increasing the levels of support.**

**Squinting modifiers.** If a modifier appears to modify the wording both before and after it, move this **squinting modifier** to eliminate the ambiguity, or rewrite.

SQUINTING    People who abuse alcohol **often** have other problems.
             READER'S REACTION: **Do they abuse alcohol *often* or *often* have other problems?**

EDITED       People who **often abuse alcohol** tend to have other problems.

REWRITTEN    People who abuse alcohol tend to have other problems **as well**.

## 2 Editing dangling modifiers

When the subject being modified does not appear in the sentence, you have a dangling modifier. You can correct the problem in three ways.

* **Add a subject** to the modifier.

DANGLING         While shopping, the stuffed alligator caught my eye.
SUBJECT ADDED    While **I was** shopping, the stuffed alligator caught my eye.

* **Change the subject** of the main clause.

DANGLING          Jumping into the water to save the drowning swimmer, the crowd applauded the lifeguard.

SUBJECT           Jumping into the water to save the drowning swimmer, **the**
CHANGED           **lifeguard** was applauded by the crowd.

* **Rewrite** the entire sentence.

DANGLING          Having debated changes in the regulations for months, the present standards were allowed to continue.
                  READER'S REACTION: ***Who* is debating? Not the standards!**

REWRITTEN         The commission debated changes in the regulations for months but decided to continue the present standards.

## 3 Editing disruptive modifiers

To correct problems caused by disruptive modifiers, move them so that sentence elements are near each other just as readers expect.

Readers expect a subject and verb to stand together and an object or complement to come right after the verb.

CLUMSY          Joanne began collecting, **using her survey form**, data for her study of dating preferences.

EDITED          **Using her survey form**, Joanne began collecting data for her study of dating preferences.

If a modifier splits the parts of an infinitive (*to* plus a verb, as in *to enjoy*), readers may have trouble relating the parts. Some readers will find any **split infinitive** irritating, clear or not.

IRRITATING      The dancers moved **to** very rapidly **align** themselves.

EDITED          The dancers moved very rapidly **to align** themselves.

At times, however, a split infinitive may be the most concise alternative.

Our goal is **to** more than **halve** our manufacturing errors.

# 28  Making Shifts Consistent

Although readers are willing to shift attention many times, they expect you to make shifts logically consistent and to signal them clearly.

SHIFTED         If **parents** would call the school board, **you** could explain why **we** oppose the proposal.
                READER'S REACTION: **I'm confused. Who's who? Who should do what?**

EDITED          If **parents** would call the school board, **they** could explain why **they** oppose the proposal.

EDITED          If **you** would call the school board, **you** could explain why **you** oppose the proposal.

EDITED          If **all of us meeting tonight** would call the school board, **we** could explain why **we** oppose the proposal.

## **SERIOUS ERROR** 28a Recognizing and editing shifts in person and number

Watch for unexpected shifts in person and number (see 22c). **Person** refers to the ways you use nouns and pronouns (*I, you, she, they*) to shape the relationship involving you, your readers, and your subject. Switching from one person to another as you refer to the same subject can be illogical. **Number** shows whether words are singular (one) or plural (two or more). Look for confusing shifts between words like *person* and *people* that identify groups or their members.

| INCONSISTENT | When **a business executive is** looking for a new job, **they** often consult a placement service. |
|---|---|
| | READER'S REACTION: **Does *they* mean business executives as a group? The sentence mentions only one executive.** |
| EDITED | When **business executives are** looking for **new jobs**, **they** often consult a placement service. |

---

**FIRST PERSON (*I, WE*).**
- Use *I* to refer to yourself as the writer or as the subject of an essay.
- Use *we* in a collaborative project when more than one person is author or subject.
- Use *we* for both yourself and your readers when discussing shared experiences or understandings.
- Use *we* in some academic fields such as the study of literature ("In this part of the poem we begin to see . . .") but not in others (for example, chemistry or engineering).
- Use *we* to represent an organization or workgroup.

**SECOND PERSON (*YOU*).**
- Use *you* to refer directly to the reader.
- Do not use *you* in most kinds of academic and professional writing unless called for by the situation, as in a set of instructions.
- Use *you* in a political, civic, or activist appeal urging readers to action.

**THIRD PERSON (*HE, SHE, IT, THEY; ONE, SOMEONE, EACH,* AND OTHER INDEFINITE PRONOUNS).**
- Use third person for the ideas, things, and people you are writing about.
- *People* and *person* are third person nouns, as are names of groups of things, ideas, and people (for example, *students, teachers, doctors*).

---

Check for illogical shifts between singular and plural forms, between first and second person, or between second and third person. Then edit to make the relationships consistent.

| INCONSISTENT NUMBER | If **a person has** some money to invest, **they** should seek advice from a financial consultant. |
|---|---|
| EDITED | If **a person has** some money to invest, **he or she** should seek advice from a financial consultant. |
| EDITED | If **people have** some money to invest, **they** should seek advice from a financial consultant. |

| INCONSISTENT PERSON | If a **person** is looking for a higher return on investments, **you** might consider mutual funds. |
|---|---|
| EDITED | If **you** are looking for a higher return on investments, **you** might consider mutual funds. |

## 28b Recognizing and editing shifts in tense and mood

When you change verb tense within a passage, you signal a change in time and the relationship of events in time. Illogical shifts can mislead your readers and contradict your meaning.

| ILLOGICAL SHIFT | Scientists digging in Montana **discovered** nests that **indicated** how some dinosaurs **take care** of their young. |
|---|---|
| LOGICAL | Scientists digging in Montana **discovered** nests that **indicate** how some dinosaurs **took care** of their young. |
| | **Although the actions of both the dinosaurs and the scientists clearly occurred in the past, *indicate* (present tense) is appropriate because researchers interpret the evidence in the present.** |

Make sure you keep verb tenses consistent and logical within a passage. If you begin narrating events in the past tense, avoid shifting suddenly to the present to try to make events more vivid.

| INCONSISTENT TENSE | We **had been searching** for a new site for the festival when Tonia **starts yelling**, "I've found the place!" |
|---|---|
| EDITED | We **had been searching** for a new site for the festival when Tonia **started yelling**, "I've found the place!" |

### ESL ADVICE: VERB TENSE AND EXPRESSIONS OF TIME

Use both verb tense and expressions of time (*yesterday*, *today*, *soon*) to indicate changes in time. Make sure the two are consistent.

| INCONSISTENT | I **study** English last year, and now **I worked** for an American company. |
|---|---|
| EDITED | I **studied** English last year, and now I **work** for an American company. |

The **mood** of a verb shows the writer's aim or attitude (see 19d-2): to command or request (**imperative**), to state or question (**indicative**), or to offer a conditional or hypothetical statement (**subjunctive**; see 20h). If you shift mood inappropriately, your sentences may be hard to follow.

**INCONSISTENT (IMPERATIVE AND INDICATIVE)**
To reduce costs, **distribute** fewer copies of drafts, and **you should encourage** employees to replace paper memos with email messages.

**CONSISTENT (IMPERATIVE)**
To reduce costs, **distribute** fewer copies of drafts, and **encourage** employees to replace paper memos with email messages.

## 28c Recognizing and editing shifts in active or passive voice

When a verb is in the **active voice,** the agent or doer of the action functions as the subject of the sentence. When a verb is in the **passive voice,** the goal of the action functions as the sentence's subject. (See 20i and 32b-3.)

|  | subject | verb | object |
|---|---|---|---|
| **ACTIVE** | The lava flow | **destroyed** | twelve houses. |
|  | agent | action | goal |

|  | subject | verb |  |
|---|---|---|---|
| **PASSIVE** | Twelve houses | **were destroyed** | [by the lava flow]. |
|  | goal | action | [agent] |

Try to focus on either active or passive voice within a sentence, rewriting if necessary, to use either active or passive voice consistently.

**INCONSISTENT**    Among the active volcanoes, Kilauea **erupts** most frequently, and over 170 houses **have been destroyed** since 1983.

**READER'S REACTION: The first part mentions Kilauea, but the second part doesn't. Did Kilauea alone destroy the houses, or were some other volcanoes also responsible?**

**EDITED**    Among the active volcanoes, Kilauea **has erupted** most frequently in recent years, and it has destroyed over 170 houses since 1983.

Sometimes you may shift voice to emphasize or highlight a subject.

active        active
**UNEMPHATIC**    Volcanic activity **built** Hawaii, and the island still **has** active volcanoes.

passive        active
**EDITED**    Hawaii **was built** by volcanic activity, and the island still **has** active volcanoes.

**The first sentence shifts subjects from *volcanic activity* to *the island*; the second shifts between passive and active to keep Hawaii as the focus.**

## 28d Recognizing and editing shifts between direct and indirect quotations

Through **direct quotation** you present someone's ideas and feelings in that person's exact words, set off with quotation marks. Through **indirect quotation** you report the substance of those words but in your own words without quotation marks. Credit your sources with either form of quotation (see Chapter 14).

| | |
|---|---|
| **DIRECT QUOTATION** | According to Aguilar, beachfront property "has wreaked havoc on sea turtle nesting patterns" (16). |
| **INDIRECT QUOTATION** | Aguilar explained how beachfront property interferes with the breeding habits of sea turtles (16). |

Within a sentence, shifts in quotation may be difficult to follow.

**STRATEGY** Rewrite awkward shifts between quotations.

| | |
|---|---|
| **AWKWARD (INDIRECT + DIRECT)** | Writing about the Teenage Mutant Ninja Turtles, Phil Patton **names** cartoonists Peter Laird and Kevin Eastman as their creators and **said**, "They were born quietly in 1983, in the kitchen of a New England farmhouse" (101). |
| **EDITED** | Phil Patton **credits** cartoonists Peter Laird and Kevin Eastman with creating the Teenage Mutant Ninja Turtles, who "were born quietly in 1983, in the kitchen of a New England farmhouse" (101). |

For indirect quotation, use past tense to report what someone has said.

| | |
|---|---|
| **DIRECT QUOTATION** | As Lan **notes**, "The region **is expected** to forfeit one of every three jobs" (4). |
| **INDIRECT QUOTATION** | Lan **projected that** the area **would lose** one-third of its jobs during the next ten years (4). |

Follow convention, however, and use present tense when you analyze events in a creative work, such as a novel, film, or television show. (See 20b.)

| | |
|---|---|
| **INCONSISTENT** | As the novel begins, Ishmael **comes** to New Bedford to ship out on a whaler, which he soon **did**. |
| **CONVENTIONAL** | As the novel begins, Ishmael **comes** to New Bedford to ship out on a whaler, which he soon **does**. |

# 29 Editing Mixed and Incomplete Sentences

When someone switches topics or jumbles a sentence during a conversation, you can ask for clarification. When you are reading, however, you can't stop in the middle of a sentence to ask the writer to explain.

**TOPIC SHIFT** One **skill** I envy is **a person** who can meet deadlines.
READER'S REACTION: **How can a *skill* be *a person?***

**EDITED** One **skill** I envy is **the ability** to meet deadlines.

Sentences with confusing shifts (called **mixed sentences**) mislead readers by undermining the patterns they rely on as they read. An **incomplete sentence** that omits wording necessary to make a logical and consistent statement does the same.

## 29a Recognizing mixed sentences

**Mixed sentences** switch topics or sentence structures without warning, for no clear reason. They throw readers off track by undermining patterns that readers rely on.

### 1 Look for topic shifts

In most sentences, the subject announces a topic, and the predicate comments on or renames the topic. In a sentence with a **topic shift** (**faulty predication**), the second part of the sentence comments on or names a topic *different* from the one first announced. As a result, readers may have trouble figuring out the true focus of the sentence.

**STRATEGY** Ask "Who does what?" or "What is it?"

If the answer to Who does what?" or "What is it?" is illogical, edit the sentence to make its meaning clear.

**TOPIC SHIFT** In this factory, **flaws** in the product noticed by any worker **can stop** the assembly line with the flip of a switch.
QUESTION: **Who does what? Flaws can't stop the line or flip a switch.**

EDITED       In this factory, **any worker** who notices flaws in the product
             **can stop** the assembly line with the flip of a switch.

## 2 Pay attention to mixed patterns

If you begin one grammatical pattern but shift to another, your sentence
may confuse readers because it doesn't follow the pattern they expect.

**STRATEGY**   **Check who does what to whom.**

• Read your sentences aloud. Pay attention to the *meaning*, especially how
  the subject and predicate relate.
• Ask, "What is the topic? How does the rest of the sentence comment on
  it or rename it?"

MIXED       By wearing bell-bottom pants and tie-dyed T-shirts was how
PATTERN     many young people challenged mainstream values in the 1960s.
            CHECK: *Who did what to whom* **is not clear.**

EDITED      By wearing bell-bottom pants and tie-dyed T-shirts, many
            young people challenged mainstream values in the 1960s.

## 29b Editing mixed sentences

In general, you can eliminate problems with topic shifts by making sure
the topic in both parts of a sentence is the same.

### 1 Rename the subject

When you use the verb *be* (*is*, *are*, *was*, *were*), you may use the sentence
predicate to rename or define the subject. Balance the topics on each side of the
verb; for example, pair a noun with a noun.

If the topics on each side of *be* are not roughly equivalent, edit the second part of the sentence to rename the topic in the first part.

TOPIC SHIFT   **Irradiation** is **food** that is preserved by radiation.

EDITED        **Irradiation** is a **process** that can be used to preserve food.

### 2 Cut *is when* or *is where*

*Is when* and *is where* make a balance on both sides of *be* impossible.

NOT           **Blocking** is **when** a television network schedules a less pop-
BALANCED      ular program between two popular ones.

EDITED        **Blocking** is the **practice** of scheduling a less popular television
              program between two popular ones.

## 3 Omit *the reason . . . is because*

Readers find *the reason . . . is because* illogical because they expect the subject (topic) to be renamed after *is*. When *because* appears there instead, it cannot logically rename the subject.

- Drop *the reason . . . is.*

  DRAFT    The **reason** he took up skating **is because** he wanted winter exercise.

  EDITED    He took up skating **because** he wanted winter exercise.

- Change *because* to *that.*

  EDITED    The **reason** he took up skating **is that** he wanted winter exercise.

## 4 Stick to a consistent sentence pattern

If you mistake words between the subject and verb for the sentence topic, you may mix up different sentence patterns.

TOPIC SHIFT    Programming **decisions** by television executives generally think about gaining audience share.
READER'S REACTION: **How can decisions think about viewers?**

EDITED    **Television executives** making programming decisions generally think about gaining audience share.

EDITED    When **they are making** programming decisions, **television executives** generally think about gaining audience share.

## 5 Be alert for sentences that begin twice

Watch for sentences in which you repeat a topic more often than the sentence structure allows or mistakenly start the sentence over again.

MIXED    **The new procedures for testing cosmetics, we** designed them to avoid cruelty to laboratory animals.

EDITED    **We** designed **the new procedures for testing cosmetics** to avoid cruelty to laboratory animals.

EDITED    **The new procedures for testing cosmetics** were designed to avoid cruelty to laboratory animals.

## 29c Recognizing and editing incomplete sentences

**Incomplete sentences** lack either grammatical (see 24a) or logical completeness. For example, if you begin a comparison with "*X* is larger," you should complete it: "*X* is larger *than Y.*"

Incomplete sentences leave out words necessary to meaning or logic, or they don't complete an expected pattern, such as a comparison. Read sentences aloud to identify missing words. Listen for omissions such as needed articles, prepositions, pronouns, parts of verbs, or parts of a comparison.

| | |
|---|---|
| INCOMPLETE | The new parking plan is much better. |
| | READER'S REACTION: **Better than what? another plan? no plan?** |
| EDITED | The new parking plan is much better **than the last plan**. |

You create an **incomplete comparison** when you omit an item being compared or the wording needed for a clear, complete comparison. To edit, supply the words that complete a comparison.

| | |
|---|---|
| INCOMPLETE | The senior members of the staff respect the new supervisor more than their co-workers. |
| | READER'S REACTION: **Do the senior staff members respect the supervisor more than they respect their co-workers? Or do they respect the supervisor more than their co-workers do?** |
| CLEAR | The senior members of the staff respect the new supervisor more **than do** their co-workers. |
| CLEAR | The senior members of the staff respect the new supervisor more **than they respect** their co-workers. |

You create an **illogical comparison** when you seem to compare things that cannot be reasonably compared. To edit, add missing words or a possessive to make a comparison logical.

| | |
|---|---|
| ILLOGICAL | The amount of fat in even a small hamburger is greater than a skinless chicken breast. |
| | READER'S REACTION: **I'm confused. Why is the writer comparing the *amount of fat* in one food to another *kind* of food (chicken breast)?** |
| EDITED (WORDS ADDED) | The amount of fat in even a small hamburger is greater than **that in** a skinless chicken breast. |
| EDITED (POSSESSIVE USED) | Even a small **hamburger's** fat content is greater than a skinless chicken **breast's**. |

# 30  Creating Parallelism

When you use consistent patterns, readers can easily follow and understand your ideas. They can concentrate on what you mean because they know just what to expect and how your ideas relate.

**WEAK**    I furnished my apartment with what I purchased at discount stores, buying items from the want ads, and gifts from my relatives.

   READER'S REACTION: **This list seems wordy and jumbled.**

**PARALLEL**    I furnished my apartment with **purchases from discount stores,**
           **items from the want ads,**
     and **gifts from my relatives.**

**Parallelism** is the expression of similar or related ideas in similar grammatical form. Besides emphasizing the relationships of ideas, parallelism can create intriguing sentence rhythms and highlights.

## 30a  Recognizing faulty parallelism

Once you begin a parallel pattern, you need to complete it. If you mix structures, creating incomplete or **faulty parallelism**, your sentences may disappoint readers' expectations and be hard to read.

**MIXED**    Consider swimming if you want an exercise that **aids** cardiovascular fitness, **develops** overall muscle strength, and **probably without causing** injuries.

**PARALLEL**    Consider swimming if you want an exercise that **aids** cardiovascular fitness, **develops** overall muscle strength, and **causes** few injuries.

## 30b  Editing for parallelism

Whether you create parallelism with words, phrases, or clauses, all the elements need to follow the same grammatical patterns.

## 1 Rework a series, pair, or list using parallel forms

When you place items in a series, pair, or list, make sure they have the same structure even if they differ in length and wording. Mixed grammatical forms can make a series clumsy and distracting.

**WORDS MIXED**

To get along with their neighbors, residents need to be patient, tactful, and to display tolerance.

**WORDS PARALLEL**

To get along with their neighbors, residents need to be patient, tactful, and **tolerant**.

**PHRASES MIXED**

The singer Jim Morrison is remembered for his innovative style, his flamboyant performances, and for behavior that was self-destructive.

**PHRASES PARALLEL**

The singer Jim Morrison is remembered for his innovative style, his flamboyant performances, and **his self-destructive behavior**.

**CLAUSES MIXED**

In assembling the research team, Cryo-Com looked for engineers whose work was creative, with broad interests, and who had boundless energy.

**CLAUSES PARALLEL**

In assembling the research team, Cryo-Com looked for engineers whose work was creative, **whose interests were broad**, **and whose energy was boundless**.

*And, but, or.* When you join sentence elements with *and, but, or, for, nor, so,* and *yet* (**coordinating conjunctions**), presenting the paired elements in parallel form can direct readers' attention to similarities or differences.

**WORDS MIXED**

A well-trained scientist keeps a detailed lab notebook and the entries made accurately.

**WORDS PARALLEL**

A well-trained scientist keeps a **detailed and accurate** lab notebook.

**PHRASES MIXED**

First-year chemistry teaches students how to take notes on an experiment and the ways of writing a lab report.

**PHRASES PARALLEL**

First-year chemistry teaches students **how to take notes on an experiment** and **how to write a lab report**.

*Both . . . and . . . .* When you wish to call special attention to a relationship or contrast, you may choose pairs of connectors such as *both . . . and, not only . . . but also, either . . . or, neither . . . nor,* or *whether . . . or* (**correlative conjunctions**). Make the joined elements parallel.

**DRAFT**

Americans claim to marry "for love," yet their pairings follow clear social patterns. They choose partners from the same social class and economic level. Most marriages bring together people with similar educational and cultural backgrounds. Similarities in race and ethnic background are important as well.

**EDITED** Americans claim to marry "for love," yet their pairings follow clear social patterns. They choose partners not only **with the same class and economic background** but also **with the same educational, cultural, racial, and ethnic background**.

**Lists.** Use parallel form for items in a list.

The early 1960s were characterized by several social changes.

**UNEDITED (CONFUSING)**
1. A growing civil rights movement
2. Emphasis increased on youth in culture and politics.
3. Taste in music and the visual arts was changing.

**EDITED FOR PARALLELISM (CLEAR)**
1. **A growing** civil rights movement
2. **An increasing** emphasis on youth in culture and politics
3. **A changing** taste in music and the visual arts

## 2 Build clear parallel patterns

**INCOMPLETE** The main character from the novel _Tarzan of the Apes_ has appeared on television, films, and comic books.
   **READER'S REACTION: I doubt he was _on_ films or _on_ comic books.**

**EDITED** The main character from the novel _Tarzan of the Apes_ has appeared **on** television, **in** films, and **in** comic books.

Repeat or state words that complete grammatical or idiomatic patterns. You needn't repeat the same lead-in word for all items in a series.

Mosquitoes can breed **in** puddles, ~~in~~ ponds, and ~~in~~ swimming pools.

## 3 Use parallelism to organize sentence clusters

You can use parallelism to strengthen **sentence clusters**, groups of sentences that develop related ideas or information. The parallel elements can clarify difficult information, highlight the overall pattern of argument or explanation, link examples, or guide readers through steps or stages.

Each of us probably belongs to groups whose values conflict. **You may belong to** a religious organization that **endorses restraint in** alcohol use or **in** relations between the sexes while **you also belong to** a social group with activities that **support contrasting values. You may**

**belong to** a sports team **that supports** competing and winning and a club **that promotes** understanding among people.

You can also use parallelism, as simple as brief opening phrases, to reinforce the overall pattern of a cluster of paragraphs.

**PARALLEL PARAGRAPH OPENERS**

**One reason for approving** this proposal now is . . .
**A second reason for action** is . . .
**The most important reason for taking immediate steps** is . . .

# 31 Using Coordination and Subordination

Suppose you were asked to rewrite the following passage, filled with short, choppy sentences that fail to emphasize connections among ideas.

California's farmers ship fresh lettuce, avocados, and other produce to supermarkets. They never send fresh olives. Fresh olives contain a substance that makes them bitter. They are very unpleasant tasting. Farmers soak fresh olives in a solution that removes oleuropein, the bitter-tasting substance. They leave just enough behind to produce the tangy "olive" taste.

You might **coordinate** the sentences, giving equal emphasis to each statement.

California's farmers ship fresh lettuce, avocados, and other produce to supermarkets **,** **but** they never send fresh olives. Fresh olives contain a substance that makes them bitter **,** **so** they are very unpleasant tasting. Farmers soak fresh olives in a solution that removes oleuropein, the bitter-tasting substance **;** **however ,** they leave just enough behind to produce the tangy "olive" taste.

Or you might show the relative importance of ideas by **subordination**, making some of the sentences modify others through the use of words like *because* and *though* (subordinating words).

California's farmers ship fresh lettuce, avocados, and other produce to supermarkets, **though** they never send fresh olives. **Because** fresh olives contain a substance that makes them bitter, they are very unpleasant tasting. **When** farmers soak fresh olives in a solution that removes oleuropein, the bitter-tasting substance, they leave just enough behind to produce the tangy "olive" taste.

## 31a Recognizing and creating coordination

When you want to link words, clauses, or phrases and emphasize their equal weight, use coordination. When you coordinate main (independent) clauses, you create a single **compound sentence** (see 19d-1).

**RELATIONSHIPS NOT SPECIFIED** — Cats have no fear of water. They do not like wet and matted fur. Cats like to feel well groomed.

**CLEAR RELATIONSHIPS** — Cats have no fear of water, **but** they do not like wet and matted fur, **for** they like to feel well groomed.

---

### CREATING AND PUNCTUATING COORDINATION

#### JOINING WORDS AND CLUSTERS OF WORDS (PHRASES)

1. Use *and, but, or, nor,* or *yet* (coordinating conjunctions).

   cut **and** hemmed     smooth **or** textured     intrigued **yet** suspicious

2. Use pairs like *either . . . or, neither . . . nor,* and *not only . . . but also.*

   **either** music therapy **or** pet therapy
   **not only** a nursing care plan **but also** a home care program

#### JOINING MAIN (INDEPENDENT) CLAUSES

1. Use *and, but, or, for, nor, so,* or *yet* (coordinating conjunctions) preceded by a comma.

   The students observed the responses of shoppers to long lines, **and** they interviewed people waiting in line. Most people in the study were irritated by the checkout lines, **yet** a considerable minority enjoyed the wait.

2. Use a semicolon (see 38a-1).

   The wait provoked physical reactions in some people; they fidgeted, grimaced, and stared at the ceiling.

3. Use words like *however, moreover, nonetheless, thus,* and *consequently* (conjunctive adverbs) preceded by a semicolon (see 38a-2).

   Store managers can take simple steps to speed up checkout lines; **however,** they seldom pay much attention to the problem.

4. Use a colon (see 38b-3).

   Tabloids and magazines in racks by the checkout counters serve a useful purpose: they give customers something to read while waiting.

---

**EXPRESSING RELATIONSHIPS THROUGH COORDINATION**

| RELATIONSHIP | COORDINATING CONJUNCTION | CONJUNCTIVE ADVERB • • • • | |
|---|---|---|---|
| addition | , and | ; in addition, | ; furthermore, |
| opposition | , but | ; in contrast, | |
| or contrast | , yet | ; however, | ; nonetheless, |
| result | , so | ; therefore, | ; consequently, ; thus, |
| cause | , for | | |
| choice | , or | ; otherwise, | |
| negation | , nor | | |

---

## 31b Recognizing and creating subordination

Use subordination to create a sentence with unequal elements: one **main or independent clause** that presents the central idea and at least one **subordinate or dependent clause** that modifies, qualifies, or comments on the main clause. You signal readers about this unequal relationship by beginning the subordinate clause with a word like *although* or *that* and by attaching it to the main clause in a **complex sentence** (see 19d-1).

MAIN CLAUSES    Malcolm uses a computer to track clinic expenses. He knows how much we pay each year for lab tests.

SUBORDINATED    **Because** Malcolm uses a computer to track clinic expenses, he knows how much we pay each year for lab tests.

READER'S REACTION: **Now I know how the ideas relate—one is a cause and the other an effect.**

---

**EXPRESSING RELATIONSHIPS THROUGH SUBORDINATION**

| | |
|---|---|
| **Time** | before, while, until, since, once, whenever, whereupon, after, when |
| **Cause** | because, since |
| **Result** | in order that, so that, that, so |
| **Concession or contrast** | although, though, even though, as if, while, even if |
| **Place** | where, wherever |
| **Condition** | if, whether, provided, unless, rather than |
| **Comparison** | as |
| **Identification** | that, which, who |

## CREATING AND PUNCTUATING SUBORDINATION

### USING SUBORDINATING CONJUNCTIONS

You can use a subordinating conjunction such as *although, because,* or *since* (see list on page 274) to create a subordinate clause at the beginning or end of a sentence (see 18g and 19c–d).

### PUNCTUATING WITH SUBORDINATING CONJUNCTIONS

Use a comma *after* an introductory clause that begins with a subordinating conjunction. At the end of a sentence, do not use commas if the clause is *essential* to the meaning of the main clause (restrictive); use commas if the clause is *not essential* (nonrestrictive). (See 25c).

BEGINNING **Once she understood the problem,** she had no trouble solving it.

END Radar tracking of flights began **after several commercial airliners collided in midair.** [Essential]

END The present air traffic control system works reasonably well, **although accidents still occur.** [Nonessential]

### USING RELATIVE PRONOUNS

You can use a relative pronoun (*who, which, that*) to create a relative clause (also called an adjective clause) at the end or in the middle of a sentence (see 18d).

### PUNCTUATING WITH RELATIVE PRONOUNS

If the modifying clause contains information that is *not essential* to the meaning of the main clause, the modifying clause is nonrestrictive and you should set it off with commas. If the information is *essential*, the modifying clause is restrictive and you should not set it off with commas. (See 25c.)

RESTRICTIVE
(ESSENTIAL)
The anthropologists discovered the site of a building **that early settlers used as a meetinghouse.**

NONRESTRICTIVE
(NONESSENTIAL)
At one end of the site they found remains of a smaller building, **which may have been a storage shed.**

RESTRICTIVE
(ESSENTIAL)
The people **who organized the project** work for the Public Archaeology Lab.

NONRESTRICTIVE
(NONESSENTIAL)
A graduate student, **who was leading a dig nearby,** first discovered signs of the meetinghouse.

## **31c** Editing coordination and subordination

How can you tell if you're using too much or too little coordination or subordination? Read your writing aloud. Watch for short, choppy sentences or long, dense passages.

### 1 Be alert for too much coordination or subordination

If you use words like *and, so,* or *but* merely to string together loosely related sentences, you risk boring readers with excessive coordination.

DRAFT

Ripe fruit spoils quickly, **and** fresh grapefruit in markets is picked before it matures to avoid spoilage, **and** it can taste bitter, **but** grapefruit in cans is picked later, **and** it tastes sweeter.

EDITED

Ripe fruit spoils quickly. Fresh grapefruit in markets is picked before it matures **, so** it may taste bitter. Grapefruit in cans is picked later **; consequently ,** it tastes sweeter.

Excessive subordination can overload readers. Divide sentences to simplify.

CONFUSING

The election for mayor will be interesting **because** the incumbent has decided to run as an independent **while** his former challenger for the Democratic nomination has decided to accept the party's endorsement **even though** the Republican nominee is her former campaign manager.

EDITED

The election for mayor will be interesting **.** The incumbent has decided to run as an independent **.** His former challenger for the Democratic nomination has decided to accept the party's endorsement **even though** she will have to run against her former campaign manager.

### 2 Watch for illogical or unclear relationships

Sometimes the subordinating word you choose may not specify a clear relationship, or it may indicate an illogical relationship. To identify such problems, state a sentence's meaning to yourself with a slightly different wording.

• Ask, "Does the original sentence convey my intended meaning?"
• Ask, "Can the subordinating word I have chosen convey several different meanings?"

UNCLEAR
EMPHASIS

Since she taught middle school, Jean developed keen insight into the behavior of twelve- and thirteen-year-olds.

READER'S REACTION: **Does *since* mean that she developed insight *because* she was a teacher or *after* she quit teaching?**

EDITED    **Because** she taught middle school, Jean developed keen insight into the behavior of twelve- and thirteen-year-olds.

## 3 Highlight important information

Subordination enables you to put some information in the foreground (in a main clause) and other information in the background (in a subordinate clause). In general, move your most important point to the main clause.

DRAFT    His training and equipment were inferior, although Jim still set a school record throwing the discus.
         READER'S REACTION: **Isn't Jim's achievement the key point?**

EDITED    **Although** his training and equipment were inferior, Jim still set a school record throwing the discus.

### ESL ADVICE: GRAMMATICAL STRUCTURES FOR COORDINATION AND SUBORDINATION

The following sentence has both a subordinator, *although*, and a coordinator, *but*. Use one pattern, not both at once.

MIXED    **Although** frogs can live both on land and in water, **but** they need to breathe oxygen.

CONSISTENT    main clause                                main clause
COORDINATION    Frogs can live both on land and in water, **but** they need to breathe oxygen.

CONSISTENT    subordinate clause                          main clause
SUBORDINATION    **Although** frogs can live both on land and in water, they need to breathe oxygen.

## 32 Creating Clear and Emphatic Sentences

Most people would find the following sentence hard to read.

INDIRECT    It is suggested that employee work cooperation encourage-
OR EVASIVE    ment be used for product quality improvement.
            READER'S REACTION: **Who is suggesting this? What is "employee work cooperation encouragement"?**

CLEAR    We will try to improve our products by encouraging employees to work cooperatively.

You can make sentences easier to read by creating clear subjects and verbs as well as direct sentence structures.

## 32a Recognizing unclear sentences

A clear sentence answers the question "Who does what (to whom)?" When a sentence doesn't readily answer this question, try to make its subject and verb easy to identify. (See 19a.)

|  | subject | verb | object |
|---|---|---|---|
| CLEAR | The research | team investigated | seizure disorders in infants. |
|  | who? | does what? | |

|  | subject | verb |
|---|---|---|
| CLEAR | The seizures | often become harmful. |
|  | who? | does what? |

You can create complex yet clear sentences by making the main elements—especially subjects and verbs—easy for readers to identify.

UNCLEAR     One suggestion offered by physicians is that there is a need to be especially observant of a child's behavior during the first six months in order to notice any evidence of seizures.

CLEAR       Physicians suggest that parents watch children carefully during the first six months for evidence of seizures.

## 32b Editing for clear sentences

As you edit for clarity, work on any recurring sentence features identified as unclear by your readers, or use the strategies below.

### 1 Concentrate on subjects

Sentences whose subjects name important ideas, people, topics, things, or events are generally easy for readers to understand.

**STRATEGY** Ask questions to clarify significant subjects.
- Who (or what) am I talking about here?
- Is this what I want to emphasize?

UNFOCUSED   You run the greatest risk if you expose yourself to tanning machines as well as the sun because both of them can damage the skin.

READER'S REACTION: **I thought the focus was the danger, whether sunbathing or tanning. Why are they both buried in the middle?**

| | |
|---|---|
| POSSIBLE REVISION | Either **the sun or a tanning machine** can damage the skin, and you run the greatest risk from exposure to **both** of them. |

**Watch out for nominalizations.** When you create a noun (*completion, happiness*) from another kind of word such as a verb (*complete*) or an adjective (*happy*), the result is a **nominalization**, often ending in *-tion, -ence, -ance, -ing*, or *-ness*. Nominalizations usefully name ideas but may obscure information or distract readers from your focus. Be sure each sentence tells who did what (to whom).

| | |
|---|---|
| USEFUL | **Sleepiness** causes accidents at work and on the road. |

Replace weak nominalizations with clear subjects.

| | |
|---|---|
| WEAK | Stimulation of the production of serotonin by a glass of milk or a carbohydrate snack causes sleepiness. |
| | READER'S REACTION: Why does this advice on getting a good night's sleep start off with *stimulation*? |
| EDITED | **A glass of milk or a carbohydrate snack** stimulates the production of serotonin and causes sleepiness. |

**Pay attention to noun strings.** Sometimes one noun modifies another or nouns plus adjectives modify other nouns: *sleep deprivation, jet lag, computer network server, triple bypass heart surgery*. Although unfamiliar **noun strings** can be hard to understand, familiar ones can be concise and clear.

To edit confusing noun strings, try turning the key word in a string (usually the last noun) into a verb. Then turn other nouns from the string into prepositional phrases.

| | |
|---|---|
| CONFUSING | The team did a ceramic valve lining design flaw analysis. |
| | READER'S REACTION: Did the team analyze flaws or use a special feature called flaw analysis? Did they study ceramic valves or valve linings made of ceramic material? |
| EDITED | The team **analyzed** flaws **in** the lining design **for** ceramic valves. |

Another option is to turn one noun into the sentence's subject.

| | |
|---|---|
| EDITED | **Flaws** in the lining design for ceramic valves were analyzed by the team. |

**Use *I, we,* and *you.*** *I, we,* and *you*, although inappropriate in some academic settings, are commonly used in work and public communities. (See 28a.)

| | |
|---|---|
| VAGUE AND WEAK | The project succeeded because of careful cost control and attention to the customer's needs. |
| CLEAR AND FORCEFUL | The project succeeded because **we** controlled costs carefully and paid attention to **our** customers' needs. |

## 2 Concentrate on verbs and predicates

Strong verbs can make sentences forceful and clear. Here are four steps you can take to strengthen your verbs.

1. Replace the verb *be* (*is, are, was, were, will be*) with a more forceful verb, especially in sentences that list or identify qualities.

   **WEAK**      Our agency **is** responsible for all aspects of disaster relief.

   **STRONGER**  Our agency **plans**, **funds**, and **delivers** disaster relief.

2. Turn nouns that follow forms of *be* into clear, specific verbs.

   **WEAK**      The new recycling system is a **money saver**.

   **STRONGER**  The new recycling system **saves money**.

3. Replace **expletive** constructions, sentences beginning with *there is, there are*, or *it is* (see 19a-1), if they are wordy or obscure. (Keep them if they add variety, build suspense, or usefully withhold information about the doer.)

   **WEAK**      **There is** a need for more classrooms at Kenny School.

   **STRONGER**  **Kenny School needs** more classrooms.

4. Eliminate general verbs (*do, give, have, get, provide, shape, make*) linked to nouns; turn the nouns into verbs.

   **WEAK**      Our company **has done a study** of the new design.

   **STRONGER**  Our company **has studied** the new design.

---

### ESL ADVICE: *THERE* AND *IT* AS SUBJECTS

When you use *there* and *it* as the subjects of sentences, these pronouns may not have the object or place meanings usually attached to them. *There* may introduce new, unknown material, while *it* may introduce environmental conditions (including distance, time, and weather).

**DRAFT**   Although there was snowing, it was dancing after dinner.

**EDITED**  Although **it** was snowing, **there** was dancing after dinner.

## 3 Select active or passive voice

When you use a verb in the **active voice** (see 20i), the agent (or doer) is also the subject of the sentence.

                  agent      action              goal
The outfielder caught the towering fly ball.
                  subject    verb                object

When you choose the **passive voice** (see 20i), you turn the sentence's goal into the subject. You de-emphasize the doer by placing it in a prepositional phrase or by dropping an unknown or unimportant agent altogether.

              goal      action          [agent]
The towering fly ball was caught [by the outfielder].
              subject   verb      [prepositional phrase]

Many writers favor the active voice because it is direct and concise, and many readers find too much passive voice weak. On the other hand, the passive voice may be favored in lab reports and other scientific or technical writing in both academic and work communities. It avoids spotlighting the researcher or repeating the researcher's actions; instead it focuses on results—what happens, not who does it. It also may be used ethically to protect someone's identity, such as a child or the victim of crime or abuse. At the same time, it may inadvertently, or even deliberately, conceal a doer (or agent), thus obscuring responsibility for actions.

**AGENT DE-EMPHASIZED**   Federal tax forms have been mailed. [By the IRS, of course.]

**AGENT CONCEALED**   Hasty decisions were made in this zoning case. [By whom?]

Rewrite sentences in the passive voice that add extra words, create inappropriate emphasis, or omit the doer (see 28c–d).

                           subject
**PASSIVE VOICE (15 WORDS)**   **Three thousand people** affected by the toxin were interviewed
                                                              agent
by **the Centers for Disease Control**.

                              agent (subject)
**ACTIVE VOICE (13 WORDS)**   **The Centers for Disease Control** interviewed three thousand people affected by the toxin.

## 4 Create variety and emphasis

If you feel that editing for clarity produces too many similar sentences, try some of the following options to direct the attention of your readers.

- Emphasize material by shifting it to the places where a reader's attention gravitates—the **sentence opening or closing**.
- **Repeat key words and ideas** within a sentence or cluster of sentences to draw attention to them. (Avoid too much repetition that calls attention to itself rather than your ideas.)

- Try **climactic sentence order**—sentences that build to a climax—to create powerful emphasis. Such sentences can stress new information at the end or focus on the last element in a series.
- Try an occasional **periodic sentence**. By piling up phrases, clauses, and words at the start, create suspense by delaying the main clause.
- Consider creating a **cumulative sentence**. Start with the main clause, and then add, bit by bit, details and ideas in the form of modifying phrases, clauses, and words to build a detailed picture, an intricate explanation, or a cluster of ideas and information.
- Vary your **sentence length**. Add short sentences for dramatic flair. Use longer ones to explore relationships among ideas and build rhythmic effects. Use middle-length sentences as workhorses, carrying the burden of explanation, but don't use too many in a sequence.
- Vary your sentence types (see 19d-2). **Declarative sentences** present, explain, and support ideas or information. An occasional exclamation (**exclamatory sentence**), a mild order (**imperative sentence**), or a question (**interrogative sentence**) can change your pace.
- Surprise your readers on occasion. Add **key words** to summarize and redirect a sentence. **Extend a sentence** that appears to have ended, adding new information or twists of thought. Use parallelism (see 30b) to highlight a contrast in a witty, dramatic, or ironic **antithesis**.

# Editing Word Choice: Matching Words to Communities

## ▼ *TAKING IT ONLINE*

**MERRIAM-WEBSTER ONLINE**
http://www.m-w.com
**THE AMERICAN HERITAGE DICTIONARY OF THE ENGLISH LANGUAGE**
http://www.bartleby.com/61/
Each dictionary site encourages you to type in a word and find its definition, history, and pronunciation.

**THESAURUS.COM**
http://www.thesaurus.com/
Simply enter a word on the site, hit "Return" to see a list of synonyms, and then click on each of those for dozens more.

**GENDER FAIR LANGUAGE**
http://www.rpi.edu/dept/llc/writecenter/web/genderfair.html
Use the suggestions on this page to avoid sexist slips.

**IDIOMS, PHRASAL VERBS, AND SLANG QUIZZES**
http://www.aitech.ac.jp/~iteslj/quizzes/idioms.html
This Web site can help ESL students and native speakers alike learn some of the most common English idioms. More than fifty links to short quizzes are sorted by category.

**WORLD WIDE WORDS**
http://www.quinion.com/words/
This engaging site encourages you to think about word choice and precise meaning. Check out the "Topical Words" and "Weird Words" sections to see how new and strange words come into use.

**A.WORD.A.DAY**
http://www.wordsmith.org/awad/
Do you want to build your vocabulary? This site archives one of the Internet's most popular mailing lists, sending out a word each day.

**PART 7**

# Editing Word Choice: Matching Words to Communities

# 33 Being Concise

Leaving extra words in your writing wastes valuable space—and your readers' time.

**WORDY**    **There is evidence that the use of** pay **as an** incentive **can be a contributing or causal factor in** improvement **of the** quality **of** work.

READER'S REACTION: **Why is this so long-winded? What's the point?**

**TRIMMED**    Incentive pay improves work quality.

READER'S REACTION: **That's short and direct—but maybe too abrupt.**

**RESHAPED**    Incentive pay **often encourages** work **of higher** quality.

READER'S REACTION: **Now I'm gaining a fuller, more subtle perspective.**

**Conciseness** means using only the words you need—not the fewest words possible, but those appropriate for your purpose, meaning, and readers. (See 32b and 34b.) Your situation may define the conciseness necessary: letters to the editor have word limits, speeches have time limits, and most grant proposals have page limits. Adhere to these limits—run a word count, rehearse an oral presentation, and check length.

## 33a Recognizing common types of wordiness

Imagine an ideal reader—a respected teacher, a savvy co-worker, or a wise civic leader. If a passage seems wordy, ask, "What would I need to tell *X* here?" Or think of *X* asking, "What's your point?"

Look for **wordy phrases** you can shrink to a word or two.

**WORDY**    Carbon 14 can be used to date a site only **in the event that** organic material has survived. **In a situation in which** rocks need dating, potassium-argon testing is used.

**CUT**    Carbon 14 can be used to date a site only **if** organic material has survived. **When** rocks need dating, potassium-argon testing is used.

Watch for **intensifying phrases** (for all intents and purposes, in my opinion), intended to add force but often carrying little meaning.

## COMMON WORDY PHRASES

| PHRASE | | REPLACEMENT |
|---|---|---|
| due to the fact that | = | because |
| at the present moment | = | now |
| a considerable proportion of | = | many, most |
| has the capability of | = | can |
| regardless of the fact that | = | although |
| concerning the matter of | = | about |

**WORDY**  **As a matter of fact**, most archaeological discoveries can be dated accurately.

**CUT**  Most archaeological discoveries can be dated accurately.

Target clutter such as **all-purpose words** (*factor, aspect, situation, type, field, range, thing, kind, nature*) and **all-purpose modifiers** (*very, totally, major, central, great, really, definitely, absolutely*).

**WORDY**  In the short story, Young Goodman Brown is so **totally** overwhelmed by **his own** guilt that he becomes **extremely** suspicious of the people around him. [25 words]

**CUT**  In the short story, Young Goodman Brown is so overwhelmed by guilt that he becomes suspicious of the people around him. [21 words]

**REWRITTEN**  In the short story, Young Goodman Brown's **overwhelming** guilt makes him **suspect everyone**. [13 words]

Simplify pairs that say the same thing twice (*each and every*) and **redundant phrases** in which adjectives repeat nouns (*final outcomes*), adverbs repeat verbs (*completely finished*), or specific words imply general (*small in size*).

**WORDY**  Because it was **sophisticated in nature** and **tolerant in style**, Kublai Khan's administration aided China's development in the 1200s.

**CUT**  Because it was **sophisticated and tolerant**, Kublai Khan's administration aided China's development in the 1200s.

**REWRITTEN**  Kublai Khan's **adept and tolerant administration** aided China's development in the 1200s.

## 33b Editing for conciseness

Edit both wordy expressions and wordy sentence patterns (see 32b).

**Trim ideas already stated or implied.** Do not cut useful repetition that helps readers follow an explanation or argument.

REPETITIVE    **Our proposal** outlines a **three-step** program for **converting the building** into a **research center** for the study of film and culture. Each of the **three steps** discussed in **our proposal** should be completed in six months. We expect that **the building** will be **converted** to a **research center** eighteen months from the time work is begun.

CUT    We propose **three steps** for **converting the building** into a center for the study of film and culture. Allowing six months for each **step**, we expect **the building** to be **converted** in eighteen months.

**Trim *which, who,* or *that* clauses and *of* phrases.** Do this by converting clauses to phrases, phrases to words.

CLAUSES    Chavez Park, **which is an extensive facility in the center of town**, was named after Cesar Chavez, **who fought for migrant farmers' rights**.

CUT TO PHRASES    Chavez Park, **an extensive facility in the center of town**, was named after Cesar Chavez, **an advocate for migrant farmers**.

CUT TO WORDS    Chavez Park, **an extensive downtown facility**, was named after **migrant advocate** Cesar Chavez.

**Replace generalities with connections and details.** First highlight the key words in a passage. Then make two changes: combine sentences to eliminate vague or repetitive wording, and add specific, concrete detail to support your main points.

WORDY    **Glaciers** were of central importance in the **shaping of the North American landscape**. They were responsible for many familiar geological features. Among the many remnants of glacial activity are **deeply carved valleys** and **immense piles of sand and rock**.

SENTENCES COMBINED    Glaciers carved deep valleys and left behind immense piles of sand and rock, shaping much of the North American landscape in the process.

DETAILS ADDED    Glaciers carved deep valleys and left behind immense piles of sand and rock, shaping much of the North American landscape in the process. **Cape Cod and Long**

> **Island are piles of gravel deposited by glaciers. The Mississippi River and the Great Lakes remained when the ice melted.**

**Reduce unnecessary writer's commentary.** Make sure your comments guide readers, but don't overdo the commentary and end up talking about yourself rather than your subject.

IRRITATING    **In my paper, I intend to show** that the benefits of placebos (pills with no physical effect) include improvements and cures, **as mentioned above**.

EDITED    The benefits of placebos (pills with no physical effect) include improvements and cures.

# 34 Choosing Appropriate Words

Edit your words so that you express what you mean correctly and appropriately for your readers.

DRAFT    Dr. Parsippani **murdered** Mr. Rollet.

READER'S REACTION: **Does the writer intend a charge of foul play? Or is this wording imprecise?**

Here, *murdered* indicates foul play, although *assassinated* might fit if Rollet were a political figure. If the writer didn't intend these meanings, *killed* might be the most precise choice. Audience expectations also affect **diction**, the choice of words and phrases. For instance, the criminal justice system defines *murder* by degree and distinguishes *homicide* from *manslaughter*.

Besides being *correct*, words need to be *appropriate*. For example, referring in an academic paper to "this guy's theories" technically isn't *incorrect* since *guy* does refer to a person. But it violates expectations and therefore is *inappropriate*. Attending to community sensitivities of this kind reassures a teacher, supervisor, or member of the public of your credibility.

## 34a Recognizing incorrect or inappropriate word choice

Select words that fit your readers, purpose, and image.

## 1 Look for diction appropriate for a specialized context

Adjust your diction to your academic discipline or your workplace, using the specialized and precise language required in that context.

TOO GENERAL [*in an analysis of a painting for an art history course*] Tiepolo's *Apotheosis of the Pisani Family* (1761) is a lively painting typical of the period when it was painted with lots of action going on and nice colors.

READER'S REACTION: **This wording seems too general for an analysis in my field of art history.**

EDITED Tiepolo's *Apotheosis of the Pisani Family* (1761) shows affinities with typical rococo frescoes of the period, including bright colors with characters in highlighted actions set against dark border accents.

## 2 Look for diction that meets your readers' expectations

In college and workplace writing that assumes a fairly formal diction, avoid **colloquialisms**, informal expressions typical of a region or group.

TOO INFORMAL The stock market crash didn't seem to **faze** many of the investors with **megabucks stashed** in property assets.

READER'S REACTION: **This seems so informal that I'm not sure I trust the writer's authority.**

EDITED The stock market crash did not profoundly affect investors with extensive property assets.

## 3 Look for diction that supports your purpose

In order to inform or persuade readers, academic, work, and public communities alike may favor balanced reasoning over highly emotional language.

BIASED Most proponents of rock-music censorship grew up listening to pablum, thinking wimpy bands like the Beach Boys were a bunch of perverts.

READER'S REACTION: **This writer seems too biased and emotional to weigh all sides of the debate.**

EDITED Proponents of rock-music censorship may unfairly stereotype all of rock-and-roll culture as degenerate or evil.

## 4 Look for diction that suits your persona

Your **persona** is the role or character you assume in your writing. For example, an objective, detached persona in a clinical report assures a reader of accuracy, but this same persona might seem cold and impersonal in the adoption column of the animal shelter newsletter.

**TOO CLINICAL FOR CONTEXT**   Three domestic canines, *Canis familiaris*, type Shetland sheepdog; age: 8 weeks; coloring: burnt umber with variegated blond diameters; behaviorally modified for urination and defecation; inoculated.

READER'S REACTION: **Why would someone at the shelter talk so uncaringly about the puppies, treating them like laboratory specimens?**

**EDITED**   Three healthy sheltie puppies 8 weeks old, brown with light spots, housebroken, all shots.

## 34b Editing for precise diction

When you choose among **synonyms**, words identical or nearly so in meaning, consider their **connotations**—"shades" of meaning or associations acquired over time. Use concrete, direct wording unless the context calls for specialized language or more abstraction.

**Choose precise, concrete, and direct words.** Here are some suggestions for editing your work.

• Replace an inexact word with an appropriate synonym.

**IMPRECISE**   The senator **retreated** from the gathering.

READER'S REACTION: **Did the senator feel attacked, bewildered, or overcome? Or did she just leave?**

**EDITED**   The senator **left** the gathering.

• Replace vague words with specific ones.

**VAGUE**   [*in a do-it-yourself brochure on bathroom remodeling*] Do not place flooring over uneven floor or damaged area.

READER'S REACTION: **What's this about a damaged area?**

**EDITED**   Do not **install** flooring over **existing** floors that are **uneven or show signs of wood rot. Replace** any damaged **flooring material before installing new flooring**.

• Stick mostly to simple, familiar words.

**STUFFY**   The reflections upon premarital cohabitation promulgated by the courts eventuated in the orientation of the population in the direction of moral relaxation on this issue.

READER'S REACTION: **How dull! Say it more plainly, please.**

**EDITED**   Court decisions about living together before marriage led to greater public acceptance of this practice.

**Idioms** are expressions, often with "forgotten histories," whose meanings differ from their literal definitions, as in *wipe the slate clean* for "start over." Overused idioms can lose their freshness, becoming trite or clichéd; replace them with precise words.

IDIOMATIC   The losers complained of **dog-eat-dog** politics.

EDITED   The losers consoled themselves after their defeat.

---

### ESL ADVICE: IDIOMS IN AMERICAN ENGLISH

Whether an expression is an **idiom** or a **phrasal verb** (see 18c), the meanings of its separate words will not reveal its meaning as a whole. Although memorizing idioms will enrich your spoken English, these expressions may be too informal in many writing situations. In class or at work, notice how many and which idioms appear in well-written papers by native speakers; adjust your usage accordingly.

---

## 35 Using Respectful Language

To represent others fairly, writers and editors eliminate sexist and discriminatory language from their work.

DRAFT   Early in his career, Lasswell published his **seminal** work on propaganda.

READER 1: **Why do you have to use this word? It's offensive to associate originality and creativity with being male.**

READER 2: **You could replace** *seminal* **with** *important* **or** *influential.*

READER 3: **Aren't you overreacting? You wouldn't throw out** *matrimony* **just because it's related to the Latin word for** *mother* **or** *patriot* **because it comes from the word for** *father.*

No matter how you feel about diversity, as a writer you *must* consider how readers react to your representation of men, women, and members of minority groups. You don't want to alienate readers, prejudice people against your ideas, or perpetuate unhealthy attitudes.

## 35a Recognizing and editing gender stereotypes

The most common form of sexist language uses *mankind* or *men* for humankind; *he, his,* or *him* for all people; and words implying men in occupations (*fireman*). When editing the generic *he*, try first to make the construction plural (for example, use *their* for *his* or for the clumsy *his or her*).

| SEXIST | Every trainee should bring **his** laptop with **him**. |
| AWKWARD | Every trainee should bring **his or her** laptop with **him or her**. |
| BETTER | All trainees should bring **their** laptops with **them**. |

Some guides suggest that a plural pronoun is better than the generic *he*, even if the pronoun does not agree in number with the subject (see 22b). Some readers, however, object more strenuously to the agreement error than to the sexist language. Reword to avoid both problems.

| ORIGINAL | **Everyone** has at some time squandered **his** money. |
| PROBLEMATIC | **Everyone** has at some time squandered **their** money. |
| BETTER | **Most people have** at some time squandered **their** money. |
| BETTER | **Everyone** has at some time squandered money. |

Your readers are likely to object to negative stereotypes based on gender, such as assumptions that men are stronger or women are worse at math.

| STEREOTYPED | The OnCall Pager is **smaller than most doctors' wallets and easier to answer than phone calls from their wives**. |
| | READER'S REACTION: **I'm a woman and a doctor. I'm insulted by the assumption that all doctors are male and by the negative reference to "wives." OnCall will never sell a pager in my office!** |
| EDITED | The OnCall Pager **will appeal to doctors because it is small and easy to operate**. |

## 35b Recognizing and editing racial, ethnic, and cultural stereotypes

Most readers won't tolerate racism and will stop reading material with discriminatory language. Don't rely on your intent; think about how your reader *might* construe your words.

| DEMEANING | My paper focuses on the **weird** courtship rituals of a **barbaric** Aboriginal tribe in southwestern Australia. |
| | READER'S REACTION: **Your paper sounds biased. How can you treat this topic fairly if you don't respect the tribe?** |

EDITED My paper focuses on the unique courtship rituals of an Aboriginal tribe in southwestern Australia.

Some racial and cultural stereotypes are so ingrained that you may not notice them at first. You may be used to hearing derogatory terms in others' speech, or you may not even know that a term is derogatory. Trusted readers can circle stereotypes and derogatory wording for you, and you can do the same for them.

RACIST The economic problems in border states are compounded by an increased number of **wetbacks** from Mexico.

READER'S REACTION: **This derogatory name is offensive. I object to characterizing a group of people this way.**

EDITED The economic problems in border states are compounded by an increased number of illegal immigrants from Mexico.

HOMOPHOBIC The talk show included a panel of **fags** who spoke about what it's like to be a **homo**.

READER'S REACTION: **Emotionally loaded names for people don't encourage reasonable discussion. You'll have to be more objective if you want me to pay attention to your ideas.**

EDITED The talk show included a panel of gay guests who shared their thoughts about homosexuality.

DEROGATORY In typical **white-male** fashion, the principal argued against the teachers' referendum.

READER'S REACTION: **The fact that white men are in the majority doesn't give you permission to stereotype them negatively.**

EDITED The principal argued against the teachers' referendum.

DISCRIMINATORY The Johnsons **welshed** on their promise.

READER'S REACTION: **What made you think that you could say this without offending people of Welsh descent? Casual stereotyping is just as offensive as deliberate insults.**

EDITED The Johnsons broke their promise.

Deciding how to identify groups may be difficult. The term *American Indian* is still widely accepted, but *Native American* is preferred. In the 1960s, *Negro* gradually gave way to *black*, but *African American* has gained popularity in its place. *Colored* has been out of use for some time, but *people of color* is now preferred for members of any "nonwhite" group (although some object to *nonwhite*). Terms for those of Hispanic descent include *Chicano* (and its feminine form, *Chicana*) for Mexicans and *Latino* and *Latina* for people from South and Central America in general.

- Whenever possible, use the term preferred by the group itself.
- When there is disagreement within the group, choose the *most widely accepted term* or one favored by a majority of the members.

# 36 Building Your Language Resources

The richer your vocabulary, the better you write and read.

**CIVIC NEWSLETTER**
Despite our efforts to lobby for a compromise, the senate engaged in an **internecine** feud over the bill.
READER'S REACTION: **I like *internecine* here to suggest the senate's destructive internal conflict.**

**WORK MEMO**
Thanks to the marketing team for its **stellar** effort.
READER'S REACTION: **What a nice way to say "job well done"!**

A varied vocabulary is essential to effective writing and easy reading in academic, work, and public communities. The more extensive your language options, the more varied, accurate, and metaphoric your prose can be. And readers will appreciate your efforts to find just the right word.

## 36a Recognizing your language resources as a writer

The writer can rework this sentence for a grant proposal *because she has options*—words like *beneficence* or *sustenance*.

Without **help**, the food-shelf program may be **ineffective**.

Without the **aid** of the Talbot Foundation, the food-shelf program may become **obsolete**.

Without the **beneficence** of the Talbot Foundation, the food-shelf program may **die**.

Without the **financial** beneficence of the Talbot Foundation, the food-shelf program in Seattle may die **of starvation**.

Without the financial **sustenance** of the Talbot Foundation, Seattle's food-shelf program may **slowly** die of starvation.

**STRATEGY** **Build a personal vocabulary list.**

Use your **journal** (a record of your observations and insights) or any notebook to list unfamiliar words. Look them up, review them, incorporate them as you write, and cross them out when you can use them comfortably.

Gather these words from whatever you read—public opinion pieces in the newspaper, textbooks for school, or technical materials at work.

## 36b Turning to the dictionary and the thesaurus

Hundreds of times you've flipped the dictionary open and checked a word's spelling or meaning. Look carefully to find much more. (See Figure 36.1, an example from *Merriam-Webster's Collegiate Dictionary*.) Like the printed versions, software dictionaries may also supply definitions, usage notes, word histories, and spelling correctors that can be personalized by adding words used often in a particular community (see 18d).

A **thesaurus**, printed or electronic, is a dictionary of **synonyms** and **antonyms**—words related or opposite in meaning. Under *funny*, for example, *Webster's Collegiate Thesaurus* lists synonyms such as *laughable, comical, ludicrous,* and *ridiculous.* Entries may also refer you to contrasted or compared words and related alternatives.

**STRATEGY**  Develop your skills as a "wordsmith."

- **Use a dictionary.** Circle any words you've learned recently or rarely used; look them up to be sure you've used them correctly. Try an ESL dictionary if you're not a native speaker.
- **Turn to a thesaurus.** Consider whether a new word choice is more accurate, more flavorful, or less redundant than your original choice. If in doubt, stick with words you know.

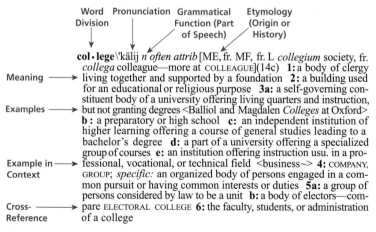

**FIGURE 36.1** Sample dictionary entry

- **Learn a new word every day**. Select a word you read or heard at school, at work, or in a public setting. Look up its definition and history. Work it into your speech or writing three times during the day, or make up sentences and repeat them to yourself.
- **Try the slash/option technique**. As you draft, note alternative words, separated with slashes. Decide later which word fits best.
- **Fight insecurity with simplicity**. Ask yourself which salesperson you would trust—one who talks in simple, honest language or one who uses fancy words for product features. Choose direct, concrete words yourself.
- **Ask a colleague or supervisor**. Someone more experienced may be able to tell you whether a term fits your community or context.

# Editing Punctuation:
# Following Community Guidelines

## ▾ *TAKING IT ONLINE*

**PUNCTUATION QUIZZES FOR ESL WRITERS**
http://www.pacificnet.net/~sperling/quiz/punctuation1.html
http://www.pacificnet.net/~sperling/quiz/punctuation2.html
These two quizzes are aimed at helping ESL students to distinguish the
comma and the semicolon and to use other marks correctly.

**PUNCTUATION MADE SIMPLE**
http://chuma.cas.usf.edu/~olson/pms/
This Web site aims to help writers overcome their fear of punctuation,
starting with a reassuring essay and covering the colon, semicolon, comma,
dash, and apostrophe.

**WRITE WORDS: THE ELUSIVE APOSTROPHE**
http://www.rightwords.co.nz/apos.html
The brief article on this New Zealand–based Web site outlines how and
when to use apostrophes.

**WHEN TO USE—AND NOT TO USE—QUOTATION MARKS**
http://www.wilbers.com/quotes.htm
This handy list of rules and instructions from the *Writing for Business and
Pleasure* Web site also includes a helpful article: "Quotation Marks Make
Reading Easy, Writing Hard."

**GRAMMAR, PUNCTUATION, AND SPELLING**
http://www.owl.english.purdue.edu/handouts/grammar/index.html
Browse here for punctuation advice and exercises.

# PART 8

# Editing Punctuation: Following Community Guidelines

# 37 | Using Commas

Of all the punctuation marks in English, the comma is probably the easiest to misuse.

**DRAFT**      During the study interviews were used to gather responses from participants and, to supplement written artifacts.

**READER'S REACTION: This sentence is hard to read. I can't tell where ideas end and begin.**

**EDITED**      During the study **,** interviews were used to gather responses from participants and to supplement written artifacts.

Readers who expect commas in certain situations are likely to find inappropriate commas confusing or disruptive.

## 37a Using commas to join sentences

When you use *and, but, or, for, nor, so,* or *yet* (**coordinating conjunctions**) to link two word groups that could stand alone as sentences (**main clauses**), place a comma *before* the conjunction.

The election was close **,** **and** he couldn't tell who was winning.

He heard no cheering **,** **yet** he decided to return to headquarters.

Precincts were still reporting **,** **but** the mayor's lead had grown.

Join main clauses with a comma *plus* a coordinating conjunction. If you omit the conjunction and join the clauses with only a comma, you create a **comma splice** (see 25a). Readers will react more strongly if you omit a conjunction than a comma, but they'll see both as errors in formal writing.

**COMMA SPLICE**      The rain soaked the soil **,** the mud slide buried the road.

**EDITED**      The rain soaked the soil **,** **and** the mud slide buried the road.

When a coordinating conjunction links two word groups, how can you decide whether to add a comma? Analyze the word groups. If both can stand on their own as sentences (main clauses), add a comma *before* the conjunction.

main clause,          (and, but, or, for,<br>
                       nor, so, yet)      main clause<br>

We wanted to deliver the order **,** **but** the weather was too bad.

If one or both of the groups *cannot* stand alone as a sentence (main clause), do *not* separate the items in the pair with a comma.

| | |
|---|---|
| **PAIR SPLIT** | We sanded **,** and stained the old oak table. |
| **EDITED** | We **sanded** and **stained** the old oak table. |
| **PAIR SPLIT** | I bought the wood stain because it was inexpensive **,** and easy to clean up. |
| **EDITED** | I bought the wood stain **because it was inexpensive** and **easy to clean up**. |

When two main clauses are very short, a comma is always appropriate but sometimes can be omitted, especially in public and informal contexts. Some academic readers, however, will expect you to use this comma in nearly every case.

The temperature dropped **and** the homeless shelters reopened.

---

## 37b Using commas to set off sentence elements

A comma can help your readers distinguish potentially confusing sentence parts. The simplest sentences, consisting of a noun phrase and a verb phrase, need no comma.

noun phrase     verb phrase<br>
Dr. Bandolo is my physician.

When you add another layer to the beginning—an **introductory word or word group**—you may need to signal the addition with a comma.

**Although I am healthy ,** I see my doctor for a regular checkup.

**For the past decade ,** Dr. Bandolo worked in an HMO.

**Nonetheless ,** she may open her own practice.

The basic structure of a sentence can be interrupted with all sorts of **parenthetical expressions** that add information: words like *however* and *moreover* (**conjunctive adverbs**, see 23a); phrases like *on the other hand* or *for example* (**transitional expressions**); and **parenthetical remarks** or **interrupters** (*in*

*fact, more importantly).* If the expression begins or ends the sentence, use one comma. If it falls in the middle, use a pair.

| | |
|---|---|
| **TRANSITIONAL** | **On the other hand,** the hail caused severe damage. |
| **INTERRUPTER** | It broke**,** **I think,** a dozen stained glass windows. |
| **CONJUNCTIVE ADVERB** | We hope**,** **therefore,** that someone starts a repair fund. |

Also set off tag questions, statements of contrast, and direct address.

| | |
|---|---|
| **TAG QUESTION** | We should contribute**,** **shouldn't we?** |
| **CONTRAST** | The church's beauty touches all of us**,** **not just the members.** |
| **DIRECT ADDRESS** | Recall**,** **friends of beauty,** that every gift helps. |

## 1 Put a comma after an introductory word or word group

Readers usually expect a comma to simplify reading by signaling where introductory wording ends and the main sentence begins. To decide whether to include a comma, consider the readability of a sentence.

| | |
|---|---|
| **CONFUSING** | Forgetting to alert the media before the rally Jessica rushed to the park. |
| **EDITED** | Forgetting to alert the media before the rally**,** Jessica rushed to the park. |

In contrast, these sentences are easy to understand without a comma.

| | |
|---|---|
| **CLEAR** | By noon Jessica will be finished with her speech. |
| **CLEAR** | Suddenly it started raining, and Jessica quit speaking. |

In general, put a comma at the end of a long introductory element introduced by words like *although, because,* and *when* (subordinators, see 31b-c); words like *during* and *without* (prepositions, see 18f); or words like *running, distracted,* and *to analyze* (verbals, see 19b-4). Also use a comma if a short introductory element might briefly confuse readers.

| | |
|---|---|
| **CONFUSING** | By six boats began showing up. |
| **EDITED** | By six**,** boats began showing up. |

## 2 Set off parenthetical expressions with commas

Use a pair of commas around a parenthetical expression or interrupter in the middle of a sentence; use a single comma with one at the beginning or end.

| | |
|---|---|
| DRAFT | Teams should meet even spontaneously as often as needed. |
| EDITED | Teams should meet **,** even spontaneously **,** as often as needed. |

## 37c Using commas to set off nonessential modifiers

Modifiers qualify or describe nouns, verbs, or other sentence elements. You change the meaning of a sentence when you decide whether to set off a modifying word or phrase with commas. You can use a **restrictive modifier** to present essential information. Add the essentials *without* commas so that readers see them as a necessary, integral part of the sentence.

RESTRICTIVE   The charts **drawn by hand** were hard to read.

> READER'S REACTION: **I assume that the other charts, maybe generated on a computer, were easier to read than these.**

You also can use a **nonrestrictive modifier** to add information that is interesting or useful but not necessary for the meaning. Set the nonessentials off *with* commas so that readers regard them as helpful but not necessary details.

NONRESTRICTIVE   The charts **,** **drawn by hand** **,** were hard to read.

> READER'S REACTION: **All the charts were hard to read. The detail that they were hand drawn doesn't necessarily relate to readability.**

---

**STRATEGY**   Test for nonrestrictive and restrictive modifiers.

Drop the test modifier from the sentence. If you can do so without altering the essential meaning, even if the sentence is less informative, the modifier is *nonrestrictive* (nonessential). Set it off with commas.

DRAFT   Their band **which performs primarily in small clubs** has gotten fine reviews.

DROP TEST   Their band has gotten fine reviews.

> **The meaning is the same, although the sentence does not offer as much interesting information. The modifier is nonrestrictive.**

COMMAS ADDED   Their band **,** **which performs primarily in small clubs** **,** has gotten fine reviews.

If dropping the modifier changes the meaning of the sentence, the modifier is *restrictive* (essential). Delete any commas with it.

DRAFT   Executives **,** **who do not know how to cope with stress** **,** are prone to stress-related illness.

**DROP TEST**     Executives are prone to stress-related illness.
**The intended meaning is that *some* executives are prone to stress-related problems; in contrast, the shortened sentence says they *all* are. The modifier is restrictive.**

**COMMAS**       Executives **who do not know how to cope with stress** are
**OMITTED**      prone to stress-related illness.

Try memorizing this formula.

*non*restrictive = *non*essential = *not* integrated (separated by commas)
restrictive     = essential     = integrated (not separated by commas)

Place commas before, after, or around nonrestrictive modifiers.

                              nonrestrictive
        main clause begins,     modifier,        main clause ends
        The public hearing, set for 7 p.m., will address cable TV rates.

        nonrestrictive modifier,                   main clause
        Because of rising costs, the companies have requested a rate hike.

             main clause,                   nonrestrictive modifier
        Many residents oppose the hike, which is larger than last year's.

**Clauses with *who*, *which*, and *that*.** Use commas to set off nonrestrictive clauses beginning with *who, which, whom, whose, when,* or *where* (see 19c). Because *that* can specify rather than simply add information, it is used in restrictive (essential) clauses. *Which* is often used to add nonessential information but can be used both ways.

**NONRESTRICTIVE**   Preventive dentistry, **which is receiving great emphasis,** may actually reduce visits to the dentist's office.

**NONRESTRICTIVE**   At the heart of preventive dentistry are toothbrushing, flossing, and rinsing, **which are all easily done.**

**RESTRICTIVE**   Dentists **who make a special effort to encourage good oral hygiene** often supply helpful pamphlets.

**RESTRICTIVE**   They also provide samples of toothbrushes and floss **that encourage preventive habits.**

**Appositives.** An **appositive** is a noun or pronoun that renames or stands for a preceding noun. Most are nonrestrictive and need commas.

**NONRESTRICTIVE**   Amy Nguyen, **a poet from Vietnam,** recently published her latest collection of verse.

**RESTRICTIVE**   The well-known executive **Louis Gerstner** went from heading RJR Nabisco to the top job at IBM.

## 37d Using commas to separate items in a series

When you list items of roughly equal status in a series, separate the items with commas. Readers expect such commas because reading a series can be difficult, even confusing, without them.

> The human relations office has forms for medical benefits **,** insurance options **, and** retirement contributions.

If an item has more than one part, put a comma after the entire unit.

> The human relations office has forms for medical and dental benefits **,** disability and insurance options **, and** retirement contributions.

Avoid confusion by placing a comma before the *and* that introduces the last item in a series. Outside the academic community, this comma is often omitted, especially in a short, clear list. Within the academic community, however, both the MLA and APA style guides recommend this comma because it reduces ambiguity (see Chapters 16 and 17).

CONFUSING     New members fill out applications, interest-group surveys, mailing labels and publication request forms.

READER'S REACTION: **Does *mailing labels and publication request forms* refer to one item or two?**

EDITED     New members fill out applications, interest-group surveys, mailing labels **,** and publication request forms.

Punctuate a numbered or lettered list in a sentence as a series. If items in a list contain commas, separate them with semicolons (see 38a-3).

> You should (a) measure the water's salinity **,** (b) weigh any waste in the filter **,** and (c) determine the amount of dissolved oxygen.

## 37e Using commas to separate adjectives in a sequence

When you use a pair of **coordinate adjectives**, each modifies the noun (or pronoun) on its own. Separate these adjectives with commas to show their equal application to the noun.

COORDINATE (EQUAL)     These drawings describe a **quick , simple** solution.

When you use **noncoordinate adjectives**, one modifies the other, and it, in turn, modifies the noun (or pronoun). Do not separate these adjectives with a comma.

| NONCOORDINATE (UNEQUAL) | We can use **flexible plastic** pipe to divert the water. |

---

**STRATEGY**    Asking questions to identify coordinate adjectives.

If you answer one of the following questions with *yes*, the adjectives are coordinate. Separate them with a comma.

- Can you place *and* or *but* between the adjectives?

| COORDINATE | Irrigation has turned dry infertile [*dry and infertile?—yes*] land into orchards. |
| EDITED | Irrigation has turned dry, infertile land into orchards. |
| NOT COORDINATE | The funds went to new computer [*new and computer?— no*] equipment. |

- Is the sense of the passage the same if you reverse the adjectives?

| COORDINATE | We left our small cramped [*cramped small?—yes, the same*] office. |
| EDITED | We left our small, cramped office. |
| NOT COORDINATE | We bought a red brick [*brick red?—no, not the same*] condo. **Because *brick red* is a color, the condo could be wooden.** |

---

## 37f Using commas with dates, numbers, addresses, place names, people's titles, and letters

Readers will expect you to follow conventional practice.

**Dates.** Put a comma between the date and the year, between the day of the week and the date, and after the year when you give a full date.

I ordered a laptop on May 3, 2004, that arrived Friday, May 21.

You don't need commas when a date is inverted (5 July 1973) or contains only month and year, month and day, or season and year.

We installed the software after its June 2003 test.

**Numbers.** To simplify long numbers for readers, use commas to create groups of three, beginning from the right. You may choose whether to use a comma with a four-digit number, but be consistent within a text.

We counted 1,746 sheep on a ranch worth $1,540,000.

Omit commas in addresses and page numbers of four digits or more.

> 18520 South Kedzie Drive        page 2054

**Addresses and place names.** Separate names of cities and states with commas. For an address within a sentence, place commas between all elements *except* the state and zip code. Do not place a comma after the zip code unless some other sentence element requires one.

> If you live in South Bend **,** Indiana **,** order locally from Frelle and Family **,** Seed Brokers **,** Box 389 **,** Holland **,** MI 30127.

**People's names and titles.** When you give a person's last name first, separate it from the first name with a comma: *Shamoon, Linda K.* Use a comma before and after a title that *follows* a person's name.

> We hired **Cris Bronkowski , A.I.A. ,** to design the building.

**Openings and closings of letters.** Use a comma after the opening of a personal letter, but use a colon in a business or formal letter. Use a comma after the closing, just before the signature.

> Dear Nan **,**      Dear Tennis Team **,**      Dear Hardware Customers **:**
>
> Sincerely **,**      Best wishes **,**      With affection **,**      Regards **,**

## 37g Using commas with quotations

When you introduce, interrupt, or conclude a quotation with a source or context, use commas to distinguish explanation from quotation.

> At the dedication, she stated **,** "This event celebrates Oakdale."
>
> "Our unity **,**" said the mayor **,** "is our strength."
>
> "Tomorrow the school can reopen **,**" the principal reported.

If your explanation ends with *that* just before a quotation, do not include a comma. If you quote a person's words indirectly (rather than word for word in quotation marks), do not use a comma after *that*.

> Lu introduced her by saying that "calamity followed Jane." Jane replied that she simply outran it.

## 37h Using commas to make your meaning clear

Even if no rule specifies a comma, add one if necessary to clarify your meaning, to remind readers of deleted words, or to emphasize.

**CONFUSING**    When food is scarce, animals that can expand their grazing territory at the expense of other species.

**EDITED**    When food is scarce, animals that can **,** expand their grazing territory at the expense of other species.

## 37i  Eliminating commas that do not belong

Avoid scattering commas through a paper; add them as required. Today most readers prefer a style in which commas are not used heavily. Too many commas, even correctly used, can create choppy prose.

**TOO MANY COMMAS (7)**    Rosa **,** always one **,** like her mother **,** to speak her mind **,** protested the use of force **,** as she called it **,** by two store detectives **,** who had been observing her.

**EDITED (2)**    Always one to speak her mind **,** like her mother **,** Rosa protested what she called the use of force by two store detectives.

- Omit commas after words like *although* and *because*. These subordinating conjunctions (see 31b–c) introduce a clause and should not be set off with commas. Conjunctive adverbs (like *however;* see 31a) and transitional expressions (like *for example*) should be set off with commas.

**EXTRA COMMA**    **Although ,** Jewel lost her luggage, she had her laptop.

**EDITED**    **Although** Jewel lost her luggage, she had her laptop.

- Remove commas between subjects and verbs unless a modifier separates them.

**SPLIT SUBJECT AND PREDICATE**    Cézanne's painting *Rocks at L'Estaque* **,** hangs in the Museu de Arte in São Paulo, Brazil.

**EDITED**    Cézanne's painting *Rocks at L'Estaque* hangs in the Museu de Arte in São Paulo, Brazil.

# 38  Using Semicolons and Colons

Semicolons and colons help readers make connections.

**TWO SENTENCES**    On April 12, 1861, one of Beauregard's batteries fired on Fort **Sumter** • **The** Civil War had begun.

READER'S REACTION: **Maybe these two sentences present a dramatic moment, or maybe they simply state facts, but they don't** *necessarily* **connect these events.**

SEMICOLON    On April 12, 1861, one of Beauregard's batteries fired on Fort **Sumter ;** **the** Civil War had begun.

READER'S REACTION: **The semicolon encourages me to link the battery firing to the Civil War beginning.**

COLON    On April 12, 1861, one of Beauregard's batteries fired on Fort **Sumter : the** Civil War had begun.

READER'S REACTION: **Now I see the guns' firing as a dramatic moment: the beginning of the Civil War.**

All three examples are correct, yet each encourages a different perspective. Readers expect you to use punctuation, especially semicolons and colons, to shape their responses and show them how your ideas relate.

 **38a** Using semicolons

A semicolon creates a brief reading pause that can dramatically highlight a close relationship or a contrast. The semicolon alone can't specify the relationship the way words like *because* or *however* can. Be sure, therefore, that the relationship you are signaling won't be puzzling to readers.

### 1 Join two sentences with a semicolon

A semicolon joins main clauses that can stand alone as complete sentences.

TWO SENTENCES    The demand for paper is at an all-time high• Businesses alone consume millions of tons each year.

ONE SENTENCE    The demand for paper is at an all-time high ; businesses alone consume millions of tons each year.

**STRATEGY**    **Test both sides of the semicolon.**

To make sure you are using the semicolon correctly, test the word groups on both sides to make sure they can stand on their own as sentences.

DRAFT    The demand for recycled paper increased greatly ; with manufacturers rushing to contract for scrap paper.

TEST CLAUSE 1    The demand for recycled paper increased greatly.
**The first clause is a complete sentence.**

TEST CLAUSE 2    With manufacturers rushing to contract for scrap paper.
**The second part is a sentence fragment.**

EDITED    The demand for recycled paper increased greatly ; manufacturers rushed to contract for scrap paper.

In some cases, elements within a second clause can be omitted if they "match" elements in the first clause. Then the two can be joined with a semicolon even though the second could not stand alone.

**ELEMENTS INCLUDED**     In winter, **the hotel guests enjoy** the log fire **;** in summer, **the hotel guests enjoy** the patio overlooking the river.

**ELEMENTS OMITTED**     In winter, **the hotel guests enjoy** the log fire **;** in summer, the patio overlooking the river.

## 2 Use a semicolon with words such as *however* and *on the other hand*

When you use a semicolon alone to link main clauses, you ask readers to recognize the logical link between the clauses. When you add words like *however* or *on the other hand*, you create a different effect on readers by specifying how the clauses relate.

assertion  →  semicolon  →  transition  →  assertion
(*pause*)     (*consider relationship*)

I like apples **;**          **however ,** I hate pears.
assertion  pause           contrast          assertion

To specify the transition between clauses, you can choose a **conjunctive adverb** such as *however, moreover, nonetheless, thus,* or *therefore* (see 31a) or a **transitional expression** like *for example, in contrast,* or *on the other hand*. Vary the punctuation depending on where you place such wording.

**BETWEEN CLAUSES**     Joe survived the flood **;** **however ,** Al was never found.

**WITHIN CLAUSE**     Joe survived the flood **;** Al **,** **however ,** was never found.

**AT END OF CLAUSE** Joe survived the flood **;** Al was never found **,** **however**.

## 3 Use a semicolon with a complex series

When items in a series contain commas, readers may have trouble deciding which commas separate parts of the series and which belong within items. To avoid confusion, put semicolons between elements in a series when one or more contain other punctuation.

**CONFUSING**     I interviewed Debbie Rios, the attorney, Rhonda Marron, the accountant, and the financial director.
        **READER'S REACTION: How many? Three, four, or five?**

**EDITED**     I interviewed Debbie Rios, the attorney **;** Rhonda Marron, the accountant **;** and the financial director.

## 38b Using colons

Use a colon to introduce, separate, or join elements.

### 1 Introducing examples, lists, and quotations

The words *before* the colon generally form a complete sentence while those after may or may not. When the words after the colon don't form a sentence, begin with a lowercase letter. When a sentence follows, begin with either a capital or lowercase letter. Stick to one style in a text.

**Examples.** Commonly, a colon follows a statement or generalization that the rest of the sentence illustrates, explains, or particularizes.

She has only one budget priority: teacher salaries.

**Lists.** A colon can introduce a list or series following a sentence. Following a word group other than a complete sentence, do not use a colon.

DRAFT      The symptoms are: sore throat, fever, and headache.

EDITED     She had three symptoms: sore throat, fever, and headache.

EDITED     The symptoms are sore throat, fever, and headache.

**Quotations.** Whether you integrate a short quotation with your own words or set off a longer one in your text (see 14b1-2), a complete sentence must precede a colon. If not, use a comma.

Ms. Nguyen outlined the plan: "Boost sales, and cut costs."

### 2 Separating titles and subtitles

Colons separate main titles from subtitles.

*Designing Your Web Site*: *A Beginner's Guide*      "Diabetes: Are You at Risk?"

Colons also separate hours from minutes (10:32); chapters from verses, as in the Bible (John 8:21–23); the salutation from the text of a business letter (Dear Ms. Billis:); parts of a ratio (2:3); parts of an electronic address (http://www.nytimes.com); and parts of references in some documentation styles (see Chapters 16–17).

### 3 Using a colon to join sentences

You can most effectively use a colon to join two word groups that can stand on their own as sentences (main clauses, see 25c). Use a colon when the second clause sharply focuses, sums up, or illustrates the first.

The blizzard swept across the prairie: **the Oregon Trail was closed**.

# 39 Using Apostrophes

Like the dot above the *i*, the apostrophe may seem trivial. But without it, readers would stumble over your sentences, growing irritated in the process.

**DRAFT** Though its an 1854 novel, Dickens *Hard Times* remain's an ageless critique of education by fact's.

> **READER'S REACTION: I can't tell possessives from plurals and contractions. This is too annoying to bother reading.**

**EDITED** Though **it 's** an 1854 novel, **Dickens 's** *Hard Times* **remains** an ageless critique of education by **facts**.

## 39a Using apostrophes that mark possession

A noun that expresses ownership is called a **possessive noun**. Mark possessive nouns to distinguish them from plurals.

**MISSING** The **cats** meow is becoming fainter.

> **READER'S REACTION: I expected something like "The cats meow all night." Do you mean many cats or the meow of one cat?**

**EDITED** The **cat 's** meow is becoming fainter.

---

**STRATEGY** Test for possession.

If you can turn a noun into a phrase using *of*, use a possessive form. If not, use a plural.

**DRAFT** The officers reports surprised the reporters.

**TEST** The reports **of** the officers? [yes, a possessive]

**TEST** Reports surprised **of** the reporters? [no, a plural]

**EDITED** The officers ' reports surprised the reporters.

### 1 Adding an apostrophe alone or an apostrophe plus *-s*

Use these guidelines to decide whether to add an apostrophe plus *-s* or an apostrophe alone.

- **Does the noun end in a letter other than -s?** When you write a singular possessive noun, usually follow it with an apostrophe plus *-s*.

  Bill**'s** coat        Connecticut**'s** taxes     the dog**'s** collar

  Possessive indefinite pronouns (see 18b) follow the same pattern.

  nobody**'s** report    everybody**'s** office     someone**'s** lunch

  A few nouns form their plurals (*mice, fish*) without ending in *-s* or *-es*.

  oxen**'s** habitat     children**'s** toys        women**'s** locker room

- **Does the noun end in -s, and is it plural** (more than one person or item)? Most plural nouns end in *-s* or *-es*. To make one possessive, simply add an apostrophe after the *-s*.

  the Solomon**s'** house     the rose**s'** petals      the bus**es'** routes

- **Does the noun end in -s, and is it singular** (one person or item)? Stick to one of two options in a paper. The preferred convention is to add an apostrophe and another *-s*, as with another singular noun.

  Chri**s's** van           Elliott Nes**s's** next move

  Alternatively, simply add an apostrophe to the final *-s*.

  Chri**s'** van            Elliott Nes**s'** next move

- **Does the noun end in -s and sound awkward?** Occasionally, adding a possessive *-s* (Hodges**'s**) to a word already ending in that sound will seem awkward to say ("Hodges-es"). If so, use only the apostrophe (Hodges**'**) to indicate only one *-s* sound, or avoid the awkwardness (*the Adams County Schools**'** policy*) by rewriting (*the policy of the Adams County Schools*).

In general, treat **hyphenated** and **multiple-word nouns** as a single unit, marking possession on the last word.

HYPHENATED    **My father-in-law's** library is extensive.

MULTIPLE-WORD    The **union leaders'** negotiations collapsed.

When you use a **compound noun phrase** (two or more nouns connected by *and* or *or*) as a possessive, decide whether the nouns function as separate items or as a single unit.

**Billy's and Harold's** lawyers were ruthless. [separate lawyers]

**Billy and Harold's** lawyers were ruthless. [same legal team]

## 2 Avoiding unnecessary apostrophes

Even though third person singular verbs end in -*s*, these are not nouns and do not have possessive forms. They don't require an apostrophe.

**DRAFT**    The contractor **order'** **s** all material early.

**EDITED**    The contractor **orders** all material early.

Don't add apostrophes to personal pronouns; they're already possessive. (See 39b.)

If this car is **yours**, why did you take **hers** and dent **its** fender?

## 39b Using apostrophes that mark contractions and omissions

You can use an apostrophe to indicate the omission of one or more letters when two words are brought together to form a **contraction**.

### 1 Using an apostrophe to contract a verb form

You can contract pronouns and verbs into a single unit (you'll = you + will) or splice nouns followed by *is*. If this informal style seems inappropriate in your class or workplace, always err on the side of formality.

**INFORMAL**      **Shoshana'** **s** going, but her **seat'** **s** in the last row.

**MORE FORMAL**   **Shoshana is** going, but her **seat is** in the last row.

---

**STRATEGY**    Expand the contraction.

To decide whether you have used a contraction appropriately, expand it.

| | | | | | |
|---|---|---|---|---|---|
| they're | = | they + are | there | = | an adverb |
| you're | = | you + are | your | = | a possessive pronoun |
| who's | = | who + is | whose | = | a possessive pronoun |
| it's | = | it + is | its | = | a possessive pronoun |

For example, test your use of the contraction *it's* by expanding the expression (*it* + *is*); if the expansion doesn't make sense, use *its*.

**DRAFT**           **Its** the best animal shelter in **its** area.

**EXPANSION TEST**  **It is** [yes, a fit] the best animal shelter in **it is** [no, not a fit] area.

**EDITED**          **It'** **s** the best animal shelter in **its** area.

## 2 Using an apostrophe to mark plural numbers and letters

Make letters and numbers plural by adding an apostrophe + -s.

**LETTERS**　Mind your **p'**s and **q'**s. The **x'**s mark missing lines.

**NUMBERS**　I'll take two size **10'**s and two size **12'**s.

Sometimes the apostrophe is omitted if it risks making a term look like a possessive (*TAs* or *TA's*). The MLA and APA styles (see Chapters 16–17) omit it from numbers and abbreviations (*1980s* and *IQs*).

## 3 Using an apostrophe to abbreviate a year or show colloquial pronunciation

Informally abbreviate years by omitting the first two numbers (*the '90s* or *the class of '05*) if the century is clear to readers. Also use apostrophes to indicate omissions in colloquial speech and dialects.

**DIALECT**　I'm **a-goin'** out for some **o'** them shrimp **an'** oysters.

# 40　Marking Quotations

Quotation marks play many conventional roles.

SERIOUS ERROR

**QUOTATION NOT FULLY MARKED**
"Thanks to the navigator," the pilot said, we made the landing.

**READER'S REACTION: Without quotation marks, I didn't realize at first that the pilot said the last part, too.**

**EDITED**
**"**Thanks to the navigator,**"** the pilot said, **"**we made the landing.**"**

Although conventions may vary slightly by field, readers in academic, work, and public settings expect you to use quotation marks precisely. How you use these marks tells readers who said what. (See 14b1–2.)

## 40a Using quotation marks

Quotation marks tell readers which words are someone else's (and which words are your own).

## 1 Identifying direct quotations and dialogue

Whenever you directly quote someone's exact words, spoken or written, use double quotation marks (" ") both before and after the quotation. Long quotations for research papers are an exception (see 14b1-2).

**SPOKEN QUOTATION**

"The loon can stay under water for a few minutes," the ranger said.

**WRITTEN QUOTATION**

Gross argues that "every generation scorns its offspring's culture" (9).

Use quotation marks within a sentence to separate quoted material from the words you use to introduce or comment on it.

**QUOTATION INTERRUPTED**

"Every generation," according to Gross, "scorns its offspring's culture" (9).

When you are writing dialogue and a new person speaks, indent as if you're starting a new paragraph. Begin with new quotation marks.

## ESL ADVICE: QUOTATION MARKS

If your native language uses other marks for quotations or if you are used to British conventions, try using your computer's search capacity to find each of the marks so you can check for American usage.

## 2 Setting off quotations inside quotations

Whenever one quotation contains another, use single marks (' ') for the inside quotation and double marks (" ") for the one enclosing it.

De Morga's account of the sinking of the *San Diego* described the battle that "caused his ship to 'burst asunder'" (Goddio 37).

## 3 Integrating indirect quotations

Whenever you paraphrase or summarize someone else's words, do not use quotation marks. (See Chapter 14.)

**INDIRECT QUOTATION (PARAPHRASE)**

The pilot told us that the navigator made the safe landing possible.

**INDIRECT QUOTATION (SUMMARY)**

Samuel Gross believes that the social consequences of a major war nearly vanish after just one generation (5).

## 40b Indicating titles of short works

Use quotation marks to enclose titles of short works, parts of a larger work or series, and unpublished works. (See also 44a.)

---

### QUOTATION MARKS WITH TITLES

**ARTICLES AND STORIES**

| | |
|---|---|
| "TV Gets Blame for Poor Reading" | newspaper article |
| "Feminism's Identity Crisis" | magazine article |
| "The Idea of the Family in the Middle East" | chapter in book |
| "Baba Yaga and the Brave Youth" | story |
| "The Rise of Germism" | essay |

**POEMS AND SONGS**

| | |
|---|---|
| "A Woman Cutting Celery" | short poem |
| "Evening" (from *Pippa Passes*) | section of a long poem |
| "Riders on the Storm" | song |

**EPISODES AND PARTS OF LONGER WORKS**

| | |
|---|---|
| "Billy's Back" | episode of a TV series |
| "All We Like Sheep" (from Handel's *Messiah*) | section of a long musical work |

**UNPUBLISHED WORKS**

| | |
|---|---|
| "Renaissance Men—and Women" | unpublished lecture |
| "Sources of the Ballads in Bishop Percy's Folio Manuscript" | unpublished dissertation |

---

Do not use quotation marks for *your* own title unless it contains the title of another work or some other element requiring quotation marks.

**DRAFT** "The Theme of the Life Voyage in Crane's story 'Open Boat'"

**EDITED** The Theme of the Life Voyage in Crane's story "Open Boat"

## 40c Highlighting words, special terms, and tone of voice

You can use quotation marks or italics (see 44b) to set off technical terms, unusual terms, or words used in a special sense. Avoid too much highlighting; it distracts readers, and most terms don't require it.

In the real estate industry, "FSBO" (sometimes pronounced as "fizbo") refers to a home that is "for sale by owner."

You can—*sparingly*—use quotation marks to indicate irony or sarcasm or to show a reader that you don't "lay claim" to an expression.

# 41 Using Periods, Question Marks, and Exclamation Points

When you speak, you mark sentence boundaries with changes in pitch or pauses. When you write, you use visual symbols—a period, a question mark, or an exclamation point. Use some of these marks sparingly, however.

**LESS FORMAL**   And why do we need your support **?** Without you, too many lovable pups will never find new homes **!**

**READER'S REACTION: This bouncy style is great for our volunteer brochure but not for our annual report.**

**MORE FORMAL**   The League's volunteers remain our most valuable asset, matching abandoned animals with suitable homes **.**

## 41a Using periods

No matter how complicated, all sentences that are *statements* must end with periods—even if they contain clauses that appear to be something other than statements. The following sentence as a whole is a statement; it reports, but does not ask, the question in the second half.

Naomi thanked her supporters profusely but wondered whether they felt responsible for her defeat **.**

Periods also mark decimal points in numbers (22.6 or 5.75) and punctuate abbreviations by letting readers know that something has been eliminated from the word or term.

Dr **.**   Ms **.**   Ph **.** D **.**   C **.** P **.** A **.**   pp **.**   etc **.**   a **.** m **.**   p **.** m **.**

Some abbreviations may not require periods, especially **acronyms** whose letters form pronounceable words (*OSHA, NATO*), terms entirely capitalized (*GOP*), and state names such as *OH*. When in doubt, turn to a dictionary.

When an abbreviation with a period occurs at the *end* of a sentence, that period will also end the sentence. If the abbreviation occurs in the *middle* of a sentence, the period may be followed by another mark, such as a comma, dash, colon, or semicolon.

Residents spoke until 10 **p .** m **. ,** and we adjourned at 11 **p .** m **.**

## 41b Using question marks

Always end a direct question with a question mark. In a sentence with several clauses, the main clause usually determines the punctuation.

**DIRECT**       When is the train leaving**?**

**DIRECT: QUOTED**   Laitan asked, "Why is the air rising so quickly**?**"

**DIRECT: TWO**    Considering that the tax break has been widely publicized, why
**CLAUSES**       have so few people filed for a refund**?**

When you present an **indirect question**—a sentence whose main clause is a statement and whose embedded clause asks a question—end with a period.

**INDIRECT**     José asked if we needed help preparing the bid**.**

A question mark also may signal an uncertain date or other fact.

David Robert Styles, 1632**?**–1676    Meadville, pop. 196**?**

Unless you're writing very informally, avoid adding question marks after other people's statements, using more than one question mark for emphasis, or combining question marks and exclamation points.

## 41c Using exclamation points

Exclamation points end emphatic statements such as commands or warnings but are rarely used in most academic or workplace writing.

Like question marks, exclamation points can be used informally. They can express dismay, outrage, shock, or strong interest. As you revise and edit, look for strong words to emphasize a point.

**DRAFT**       Rescuers spent hours (**!**) trying to reach the child.

**EDITED**       Rescuers spent **agonizing** hours trying to reach the child.

# 42   Using Other Punctuation Marks

Most punctuation symbols make up a kind of toolbox for writing. You can use the tools to change the style, sense, and effect of your prose.

DASHES | When the boy—clutching three weeks' allowance—returned to the store, it had already closed.
READER'S REACTION: **Dashes emphasize how hard the boy worked to save his allowance.**

PARENTHESES | When the boy (clutching three weeks' allowance) returned to the store, it had already closed.
READER'S REACTION: **The parentheses de-emphasize the boy's savings, making the store hours seem more important.**

COMMAS | When the boy, clutching three weeks' allowance, returned to the store, it had already closed.
READER'S REACTION: **This straightforward account doesn't emphasize either the allowance or the store hours.**

Punctuation marks help guide readers through complex sentences.

## 42a Using parentheses

Parentheses *enclose* a word, sentence, or clause: you can't use just one. Readers interpret whatever falls between as an aside. Omit a comma *before* a parenthetical statement in the middle of a sentence. *After* the closing parenthesis, use whatever punctuation would otherwise occur.

WITHOUT PARENTHESES | When you sign up for Telepick, including Internet access, you will receive an hour of free calls.

WITH PARENTHESES | When you sign up for Telepick (including Internet access), you will receive an hour of free calls.

When parentheses *inside a sentence* come at the end, place the end punctuation *after* the closing mark. When enclosing a *freestanding sentence*, place end punctuation *inside* the closing parenthesis.

INSIDE SENTENCE | People on your Telepick list also get discounts (once they sign up).

SEPARATE SENTENCE | Try Telepick now. (This offer excludes international calls.)

You can also use parentheses to mark numbered or lettered lists or to enclose detail that is not part of the structure of a sentence.

DETAIL AND LIST | Harry's Bookstore has a fax number (555-0934) for (1) ordering books, (2) asking about new items, or (3) signing up for store events.

## 42b Using brackets

When you add your own words to a quotation for clarity or background, enclose this **interpolation** in brackets. Also bracket the word *sic* (Latin for "so" or "thus") after an error within a quotation from a source to confirm that you've quoted accurately. If *sic* appears after the quotation, enclose it in parentheses.

INTERPOLATION   As Walters explains, "When Catholic Europe adopted the Gregorian calendar in 1582 and dropped ten days in October, Protestant England ignored the shift, still following October 4 by October 5 [Julian calendar]" (71).

Academic readers expect you to use brackets scrupulously to distinguish your words from those of a source (although nonacademic readers may find them pretentious).

If one parenthetical statement falls *within* another, use brackets for the inner statement.

Contact Rick Daggett (Municipal Lumber Council [Violations Division], Stinson County Center) to report logging violations.

## 42c Using dashes

Dashes set off material with more emphasis or spark than parentheses supply. Too many dashes may strike academic readers as informal. In contrast, dashes add flair to work and public appeals, ads, or brochures. Use your software's dash character, or type a dash as two unspaced hyphens, without space before or after: --. In print, the dash appears as a single line: —.

Dashes can set off an idea or a series of items, especially to open or close dramatically or call attention to an assertion. Use one dash to introduce material that concludes a sentence; use a pair of dashes to highlight words in the middle.

MATERIAL IN THE MIDDLE
After hours of service to two groups—**Kids First and Food Basket**—Olivia was voted Volunteer of the Year.

OPENING LIST
**Extended visitation hours**, **better meals**, and **more exercise**—these were the inmates' major demands.

> **STRATEGY** Convert excessive dashes to other marks.
>
> If your draft is full of dashes, circle those that seem truly valuable—maybe setting off a key point. Replace the others with commas, colons, parentheses, or more emphatic wording.

## 42d Using ellipses

The **ellipsis** (from Greek *elleipsis*, "an omission") is a series of three *spaced* periods showing that something has been left out. Academic readers expect you to use ellipses to mark omissions from a quotation. Readers in other communities may prefer complete quotations to ellipses.

---

**PLACEMENT OF ELLIPSIS MARKS**

- Use three spaced periods • • • for ellipses within a sentence or line of poetry. In quoting a text that already uses ellipses, bracket yours (MLA style).
- Use a period before an ellipsis that ends a sentence• • • •
- Leave a space before the first period • • • and after the last unless the ellipsis is bracketed.
- Omit ellipses when you begin quotations (unless needed for clarity), or use words or phrases that are clearly incomplete.
- Retain another punctuation mark before omitted words if needed for the sentence structure; • • • omit it otherwise.
- Supply a series of spaced periods (MLA style) to show an omitted line (or more) of poetry in a block quotation.

---

Ellipses mark material omitted from a quotation because it is irrelevant, too long, or located between two useful parts of the quotation. When you drop *part* of a sentence, keep a normal structure that readers can follow.

**ORIGINAL INTERVIEW NOTES**
Museum director: "We expect the Inca pottery in our special exhibit to attract art historians from as far away as Chicago, while the colorful jewelry draws the general public."

**CONFUSING DRAFT**
The museum director hopes "the Inca pottery • • • art historians • • • the colorful jewelry • • • the general public."

**EDITED**
The museum director "expect[s] the Inca pottery • • • to attract art historians • • • while the colorful jewelry draws the general public."

In fictional or personal narrative, you may want to indicate a pause or gap showing suspense, hesitation, uncertainty, or ongoing action.

**FOR SUSPENSE**  Large paw prints led to the tent• • • •

## 42e Using slashes

When indicating alternatives, the slash may translate as *or* or *and*.

Be certain that the **on/off** switch is in the vertical position.

This shorthand is common in technical documents, but some readers object to its informality or imprecision (and prefer *or* in its place).

To quote poetry *within* your text instead of using a block quotation (see 14b1–2), separate lines of verse with a slash, with spaces before and after.

The speaker in Sidney's sonnet hails the moon: "O Moon, thou climb'st the skies! / How silently, and with how wan a face!" (1–2).

## 42f  Using symbols in electronic addresses

When you note an electronic address, record its characters exactly—including slashes, @ ("*at*") signs, underscores, colons, and periods.

j.bon@ceo.uc.edu

http://www.access.gpo.gov/su__docs

## 42g  Combining punctuation marks

Follow the conventions your readers expect.

- **Pair marks that enclose:** ( ) [ ] " " ' ' Pair commas and dashes to enclose midsentence elements. Type a dash as a pair—of hyphens.
- **Use multiple marks when each plays its own role**. If an abbreviation with a period falls in the *middle* of a sentence, the period may be followed by another mark.

  Lunch begins at **11 a.m.,** right after the lab.

- **Eliminate multiple marks when their roles overlap**. When an abbreviation with a period concludes a sentence, that one period also ends the sentence. Omit a comma *before* parentheses; *after* the parentheses, use whatever mark would otherwise occur.
- **Avoid confusing duplications**. If items listed within a sentence include commas, separate them with semicolons, not more commas.

  ____, ____, and ____; ____, ____, and ____; and ____.

  If one set of parentheses falls within another, use brackets to enclose the internal element.

  ──(──[──]──).

  Use one pair of dashes at a time, not dashes within dashes.

  ____ ── ____ ── ____.

# Proofreading for Mechanics and Spelling: Respecting Community Conventions

## ▼ TAKING IT ONLINE

**PROOFREADING**

http://www.bgsu.edu/departments/writing-lab/goproofreading.html
http://reach.ucf.edu/~uwc/Writing%20Resources/handout_home.htm
Both sites supply practical tips to help you proofread more accurately
and efficiently.

**ACRONYM SERVER**

http://www.ucc.ie/cgi-bin/acronym/
The meanings of acronyms and abbreviations can differ from community
to community. To a sportswriter, *ERA* means something different from what
it means in a discussion about gender equality. Use this searchable database
to find out what acronyms or abbreviations mean.

**A SPELLING TEST**

http://www.sentex.net/~mmcadams/spelling.html
This interactive spelling test of fifty of the most commonly misspelled
words in American English will tabulate your score automatically.
The site also offers advice on ways to become a better speller.

**CANDIDATE FOR A PULLET SURPRISE**

http://tenderbytes.net/rhymeworld/feeder/teacher/pullet.htm
There are many versions of this humorous but enlightening poem
published on the Internet. It reveals just how unreliable computer
spelling checkers can be. Can ewe right another verse or too?

# PART 9

# Proofreading for Mechanics and Spelling: Respecting Community Conventions

# 43 Capitalizing

Capitalization makes reading easier. Readers expect capital letters to signal where sentences start or to identify specific people, places, and things.

**CAPITALS MISSING** thanks, ahmed, for attaching a copy of the 2004 plant safety guidelines. i'll review this file by tuesday.

**READER'S REACTION: Even though email may be informal, the missing capitals here distract me from the message.**

**CAPITALS IN PLACE** Thanks, Ahmed, for attaching a copy of the 2004 Plant Safety Guidelines. I'll review this file by Tuesday.

If you ignore conventions for capitals, readers may assume that you are careless. Be especially alert to conventions for capitalizing titles, company divisions, and the like.

## 43a Capitalizing to begin sentences

Sentences begin with capital letters, whether complete sentences or fragments used appropriately as partial sentences. (See 24c.)

Two national parks, Yellowstone and Grand Teton, are in Wyoming.

### 1 Capitalize the opening word in a quoted sentence

Capitalization varies with the completeness of a quotation. The following examples include MLA style page citations (see 16a).

Capitalize when a quotation is a complete sentence or begins your sentence.

**QUOTED SENTENCE** As Galloway observes, "The novel opens with an unusual chapter" (18).

**SENTENCE OPENER** "An unusual chapter" (Galloway 18) opens the novel.

Do not capitalize after you interrupt a quotation with your own words or as you integrate a quotation into the structure of your own sentence.

| | |
|---|---|
| **INTERRUPTED QUOTATION** | "The novel," claims Galloway, "opens with an unusual chapter" (18). |
| **INTEGRATED QUOTATION** | Galloway notes that the book "opens with an unusual chapter" (18). |

## 2 Capitalize a freestanding sentence in parentheses

Capitalize the first word of a sentence if it stands on its own in parentheses but not if it falls *inside* another sentence.

| | |
|---|---|
| **FREESTANDING SENTENCE** | The Union forces were split up into nineteen sections. (Nevertheless, Grant was determined to unite them.) |
| **ENCLOSED SENTENCE** | Saskatchewan's economy depends on farming (over half of Canada's wheat crop comes from the province). |

## 3 Capitalize the first word of a line of poetry

Lines of poetry traditionally begin with a capital letter.

We said goodbye at the barrier,
And she slipped away. . . .
　　　　　　　　—ROBERT DASELER, "At the Barrier," *Levering Avenue*

If a poem ignores this or other conventions, follow the poet's practice.

new hampshire explodes into radio primary,
newspaper headlines & beer—
well-weathered tag-lines from lips of schoolchildren.
　　　　　　　　—T. R. MAYERS, "(snap)shots"

## 4 Use consistent capitalization

When capitalization is flexible, be consistent within a document.

**Complete sentence after a colon.** When a *sentence* follows a colon (see 38b), you can use lowercase (as for other words after a colon) or capitalize.

| | |
|---|---|
| **OPTION 1** | The population of New Brunswick is bilingual: one-third is French-speaking and the rest English-speaking. |
| **OPTION 2** | The population of New Brunswick is bilingual: One-third is French-speaking and the rest English-speaking. |

**Questions in a series.** Capitalize or lowercase a sequence of questions.

| | |
|---|---|
| **OPTION 1** | Should we order posters? Billboards? Flyers? |
| **OPTION 2** | Should we order posters? billboards? flyers? |

**Run-in lists.** When items are not listed on separate lines, you may separate them with commas, semicolons (if they are complex), or periods (if they are sentences). Capitalize the first letters of sentences standing alone. Don't capitalize words, partial sentences, or a series of embedded sentences.

In estimating costs, remember the following: (a) **l**ab facilities must be rented, (b) **u**tilities are charged to the project's account, and (c) **m**easuring equipment has to be leased.

In estimating costs, remember to include (a) **l**ab facilities, (b) **u**tilities, and (c) **m**easuring equipment.

**Vertical lists.** Choose whether to capitalize words or partial sentences, but capitalize complete sentences except in an outline without periods.

| OPTION 1 | OPTION 2 |
|---|---|
| 1. **L**ab facilities | 1. **l**ab facilities |
| 2. **U**tilities | 2. **u**tilities |
| 3. **M**easuring equipment | 3. **m**easuring equipment |

## 43b Capitalizing proper names and titles

Capitalize the names of specific people, places, and things (**proper nouns**) as well as **proper adjectives** derived from them.

Brazil, Dickens          Brazilian music, Dickensian plot

In titles, capitalize the first word, the last word, and all words in between *except* articles (*a, an, the*), prepositions under five letters (*in, of, to*), and coordinating conjunctions (*and, but*). These rules apply to titles of long, short, and partial works as well as your own papers. Capitalize the first word after a colon that divides the title.

*The Mill on the Floss*          "Civil Rights: What Now?"

Developing a Growth Plan for a Small Business [your own title]

In an APA reference list, however, capitalize only proper nouns and the first letters of titles and subtitles of full works (books, articles) (see 17b).

### CAPITALIZATION OF NOUNS AND ADJECTIVES

| CAPITALIZED | LOWERCASE |
|---|---|
| **INDIVIDUALS AND RELATIVES** | |
| Georgia O'Keeffe | my teacher's father |
| Uncle Jack, Mother | my cousin, her dad          *(Continued)* |

## CAPITALIZATION OF NOUNS AND ADJECTIVES (Continued)

| CAPITALIZED | LOWERCASE |
|---|---|
| **GROUPS OF PEOPLE AND LANGUAGES** | |
| Maori, African American | the language, the people |
| **TIME PERIODS AND SEASONS** | |
| October, Fall Orientation | spring, summer, fall, winter |
| Easter, Ramadan | holiday |
| **RELIGIONS AND RELATED SUBJECTS** | |
| Buddhism, Catholic | catholic (meaning "universal") |
| Talmud, Bible, God | talmudic, biblical, a god |
| **ORGANIZATIONS, INSTITUTIONS, AND MEMBERS** | |
| U.S. Senate, Senator Hayes | a senator |
| Air Line Pilots Association | the union, a union member |
| **PLACES, THEIR RESIDENTS, AND GEOGRAPHIC REGIONS** | |
| Malaysia, Erie County | the country, the county |
| the Southwest, East Coast | southwestern, eastern |
| **BUILDINGS AND MONUMENTS** | |
| Taj Mahal, Getty Museum | the tower, a museum |
| **HISTORICAL PERIODS, EVENTS, AND MOVEMENTS** | |
| Algerian Revolution, Jazz Age | the revolution, a trend |
| **ACADEMIC INSTITUTIONS AND COURSES** | |
| Auburn University | a university, the college |
| Sociology 203, Art 101 | sociology or art course |
| **VEHICLES** | |
| Pontiac Bonneville SSE | my car, an automobile |
| **COMPANY NAMES AND TRADE NAMES** | |
| Siemens, Kleenex | the company, tissues |
| **SCIENTIFIC, TECHNICAL, AND MEDICAL TERMS** | |
| Big Dipper, Earth (planet) | star, earth (ground) |

# 44 Italicizing (Underlining)

Type that slants to the right—*italic type*—emphasizes words and ideas. In texts that are handwritten, typed, or prepared in MLA style (see 16c), underlining is its equivalent: The Color Purple = *The Color Purple*.

UNDERLINING    Walker's novel <u>The Color Purple</u> has been praised since 1982.

READER'S REACTION: **I can spot the title right away.**

Some readers, including many college instructors, prefer underlining because it's easy to see. Observe the conventions your community expects.

## 44a  Using italics (underlining) in titles

Italicize (underline) titles of most long works (books, magazines, films) and complete works (paintings, sculptures). Enclose titles of parts of works and short works (stories, reports, articles) in quotation marks (see 40b).

---

### TREATMENT OF TITLES

| ITALICS OR UNDERLINING | QUOTATION MARKS |
|---|---|
| **BOOKS AND PAMPHLETS** | |
| *Maggie: A Girl of the Streets* (book) | "Youth" (chapter in book) |
| *Beetroot* (story collection) | "The Purloined Letter" (story) |
| *The White Album* (essay collection) | "Once More to the Lake" (essay) |
| *Guide for Surgery Patients* (pamphlet) | "Anesthesia" (section of pamphlet) |
| | |
| **POEMS** | |
| *Paradise Lost* (long poem) | "Richard Cory" (short poem) |
| *The One Day* (long poem) | "Whoso list to hunt" (first line as title) |
| | |
| **PLAYS AND FILMS** | |
| *King Lear* (play) | |
| *Star Wars* (film) | |
| | |
| **RADIO AND TELEVISION PROGRAMS** | |
| *The West Wing* (TV series) | "Gone Quiet" (episode) |
| *20/20* (TV news show) | "Binge Drinking" (news report) |
| | |
| **PAINTINGS AND SCULPTURES** | |
| *Winged Victory* (sculpture) | |
| | |
| **MUSICAL WORKS** | |
| *Nutcracker Suite* (work for orchestra) | "Waltz of the Flowers" (section of longer work) |
| *Master of Puppets* (CD) | "Orion" (song on CD) |
| Camille Saint-Saëns's *Organ Symphony* | BUT Saint-Saëns, Symphony no. 3 in C Minor, op. 78 |
| | |
| **MAGAZINES AND NEWSPAPERS** | |
| *Discover* (magazine) | "How Baby Learns" (article) |

(Continued)

---

**TREATMENT OF TITLES** *(Continued)*

*Review of Contemporary Fiction*      "Our Students Write with
  (scholarly journal)                  Accents" (scholarly article)
the *Denver Post* (newspaper)        "All the Rage" (article)

**NO ITALICS, UNDERLINING, OR QUOTATION MARKS**

**SACRED BOOKS AND PUBLIC, LEGAL, OR WELL-KNOWN DOCUMENTS**
Bible, Koran, Talmud, United States Constitution

**TITLE OF YOUR OWN PAPER (UNLESS PUBLISHED)**
Attitudes of College Students Toward Intramural Sports
Verbal Abuse in <u>The Color Purple</u> (title of work discussed is underlined)

---

## 44b Using italics for specific terms

Italicize (underline) the names of specific ships, airplanes, trains, and spacecraft (*Voyager VI, Orient Express*) but not *types* of vehicles (Boeing 767, Chris Craft) or *USS* and *SS* (USS *Corpus Christi*). Italicize a foreign word or phrase that has not moved into common use (*omertà*) but not common words such as quiche, junta, taco, and kvetch. Italicize scientific names for plants (*Chrodus crispus*) and animals (*Gazella dorcas*) but not common names (seaweed, gazelle).

Focus attention on a word, letter, number as itself, or defined term by italicizing (underlining) it.

In Boston, *r* is pronounced *ah* so that the word *car* becomes *cah* and *park* becomes *pahk*.

A *piezoelectric crystal* is a piece of quartz or similar material that responds to pressure by producing electric current.

You may italicize a word or phrase for stylistic emphasis, but readers become annoyed if you do this too often.

**EMPHASIS**   The letter's praise is *faint*, not fulsome.

## 44c Underlining for emphasis

Notes, personal letters, and other informal writing may use underlining to add "oral" emphasis. Avoid this in formal writing.

**INFORMAL**   *Hand* the receipts to me.

**MORE FORMAL**   Give the receipts to me personally.

# 45 Hyphenating

Readers expect hyphens to play two different roles—dividing words and tying them together.

**CONFUSING**    The Japanese language proposal is well prepared.

**READER'S REACTION: Is the proposal *in* Japanese or *about* the Japanese language?**

**CLARIFIED**    The Japanese-language proposal is well prepared.

Type a hyphen as a *single* line (-) with no space on either side.

**FAULTY HYPHEN**    well — trained engineer

**EDITED**    well-trained engineer

## 45a Hyphenating to join words

Hyphens often tie together the elements of compound words and phrases. A **compound word** is made from two or more words tied together by hyphens (*double-decker*), combined as one word (*timekeeper*), or treated as separate words (*letter carrier*). These conventions may vary or change rapidly; check an academic style guide, observe accepted practice in work or public contexts, or use an up-to-date dictionary.

**Numbers.** In general writing, hyphenate numbers between twenty-one and ninety-nine, even if the number is part of a larger one. Academic and workplace readers in certain fields, however, expect numbers in figures (not spelled out) (see 46b).

    forty-one      fifty-eight thousand   sixty-three million

Use a hyphen for inclusive numbers (pages 163-78, volumes 9-14) and generally for fractions spelled out (one-half).

**Prefixes and suffixes.** Hyphenate a prefix that comes before a capitalized word or a number.

    Cro-Magnon    non-Euclidean     post-Victorian     pre-1989

Hyphenate with *ex-, self-, all-, -elect,* and *-odd.*

self‑centered    all‑encompassing    president‑elect

**Letters with words.** Hyphenate a letter and a word forming a compound, except in music terms.

A‑frame    T‑shirt    A minor    G sharp

**Compound modifiers.** Hyphenate two or more words working as a single modifier when you place them *before* a noun. When the modifiers come *after* a noun, generally do not hyphenate them.

**BEFORE NOUN**    The **second‑largest** supplier of crude oil is Nigeria.

**AFTER NOUN**    Many cancer treatments are **nausea inducing**.

Do not hyphenate *-ly* adverbs or comparative and superlative forms.

Our **highly regarded** research team developed them.

Hyphens help readers know which meaning to assign a compound.

The scene required three **extra wild** monkeys.

The scene required three **extra‑wild** monkeys.

**Strings of modifiers.** Reduce repetition with hyphens that signal the suspension of an element until the end of a series of parallel compound modifiers. Leave a space after the hyphen and before *and*, but not before a comma.

The process works with **oil‑ and water‑based** compounds.

## 45b Hyphenating to divide words

Hyphens help distinguish different words with the same spelling.

For **recreation,** they staged a comic **re‑creation** of events.

They clarify words with repeated combinations of letters.

anti‑imperialism    post‑traumatic    co‑owner

Traditionally you could use a hyphen to split a word at the end of a line, marking a break *between syllables.* Now word processors include **automatic hyphenation**, dividing words at the ends of lines but sometimes creating hard-to-read lines or splitting words incorrectly. Many writers turn off this feature, preferring a "ragged" (unjustified) right margin. Style guides such as MLA and APA advise the same.

- Divide words only between syllables (for example, *ad-just-able*).
- Check divisions in a dictionary (*ir-re-vo-ca-ble*, not *ir-rev-oc-able*).
- Leave more than one letter at the end of a line and more than two at the beginning (not *a-greement* or *disconnect-ed*).
- Divide at natural breaks between words in compounds (*Volks-wagen*, not *Volkswa-gen*) or after hyphens (*accident-prone*, not *acci-dent-prone*).
- Don't divide one-syllable words (*touched, drought, kicked, through*).
- Avoid confusing divisions that form distracting words (*sin-gle*).
- Don't split acronyms and abbreviations (*NATO, NCAA*), numerals (*100,000*), and contractions (*didn't*).
- Don't hyphenate an electronic address; simply divide it after a slash.

## 46 Using Numbers

You can convey numbers with numerals (*37, 18.6*), words (*eighty-one, two million*), or a combination (*7th, 2nd, 25 billion*).

**GENERAL TEXT**  These **fifty-nine** scientists represented **fourteen** states.

READER'S REACTION: **In general academic or other texts, I expect most numbers to be spelled out.**

**TECHNICAL**  These **59** scientists represented **14** states.

READER'S REACTION: **When I read a scientific or technical report, I expect more numerals.**

This chapter shows you how to present numbers in general writing. For conventions expected in specific technical, business, or scientific contexts, seek advice from your instructor, supervisor, colleagues, or style guide (see Chapters 16–17). Unconventional or inconsistent usage can mislead readers or undermine your authority as a writer.

## 46a Spelling out numbers

Spell out a number of one or two words, counting hyphenated compounds as a single word.

**twenty-two** computers        **seventy thousand** eggs        **306** books

Treat numbers in the same category consistently in a passage, either as numerals (if required for one number, use them for all) or as words.

**CONSISTENT**    Café Luna's menu soon expanded from **48** to **104** items.

Spell out numbers according to the following conventions.

**DATES AND TIMES**
October seventh    nineteenth century    the sixties
four o'clock, *not* 4 o'clock    four in the morning
half past eight, a quarter after one (rounded to the quarter hour)

**ROUNDED NUMBERS OR ROUNDED AMOUNTS OF MONEY**
three hundred thousand citizens    nearly eleven thousand dollars
sixty cents (and other small dollar or cent amounts)

**LARGE NUMBERS**
For large numbers, combine numerals and words.
75 million years    2.3 million members

| **STRATEGY** | Spell out an opening number, or rewrite. |
|---|---|

**INAPPROPRIATE**    **428** houses in Talcott are built on leased land.

**DISTRACTING**    **Four hundred twenty-eight** houses in Talcott are built on leased land.

**EASY TO READ**    **In Talcott, 428** houses are built on leased land.

## 46b Using numerals

Use numerals according to the following conventions.

**ADDRESSES, ROUTES**
2450 Ridge Road, Alhambra, CA 91801    Interstate 6

**DATES**
September 7, 1976    1880–1910    from 1955 to 1957
1930s    class of '97    the '80s (informal)
486 BC (or BCE)    AD (or CE) 980

**PARTS OF A WRITTEN WORK**
Chapter 12    Genesis 1:1–6 or Gen. 1.1–6 (MLA style)
*Macbeth* 2.4.25–28 (or act II, scene iv, lines 25–28)

**MEASUREMENTS WITH ABBREVIATIONS**
55 mph    6'4"    47 psi    21 ml    80 kph

**FRACTIONS, DECIMALS, PERCENTAGES**
7 5/8     27.3     67 percent (or 67%)

**TIME OF DAY**
10:52     6:17 a.m.     12 p.m. (noon)     12 a.m. (midnight)

**MONEY (SPECIFIC AMOUNTS)**
$7,883 (or $7883)     $4.29     $7.2 million (or $7,200,000)

**SURVEYS, RATIOS, STATISTICS, SCORES**
7 out of 10     3 to 1 (or 3:1)     a mean of 23
a standard deviation of 2.5     won 21 to 17

**CLUSTERED NUMBERS**
paragraphs 2, 9, and 13 through 15 (or 13–15)
units 23, 145, and 210

**RANGES OF NUMBERS**
**LESS THAN 100**     Supply the complete second number.
                9–13     27–34     58–79     94–95

**OVER 100**     Simply supply the last two figures in the second number unless
            readers need more to avoid confusion. Do not use commas in
            four-digit page numbers.
            134–45     95–102 (not 95–02)     370–420
            1534–620 (not 1534–20)     1007–09

**YEARS**     Supply all digits of both years in a range unless they belong
        to the same century.
        1890–1920     1770–86     476–823     42–38 BC

## 47   Abbreviating

When they are accepted by both writer and reader, abbreviations act as
a shorthand, making a sentence easy to write and read. Inappropriate or badly
placed abbreviations, however, can make a sentence *harder* to read.

CONFUSING    **Jg.** **Rich.** Posner was a **U of C** law **prof.**

             READER'S REACTION: **Am I supposed to know all these abbreviations? What is "Jg."? Is "U of C" the University of California?**

CLEAR    **Judge Richard** Posner was a **University of Chicago** law **professor**.

Abbreviations should aid readers, not baffle them.

## 47a Using familiar abbreviations

Many abbreviations are so widely used that readers have no trouble recognizing them. These abbreviations are acceptable in all kinds of writing as long as you present them in standard form.

### 1 Abbreviate titles with proper names

Abbreviate titles just before or after people's names.

    **Ms.** Rutkowski    Cathy Harr, **D.V.M.**    James Guptil, **Sr.**

With a person's full name, you may abbreviate a title. Spell out a title used as *part of your reference to the person* or placed away from a proper name.

FAULTY    We invited **Prof.** Leves and **Rep.** Drew.

ACCEPTABLE    We invited **Professor** Leves and **Representative** Drew.

ALTERNATIVE    We invited **Prof. Roland** Leves and **Rep. John** Drew.

EXCEPTIONS    **Rev.** Mills and **Dr.** Smith were not invited.

Use only one form of a person's title at a time.

FAULTY    **Dr.** Vonetta McGee, **D.D.S.**

EDITED    **Dr.** Vonetta McGee or Vonetta McGee, **D.D.S.**

Abbreviated academic degrees such as *M.A.*, *Ph.D.*, *B.S.*, and *M.D.* can be used as titles or on their own.

ACCEPTABLE    The **Ed.D.** is designed for school administrators.

---

**ESL ADVICE:** ABBREVIATED TITLES

In some languages, abbreviated titles such as *Dr.* or *Mrs.* do not require periods as they do in English. If this is true in your first language, proofread carefully.

## 2 Abbreviate references to people and organizations

Readers generally accept abbreviations that are familiar (*3M, IBM*), simple (*AFL-CIO*), or standard in specific contexts (*FAFSA*). Abbreviations in which the letters are pronounced singly (*USDA*) and **acronyms** in which they form a pronounceable word (*NATO*) usually use capitals without periods (but note *laser, radar*).

| | |
|---|---|
| **ORGANIZATIONS** | NAACP, AMA, NBA, FDA, NCAA, UNESCO, IBEW |
| **CORPORATIONS** | GTE, USX, PBS, GM, CNN, AT&T, CBS, BBC |
| **COUNTRIES** | USA (*or* U.S.A.), UK (*or* U.K.) |
| **PEOPLE** | JFK, LBJ, FDR, MLK |
| **THINGS OR EVENTS** | FM, AM, TB, MRI, AWOL, DUI, TGIF |

**STRATEGY** Introduce an unfamiliar abbreviation.

Give the full term when you first use it; show the abbreviation in parentheses. From then on, use the abbreviation to avoid tedious repetition.

The **American Library Association (ALA)** has taken stands on access to information. For example, the **ALA** opposes book censorship.

## 3 Abbreviate terms with dates and numbers

Abbreviations that *specify* a number or amount may be used with dates and numbers; don't substitute them for general terms. For example, use *the morning*, not *the a.m.* (See 46b.)

| **ABBREVIATION** | **MEANING** |
|---|---|
| AD | *anno Domini*, meaning "in the year of Our Lord" |
| BC | *before* Christ |
| BCE | *before common era* (alternative to BC) |
| CE | *common era* (alternative to AD) |
| a.m. | *ante meridiem* for "morning" (A.M. in print) |
| p.m. | *post meridiem* for "after noon" (P.M. in print) |
| no., $ | number, dollars |

## 47b Proofreading for appropriate abbreviations

In most formal writing, readers expect words in full form except for familiar abbreviations. In research, scientific, or technical writing, you can use more abbreviations to save space, particularly in documenting sources (see Chapters 16–17). Abbreviations may also be accepted in specific contexts—for example, OT (occupational therapy) in medical reports.

**DAYS, MONTHS, AND HOLIDAYS**

| DRAFT | Thurs., Thur., Th | Oct. | Xmas |
|---|---|---|---|
| EDITED | Thursday | October | Christmas |

**PLACES**

| DRAFT | Wasatch Mts. | Lk. Erie | Ont. Ave. |
|---|---|---|---|
| EDITED | Wasatch Mountains | Lake Erie | Ontario Avenue |

EXCEPTION  988 Dunkerhook Road, Paramus, **NJ** 07652
**Use accepted postal abbreviations in all addresses with zip codes.**

**COMPANY NAMES**

QUESTIONABLE  LaForce Bros. Electrical Conts.

EDITED  LaForce Brothers Electrical Contractors
**Use abbreviations only if they are part of the official name.**

**PEOPLE'S NAMES**

DRAFT  Wm. and Kath. Newholtz will attend.

EDITED  William and Katherine Newholtz will attend.

**DISCIPLINES AND PROFESSIONS**

| DRAFT | econ., bio. | poli. sci. | phys. ed. | PT |
|---|---|---|---|---|
| EDITED | economics, biology | political science | physical education | physical therapy |

**SYMBOLS AND UNITS OF MEASUREMENT**

In general writing, reserve symbols (@, #, =, –, +) for tables or graphs. Spell out units of measurement (*mile*). Abbreviate phrases such as *rpm* and *mph*, with or without periods, but be consistent in a text.

| AVOID IN TEXT | pt. | qt. | in. | mi. | kg. |
|---|---|---|---|---|---|
| USE IN TEXT | pint | quart | inch | mile | kilogram |

**PARTS OF WRITTEN WORKS**

Follow your instructor's advice or the style guide for the field.

| IN DOCUMENTATION | ch. | p. | pp. | fig. |
|---|---|---|---|---|
| IN WRITTEN TEXT | chapter | page | pages | figure |

**LATIN ABBREVIATIONS**

Reserve these for documentation and parenthetical comments.

| cf. | compare (*confer*) | i.e. | that is (*id est*) | e.g. | for example (*exempli gratia*) |
|---|---|---|---|---|---|
| N.B. | note well (*nota bene*) | et al. | and others (*et alii*) | etc. | and so forth (*et cetera*) |

**48** Spelling

Readers in academic, public, and work settings notice how accurately you spell.

**INCORRECT**        The city will not **except** any late bids for the project.

**READER'S REACTION: I get annoyed when careless or lazy writers won't correct their spelling.**

**PROOFREAD**        The city will not **accept** any late bids for the project.

Readers may ignore or laugh at a newspaper misspelling. For academic and work documents, however, they may consider a writer who misspells lazy, ignorant, or disrespectful.

## 48a Recognizing spelling errors

Correct the errors you see; then ask readers to spot others.

### 1 Start with your spelling checker

When you use a spelling checker, the computer compares the words in your text with those in its dictionary. If it finds a match, it assumes your word is correctly spelled. If it does *not* find a match, it questions the word so you can select an alternative spelling or make a correction. What it can't reveal are words properly spelled but used incorrectly, such as *lead* for *led*. When in doubt, check a dictionary.

---

**STRATEGY** Go beyond the spelling checker.

- List as many possible spellings as you can. Look them up. Once you're in the right area in the dictionary, you may find the word.
- Try a special dictionary for poor spellers, listing words under both correct spelling (*phantom*) and likely misspellings (*fantom*).
- Try a thesaurus (see 36b); the word may be listed with a synonym.
- Ask classmates or co-workers about the preferred or correct spellings, especially for technical terms; verify their information in the dictionary.

- Check the indexes of books that treat the topic the word relates to.
- Look for the word in textbooks, company materials, or newspapers.
- Add tricky words to your own spelling list. Look for ways to recall them. For example, you might associate the two z's in *quizzes* with boredom (*zzzz*).

## 2 Watch for common patterns of misspelling

Many groups of letters can trip up even the best spellers.

**Plurals.** You form most plurals simply by adding -s (*novel, novels*).

- For words ending in a consonant plus -*o*, often add -*es*.

**ADD -es**    potato, potatoes    hero, heroes

**ADD -s**     cello, cellos       memo, memos

When a vowel comes before the -*o*, add -*s*.

**ADD -s**     stereo, stereos     video, videos

- For words ending in a consonant plus -*y*, change *y* to *i*, and add -*es*.

etiology, etiologies    gallery, galleries    notary, notaries

**EXCEPTION**    Add -*s* for proper nouns (*Kennedy, Kennedys*).

- For words ending in a vowel plus -*y*, keep the *y*, and add -*s*.

day, days    journey, journeys    pulley, pulleys

- For words ending in -*f* or -*fe*, often change *f* to *v*, and add -*s* or -*es*.

knife, knives    life, lives    self, selves

Some words simply add -*s*.

belief, beliefs    roof, roofs    turf, turfs

- For words ending with a hiss (-*ch*, -*s*, -*ss*, -*sh*, -*x*, -*z*), usually add -*es*.

bench, benches    bus, buses    bush, bushes

buzz, buzzes    fox, foxes    kiss, kisses

One-syllable words may double a final -*s* or -*z*: *quiz, quizzes*.

- Words with foreign roots often follow the original language.

alumna, alumnae     criterion, criteria     datum, data

- Some familiar plurals are irregular.

foot, feet     mouse, mice     man, men

- In a compound, make the last word plural unless the first is more important.

basketball, basketballs     sister-in-law, sisters-in-law

**Word beginnings and endings. Prefixes** do not change the spelling of the root word that follows: *precut, post-traumatic, misspell.*

- *In-* and *im-* have the same meaning; use *im-* before *b, m,* and *p.*

| USE ***in-*** | incorrect | inadequate | incumbent |
|---|---|---|---|
| USE ***im-*** | imbalance | immobile | impatient |

**Suffixes** may change the root word that comes before, or they may pose spelling problems in themselves.

- Retain a word's final silent *-e* when a suffix begins with a consonant.

| KEEP ***-e*** | fate, fateful     gentle, gentleness |
|---|---|
| EXCEPTIONS | words like *judgment, argument, truly,* and *ninth* |

- Drop the silent *-e* when a suffix begins with a vowel.

| DROP ***-e*** | imagine, imaginary     decrease, decreasing |
|---|---|
| EXCEPTIONS | words like *noticeable* and *changeable* |

- Four familiar words end in *-ery: stationery* (paper), *cemetery, monastery, millinery.* Most others end in *-ary: stationary* (fixed in place), *secretary, primary, military, culinary.*
- Most words with a final "seed" sound end in *-cede,* such as *precede, recede,* and *intercede.* Only three are spelled *-ceed: proceed, succeed,* and *exceed.* One is spelled *-sede: supersede.*
- Add *-able* if word roots can stand on their own and *-ible* if they can't.

| USE ***-able*** | charitable, habitable, advisable, mendable |
|---|---|
| | **Drop the e for word roots ending in one e (*comparable, debatable*). Keep it for words ending in double e (*agreeable*).** |
| USE ***-ible*** | credible, irreducible |

**Words containing *ie* and *ei*.** Most words follow the old rhyme: *I* before *e* / Except after *c*, / Or when sounding like *a* / As in n*ei*ghbor and w*ei*gh.

USE *ie*    believe, thief, grief, friend, chief, field, niece

USE *ei*    receive, deceit, perceive, ceiling, conceited

EXCEPTIONS    weird, seize, foreign, ancient, height, either, neither, their, leisure, forfeit

## **48b** Proofreading for commonly misspelled words

Words that sound like each other but are spelled differently (*accept/except, assent/ascent*) are known as **homophones**.

---

### COMMONLY MISSPELLED OR CONFUSED WORD PAIRS

| WORD | MEANING |
| --- | --- |
| accept | receive |
| except | other than |
| affect | to influence; an emotional response |
| effect | result |
| all ready | prepared |
| already | by this time |
| allusion | indirect reference |
| illusion | faulty belief or perception |
| assure | state positively |
| ensure | make certain |
| insure | indemnify |
| bare | naked |
| bear | carry; an animal |
| board | get on; flat piece of wood |
| bored | not interested |
| brake | stop |
| break | shatter, destroy; a gap; a pause |
| capital | seat of government; monetary resources |
| capitol | building that houses government |
| cite | credit an authority |
| sight | ability to see; a view |
| site | a place |
| complement | to complete or supplement |
| compliment | to praise |

*(Continued)*

| WORD | MEANING |
|------|---------|
| desert | abandon; sandy wasteland |
| dessert | sweet course at conclusion of meal |
| discreet | tactful, reserved |
| discrete | separate or distinct |
| elicit | draw out, evoke |
| illicit | illegal |
| eminent | well known, respected |
| immanent | inherent |
| imminent | about to happen |
| fair | lovely; light-colored; just |
| fare | fee for transportation |
| forth | forward |
| fourth | after *third* |
| gorilla | an ape |
| guerrilla | kind of soldier or warfare |
| hear | perceive sound |
| here | in this place |
| heard | past tense of *hear* |
| herd | group of animals |
| hole | opening |
| whole | complete |
| its | possessive form of *it* |
| it's | contraction for *it is* |
| know | understand or be aware of |
| no | negative |
| later | following in time |
| latter | last in a series |
| lessen | make less |
| lesson | something learned |
| loose | not tight |
| lose | misplace |
| passed | past tense of *pass* |
| past | after; events occurring at a prior time |
| patience | calm endurance |
| patients | people getting medical treatment |
| peace | calm or absence of war |
| piece | part of something |
| plain | clear, unadorned |
| plane | woodworking tool; airplane |

(Continued)

## COMMONLY MISSPELLED OR CONFUSED WORD PAIRS (Continued)

| WORD | MEANING |
|------|---------|
| persecute | harass |
| prosecute | take legal action against |
| personal | relating to oneself |
| personnel | employees |
| precede | come before |
| proceed | go ahead, continue |
| principal | most important; head of a school |
| principle | basic truth, rule of behavior |
| raise | lift up or build up |
| raze | tear down |
| right | correct |
| rite | ritual |
| write | compose; put words into a text |
| scene | section of a play; setting of an action |
| seen | visible |
| stationary | fixed in place or still |
| stationery | paper for writing |
| straight | unbending |
| strait | water passageway |
| than | compared with |
| then | at that time; next |
| their | possessive form of *they* |
| there | in that place |
| they're | contraction for *they are* |
| to | toward |
| too | in addition, also |
| two | number after *one* |
| waist | middle of body |
| waste | leftover or discarded material |
| which | one of a group |
| witch | person with magical powers |
| who's | contraction for *who is* |
| whose | possessive of *who* |
| your | possessive of *you* |
| you're | contraction for *you are* |

# Glossary and Index

▼ **TAKING IT ONLINE**

**COMMON ERRORS IN ENGLISH**
http://www.wsu.edu/~brians/errors/
Devoted to errors in usage, this site lists hundreds of potentially troublesome words and expressions.

**THE SLOT: A SPOT FOR COPY EDITORS**
http://www.theslot.com/
Here, you can access usage issues and pesky expressions by searching the site.

**THE VOCABULA REVIEW**
http://www.vocabula.com/
This electronic publication regularly includes articles on word origins, common errors in grammar and usage, and advice about succinct and stylish writing. Its Language Links will connect you to a wide variety of sites—classics, language resources, periodicals, media sites, and quick references.

**THE GLOSSARIST**
http://www.glossarist.com
The site collects glossaries of terms for topics and fields—from Arts and Culture to World Regions, Countries, and Travel.

**ENGLISH USAGE, STYLE, AND COMPOSITION**
http://www.bartleby.com/usage
At this site, you can search for usage issues or access guides to language and usage.

**GUIDE TO GRAMMAR AND STYLE**
http://www.andromeda.rutgers.edu/~jlynch/Writing/index.html
Check here for grammar terms, comments on style, and usage notes.

# Proofreading for Mechanics and Spelling: Respecting Community Conventions

# GLOSSARY OF USAGE

**a, an** When the word after *a* or *an* begins with a vowel sound, use *an*: *an outrageous film*. Use *a* before consonants: *a shocking film*. (See 18a.)

**accept, except** *Accept* means "to take or receive"; *except* means "excluding."

Everyone **accepted** the invitation **except** Larry.

**adverse, averse** Someone opposed to something is *averse* to it; if conditions stand in opposition to achieving a goal, they are *adverse*.

**advice, advise** *Advice* is a noun meaning "counsel" or "recommendations." *Advise* is a verb meaning "to give counsel or recommendations."

Raul wanted to **advise** his students, but they wanted no **advice**.

**affect, effect** *Affect* is a verb meaning "to influence." *Effect* is a noun meaning "a result." More rarely, *effect* is a verb meaning "to cause something to happen."

CFCs may **affect** the deterioration of the ozone layer. The **effect** of that deterioration on global warming is uncertain. Lawmakers need to **effect** changes in public attitudes toward our environment.

**aggravate, irritate** *Aggravate* means "to worsen"; *irritate* means "to bother or pester."

**ain't** Although widely used, *ain't* is inappropriate in formal writing. Use *am not, is not,* or *are not*; the contracted forms *aren't* and *isn't* are more acceptable than *ain't* but may still be too informal in some contexts. (See 39b.)

**all ready, already** *All ready* means "prepared for"; *already* means "by that time."

Sam was **all ready** for the meeting, but it had **already** started.

**all right** This expression is always spelled as two words, not as *alright*.

**all together, altogether** Use *all together* to mean "everyone"; use *altogether* to mean "completely."

We were **all together** on our decision to support the center, but it was **altogether** too hard for us to organize a fund-raiser in a week.

**allude, elude** *Allude* means "hint at" or "refer to indirectly"; *elude* means "escape."

**allusion, illusion** An *allusion* is a reference to something; an *illusion* is a vision or a false belief.

**a lot** This expression is always spelled as two words, not as *alot*. Because *a lot* may be too informal for some writing, consider *many, much,* or another modifier instead.

**a.m., p.m.** These abbreviations may be capital or lowercase letters (see 47a).

**among, between** Use *between* to describe something involving two people, things, or ideas; use *among* to refer to three or more.

The fight **between** the umpire and the catcher was followed by a discussion **among** the catcher, the umpire, and the managers.

**amount, number** Use *amount* for a quantity of something that can't be divided into separate units. Use *number* for countable objects.

A large **number** of spices may be used in Thai dishes. This recipe calls for a small **amount** of coconut milk.

**an, a** (See **a, an**.)

**and etc.** (See **etc.**)

**and/or** Although widely used, *and/or* is usually imprecise and may distract your reader. Choose one of the words, or revise your sentence. (See 42c.)

**ante-, anti-** Use *ante-* as a prefix to mean "before" or "predating"; use *anti-* to mean "against" or "opposed."

**anyone, any one** *Anyone* as one word is an indefinite pronoun. Occasionally you may want to use *any* to modify *one*, in the sense of "any individual thing or person." (The same distinction applies to **everyone**, **every one**; *somebody*, *some body*; and *someone*, *some one*.)

**Anyone** can learn to parachute without fear. But the instructors are told not to spend too much time with **any one** person.

**anyplace** Replace this term in formal writing with *anywhere*, or revise.

**anyways, anywheres** Avoid these incorrect versions of *anyway* and *anywhere*.

**as, like** Used as a preposition, *as* indicates a precise comparison. *Like* indicates a resemblance or similarity.

Remembered **as** a man of habit, Kant took a walk at the same time each day. He, **like** many other philosophers, was thoughtful and intense.

**as to** *As to* is considered informal in many contexts.

| INFORMAL | The media speculated **as to** the film's success. |
| EDITED | The media speculated **about** the film's success. |

**assure, ensure, insure** Use *assure* to imply a promise; use *ensure* to imply a certain outcome. Use *insure* only when you imply something legal or financial.

The surgeon **assured** the pianist that his fingers would heal in time for the concert. To **ensure** that, the pianist did not practice for three weeks and **insured** his hands with Lloyd's of London.

**at** In any writing, avoid using *at* in direct and indirect questions.

| COLLOQUIAL | Jones wondered where his attorney was **at**. |
| EDITED | Jones wondered where his attorney **was**. |

**awful, awfully** Use *awful* as an adjective modifying a noun or pronoun; use *awfully* as an adverb modifying a verb, adjective, or other adverb. (See 23b.)

Sanders played **awfully** at the golf tournament. On the sixth hole, an **awful** shot landed his ball in the pond.

**awhile, a while** *Awhile* (as one word) functions as an adverb; it is not preceded by a preposition. *A while* functions as a noun (preceded by *a*, an article) and is often used in prepositional phrases.

The shelter suggested that the homeless family stay **awhile**. It turned out that the children had not eaten for **a while**.

**bad, badly** Use *bad* as an adjective that modifies nouns or with a linking verb expressing feelings. Use *badly* as an adverb. (See 23b-3.)

**because, since** In general, avoid using *since* in place of *because*, which is more formal and precise. Use *since* to indicate time, not causality.

**being as, being that** Avoid both in formal writing when you mean *because*.

**beside, besides** Use *beside* as a preposition to mean "next to." Use *besides* as an adverb meaning "also" or an adjective meaning "except."

> Betsy placed the documents **beside** Mr. Klein. **Besides** being the best lawyer at the firm, Klein was also the most cautious.

**better, had better** Avoid using *better* or *had better* in place of *ought to* or *should* in formal writing.

| | |
|---|---|
| COLLOQUIAL | Fast-food chains **better** realize that Americans are more health-conscious today. |
| EDITED | Fast-food chains **ought to** realize that Americans are more health-conscious today. |

**between, among** (See **among, between**.)

**bring, take** *Bring* implies a movement from somewhere else to close at hand; *take* implies a movement in the opposite direction.

> Please **bring** me a coffee refill, and **take** away these leftover muffins.

**broke** *Broke* is the past tense of *break*; avoid using it as the past participle.

| | |
|---|---|
| DRAFT | The computer was **broke**. |
| EDITED | The computer was **broken**. |

**burst, bursted** *Burst* implies an outward explosion. Do not use the form *bursted* for the past tense.

> The gang of boys **burst** the balloon.

**bust, busted** Avoid the use of *bust* or *busted* to mean "broke."

| | |
|---|---|
| COLLOQUIAL | The senator's limousine **bust** down on the trip. |
| EDITED | The senator's limousine **broke** down on the trip. |

**but however, but yet** Choose one word of each pair, not both.

**can, may** *Can* implies ability; *may* implies permission or uncertainty.

> Bart **can** drive now, but his parents **may** not lend him their new car.

**can't hardly, can't scarcely** Use these pairs positively, not negatively: *can hardly* and *can scarcely*, or simply *can't*. (See 23b-4.)

**capital, capitol** *Capital* refers to a government center or to money; *capitol* refers to a government building.

**censor, censure** *Censor* means the act of shielding something from the public, such as a movie. *Censure* implies punishment or critical labeling.

**center around** Use *center on* or *focus on*, or reword as *revolve around*.

**choose, chose** Watch for spelling errors; use *choose* for the present tense form of the verb and *chose* for the past tense.

**cite, site** *Cite* means to acknowledge someone else's work; *site* means a place or location.

Phil decided to **cite** Chomsky's theory of syntax.

We chose the perfect **site** to pitch our tent.

**climactic, climatic** *Climactic* refers to the culmination of something; *climatic* refers to weather conditions.

**compare to, compare with** Use *compare to* when you want to imply similarities between two things—the phrase is close in meaning to *liken to*. Use *compare with* to imply both similarities and differences.

The doctor **compared** the boy's virus **to** a tiny army in his body. **Compared with** his last illness, this one was mild.

**complement, compliment** *Complement* means "an accompaniment"; *compliment* means "words of praise."

The diplomats **complimented** the ambassador on her menu. The dessert **complemented** the main course perfectly.

**continual, continuous** *Continual* implies that something is recurring; *continuous* implies that something is constant and unceasing.

Local residents found the **continual** noise of landing jets less annoying than the traffic that **continuously** circled the airport.

**could of, would of** These incorrect pairs are common because they are often pronounced as if they are spelled this way. Use the correct verb forms *could have* and *would have*.

DRAFT          I **could of** written a letter to the editor.

EDITED         I **could have** written a letter to the editor.

**couple, couple of** In formal writing, use a *few* or *two* instead.

COLLOQUIAL     Watson took a **couple of** days to examine the data.

EDITED         Watson took **a few** days to examine the data.

**criteria** *Criteria* is the plural form of *criterion*. Make sure your verbs agree in number with this noun.

SINGULAR       One **criterion** for the bonus was selling ten cars.

PLURAL         The **criteria** were too strict to follow.

**curriculum** *Curriculum* is the singular form of this noun. For the plural, use either *curricula* or *curriculums*, but be consistent.

**data** Although widely used for both the singular and plural, *data* technically is a plural noun; *datum* refers to a single piece of data. If in doubt, use the formal distinction, and make sure your verbs agree in number.

SINGULAR       This one **datum** was unexpected.

PLURAL         These **data** are not very revealing.

**different from, different than** Use *different from* when an object follows, and use *different than* when an entire clause follows.

Jack's proposal is **different from** Marlene's, but his ideas are now **different than** they were when he first joined the sales team.

**discreet, discrete** *Discreet* means "reserved or cautious"; *discrete* means "distinctive, different, or explicit."

**disinterested, uninterested** *Uninterested* implies boredom or lack of interest; *disinterested* implies impartiality or objectivity.

**done** Avoid using *done* as a simple past tense; it is a *past participle* (see 20c).

DRAFT    The skater **done** the best she could at the Olympics.

EDITED    The skater **did** the best she could at the Olympics.

**don't, doesn't** Contractions like these may strike some readers as too informal. Err on the side of formality (*do not, does not*) when in doubt. (See 39b.)

**due to** When meaning "because," use *due to* only after some form of the verb *be*. Avoid *due to the fact that*, which is wordy.

DRAFT    The mayor collapsed **due to** campaign fatigue.

EDITED    The mayor's collapse was **due to** campaign fatigue.

EDITED    The mayor collapsed **because** of campaign fatigue.

**effect, affect** (See **affect, effect**.)

**e.g.** Avoid this abbreviation (from Latin, "for example") when possible. (See 47b.)

AWKWARD    Her positions on major issues, **e.g.**, gun control, abortion, and the death penalty, are very liberal.

EDITED    Her positions on major issues **such as** gun control, abortion, and the death penalty are very liberal.

**emigrate from, immigrate to** Foreigners *emigrate from* one country and *immigrate to* another. *Migrate* implies moving around (as in *migrant workers*) or settling temporarily.

**ensure, assure, insure** (See **assure, ensure, insure**.)

**enthused** Avoid *enthused* to mean *enthusiastic* in formal writing.

**especially, specially** *Especially* implies "in particular"; *specially* means "for a specific purpose."

It is **especially** important that Jo follow her **specially** designed workouts.

**etc.** Avoid this abbreviation in formal writing by supplying a complete list of items or by using a phrase like *so forth*. (See 47b.)

INFORMAL    The Washington march was a disaster: it was cold and rainy, the protesters had no food, **etc.**

EDITED    The Washington march was a disaster: the protesters were cold, wet, and hungry.

**eventually, ultimately** Use *eventually* to imply that an outcome follows a series of events or a lapse of events. Use *ultimately* to imply that a final or culminating act ends a series of events.

**Eventually**, the rescue team managed to pull the last of the survivors from the wreck, and **ultimately** there were no casualties.

**everyday, every day** *Everyday* is an adjective that modifies a noun. *Every day* is a noun (*day*) modified by an adjective (*every*).

**Every day** in the Peace Corps, Monique faced the **everyday** task of boiling her drinking water.

**everyone, every one** *Everyone* is a pronoun; *every one* is an adjective (*every*) followed by a noun (*one*). (See also **anyone, any one**.)

**Everyone** was tantalized by **every one** of the desserts on the menu.

**exam** In formal writing, some readers may be bothered by this abbreviation of *examination*.

**except, accept** (See **accept, except**.)

**explicit, implicit** *Explicit* means that something is outwardly or openly stated; *implicit* means that it is implied or suggested.

**farther, further** *Farther* implies a measurable distance; *further* implies something that cannot be measured.

The **farther** they trekked into the wilderness, the **further** their relationship deteriorated.

**female, male** Use these terms only when you want to call attention to gender specifically, as in a research report. Otherwise, use the simpler *man* and *woman* or *boy* and *girl* unless such usage is sexist (see 35a).

**fewer, less** Use *fewer* for things that can be counted, and use *less* for quantities that cannot be divided. (See 23a.)

The new bill had **fewer** supporters and **less** media coverage.

**finalize** Some readers object to adjectives and nouns that are turned into verbs ending in -ize (*finalize, prioritize, objectivize*). When in doubt, use *make final* or some other construction.

**firstly** Use *first, second, third*, and so forth when enumerating points in writing.

**former, latter** *Former* means "the one before" and *latter* means "the one after." They can be used only when referring to two things.

**freshman, freshmen** Many readers consider these terms sexist and archaic. Unless you are citing an established term or group (such as the Freshman Colloquium at Midwest University), use *first-year student* instead.

**get** Avoid imprecise or frequent use of *get* in formal writing.

INFORMAL    Martin Luther King had a premonition that he would **get** shot; his speeches before his death **got** nostalgic.

EDITED    Martin Luther King had a premonition that he would **be** shot; his speeches before his death **waxed** nostalgic.

**go, say** In very informal contexts, some speakers use **go** and **goes** to mean *say* and *says*. This usage is considered inappropriate in all writing.

INAPPROPRIATE    Hjalmar **goes** to Gregers, "I thought this was my account."

EDITED    Hjalmar **says** to Gregers, "I thought this was my account."

**gone, went** Do not use *went* (the past tense of *go*) in place of the past participle form *gone*. (See 20c–d.)

DRAFT    The officers **should have went** to their captain.

EDITED    The officers **should have gone** to their captain.

**good, well** *Good* is an adjective meaning "favorable" (a *good* trip). *Well* is an adverb meaning "done favorably." (See 23b-3.)

**good and** This is a colloquial term when used to mean "very" (*good and* tired; *good and* hot). Avoid it in formal writing.

**got to** Avoid the colloquial use of *got* or *got to* in place of *must* or *have to*.

COLLOQUIAL    I **got to** improve my ratings in the opinion polls.

EDITED    I **must** improve my ratings in the opinion polls.

**great** In formal writing, avoid using *great* as an adjective meaning "wonderful." Use *great* in the sense of "large" or "monumental."

**hanged, hung** Although the distinction between these terms is disappearing, some readers may expect you to use **hanged** exclusively to mean execution by hanging and **hung** to refer to anything else.

**have, got** (See **got to**.)

**have, of** (See **could of, would of**.)

**he, she, he or she, his/her** When you use gender-specific pronouns, be careful not to privilege the male versions (see 35a).

**hopefully** Although the word is widely used to modify entire clauses (as in "Hopefully, her condition will improve"), some readers may object. When in doubt, use *hopefully* only to mean "feeling hopeful."

Bystanders watched **hopefully** as the workers continued to dig.

**however, yet, but** (See **but however, but yet**.)

**hung, hanged** (See **hanged, hung**.)

**if, whether** Use *if* before a specific outcome (either stated or implied); use *whether* when you are considering alternatives.

**If** holographic technology can be perfected, we may soon be watching three-dimensional television. But **whether** we will be able to afford it is another question.

**illusion, allusion** (See **allusion, illusion**.)

**immigrate to, emigrate from** (See **emigrate from, immigrate to**.)

**implicit, explicit** (See **explicit, implicit**.)

**in regard to** Although it may sound sophisticated, *in regard to* is wordy. Use *about* instead.

**inside of, outside of**  When you use *inside* or *outside* to mark locations, do not pair them with *of.*

UNNEEDED            **Inside of** the hut was a large stock of rootwater.

EDITED              **Inside** the hut was a large stock of rootwater.

**insure, assure, ensure**  (See **assure, ensure, insure**.)

**irregardless**  Avoid this erroneous form of the word *regardless*, commonly used because *regardless* and *irrespective* are often used synonymously.

**irritate, aggravate**  (See **aggravate, irritate**.)

**its, it's**  *Its* is a possessive pronoun, and *it's* contracts *it is* (see 13a-3 and 39e). (Some readers may also object to *it's* for *it is* in formal writing.)

**-ize, -wise**  Some readers object to nouns or adjectives turned into verbs by adding *-ize* (*finalize, itemize, computerize*). Also avoid adding *-wise* to words, as in "Weather-*wise*, it will be chilly."

**kind, sort, type**  These words are singular nouns; precede them with *this*, not *these*. In general, use more precise words.

**kind of, sort of**  Considered by most readers to be informal, these phrases should be avoided in academic and workplace writing.

**latter, former**  (See **former, latter**.)

**lay, lie**  *Lay* is a transitive verb requiring a direct object (but not the self). *Lie*, when used to mean "place in a resting position," refers to the self but takes the form *lay* in the past tense. (See 20f.)

**less, fewer**  (See **fewer, less**.)

**lie, lay**  (See **lay, lie**.)

**like, as**  (See **as, like**.)

**literally**  Avoid using *literally* in a figurative statement (one that is not true to fact). Even when used correctly, *literally* is redundant because the statement will be taken as fact anyway.

DRAFT              The visitors **literally** died when they saw their hotel.

REDUNDANT          The visitors **literally gasped** when they saw their hotel.

EDITED             The visitors gasped when they saw their hotel.

**loose, lose**  Commonly misspelled, these words are pronounced differently. *Loose* (rhyming with *moose*) is an adjective meaning "not tight." *Lose* (rhyming with *snooze*) is a present tense verb meaning "to misplace."

**lots, lots of, a lot of**  (See **a lot**.)

**may, can**  (See **can, may**.)

**maybe, may be**  *Maybe* means *possibly*; *may be* is part of a verb structure.

The President **may be** speaking now, so **maybe** we should turn on the news.

**media, medium**  Technically, *media* is a plural noun requiring a verb that agrees in number. Many people now use *media* as a singular noun when referring to the press. *Medium* generally refers to a conduit or method of transmission.

The **media** is not covering the story accurately.

The telephone was not a good **medium** for reviewing the budget.

**might of, may of** (See **could of, would of.**)

**mighty** Avoid this adjective in formal writing; omit it or use *very.*

**Ms.** To avoid the sexist labeling of women as "married" or "unmarried" (a condition not marked in men's titles), use *Ms.* unless you have reason to use *Miss* or *Mrs.* (for example, when giving the name of a character such as *Mrs. Dalloway*). Use professional titles when appropriate (*Doctor, Professor, Senator, Mayor*). (See 35a.)

**must of, must have** (See **could of, would of.**)

**nor, or** Use *nor* in negative constructions and *or* in positive ones.

> NEGATIVE     Neither rain **nor** snow will slow the team.

> POSITIVE     Either rain **or** snow may delay the game.

**nothing like, nowhere near** These are considered informal phases when used to compare two things (as in "Gibbon's position is **nowhere near** as justified as Carlyle's"). Avoid them in formal writing.

**nowheres** Use *nowhere* instead.

**number, amount** (See **amount, number.**)

**of, have** (See **could of, would of.**)

**off of** Use simply *off* instead.

**OK** When you write formally, use *OK* only in dialogue. If you mean "good" or "acceptable," use these terms.

**on account of** Avoid this expression in formal writing. Use *because* instead.

**outside of, inside of** (See **inside of, outside of.**)

**per** Use *per* only to mean "by the," as in *per hour* or *per day.* Avoid using it to mean "according to," as in "per your instructions."

**percent, percentage** Use *percent* only with numerical data. Use *percentage* for a statistical part of something, not simply to mean *some* or *part.*

Ten **percent** of the sample returned the questionnaire.

A large **percentage** of the parking revenue was stolen.

**plus** Avoid using *plus* as a conjunction joining two independent clauses.

> INFORMAL     The school saved money through its "lights off" campaign, **plus** it generated income by recycling aluminum cans.

> EDITED     The school saved money through its "lights off" campaign and also generated income by recycling aluminum cans.

Use *plus* only to mean "in addition to."

The wearisome campaign, **plus** the media pressures, exhausted her.

**precede, proceed** *Precede* means "come before"; *proceed* means "go ahead."

**pretty** Avoid using *pretty* (as in *pretty good, pretty hungry, pretty sad*) to mean "somewhat" or "rather." Use *pretty* in the sense of "attractive."

**principal, principle** *Principal* is a noun meaning "an authority" or "head of a school" or an adjective meaning "leading" ("a *principal* objection to the testimony"). *Principle* is a noun meaning "belief or conviction."

**proceed, precede** (See **precede, proceed.**)

**quote, quotation**  Formally, *quote* is a verb and *quotation* is a noun. *Quote* is sometimes used as a short version of the noun *quotation*, but this may bother some readers. Use *quotation* instead.

**raise, rise**  *Raise* is a transitive verb meaning "to lift up." *Rise* is an intransitive verb (it takes no object) meaning "to get up or move up."

He **raised** his head and watched the fog **rise** from the lake.

**rarely ever**  Use *rarely* alone, not paired with *ever*.

**real, really**  Use *real* as an adjective and *really* as an adverb. (See 23b-3)

**reason is because, reason is that**  Avoid these wordy phrases. (See 29b-1.)

**regarding, in regard, with regard to**  (See **in regard to**.)

**regardless, irregardless**  (See **irregardless**.)

**respectfully, respectively**  *Respectfully* means "with respect"; *respectively* implies a certain order for events or things.

The senior class **respectfully** submitted the planning document. The administration considered items 3, 6, and 10, **respectively**.

**rise, raise**  (See **raise, rise**.)

**says, goes**  (See **go, say**.)

**set, sit**  *Set* means "to place"; *sit* means "to place oneself." (See 20f.)

**should of**  (See **could of, would of**.)

**since, because**  (See **because, since**.)

**sit, set**  (See **set, sit**.)

**site, cite**  (See **cite, site**.)

**so**  Some readers object to the use of *so* in place of *very*.

INFORMAL     The filmmaker is **so** thoughtful about his films' themes.

EDITED     The filmmaker is **very** thoughtful about his films' themes.

**somebody, some body**  (See **anyone, any one**.)

**someone, some one**  (See **anyone, any one**.)

**sometime, some time, sometimes**  *Sometime* refers to an indistinct time in the future; *sometimes* means "every once in a while." *Some time* is an adjective (*some*) modifying a noun (*time*).

The probe will reach the nebula **sometime** in the next decade. **Sometimes** such probes fail to send back any data. It takes **some time** before images will return from Neptune.

**sort, kind, type**  (See **kind, sort, type**.)

**specially, especially**  (See **especially, specially**.)

**stationary, stationery**  *Stationary* means "standing still"; *stationery* refers to writing paper.

**such**  Some readers will expect you to avoid using *such* without *that*.

INFORMAL     Anne Frank had **such** a difficult time.

EDITED     Anne Frank had **such** a difficult time growing up **that** her diary writing became her only solace.

**suppose to, supposed to** The correct form of this phrase is *supposed to*; the *-d* is sometimes mistakenly left off because it is not always heard. (See 20c.)

**sure, surely** In formal writing, use *sure* to mean "certain." *Surely* is an adverb; don't use *sure* in its place. (See 23b-3.)

He has **surely** studied hard for the exam; he is **sure** to pass.

**sure and, try and** With *sure* and *try*, replace *and* with *to*.

**take, bring** (See **bring, take**.)

**than, then** *Than* is used to compare; *then* implies a sequence of events or a causal relationship.

West played harder **than** East, but **then** the rain began.

**that, which** Although the distinction between *that* and *which* is weakening in many contexts, formal writing often requires you to know the difference. Use *that* in a clause that is essential to the meaning of a sentence (restrictive modifier); use *which* with a clause that does not provide essential information (nonrestrictive modifier). (See 37c–d.)

**theirself, theirselves, themself** All these forms are incorrect; use *themselves* to refer to more than one person, and *himself* or *herself* to refer to one.

**them** Avoid using *them* as a subject or to modify a subject, as in "*Them* are delicious" or "*Them* apples are very crisp."

**then, than** (See **than, then**.)

**there, their, they're** These forms are often confused in spelling because they all sound alike. *There* is a preposition of location; *their* is a possessive pronoun; *they're* is a contraction of *they* and *are*. (See 39b.)

Look **over there**.

**Their** car ran out of gas.

**They're** not eager to hike to the nearest gas station.

**thusly** Avoid this term; use *thus* or *therefore* instead.

**till, 'til, until** Some readers will find *till* and *'til* too informal; use *until*.

**to, too, two** Because these words sound the same, they may be confused. *To* is a preposition indicating direction or location. *Too* means "also." *Two* is a number.

The Birdsalls went **to** their lake cabin. They invited the Corbetts **too**. That made **two** trips so far this season.

**toward, towards** Prefer *toward* in formal writing. (You may see *towards* in England and Canada.)

**try and, try to, sure and** (See **sure and, try and**.)

**ultimately, eventually** (See **eventually, ultimately**.)

**uninterested, disinterested** (See **disinterested, uninterested**.)

**unique** Use *unique* alone, not *most unique* or *more unique*. (See 23b-4.)

**until, till** (See **till, 'til, until**.)

**use to, used to** Like *supposed to*, this phrase may be mistakenly written as *use to* because the *-d* is not always clearly pronounced. Write *used to*. (See 20c.)

**wait for, wait on** Use *wait on* only to refer to a clerk's or server's job; use *wait for* to mean "to await someone's arrival."

**well, good** (See **good, well**.)

**went, gone** (See **gone, went**.)

**were, we're** *Were* is the past plural form of *was; we're* contracts *we are*. (See 39a.)

**We're** going to the ruins where the fiercest battles **were**.

**where . . . at** (See **at**.)

**whether, if** (See **if, whether**.)

**which, that** (See **that, which**.)

**who, whom** Although the distinction between these words is slowly disappearing from the language, many readers will expect you to use *whom* as the objective form. When in doubt, err on the side of formality. (Sometimes editing can eliminate the need to choose.) (See 21b-4.)

**who's, whose** *Who's* contracts *who is. Whose* indicates possession. (See 39c.)

The programmer **who's** joining our division hunted for the person **whose** bag he took by mistake.

**wise, -ize** (See **-ize, -wise**.)

**would of, could of** (See **could of, would of**.)

**yet, however, but** (See **but however, but yet**.)

**your, you're** *Your* is a possessive pronoun; *you're* contracts *you are*. (See 21a-3 and 39c.)

If **you're** going to take physics, you'd better know **your** math.

# CREDITS

American Psychological Assocation (APA) home page (www.apa.org). Copyright © 2004 by the American Psychological Association. Reproduced with permission.

*Atlanta Journal and Constitution*, Staff Writer. "Restrict Right to Sue or We'll Pay in the End." Copyright © 2001 by Atlanta Jour-Constitution. Reproduced with permission of Atlanta Journal-Constitution in the format Textbook via Copyright Clearance Center.

Berendt, John. "Class Acts." *Esquire*, 1991.

Boutron, Claude F., et al. "Decrease in Anthropogenic Lead, Cadmium, and Zinc in Greenland Snows since the Late 1960's." *Nature*, Vol. 353, 1991.

Bright, Michael. *Animal Language.* (Ithaca, NY: Cornell University Press, 1984).

Colorado Division of Wildlife. "Tips." *The Denver Post*, July 30, 1998, p. 15. Reprinted by permission of the Colorado Division of Wildlife.

Committee of Concerned Journalists. "A Statement of Concern," in *The Media and Morality.* Robert M. Baird, William E. Loges, and Stuart E. Rosenbaum, eds. (New York: Prometheus Books, 1999).

CRITT Web site (Critical Resources in Teaching with Technology), 1997. http://www.engl.uic.edu/~stp/.

Curtin, Sharon R. Nobody Ever Died of Old Age. (Boston: Little, Brown, 1972).

Daseler, Robert. *Levering Avenue Poems.* ( Evansville: The University of Evansville Press, 1998).

Database Health Reference Center-Academic. Sample of Abstracts. Courtesy of Providence Public Library.

Davis, Mike. "House of Cards." *Sierra* © 1995.

Fast-Track Recalls. *Consumer Product Safety Review*, Fall, 1998 issue, Vol. 3, No.1.

Flippen, Royce. "Tossing and Turning." *American Health*, May 1992. Copyright © 1992 by American Health.

Francione, Gary L., and Charlton, Anna E. From Animal Rights Project Website. Copyright © Reprinted by permission.

GlobalReach Website (http://global-reach.biz) Reprinted by permission of Global Reach.

Gmelch, George. "Baseball Magic." *Transaction*, 1971.

Goieman, Daniel. "Too Little, Too Late." *American Health* © 1992 by American Health.

Goddio, Frank. "San Diego: An Account of Adventure, Deceit, and Intrigue." *National Geographic*, 1994.

Gonzalez, Anson. "The Little Rosebud Girl" Copyright © 1972 by Anson Gonzalez. Reprinted by permission.

Google Logo and Search Code Copyright © 2000 Google. The Google search code and Google Logo used on the main page of this site are provided by and used with permission of www.google.com.

Gore, Al. *Earth in Balance.* (Boston, MA: Houghton Mifflin, 1992).

Gorman, Christine. Excerpt from "Sizing Up the Sexes," from the January 20, 1992 issue of *Time.* Reprinted by permission of Time Inc.

Green, Kenneth C. Chart from The Campus Computing Project. Copyright © 1998 by Kenneth C. Green. Reprinted by permission.

Gregor, Michael. Excerpt from "Milk…Help Yourself (To Cancer, AIDS and Multiple Sclerosis?)" from *Animal Life*, Fall 1994, Vol. 5, No. 1. Reprinted by permission of the publisher.

Haines, John. Excerpt from "Three Days." Copyright © 1989 by John Haines. Reprinted from *The Stars, The Snow, the Fire* with the permission of Graywolf Press, Saint Paul, Minnesota.

Hall, Donald. Excerpt from "The Black-Faced Sheep" from *Old and New Poems* by Donald Hall. Copyright © 1990 by Donald Hall. Reprinted by permission of Houghton Mifflin Company. All rights reserved.

Hand, Wayland D. "Folk Medical Magic and Symbolism in the West," in *Magic, Witchcraft and Religion: An Anthropological Study of the Supernatural*, 3rd ed., Arthur C. Lehmann and James E. Myers, eds. (Mayfield Publishing, 1993).

Hermann, Andrea. "When you hear the word crystal…" Reprinted by permission of the author.

Honey, Maureen. *Creating Rosie the Riveter*. (University of Massachusetts Press, 1984).

Mayers, T.R. From "(snap) shots." Reprinted by permission of the author.

Merriam-Webster, Incorporated. *Merriam-Webster's Collegiate®Dictionary, Eleventh Edition* © 2004 by Merriam-Webster, Inc. (www.Meriam-Webster.com).

Merriam-Webster, Incorporated. By permission, from *Webster's Third New International® Dictionary, Unabridged* © 1993 by Merriam-Webster, Inc. (www.Merriam-Webster.com).

MountainLion Foundation Website (www.mountainlion.org) Reprinted by permission.

Peterson, Brenda. *Nature and Other Mothers*. (New York: Harper Collins, 1992).

Phillips Park Zoolennium Fall Festival 2004! Website. Reprinted by permission of City of Aurora, IL Parks Department, www.aurora-il.org/parks.

Prevention Magazine. "Zero in on Hidden Fats." Reprinted by permission of Prevention Magazine. © 2003 by Rodale Inc. All rights reserved. Prevention® is a registered trademark of Rodale Inc.

Reisberg, Leo. "Colleges Step Up Efforts to Combat Alcohol Abuse." *The Chronicle of Higher Education*, June 12, 1998, Vol. 44, No. 44. Copyright © 1998 by The Chronicle of Higher Education. Reprinted by permission.

Russell, Peter. *The Brain Book*. Copyright © 1979 by Peter Russell. Used by permission of Dutton Signet, a division of Penguin Group (USA) Inc.

Sadeh, Avi, Raviv, Amiram, and Gruber, Reut. "Sleep Patterns and Sleep Disruptions in School-Age Children." *Developmental Psychology*, Vol. 36, No. 3, May 2000.

Sankey, Jay. *Zen and the Art of Stand-Up Comedy*. Copyright © 1998 by Jay Sankey. Reproduced by permission of Routledge/Taylor & Francis Books, Inc.

Schor, Juliet B. The Overworked American. (New York: Harper Collins, 1998).

Schwegler, Brian. "Character Development Sketch: Dave The Guesser." *Salt Magazine*, August, 1994. Reprinted by permission of the author and SALT Center for Documentary Field Studies.

Sidney, Sir Phillip. "His Lady's Cruelty," from *The Oxford Book of English Verse 1250-1918*. (London; Oxford University Press, 1973).

Tannen, Deborah. *You Just Don't Understand: Women and Men in Conversation*. (New York: Morrow, 1990).

The Jane Austen Society of Australia Inc. website. Reprinted by permission. 45 Sylvan Avenue, Linefield NSW 2070, Australia, info @jasa.net.au.

"Why Does Milk Bother Me?" from National Digestive Diseases Information Clearinghouse, National Institutes of Health, www.niddk,gov/health/digest/pubs/whymilk/index.html. Reprinted with permission.

Whymilk Webpage, www.whymilk.com. Reprinted by permission of Weber Shandwick, Chicago, IL.

Wideman, John Edgar. *Brothers and Keepers*. (New York: Random House, 1984).

Student Acknowledgements: David Aharonian, Summer Arrigo-Nelson, Jeanne Brown, Zachary Carter, Pam Copass, Melanie Dedecker, Jennifer Figliozzi, Daisy Garcia, Shane Hand, Andrea Herrmann, Steven King, Jenny Latimer, Fredza Leger, Kris Lundell, Jennifer O'Berry, Ian Preston, Paul Pusateri, Sam Roles, Brian Schwegler, Ted Wolfe, Tou Yang.

# INDEX

*Note:* The index is sorted by word order. **Bold** page numbers indicate definitions in the text. Page numbers followed by *G* indicate entries in the glossary. *See* references refer you to appropriate or related index entries.